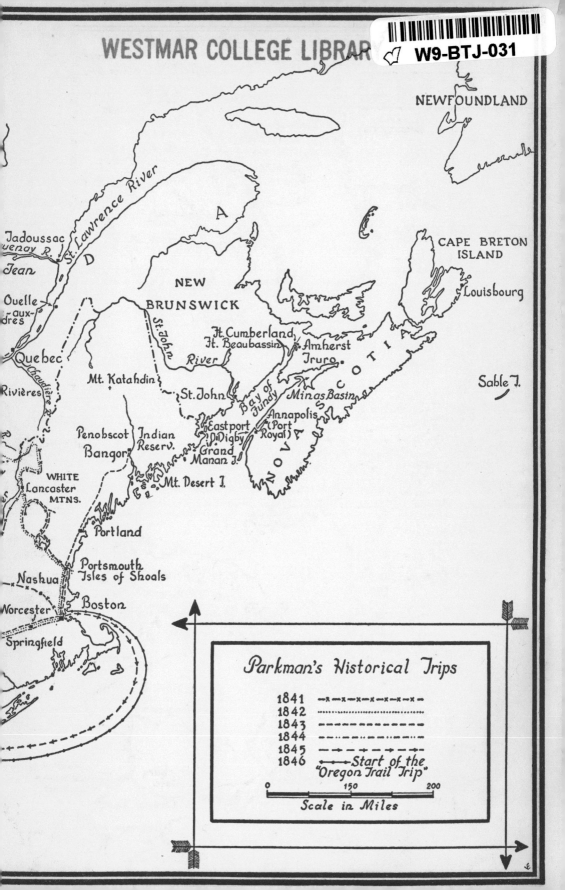

NEWFOUNDLAND

A

C

CAPE BRETON
ISLAND

St. Lawrence River

Tadoussac
Suenay R.

D

Jean

NEW
BRUNSWICK

Louisbourg

Ouelle
aux-
dres

St. John

Quebec

Chaudiere

River

Ft. Cumberland
Ft. Beaubassin
Amherst
Truro

NOVA SCOTIA

Rivières

Mt. Katahdin

St. John

Bay of Fundy

Minas Basin

Sable I.

Penobscot Indian
Reserv.

Bangor

Eastport
Digby

Annapolis
(Port
Royal)

Grand
Manan I.

WHITE
Lancaster
MTNS.

Mt. Desert I.

Portland

Portsmouth
Isles of Shoals

Nashua

Worcester

Boston

Springfield

Parkman's Historical Trips

1841 —x—x—x—x—x—x—x—x
1842 ••••••••••••••••
1843 — — — — — — —
1844 —·—·—·—·—·—·
1845 —▸—▸—▸—▸—▸
1846 •—▸ Start of the
"Oregon Trail Trip"

0   150   200

Scale in Miles

THE
JOURNALS
OF
FRANCIS PARKMAN

———

VOLUME I

Francis Parkman at Twenty
From C. H. Farnham's Francis Parkman
(Little, Brown, and Company)

THE
JOURNALS
OF
FRANCIS PARKMAN

Edited by MASON WADE

Author of
FRANCIS PARKMAN: HEROIC HISTORIAN

ILLUSTRATED

VOLUME I

NEW YORK AND LONDON
HARPER & BROTHERS PUBLISHERS
MCMXLVII

TABLE OF CONTENTS

VOLUME I

VOLUME II

LIST OF ILLUSTRATIONS

VOLUME I

VOLUME II

Preface

FRANCIS PARKMAN is the greatest writer among American historians; the "climax and the crown," as Van Wyck Brooks has pointed out, of that notable nineteenth century Boston school of historians which included Jared Sparks, John Gorham Palfrey, George Bancroft, William Hickling Prescott, and John Lothrop Motley. He is alone among this goodly company in that his books still live today, while those of his greatest rivals, Prescott and Motley, seem stiffly rhetorical and unduly romantic. As history his work has also stood the test of time, for much later research and investigation have disproved only a detail or two in the vast field in which he was a pioneer. History has become more factual and scientific since Parkman's day, but the new historians have not been able to make sound scholarship dramatic and exciting, as this romantic rationalist did. Parkman's newly rediscovered journals have a twofold importance: they constitute both a partial autobiography of one of America's greatest writers and the raw material of his work. From them emerges a remarkable picture of North America in the mid-nineteenth century, as seen by a great writer who was familiar through long and loving study with the history of the regions he describes. They are of enormous literary and historical interest, since they reveal the development of the vivid style for which Parkman is famed, and his methods of research and investigation. The journals constitute one of the finest descriptions and interpretations of the American scene of the period; and they throw a great flood of light upon Parkman's books, which are so notable a part of the American cultural heritage.

Francis Parkman was a Boston Brahmin, and his New England reticence allowed little of himself to appear in his formal works, the seven-part history of *France and England in North America* and its epilogue, *The Conspiracy of Pontiac*. But like so many of the great figures of that nineteenth century Boston which has set a lasting mark upon American thought, Parkman revealed himself more fully in his private journals than it was ever possible for him to do when writing for the public. And like Emerson, Thoreau, and Hawthorne, once the wall of Puritan reticence had been broken down in private, he was too much of a literary man to let his words go unread; and so he made use of passages from his journals in works destined for an audience. Thus his first book, *The Oregon Trail*, a youthful effort which has been more widely read than the formal histories, is wholly based upon the diary that Parkman kept during his great adventure in the West; and his only novel, the forgotten *Vassall Morton* in which is buried his personal philosophy, takes over much material and many incidents recorded in unfictionalized form in the journals. Most of the few personal references which Parkman permitted himself in his historical works are drawn from the journals, which enable us to follow his intellectual development and to discover the reticent man who hid behind the objective historian.

The main function of the journals was to record Parkman's researches in the field. The historian early settled upon his lifework, and his youthful journals were a part of the exhaustive preparation which he imposed upon himself for the task that lay ahead. One of the teachers of his boyhood, Thomas Cushing, recalls somewhat ponderously that his pupil shone "in the rhetorical department," and that "he might have excelled in narrative and descriptive poetry (the poetry of action) had he not early imbibed the historical idea." Poetry was indeed Parkman's first love, but considering the faultiness of his ear, witnessed in the journals by extremely rough phonetic equivalents for unfamiliar foreign words and names, it is doubtless fortunate that he decided, in his own words, "to confine his homage to the Muse of History, as being less apt than her wayward sisters to requite his devotion with a mortifying rebuff." But his early fondness for Byron, Scott, and Cooper never left him, and their romantic influence is evident in his lifelong love of the dramatic and the vivid. Once history had been settled upon as his chosen field, there remained the choice of a subject. This was strongly influenced by

Parkman's early passion for the wilds and by the active interest of his Harvard history teacher, Jared Sparks, in the American past, which had previously been neglected and largely forgotten in a colonial culture's preoccupation with the European tradition. Sparks, a Unitarian minister turned editor and writer, was the first American academic figure to concern himself seriously with the history of his country. Parkman fell under his influence as an undergraduate; did further historical work under his guidance while nominally studying law; and acknowledged his assistance in *The Conspiracy of Pontiac* by dedicating that first-written of the histories to the new president of Harvard "as a testimonial of high personal regard and a tribute of respect for his distinguished services to American history." But however great the influence of Sparks may have been, the choice of subject was primarily Parkman's:

Before the end of my sophomore year my various schemes had crystalized into a plan of writing a story of what was then known as the "Old French War"—that is, the War that ended in the conquest of Canada—for here, as it seemed to me, the forest drama was more stirring and the forest stage more thronged with appropriate actors than in any other passage of our history. It was not until some years later that I enlarged the plan to include the whole course of the American conflict between France and England, or, in other words, the history of the American forest; for this was the light in which I regarded it.

—Letter to Martin Brimmer, 1886

Thus from an early fascination with the wilderness and with the obscure border battles of the Seven Years' War developed Parkman's great historical epic, which covers a much broader canvas.

John Fiske, who habitually ranked Parkman's work with that of Herodotus, Thucydides, and Gibbon, stressed its scope: "The book which depicts at once the social life of the Stone Age and the victory of the English political ideal over the ideal which France inherited from imperial Rome, is a book for all mankind and for all time." Fiske's judgment of Parkman's work is somewhat excessive, for *France and England in North America* lacks the unity of the great histories of Herodotus and Thucydides and the sweep of Gibbon's masterpiece. Parkman was plagued by ill-health, both mental and physical, during his entire writing life; and though he early planned out his lifework as a whole, he was forced to do it piecemeal, struggling against almost overwhelming odds that he would never live to complete it. He did finish the last link in the chain of volumes, and revised many of the earlier ones, but he had neither time nor energy left for the final revision in which he planned, on Henry Adams' advice, to weld the parts together into a single work. The theme was essentially episodic, for the conflict between France and England was fitfully waged over half a continent for a century; and most of its major episodes could be grouped about single central figures, a method which Parkman, with his romantic devotion to the great-man theory of history, found the most satisfactory principle of organization. What Parkman thus lost in majestic perspective over the chain of events, he gained in the vividness of the episodes. Fiske justly referred to the seven-part series as a book, for *France and England in North America* has a dramatic unity which offsets its division into studies of individual figures or topics. Parkman thought of it at first as the epic of the struggle between "feudal, militant, and Catholic" France and "democratic, industrial, and Protestant" England for domination of the New World. But later he saw that the American Hundred Years' War was a "contest for colonial and maritime supremacy," and that the struggle in America was intricately linked with the struggle for power in Europe. One of Parkman's great historical contributions was the demonstration that obscure events in America had a vital effect upon the course of history in Europe, as those in Europe did in America. Parkman was one of the first historians to take a continental view of North America, but that view did not prevent him from recognizing the influence of nationalism and internationalism.

The great history extends from the dawn of French colonization in America to the eclipse of New France with the English conquest of 1760. The first part, *The Pioneers of France in the New World*, deals with the tentative settlement of Florida and Carolina by the French Huguenots and their bitter struggle with the Spaniards in the latter half of the sixteenth century; and with the enduring colonization of Champlain and his associates in Acadia and Canada at the outset of the seventeenth century. The second, *The Jesuits in North America*, carries the story on to 1675, with a moving account of the missionaries' heroic but short-lived effort to convert the Hurons and the Iroquois, and to make Canada a New Paraguay rather than a New France. The third, *La Salle and the Discovery of the Great West*, is the story of the French exploration and token colonization of the Great Lakes and the Mississippi Valley, the heart of the continent. It is also an account of the conflict of the religious and commercial ideals in New France, the incompatible ideals of the Jesuit and of the fur trader. The fourth, *The Old Regime in Canada*—a pioneer American essay in social history—falls into three divisions: the first dealing with the semifeudalism of Canada, the second with New France as a mission, and the third with the royal exploitation of the colony for the benefit of the mother country. The fifth, *Count Frontenac and New France under Louis XIV*, is an account of the colony in its heyday, with the conflict between State and Church already straining its top-heavy structure as England and France formally began their great American struggle in King William's War (1689-97). The sixth, *A Half-Century of Conflict*, covers the years between 1700 and 1748, which were filled with border strife as well as Queen Anne's War (War of the Spanish Succession, 1702-13) and King George's War (War of the Austrian Succession, 1744-48). At the outset of this work, Parkman indicated that he had adopted a broader view of the great struggle which he was chronicling. He considered Queen Anne's War to be "the second of a series of four conflicts which ended in giving to Great Britain a maritime and colonial preponderance over France and Spain. So far as concerns the colonies and the seas, these several wars may be regarded as a single protracted one, broken by intervals of truce. The three earlier of them, it is true, were European contests, begun and waged on European disputes. Their American part was incidental and apparently subordinate, yet it involved questions of prime importance in the history of the world." The seventh and final work, *Montcalm and Wolfe*—considered the finest of the series—is an account of the climactic struggle of the Seven Years' War (1756-63), that "Old French War" on which he had first planned to write, ending in the downfall of New France on the Plains of Abraham. This conflict, unlike the earlier ones, started in America with Washington's attack on Jumonville on the Monongahela in 1754; an "obscure skirmish began the war that set the world on fire" two years later. *The Conspiracy of Pontiac*, which is not formally a part of *France and*

England in North America, fills out the story of the English conquest with an account of the subsequent Indian uprising against the new rulers of North America. It was Parkman's first historical book, written when he thought himself doomed to death before he could write the greater work on which his heart was set; and so its introductory chapters briefly sum up the great three-cornered struggle for the continent among the Indians, the French, and the English. If only one of Parkman's books can be read, this is perhaps the best choice, for it is at once a summary and the crown of the great epic of *France and England in North America*, and an excellent introduction to the pre-Revolutionary history of America. As that acute critic Theodore Parker pointed out to his young friend, however, it was unjust to the Indians and the Quakers; it lacked the dramatic unity which so notably characterized most of Parkman's later books; and its style was too florid, inexact, and hasty—characteristics not evident in the later books, in which his early tendency to overwrite and to be romantically picturesque was restrained.

So vast a project demanded the broadest sort of preparation, and Parkman was blessed with the social position, means, and opportunities which could provide it. He was the son of a leading Unitarian minister in Boston, the grandson of one of Boston's merchant princes, and an heir of the Brahmin tradition, with its pride of learning and its pride of power. His ancestry gave him a personal interest in the early history of America, in which his forebears had taken notable parts. His share of his grandfather's wealth relieved him of the necessity for making a living and enabled him to devote his life to a self-imposed task for which he received only a slight return—and that in reputation rather than in money. As a boy he roamed the Middlesex Fells near his grandfather's Medford farm and developed his lifelong fondness for the wilds. At Harvard he slighted all studies that did not further the purpose he had formed, and eagerly pursued those which promoted it. At eighteen Parkman set about preparing himself to treat the great theme which obsessed him. He did a vast amount of historical reading outside his college and law school courses, being blessed, as Sparks had been, with access to the collections of Harvard, the Athenaeum, and the Massachusetts Historical Society, which afforded facilities which then could not be enjoyed elsewhere

in America. He also undertook a rigorous program of physical training designed to harden him for research in the field, for it was evident to him that "other study than that of the closet" was necessary
for success in his attempt to write the history of the American forest.
Rowing, riding, and boxing were supplemented by long walks and
hunting expeditions through the countryside about Cambridge during term time; and all his college vacations were devoted to more
ambitious and strenuous expeditions, for Parkman was determined
to know the wilderness as well as the heroes of his history. Such was
the origin of the series of forest journeys recorded in the early journals.
In them research and recreation were combined, for most of the
scenes of the struggle that dominated Parkman's thoughts lay in
frontier regions, still almost untouched in the mid-nineteenth
century by the advance of industrial civilization, and were in any
case the places to which his innate love of the wilds would have led
him. Indians and pioneers, two great categories in his cast of characters, could still be found on the New England frontier in the 1840's;
and it was to these regions that Parkman first turned.

After his freshman year at Harvard, he spent the summer of 1841
in the wilds of northern New Hampshire and Maine; in the following
year he visited Lake George and Lake Champlain, the scene of so
many battles in the French and Indian War, and then followed the
Canadian border eastward to the sources of the Connecticut River,
returning home by his 1841 route. In the following summer he
inspected the old forts on the lakes once more, and then passed
northward by the Richelieu to Montreal and Quebec, returning by
way of the White Mountains and later visiting an Indian reservation
in Maine. In his desire to emulate the life of the hardy heroes who
preoccupied his mind, he drove himself too sternly and nearly ruined
his health; and so was packed off to Europe by his family for a rest
and change. There, while touring Sicily, Italy, Switzerland, France,
and Great Britain, he took advantage of his opportunity to familiarize
himself with Catholicism, a potent force in his chosen field of history,
and thus rid himself of some of the provincialism inherent in his
make-up. In the summer of 1844, following his return from Europe
and the completion of his college studies, he wandered through the
Berkshire Hills, rounding out his acquaintance with the old New

England frontier. During the following summer he visited the Alleghany frontier and the old forts and trading posts of the Great Lakes, returning by way of the Mohawk Valley, the home of the Iroquois who played a role second only to that of the French and English in his history. And then in 1846 he made the greatest of his expeditions, a seven months' trip in the West over the Oregon and Santa Fe trails, in order to perfect his knowledge of the Indians. This journey brought about the collapse of a constitution already strained by ill-advised attempts to strengthen it, and so ended the series of wilderness journeys which gave Parkman a firsthand knowledge of the chief scenes of his history. No historian has ever covered the ground he was to write about as thoroughly as Parkman did, and none has left so rich a record of his preparation for his lifework.

With the long illness that followed, whose mental and physical manifestations tried his fighter's heart, Parkman lost much of the energy and vitality which make the early journals such absorbing reading. When interludes of improved health permitted travel for historical research, he was content to jot down rough notes and references in his notebooks, rather than to write full narratives, as before. All his slender store of impaired sight and diminished energy had to be concentrated on the production of the histories; there was none to squander on journalizing. These later notebooks, which record his frequent visits to Canada, his occasional forays to the French and British archives in Paris and London, and an expedition late in life to Carolina and Florida (to correct the descriptions of the one book he wrote without first going over the ground himself), are of less interest to the general reader than the early journals, though they are occasionally lit up by flashes of the prose poetry which has given an enduring vitality to Parkman's books. But they will delight the historian, who can form from them a remarkably detailed picture of Parkman's methods, sources, contacts with fellow workers, and the shoptalk of a master of the craft. And then, since Parkman was a pioneer in a virtually untouched field of history, his notes have a certain documentary value.

After 1862, when the illness which Parkman called "The Enemy" had been mastered and he began to write the books for which he had been so long preparing, he turned to the early journals for firsthand impressions and observations to supplement the facts he had laboriously mined out of the mass of manuscripts, books, and pamphlets bearing on his subject which he had accumulated. This practice does much to explain the extraordinary vividness of his descriptions: through the use of the journals he was able to recapture the freshness of vision with which he first saw the chief scenes of the great historical drama. He had lived the same adventurous life as the *coureurs de bois*, partisans, and missionaries whom he wrote about, and thus he was able to invest his accounts of them with an immediacy and vigor which make novels pall. The journals also served him well in another more personal fashion: through rereading them when housebound by illness he could relive the strenuous days of his youth amid the wilderness of which he was a lifelong lover. First ill-health and then age barred him from the life of action that would have been his choice, but he never ceased to regret being obliged to hold "the pen with the hand that should have grasped the sword." He found compensation for his confinement in imaginative journeys, and this mental habit stood him in good stead when he described the epic wanderings of the French explorers and missionaries. Sometimes he regaled his family or a close friend with a reading from one of the early journals; sometimes, as in *Vassall Morton* or his *Harper's* articles, he reworked these early writings for publication. The journals were always at hand when the little world of Boston pressed too closely upon him; he kept them in a drawer of his desk in the Beacon Hill attic study which was decorated with trophies from the expeditions they chronicled: an Indian shield and lance, bows and arrows, a calumet, and pictures of some of the far places he had known in his youth, before being confined in what he called the "Dungeon of the Spirit." After necessity made him an armchair traveler, he developed a great fondness for travel books. He also carried on a large correspondence with explorers such as E. G. Squier, Adolph Bandelier, and Captain John Bourke, whom he aided in the field researches which he himself would have liked to pursue. In his closing years some improvement in his health permitted him another taste or two of wilderness life: in October 1883 he made a six-day horseback trip from Portsmouth, New Hampshire, to Crawford Notch and back, and reported proudly that "although I am a sixty-year-old grandfather, I was not upset by the adventure." Again, three years later, he spent the month of June camping on the Batiscan in Quebec, canoeing amid the furious eddies of that wild river, fishing, and trying his hand once more as a marksman, though his lameness confined his shooting to target practice—tame sport for one who had hunted buffalo on horseback! He spent the latter part of that same summer on the Rangeley Lakes in Maine, not far from the scenes of his youthful adventures on the Magalloway; and here he hoped to return each summer, but his health never again permitted it. His dying words concerned a dream he had had of killing a bear; his last thought was of the American forest which he has immortalized for those who can know it only by the printed page. There is no better picture of the wilderness among all Parkman's writings than that found in these journals, which are also the unassuming record of a lifetime's devotion to a single purpose that was fulfilled with a completeness rare in the annals of American letters.

II

Some account of the history of these journals is demanded by the fact that, with all their obvious value and importance, they have gone so long unpublished. Parkman's will provided that his historical papers should be turned over to the Massachusetts Historical Society upon his death, while his historical library and maps went to Harvard. The historical importance of the journals was not fully recognized by his family and early biographers. They were duly put at the disposal of Charles Haight Farnham, a former secretary who was appointed official biographer shortly after Parkman's death in 1893. Confronted with this treasure trove and a vast mass of correspondence, Farnham astigmatically characterized the materials for a life of Parkman as "extraordinarily scanty." The second biographer, Henry Dwight Sedgwick, saw the importance of the journals far more clearly, and used as many excerpts from them as the brief scope of his sketch in the American Men of Letters series permitted. It is not clear, however, whether he or Farnham ever saw all the notebooks, for they neither mention nor quote from some of them. After 1904 the journals dropped out of sight and out of memory.

In 1940, when the present writer set about the preparation of a new life of Parkman, he was unable to find any trace of these documents so essential to his purpose. They were not with the rest of the Parkman Papers at the Massachusetts Historical Society, nor among his books and maps at Harvard. The Parkman family knew nothing of their whereabouts, and was firmly convinced that all his papers had been turned over to the Historical Society. Further research in the United States and Canada offered no clue, except the evident fact that a considerable and important part of Parkman's correspondence was not with the rest of his papers at the Historical Society. Finally a visit to Parkman's old Boston home on Chestnut Street, by the kind permission of Parkman's niece, Miss Elizabeth Cordner, resulted in an inspection of his attic study, closed for the summer in 1893 and, because of his death that fall at his country home at Jamaica Plain, never since disturbed except for use as a storeroom. Parkman's Indian trophies still hung on the walls; the bookcases still held the well-worn editions of Byron, Cooper, and Scott which were his lifelong favorites; and in the center of the room, covered with a dust sheet, stood the desk on which the great histories had been written. This desk was two-sided; the drawers on one side had obviously been inspected and emptied of most of their contents, though in one was found the wire grid he used to guide his pencil when he could not see to write. The drawers on the other side had been overlooked; they contained the missing journals and a great mass of correspondence, including some of the most important letters Parkman wrote and received. Evidently, when Sedgwick returned the materials loaned him for the writing of his biographical sketch, the manuscripts had been returned to their accustomed place in the desk; and with the death of Parkman's sister, who had acted as his secretary, their hiding place had been forgotten. Miss Cordner graciously put the rediscovered material at my temporary disposal for the writing of my biography of Parkman; and then the manuscripts passed into the possession of the Massachusetts Historical Society, where it was agreed that they belonged under the spirit of Parkman's will.

III

The editing of the journals has presented certain problems. Some may consider the verbatim publication of such material, largely

written in youth and for the author's eye alone, as a disservice to
the memory of a great writer. But the polished and revised version
of many a passage from the journals may be found in the standard
sets of Parkman's works; and much of the special quality of these
informal notes taken on the spot would be lost if the text were edited
in accordance with modern usages. In addition, the historian would
not be served, since he prefers the original text. Therefore, since the
general reader (for whom Parkman wrote, scandalous as that may
seem today) will not be particularly inconvenienced by slight variations from modern usage, and may be consoled by the discovery that
even the greatest writers fall prey to slips of the pen, it has seemed
best to present the text of the journals as Parkman wrote and hastily
revised it. Punctuation has been modernized and such emendations
made as were demanded for clarity. All such editorial emendations
are in brackets, while parentheses have been used to indicate the
omissions practiced in modern or correct spelling of the text. Parkman's footnotes are signed with his initials; those of the editor are
indicated. Alternative readings rejected by Parkman have not been
preserved, except in the 1870 Notebook, as a sample of his method of
writing. Proper names have been given in their correct form in
brackets upon their first appearance in each journal, and identified
on the same basis in the footnotes when necessary or possible. Page
references to the original MMS. are supplied in the running-heads.

Since the book is intended both for the general reader and the
historical student, the editorial notes have not been allowed to
encumber the text, but have been grouped at the back of the book,
except for those necessary to follow the text, or cross references. In
the course of six years' work on Parkman, the editor has accumulated
considerable detailed information which, while wearisome to the
general reader, may prove of service to the student not familiar with
the mass of Parkman manuscript material or with the bypaths of
Canadian history. This accounts for the fact that the notes sometimes
bulk larger than the text of the terse later notebooks, which are largely
concerned with historical matters. This material has been relegated
where it will not obstruct the path of the general reader, while it
remains accessible to the specialist or the curious. An introduction
to each journal places it in relation to Parkman's life and works, and

supplies general background material. Since the journals so closely approximate an autobiography, a chronological table is the chief biographical material here supplied. Further facts and theories on Parkman's life are available in the editor's *Francis Parkman: Heroic Historian* (New York, 1942). All references to Parkman's books are to the Frontenac edition, the last revision by the author.

The journals are published with the permission of the owners, the Massachusetts Historical Society, and with the consent of the Parkman family. For permission to reprint excerpts which have already appeared in print, the editor makes grateful acknowledgment to the Viking Press, the Limited Editions Club, Little, Brown & Company, and the Houghton Mifflin Company. The illustrations, aside from those by Parkman and the portrait of him, have been drawn from the William H. Coverdale Collection of Canadiana at the Manoir Richelieu, Murray Bay, P.Q., by courtesy of Canada Steamship Lines, Montreal. The editor is greatly indebted to the Western historical scholarship of Bernard DeVoto for aid with the Introduction and Notes of the Oregon Trail Journal, and to the cartographic knowledge of Norman Fee of the Public Archives of Canada for map references. The maps of Parkman's travels have been drawn by Van H. English of the Department of Geography, Dartmouth College. The editor welcomes this opportunity to express his thanks to a host of individuals who have aided his work and made this book possible; he is under particular obligation to Daniel Sargent, Bernard DeVoto, the late Eugene Saxton, Allyn B. Forbes, J. Bartlet Brebner, Antoine Roy, Père René Baudry, Joseph Belleau, and Alexander Laing. He is indebted for assistance and many courtesies to the staffs of the Massachusetts Historical Society, the Harvard College Library, the Dartmouth College Library, the Public Archives of Canada, the Archives of the Province of Quebec, the McGill University Library, and the Quebec Literary and Historical Society. He particularly thanks Mlles. B. Binet and B. Labrecque for assistance in preparing the manuscript, and Miss Caroline Neef for reference work.

MASON WADE

Quebec 1943–
Cornish 1946

Chronological Table

1823. Born September 16 on Beacon Hill, Boston, eldest son of the Rev. Francis Parkman and Caroline Hall Parkman, descendants of Elias Parkman and John Cotton.

1831-35. Parkman lived during these years on his grandfather Hall's farm at Medford and developed an interest in nature while roaming the Middlesex Fells.

1838. Family moved to grandfather Samuel Parkman's mansion in Bowdoin Square, Boston.

1840-41. Entered Harvard. Spent summer vacation of his freshman year in the White Mountains and Maine with Daniel Denison Slade.

1842. Spent his summer vacation with Henry Orne White visiting Lake George and Lake Champlain, northern Vermont, the Eastern Townships of Quebec, the Connecticut Lakes, and then retraced the course of the previous summer's journey.

1843. First trip to Canada: Lake George, Lake Champlain, St. John's, Chambly, Montreal, Quebec, White Mountains. After return to Boston, visited Penobscot Indians at Bangor, Maine.

1843-44. European Tour, November-June: Gibraltar, Malta, Sicily, Italy, Switzerland, France, and Great Britain.

1844. Visited Berkshire Hills. Graduated from Harvard College and entered Dane Law School.

1845. Visited Pennsylvania, western New York, Detroit, Mackinac, Sault Ste. Marie, and returned home by way of the Mohawk Valley. Wrote sketches of frontier life for the *Knickerbocker Review*.

1846-47. Wrote first version of *The Oregon Trail*, which appeared serially in the *Knickerbocker* during 1847-49.

1849. *The Oregon Trail* published in book form.

1850. Married Catherine Scollay Bigelow, daughter of Dr. Jacob Bigelow of Boston.

1851. Published *The Conspiracy of Pontiac*, first historical work. Wrote on Indians for the *Christian Examiner*.

1852. First contribution to the *North American Review*: critical article on Fenimore Cooper.

1856.   Published only novel, *Vassall Morton*. Visited Montreal, Quebec, and Ottawa Valley.

1857.   Only son, Francis, Jr., died.

1858.   His wife, Catherine Scollay Bigelow died. Parkman spent winter of 1858-59 in Paris under treatment of French neurologists.

1858-63.   Worst period of health. Chief concern horticulture.

1863-64.   Contributed a revision of his 1841 journal and advance chapters of *The Pioneers of France* to *Harper's* and the *Atlantic*.

1865.   Published *The Pioneers of France*, Part I of *France and England in North America*.

1866.   Published *The Book of Roses*. Visited Montreal and Quebec. Began to review historical books in the *Atlantic*.

1867.   Published *The Jesuits in North America*. Visited Middle West and Great Lakes region for La Salle material.

1868.   Elected overseer of Harvard. Wrote preface for William Smith's *Historical Account of Bouquet's Expedition against the Ohio Indians*. Spent winter in Paris and London.

1869.   Published *The Discovery of the Great West* (later called *La Salle*). Began contributing to Godkin's *Nation*.

1870.   Visited Mt. Desert and Grand Manan.

1871.   Professor of horticulture, Bussey Institution, Harvard. Visited Acadia.

1872.   Visited Europe, working in Paris archives.

1873.   Visited Quebec, lower St. Lawrence, Acadia.

1874.   Published *The Old Regime in Canada*.

1875.   Chosen Fellow of Harvard Corporation, President of Massachusetts Historical Society.

1876.   Developed *lilium Parkmanii*.

1877.   Published *Frontenac and New France under Louis XIV*.

1878.   Visited Lake George, Lake Champlain, and Quebec.

1879.   Visited Quebec, Louisburg, and Acadia.

1880.   Summer trip to Europe.

1881.   Summer trip to Europe.

1884.   Published *Montcalm and Wolfe*.

1885.   Visited Beaufort, South Carolina, and Florida east coast to revise *Pioneers*.

1886.   Camped on Batiscan River in Canada. Visited Rangeley Lakes in Maine.

1887.   Last journey to Europe.

1888.   Began to spend summers at Portsmouth, New Hampshire.

1890.   Published revision of his Roman journal in *Harper's*.

1892.   Published *A Half-Century of Conflict*, thus completing *France and England in North America*.

1893.   November 8, died at his country home at Jamaica Plain, near Boston.

1841 Journal

White Mountains and Maine

Introduction

IN THE summer vacation of his freshman year at Harvard, Parkman made the first of that remarkable series of journeys which were a major part of his self-imposed preparation for his life-work. For he never could have written so vividly of the forest if he had not known wilderness life at first hand; and this excursion of July and August 1841 to the White Mountains and Maine was no mere pleasure trip, though it fulfilled Parkman's strongest desires. In an autobiographic letter, written in 1864—with characteristic reticence, in the third person—to his friend Dr. George Ellis, Parkman thus describes his youthful preoccupation with the wilderness: "His thoughts were always in the forest, whose features possessed his waking and sleeping dreams, filling him with vague cravings impossible to satisfy." But in concluding this spirited journal of his holiday, he stresses his basic purpose: "My chief object in coming so far was merely to have a taste of the half-savage kind of life necessary to be led, and to see the wilderness where it was as yet uninvaded by the hand of man." He was already thinking of that "history of the American forest" which he later planned out in detail.

So, with his classmate Daniel Denison Slade, who was equally fond of the wilderness—at least in theory—Parkman spent a month traveling by stage, foot, and skiff through the then unfrequented wilds of northern New Hampshire and Maine, indulging his liking for fishing and hunting, and living the life of the forest dweller. Journeying by train from Charlestown to Dover, New Hampshire, the two young men took first to a stage and then to shank's mare, reaching Lake Winnipesaukee in the midst of an overpowering hot spell. Thence, by way of Conway and Bartlett, they continued to Crawford Notch, long to be Parkman's favorite center for excursions in the White Mountains. Here he scrambled about the cliffs

3

in the Notch, almost killing himself in one climb which he describes so vividly that it is clear that at seventeen the future historian knew singularly well how to paint action in words. Then he rode up to the summit of Mt. Washington on the newly opened Crawford bridle path. (Incidentally, he was so charmed by the "strength and spirit and good humor" of one of his companions here, a Miss Prentiss of Keene, that he became her devoted admirer for some five or six years.) Then he and Slade walked over to Franconia Notch, where they saw the sights and tried their hand with rod and gun.

Having been told of the existence of Dixville Notch while at Crawford's, and learning that moose and other big game were to be found there, Parkman dragged the increasingly reluctant Slade northward by way of Lancaster and Colebrook. At Lancaster he fell in with the State Geological Survey party under Dr. Charles T. Jackson, and got a full account of the country to the north and of the requisites for those who would travel there. Slade found this alarming, "as if we were bound for an exploring expedition to Hudson's Bay," and displayed a strong desire to go home rather than into the wilderness. But by means of alternate taunts and appeals he was induced to continue. After the pair left Colebrook, they were really in the wilds, for there was then only a handful of settlers in this region. Passing through Dixville Notch, where a road of sorts was first opened in this same year to Bragg's Settlement (Errol), Parkman and Slade followed the Androscoggin upstream to its source, at the juncture of the Magalloway River with the outlet of Lake Umbagog, near the Maine border. Somewhere below the present Wilsons Mills, Maine, they and their guide took to a skiff and followed the Magalloway northward to its forks, not far from the Canadian boundary. It is impossible to trace the route on a modern map, since the damming of the Magalloway above Wilsons Mills has covered Parkman's path with the waters of Aziscoos Lake. Without proper equipment and supplies, Parkman and Slade journeyed much as the Jesuit missionary and the *coureur de bois* had done, depending upon fish and game to swell their meager larder. Only the absence of blankets and bread, and the complete discouragement of Slade, deterred Parkman from continuing on to Canada by way of the St. Francis or Chaudière rivers.

Turning back, they retraced their route as far as Lancaster; and thence Parkman proceeded to Boston by stage down the Connecticut Valley, through Littleton, Haverhill, Hanover, and Windsor, and then to Nashua, where he took the train. Despite the rigors of this journey—no small feat for a gently nurtured seventeen-year-old, accustomed to the soft life of a student—Parkman viewed this journey "as the beginning of greater things" and "as merely prefatory to longer wanderings." Far from being worn out or weary of the wilderness, he expressed a wish soon to pass another month as pleasantly, as he initialed the last page of the journal with two triumphant flourishes. This hope had to be deferred until the following summer, when he returned to Boston by the Magalloway route after a far more ambitious journey along the Canadian border.

Aside from its interest as an early account of the best-known places in the White Mountains by one of their most ardent and eloquent admirers, this journal is notable for its picture of Parkman as a man and as a writer at the age of seventeen. Here are revealed the qualities of solitary courage and perseverance which enabled him to accomplish his lifework despite the almost insuperable difficulties which beset his path. And here, in this joyous and vivid narrative set down with only a few slips of the pen, is the measure of Parkman's precocious ability to use words effectively, and to make the unfamiliar world of the wilderness come alive for the armchair wanderer. The historian still had much to learn, but the writer was ready for the task that lay ahead.

The journal is written in ink in a $6\frac{3}{8}$ by $7\frac{7}{8}$ inches copybook, with marbled paper covers. In September, soon after his return to Boston, Parkman rewrote the account of the Magalloway portion of the journey in ink on gray paper. This revised version is inferior to the original, losing the simplicity and vigor of the first in an effort to be literary; and since it incorporates no new material, it is not reproduced here. Twenty-three years later Parkman published in *Harper's Magazine* for November 1864 (XXIX, 735-41) an anonymous sketch, "Exploring the Magalloway," which is based upon these youthful notes, and those of the 1842 journal. His companion Slade wrote an account of the trip ("In the White Mountains with Francis Parkman in 1841," *New England Magazine*, New Series, Vol. XI, 1 [September 1894], 94-9), supposedly based on his own diary but really on Parkman's. Slade's essay has little value, since it romanticizes in retrospect: "The entire journey was a delight to us"!

1841

July 19th, Monday. I was disappointed of one of my companions, Tower,[1] who fell sick this morning, having imprudently gorged himself with pie yesterday. Dan Slade's[2] horror at so inauspicious an occurrence damped his own ardor and somewhat retarded his preparations, insomuch that I watched from the window, quarter of an hour after the specified time, without beholding the approach of either of my fellow travelers. At length Dan appeared alone, striding along like the colossus; and truly there was need, for we had just five minutes to reach the depot of the railroad, three-quarters of a mile off. By a special providence, a hack was passing; we jumped in, exhorted the driver to use his best speed, and reached the railroad boat at the instant she was leaving the wharf. This was at seven o'clock—at ten we were at Portsmouth—at half-past eleven we were at Dover,[3] and at twelve, *cibo et poto graves,*[a] were on the way to Alton. Our conveyance was none of the most agreeable. A little carryall, whose legitimate freight was four persons, was doomed to transport seven, with baggage more than proportional. Four ladies, or women, were deposited behind, politeness, of course, forbidding Dan and myself to lay claim to back seats. The front seat was all that remained and the driver was a portly man—imagine, then, our condition—uncomfortable, at any rate, but almost insufferable when it be considered that beside being jammed by our disagreeable propinquity, we were obliged to sit bolt upright, for two of the "ladies" occupied the seat just behind, so that we sat back to back with these fair ones, with no guard between; consequently an attempt on our part to lean would have pitched the nymp(t)hs, head first, into the laps of their neighbors opposite. This state of thing endured for twenty miles, but the driver being pleasant, civil, and accommodating, the matter

[a] "Full of food and drink."—Ed.

7

was not so bad as it might have been. This "extra accommodation"—for such it was—carried us within twelve miles of Alton.⁴ Here we got out, glad of any change, strapped on knapsacks, and entered upon our pedestrian experiences. The way was long and the burden heavy; I particularly had, beside my knapsack, a heavy gun, a ponderous double shot-pouch, well filled, an[d] a powder flask. We travelled on at a tolerably easy rate, until Dan, seating himself on a stone, complained that his darned knapsack hurt his shoulders. He accordingly carried it in his hand a space, but finding this method still more annoying, he again restored it to its rightful position.

"How far to Alton Bay?" we inquired of a rustic who was raking hay in a field. "Two mile strong." "Two miles what?" said we in astonishment. "Two mile strong—rather more nor two mile"; and, accordingly, we found ourselves entering a valley between two ranges of high hills which had appeared to us first, a few hours before, like blue clouds in the distance. The road, flanked by thick woods, wound downwards through the valley; at length we turned an angle of it and saw the waters of the lake glistening through the trees. "There!" cried Dan in exstacy, "there's the lake at last—hope we shall get some good supper—Frank, is my face clean?" Having satisfied Dan on the important subject of his question, I proceeded down with him to a most unpromising-looking tavern on the lake shore. Nevertheless, our lodgings are good and our supper was excellent. We have travelled upwards of a hundred miles today, twelve of them on foot.

July 20ᵗʰ. The Winnipissiogeeᵇ steamboat foundered last year, the only sail-boat at Alton was out of repair, and our only alternative was a walk to Senter [Center] Harbor. There runs a road along the western banks of the lake, but little travelled, for the first eight or ten miles at least, and commanding fine views of the water and mountains. We left Alton by this path in the morning, doubting nothing to reach Senter Harbor by night, albeit it was a distance of nearly thirty miles. At first we were cool enough, for the road was flanked by deep and dark forests and shaded by wild hills, winding

ᵇ *Winnipisseogee* was the most common variant spelling of *Winnipesaukee* in nine-teenth-century usage.—Ed.

at one time along the edge of the lake and then passing through shaded vallies. But this happy condition of things was not destined to last. The sun grew hotter and hotter and the road more and more open. For the first hour or two, we passed no dwellings but a few log-cabins, with a little clearing in the forest around them. But, alas, the little pathway was widened by the junction of others, and farm houses began to appear, first singly, then in clusters, with clearings extending for miles. The road, too, began to turn from the edge of the lake and to run inland, so that the scenery was no ways so interesting as before. It was almost noon and we toiled up the scorching road, sweating and grumbling at the folly which had deprived us of shelter and comfort by ridiculously burning the forests, in the zeal for making clearings, though the burnt land lays utterly waste and the sole effect of the operation is to ruin the scene and lay the road open to the baking sun. The thermometer was at about 90° and the road had become most disgustingly hilly and dreary. We reached the lake again and bathed—no small relief, for our clothes clung to us with sweat. Next we stopped at a farm house and got some bread and milk, and next made a temporary encampment in a cool piece of wood and rested some time. Then we journeyed on again, and that part of us left undissolved by the heat arrived early in the afternoon at Meredith Bridge, where we lost no time in establishing ourselves at the tavern, wisely relinquishing our purpose of proceeding further. "Last time you catch me walking this time of day," said Dan from his easy chair in the tavern parlor. "Amen," said I, "we will set out before sunrise tomorrow." Meredith Bridge, by the way, is a disgusting little manufacturing village, with no single point of attraction, either as concerns scenery or anything else, if we set aside the six-pound trout sometimes taken there. Indeed, we heard an apocryphal story of a trout of ten pounds caught a day or two ago.

July 21ˢᵗ, Wednesday. Agreeably to our resolutions of last night we were up early; nevertheless, the sun from its very rising was insufferably hot, and every well we passed was called upon for our relief. The inhabitants were a kind and hospitable race, to talk like the geography. When we stopped at the cistern, a white-headed brat would generally be despatched out to us with a mug, that we might quench our thirst with the greater convenience, or the master of the house would come himself and hold a talk with us.

We toiled on to Meredith Village—nine miles—where we breakfasted, and finding that we were losing flesh with astounding rapidity and gaining nothing to counterbalance it, we hired a waggon and rode the remaining four miles to Senter Harbor. Here we got rooms, and finding it impossible to stir on account of the heat, we amused ourselves indoors as we best might, Dan with snoring on his bed and I with reading the *Alhambra*[5] on the balcony. There I sat watching the heated air rising from the road and fences, and the lake as it lay enduring the heat with Christian resignation, with its surface like glass and all its trees wilting over it. There has been no rain here for weeks; the crops are dried up and all the grass of a straw color. The evening brought some relief, for a party of us, having obtained a leaky boat with infinite difficulty, went out on the pond and landed on some of the islands. Returning, we bathed, to the indescribable horror and inexpressible consternation of a party of ladies who had been out in a leakier boat, and who were advancing in the darkness directly into the midst of us until we signified the peculiar delicacy of our situation by splashings in the water and unequivocal callings to one another. Then, indeed, arose a suppressed murmuring of "Oh's!" and "Ah's!" and "Did you ever's!" as the boat sheered off.

July 22nd, Thursday. We set out before sunrise this morning for Red Hill[6] in a waggon. The waggon and the early hour were both adopted from prudential motives, for we remembered our roasting of yesterday. We arrived at the foot of the hill a little after sunrise, fastened our horse, and began the ascent. The road is still shadowed by the forests, though it is extremely doubtful how long it will remain so. The unsightly "cleared land" is constantly extending its bounds up the side of the hill, and the smoke of the fires which are destroying the chief ornament of the country fills the air. So much for the Yankee spirit of improvement. The path at first is not steep. Half way up the mountain stands the house of the Cooke family, of whom we found only the deaf and dumb daughter at home. We made her comprehend that we wanted something to eat, and by imitating the motion of milking and other pantomimic representations, that bread and milk was what we particularly desired. She bestirred herself with the greatest alacrity, and we pursued our journey upwards marvellously refreshed. We reached the top but were disappointed. The air was filled with vapour, and thin dull clouds were hanging around the mountains. Even the near ridge of Ossipee looked like a huge, indistinct, ragged wall, and the lake—visible in clear weather through its whole extent—could now scarcely be seen at a distance of ten miles. The whole landscape was dim and dull as if seen through smoke. I had seen it once before in its perfection,[7] and knew what we lost; as for Dan, he appeared to care little one way or other.

He sat him on a stone, and gave one glance at the view—"First-rate prospect!—I tell you what, Frank, I guess my shoes won't stand this much longer." "Dan," said I, as we went down, "I shall start for the White Mountains this noon—you had better wait here a day or two for Tower; you can join me again, if you want to, at Crawford's." "Darne it!" responded my fellow traveller, "you don't suppose I am going to stay alone in this dirty hole, do you? If you go, I'll go too."[c]

At two o'clock we took stage for Conway, having spent the interim since the morning in sleeping and reading, for the heat is Tartarean, and being out of doors at noon is out of the question. The country was extremely wild and beautiful—more so than my recollection of my former journey had prepared me for. Ossipee Pond is a magnificent sheet of water, girt by mountains, and not choked up, like Winnipissiogee, by a too-great number of islands. We passed, too, Chicoriuya, alias Chorcorua, Mountain, the highest peak of a noble range, from whose summit the Indian chief who has given it his name flung himself in dispair at the encroachments of the white men.[8] But all these scenes are impaired by wide patches of burnt wood and the half-cultivated lands which increase continually and disfigure them more and more. We arrived at Conway at eight, and I occupied myself with writing a letter home.

[c] Ten lines have been inked out here in the journal, and are largely illegible. They open with a regret that Tower had not come along, so that Parkman could have left his companions whenever he felt like it.—Ed.

July 23rd, Friday. Set out from Conway at six, breakfasted at Bartlett at eight, and proceeded onward for the mountains. The weather was cloudy and threatening, and passing a valley in the mountains, it began to rain. It soon ceased and we kept on through a country ten times wilder and more mountainous than we passed yesterday. The forests were untouched, and the hills, in place of the coat of green woods, were broken with precipices and crowned with shattered crags. The clouds were around most of them, and the view was indistinct with the mist, yet sometimes the more interesting on that very account. We reached (the) old man Crawford's,[9] eight miles from the Notch, and it began to rain in good earnest. I was on the outside; so was Slade; so were two ladies. At first we put up umbrellas; but the rain came down like a thunder shower, and I, who sat on the driver's seat, and whose umbrella, consequently, conducted a small torrent of dirty water directly into the laps of the ladies behind, judged it expedient to lower my miserable shelter and receive the bounty of heaven in full. This, indeed, subjected me to no additional drenching for, in the situation in which I was, the umbrella was like a dam of bulrushes against the Nile. We made sport of the matter, although the driver averred he had not gotten such a ducking for four years—the ladies especially exhibited much philosophy, though of the kind denominated "laughing philosophy," and, altogether, the ducking was an extremely agreeable affair. We entered the Notch; the clouds lay over the mountains from top to bottom, but occasionally, as some heavy mass was rolled aside, we caught a view of the craggy and savage hill, scored with avalanche tracks, and white with torrents. The little streams, parched up by the heat, were swoln on a sudden and went foaming about us, and rising every instant more and more. We reached the Notch House[10] in pretty plight. For myself, not a thread of my thin clothing was dry, and the heroic ladies were wet to the skin. A little brandy and water, with a change of clothing, revived us, though a reviving process was almost needless.

July 24. This morning I went fishing, following downwards the stream of the waterfall which comes down through the Floom [Flume]. I basketed about thirty trout. The weather was dull and cloudy; the clouds hid the peaks of the mountains and rolled in huge masses along their sides. Early in the morning the mist was rolling, in a constant stream, from the narrow opening of the Notch, like a furnace disgorging its smoke.

This afternoon I achieved the most serious adventure it was ever my lot to encounter. I walked down the Notch to the Willey House[11] and, out of curiosity, began to ascend in the pathway of the avalanche on the mountain directly behind. This pathway is a deep ravine, channelled in the side of the mountain which in this place is extremely steep. In the bottom of this gulf a little stream comes down from a spring above and renders the precipitous rock as slippery as clay. The sides of the ravine, which runs directly up and down the mountain, are of decaying granite, while the bottom is formed by a trap-dike. I ascended at first easily, but the way began to be steeper and the walls on each side more precipitous. Still I kept on until I came to a precipice about forty feet high and not far from perpendicular. I could see that this was followed by a similar one above. Professor Silliman,[12] a year or two ago, ascended in this place, until, as he says, "further progress was prevented by inaccessible precipices of the trap rock." The exploit of the professor occurred to me as I stood below and I determined that "inaccessible precipices" which had cooled his scientific ardor should prove no barrier to me. I began to climb; and with considerable difficulty and danger, and with the loss of my stick, which went rattling and bounding down the ravine many rods before it found a resting place, I surmounted both precipices. I climbed on; but finding that I was becoming drenched by the scanty stream, and seeing, moreover, a huge cloud, not far up, settling slowly towards me, I bethought me of retracing my steps. I knew that it would be impossible to descend by the way I had come, and, accordingly, I tried to get out of the ravine to the side of the mountain which was covered with wood, which I could grasp hold of to assist me. But I was enclosed between two walls, (of) fifty feet high and so steep and composed of such material that an attempt to climb would only bring down the rotting granite upon my head. So I began to descend the ravine, nothing doubting that I should find some means of getting out before reaching the critical point. But it was impossible, and I found myself at the top of the precipice with no alternative but to slide down, or clamber the perpendicular and decaying walls to the surface of the mountain. The former was certain destruction, as I proved by suffering a rotten log to slide down. It glanced by the first descent like an arrow, struck at the bottom, bounded six feet into the air, and leaped down the mountain, splintering into twenty pieces as it went. The other method was scarcely less dangerous, but it was my only chance, and I braced my nerves and began to climb. Down went stones and pebbles, clattering hundreds of feet below and giving me a grateful indication of my inevitable fate in case my head should swim or my courage fail. I had got half way up and was clinging to the face of the precipice, when the two stones which supported my feet loosened and leaped down the ravine. My finger-ends, among the rotten gravel, were all which sustained me, and they, of course, would have failed, had I not thought, on the instant, of lowering my body gradually, and so diminishing its weight, until my feet found new supporters. I sank the length of my arms and then hung, for the time, in tolerable safety, with one foot resting on a projecting stone. Loosening the hold of one hand, I took my large jack-knife from my pocket, opened it with the assistance of my teeth, and dug with it a hollow among the decayed stones large enough to receive and support one foot. Then, thrusting the knife as far as possible into the wall to assist my hold, I grasped it and the stones with the unoccupied hand and raised my foot to the hollow prepared for it. Thus, foot by foot, I made my way, and in ten minutes, as time seemed to me, I siezed a projecting root at the top and drew myself up. During the whole time of climbing, I felt perfectly cool, but when fairly up, I confess I shuddered as I looked down at the gulf I had escaped. A large stone, weighing, perhaps, a hundred pounds, lay on the edge. I thrust it off with my foot and down it went, struck the bottom of the ravine with a tremendous crash, and thundered down, leaping from side to side, until it lodged at last, far below, against a projecting rock. I descended the mountain by means of the trees and bushes; cut a fishing pole at the bottom; and, having amused myself with an hour's fishing, went to the tavern, and astonished the company with a recital of my adventure. Crawford expressed considerable astonishment at my escape, and the young lady in whose company I got my ducking on the stage transferred an account to her journal, but refused to let me see it, promising to send me a copy the moment her book was out of the press. Crawford's house, by the way, is full of pleasant company, and an ascent of Mount Washington is in agitation tomorrow.

July 25th. This morning proving tolerably fair, we set out for the mountain—an army of ten strong, horse[13] and foot, male and female. The first two miles (the entire distance is six miles) are through a dense forest—an ascent the whole distance. As we went on, the trees grew smaller and smaller, until we arrived in two hours at a height where the path ascended through a forest of the gigantic height of two feet—a complete miniature of the larger wood we had passed. Ten minutes more and we were on the summit of Mt. Clinton [Pierce][d] with a long succession of wild and rocky peaks stretching before. We descended Mount Clinton and mounted the higher summit of Mount Pleasant, and here a most glorious scene presented itself to us. On each side, thousands of feet below, stretched a wide valley, girt with an amphitheatre of mountains rising peak after peak like the black waves of the sea, the clouds now sinking over their summits, now rising and breaking, disclosing yet more distant ranges, and then settling thick and heavy so that nothing was visible but the savage rocks and avalanche slides of the neighboring mountains looming dimly through the mist. At length the clouds closed around and we could not even see one another and we descended Mount Pleasant in darkness. But as we mount[ed] up the steep ascent of Mount Monroe [Franklin] the sun broke out bright and clear; the mists gathered themselves and rolled down the mountain sides, quivered an instant, then boiled up through the ravines and gorges, scattered, and were borne along glistening in the sun, among the thousand mountains that lay beneath and around us. At the same moment, a peal of thunder sounded below and a rainbow arched, for an instant, the peak before us. I stopped my horse on the ridge where we stood and watched the rest, as they wound in a long line up the mountain. The side was steep and the path ran zig-zag up. No scene among the Andes could have been wilder or more picturesque. They moved, one by one, up the steep, bending and winding in twenty directions, the outlandish habits of the gentlemen and

[d] Mt. Pierce was known at this time as Mt. Clinton.—Ed.

the fluttering shawls of the ladies suiting well with the scene, until they stood against the sky on the summit. I followed, and the scene appeared yet sublimer and more extensive. The mountains were like a sea of lashing waves; the valley of the Connecticut was visible for fifty miles, with the river winding through it like a thread; while in the valley below, the forests seemed, from the tremendous height we stood upon, like fields of mown grass intersected by the channels of streams whose waters, at intervals, flashed in the sun. Two peaks were still before us, the highest and most distant topped with clouds, and this was Mt. Washington. We reached the first, Mt. Franklin [Monroe], and the path led along a ledge on a high precipice at its summit. The ledge overhung the valley beneath—deeper even than that on the other side, and in place of the extensive prospect there visible, a huge range of mountains, marked with avalanches and capped with clouds, heaved up like a wall.

We passed the Lake of the Clouds, near the summit of the Mountain—the source of the Amonioosack [Ammonoosuc] and another large stream. The lake is small but very deep and its waters extremely cold. Mount Washington now rose before us, still covered with clouds, and with patches of snow laying in its sheltered hollows. We mounted, and in a moment entered the clouds again. We could hear each other's voices but see nothing. The path wound among bare rocks scantily covered with moss, with here and there a stunted blade of coarse grass, and no other sign of vegetation. The wind was strong and cold and sleet was mixed with the mist that drove along the mountain. We reached the top at last—a pyramid of huge rocks through which the wind was whistling like the shrieking of a storm and faintly bore down to us the voices of some of the party who had reached the top before us and were singing "Old Hundred" to the winds. Crawford brought us provisions, with a stock of brandy, which he served out to us in a sheltered spot, as we sat round a flat rock which was his table. We remained there three-quarters of an hour in the vain hope of its clearing, but a storm of sleet and rain came on and we began our descent. We soon reached warmth and sunlight, and the scenes we had passed in ascending appeared to yet greater advantage now. Two of the party fell from their horses, three of the ladies were faint-hearted, and all of them tired with one exception—Miss Prentiss[14] of Keene, whose strength and spirit and good humor would have invigorated at least a dozen feeble damsels. We passed the mountains, entered the forest, and reached the tavern, having set out at ten in the morning and returned at seven in the evening. I walked, from choice, all but a mile in going, and all but about twice that distance in returning, the entire distance being twelve miles of ascent and descent.

July 26. A dull rain. It held up in the morning and I ascended the High Rock[15] in the Notch, whence I had a noble view. As in my former more critical adventure, ascending was passable, but coming down abominable. The way was through a tangled wood, rocky, bushy, and strewed in all directions with rotten trunks, many of which, when stepped upon, straightway burst to pieces, and, unless I was extremely careful, seated me among their rot. There was a path, but I did not avail myself of it. Coming down, I found dinner over and all the pleasant company gone to Franconia, whither I shall go tomorrow, weather permitting. And now, having made up for former neglect by writing 9 pages at a sitting, I begin to feel tired and more disposed to curse the weather than ever before, and the prospect of an evening almost solitary in no wise tends to improve my temper. Heaven send that I be not obliged to spend another day here at the Notch House—a place which, though one of the pleasant-est in the world at other times, is the perfection of dulness in bad weather.

July 27th. We spent the last evening in the desirable company of Mr. and Mrs. Plummer—a couple of the most consummate fools I ever saw. They set out for the mountain this morning, though the lady uttered the most piercing shrieks her limited power of lungs could compass the instant she was seated in the saddle. A fit person she is, truly, to climb a mountain of seven thousand feet![e] We left Crawford's early this morning, on foot, for Franconia. The morning was the finest we have had yet; so was the road. At Fabyan's, where we stopped a few minutes, we heard that our intended companion, Tower, had arrived before us, having recovered from his illness; and

e Mt. Washington's real height is 6,288 feet.—Ed.

was then gone, with a party, to Mt. Washington. He passed Crawford's without thinking to inquire there for us. We found, to our surprise, that George Cary, Henry Parker, and Wheelright[16] were at the tavern in the morning, but were now absent on the mountain. We walked on. I shot a partridge and a wild pigeon, and we stopped at noon in the woods on the bank of the Amonoosuck, kindled a fire, cooked our game, and made a good dinner with the assistance of some crackers. Eight miles further on, and we arrived at Franconia Village—a distance of twenty-two miles from our morning starting place.

July 28th. Left Franconia Village for the Notch this morning, having first committed my imbecile shoes to the care of a competent cobbler and substituted a new straw hat—the only one in the town—for my damaged old one. We reached the Notch and dined on bread and milk, then visited the curiosities of the place. The Old Man of the Mountain scowled as fixedly as ever, and the mountains, with their forest-covered sides and bare white peaks, presented the same aspect as when I had seen them three years before. We found a boat on one of the little lakes and circumnavigated it for some time, at the great risk of capsizing, for the boat was a wretched affair. Spite of its fine scenery, the place began to grow dull, and we walked on to Lincoln, in order to see the Flume in the morning.

At Lincoln the sole tavern and the sole house presented rather discouraging aspect; nevertheless, enter we must and make the best of it we could. The interior arrangements in no wise belied external appearances. In company with a most comical looking Yankee pedlar, we were served with a supper whereof the chief item was raw cucumbers, backed by an anonymous pie with a crust like lignum-vitae. We survived it, not being fastidious, and having the anticipation of a good breakfast, provided it be not spoiled in the cooking, for I shot on the road a large partridge and several wild-pigeons which I delivered to the hostess for preparation. In addition to the other slight drawbacks to comfort, we found the host[f] drunk; and it was with difficulty that we made him comprehend that clean sheets, a couple of chairs, and a table were indispensable requisites.

[f] Referred to as Gurnsey in the 1842 Journal.—Ed.

As to a washstand, there was no such thing in the house; so we must e'en be content with the pump.

July 29ᵗʰ. We set out this morning, before breakfast, to see the Flume. Half-way through the woods, we missed the path, but, guided by the roaring of the water, we found the banks of the Pemigewasset and determined to follow them up until we reach the Flume. Now we were making a grievous mistake, for the Flume is not on the main stream, but on a branch of it in an opposite direction from the one we were pursuing. The forest was dense and dark, and the ground strewed with fallen trunks in various states of decay. The ground was rocky, moreover, and full of ravines and deep holes; and the thick matted undergrowth in nowise facilitated our progress. On we went, stumbling amongst piles of rotten logs, and switched in all directions by the recoiling twigs. The forest was almost impassable, so we essayed the bank of the river. But the river was full of huge rocks and stones, amongst which the water came racing and foaming down, so that even wading up its bed was impossible. Cliffs (of) sixty feet high, damp and green with moss, and with pine and birch trees growing from their fissures in many places, overhung the water; and along their edges and up and down their sides we must make our way. I was encumbered with gun and shot pouch, which was a still farther aggravation of my difficulties. Dan stopped short: "Hang your dirty Flume! I move we go back to the house and get the old man to show us the way as he said he would." "We could not find the house, Dan; our only way is to keep on till we come to the Flume. It can't be more than a few rods further."

There was a kind of natural pathway at the foot of the cliffs and we followed it, making our way with difficulty between the rocks on one side and the roaring water on the other. A projecting rock and a slight bend in the stream prevented our seeing further before us, but we heard a loud heavy plunging of water. By swinging from a projecting branch and making a long leap, we gained a flat rock in the middle of the river, and beheld a scene which paid us for our trouble. A broad circular basin[17] of water was before us, so deep that its waves were of a dark green, with huge perpendicular cliffs rising on each hand above it. From the top of the cliffs, trees started out obliquely against the sky and dripping festoons of moss were hanging from every cleft. In front, these same cliffs swept round until they almost met, leaving a narrow passage for the river, through which it plunged, over a wall of rocks, into the basin below. Above, it might be seen again, foaming over a bed of steep rocks, and closing the perspective with a smooth unbroken fall contrasted well with its lashing and white rapids. We looked at it for some time and then began to devise some method of proceeding. It was no easy matter, for the cliffs rose directly from the water and their sides were so steep and smooth that they offered no hold to one passing them. Our only alternative was to scale them where they were less steep, a little way below. We got to the top and began to force our way through the forest again. "Damn the Flume," said Dan, when we had proceeded about quarter of a mile. "We must have missed it," said I, "it can't be farther on than this. This river strikes the road about a mile from here—we had better keep on till we reach it." "Devil take the Flume —I wish we had never come, or else had brought a guide." Thus profanely spoke Dan, but we kept on for half an hour, with toil and suffering, and emerged at length on the road, two miles from the tavern, having forced our way through a mile and a half of forest in the whole, and having two miles more, on the road, to walk before we reached the tavern again. We got there at last, took breakfast, procured a guide, and set out for the Flume a second time. We found, to our great satisfaction, that visitors seldom attempted, unattended, to find the place we were searching for, and that when they did they usually returned discouraged and frightened, or else became lost and had to be searched for with shoutings and firings of guns. This Flume is a huge natural trough of rock through which runs, in a succession of falls and rapids, a branch of the river Pemigewasset. On each side of the stream high cliffs rise perpendicularly and run for many rods facing each other. Their black sides are smooth, and continually dropping moisture, for the forest above extends its branches from their edges so that the light of the sun can scarcely penetrate the ravine. Standing on the rocks at the bottom and looking up, you see huge decayed trunks and branches extending across the narrow strip of sky visible between the edges of the cliffs, and the edges themselves overgrown with masses of wet and green moss which hang dripping from them. Knotted and distorted pines, rooted in the crevices, fling their boughs across; and even these, though living, are covered with damp mosses. Midway between the top of the cliffs and the water, and closing the spectator's onward view, hangs a rock, hurled by some convulsion down the ravine and intercepted between its approaching sides. Just beneath this, the stream foams down over a bed of rocks into a deep basin at their foot, then leaps from the basin and rushes forward among the stones and accumulated trunks of trees which intercept its course.

We returned from the Flume and walked back to Franconia Notch, where the tavern is kept by a man named Fifield.[18] He went with us fishing in the afternoon to a little brook at some distance in the woods. I followed the stream upward, while Fifield and Slade went in an opposite direction. Just before sunset, I was half a mile up the brook, with a long string of trout and with the full belief that I knew the direction in which the road lay. I accordingly made all speed through the forest, lest I should be overtaken by the dark. I travelled about a mile, guiding my course by the sun, but the forest seemed deeper and wilder the further I went. At length I caught sight of a mountain peak which I knew, and shaping my course by that, in a few minutes reached the road.

July 30th, Lancaster. It was a week ago that I first heard of the existence of a pass in the mountains, in the town of Dixville, said by those who have visited it to be equal or superior in grandeur to the Notch of the White Mountains. Mr. Prentiss[19] from Keene, whom I met at Crawford's, first told me of it and advised me to visit it. The country about it is a wilderness where moose and other wild game are still common, though it is traversed by a new and almost impassable road. I determined from the first to go if possible, and came to Lancaster today to secure the services of an Indian named Anantz [Annance][20] as a guide. He was by far the best hunter in this part of the country, and lived, in part, by guiding parties through the wildernesses on the borders of New Hampshire and Canada. He was an educated man, moreover, having passed through Dartmouth College, and celebrated through the country for his skill, faithfulness, and courage. But arriving at Lancaster, I found that he was absent in Vermont and that there was no other man to supply his place. Luckily, Dr. Jackson[21] and his assistants in the state survey were in the town, and from them I got a full and accurate account of the country and of the requisites for my expedition. Mr. Williams,[22] one of his assistants, hunted there under the guidance of Anantz last season, and, between them, they shot two moose! He showed me a map of my course, of which I took a copy; told me the places where temporary guides might be engaged; and, more than all, acquainted me with the usual prices of their services—a most valuable piece of information, for otherwise I could not guard myself against imposition. As for Dr. Jackson, he most kindly gave us the full fruits of his experience—and a most ample one it has been—in the matters of provision, camps, canoes, guns, guides, and a thousand other things, as if we were bound on an exploring expedition to Hudson's Bay. Dan Slade was frightened by the formidable catalogue. He muttered several dark hints about his "not entering into the spirit of it," his "not engaging to come so far," "starting off without any preparation," &c., &c. I was obliged to accuse him of a tendency to "funk out" and open upon him a full battery of arguments before he would yield a reluctant consent. I took such pains for a double reason—first, I am unwilling to travel wholly alone through the wilderness, and I do not propose to secure a guide until I have visited the pass and penetrated yet deeper—secondly, the hire for transportation and guides will amount to just half the sum; that is, I shall pay one half, and he the other.

Our course lies first to Colebrook, a town thirty-five miles north of this place, on the Connecticut; thence we proceed on foot in an easterly direction by a road little travelled which brings us to the pass. Thence keeping on, we strike the Umbagog Lake and the Ma(r)galloway river. Here there is a small settlement, where a guide may be had, and from here our journey lies—the Lord knows where. We have just engaged a private waggon for Colebrook, for no public conveyance is to be had, and we leave Lancaster for that town at seven tomorrow.

By the way, we met Tower at Littleton today. He is sick and discouraged and on his way home.

Sir William Johnson, Baronet
Engraving
(Coverdale Collection No. 72)

July 31st, Colebrook. We reached this place at two o'clock. It is a town of a few hundred inhabitants—the largest north of Lancaster—and lies on the Connecticut opposite Monadnock Mountain on the Vermont shore. It is watered, moreover, by the Mohawk River, a mighty stream at present about four inches deep. Our journey hither lay along the east bank of the Connecticut, through a country fertile and by no means thinly inhabited. The high mountains in the town of Stark lay on our right, and the river, fallen extremely low and full of rapids, on our left. We found a neat little tavern where we are at present stopping.

Sunday, Aug. 1st. Sunday in the country is a day of most unmitigated and abominable dulness. By a strong and desperate effort, I nerved myself to endure, being greatly assisted in my resolve by the discovery of several numbers of a Baltimore magazine[23] in the house. I went to church in the morning, but the minister being unfortunately an Unitarian, the dulness of his discourse and the squall of his choir were not varied and relieved by any novel fanaticism or methodistical blunders. This being the case, I determined not to go again but to stay at home and amuse myself with writing a letter.

Aug. 2nd, Captain Brag[g]'s Settlement [Errol, N. H.].[24] We left Colebrook and civilization this morning, and now a new epoch of this interesting history commences. Our journey lieth not, henceforward, through pleasant villages and cultivated fields, but through the wild forest and among lakes and streams which have borne no bark but the canoe of the Indian or the hunter. This is probably the last night for some time which we shall spend under a roof. Our road ran eastward towards Maine. A few farm houses were at first scattered along its side, but they became more and more distant as we went on, and at last the way was flanked by a forest so thickset and tangled that we could scarcely see two rods in any direction, excepting before and behind. We were traveling what was called a road, but the term was grievously misapplied. By dint of great exertion, a strong waggon might possibly be forced over the stones and stumps and roots and through the overhanging boughs which formed a complete arch overhead, but the attempt would be destruction to a carriage or chaise. Ruts on each side showed that it was occcasionally travelled, but that this was very seldom was evident from the grass which almost covered it. As we were sitting on a log to rest, we heard a clatter of hoofs, and in a moment a man, mounted and bearing a gun, appeared through the trees, advancing towards us. He was from Brag's settlement, thirteen miles further on, and going to Cole-brook for employment. The pass, he told us, was but a few miles before us, and accordingly, through an opening in the trees, we saw the mountains extended before us like a green wall and apparently blocking our passage. A little further, and we emerged upon a plain almost free of wood; and now a gap in the range appeared, with bare and pointed rocks starting upward from the forests that covered the mountains and looking down upon us as we entered the passage. These rocks were many hundred feet high and the pass between extremely narrow. Looking upward on either side, the mountains were almost perpendicular. Fire had stripped them of their verdure and left them covered with blackened trunks and rocks rolled from the sharp peaks above. In picturesque effect the scene was superior to the Notch of the White Mountains, but in grandeur it fell far below it. Instead of the vast rounded summits of the Notch, these mountains were surmounted by peaks and needles of rock, which from below looked like ruined towers standing out in relief against the sky.

We were in want of a dinner, and so, catching some trout and shooting some pigeons, we cooked them after a style wholly original, and stayed for a time the inroads of appetite. While Dan sat still to digest his dinner, I ascended one of the mountains and had a fine view of the pass and the neighboring country. We proceeded, passed some few houses, mostly log cabins, and reached at sunset the settle-ment of Capt. Brag on the Amorescoggin [Androscoggin]. Here we got tolerable accommodation, and slept to the roar of the rapids of the river which ran close to the house.

The Captain slew a bear day before yesterday, and his fresh skin was nailed on the barn to dry. I write this on the morning of the 4th—having got somewhat behind-hand—by the blaze of our camp-fire in the forest.

And now, the life I have led for the past week having prevented my recording my experiences from day to day, I take this first opportunity for making up for former neglect. Beginning where I left off:

Tuesday, Aug. 3ʳᵈ. Brag's settlement is on the Amariscoggin River, not far from Lake Umbagog and a few miles west of the mouth of the Margalloway. The Amariscoggin at this place is a succession of rapids extending more than a mile. On the Margalloway, too, some miles above its junction with the Ameriscoggin, are rapids of two miles in length and passable only by means of a rugged and difficult portage. Our intention was to take a boat and a guide at Brag's, ascend the Margalloway as far as the rapids, have the boat drawn round them and launched above, and then keep on up the river, which is navigable for thirty miles above without serious obstruction. But we found it impossible to procure here a good guide and boat, though both, they told us, were to be had at settlements on the Margalloway. Could they convey us to these settlements? Brag had but few men with him and these occupied in necessary work; moreover, there was a path through the forest several miles less than the passage by water, and by this we might reach the settlements in half a day. We determined on this route, and Brag accompanied us a mile or two on our way to point out its difficulties and to prevent our plunging into quagmires or mistaking a rabbit track or a cattle path for the road.

"The first house," said he, "is five or six miles further on. When you get about a mile, you will have to cross a brook.ᵍ On the other side there are logging paths and one thing another branching out like, right and left. All you have got to do is to pick out the one that you see has been most travelled by the cattle, because all the others run a little ways and then come to nothing. Then go on a little further and you will come to a guzzle that they say is pretty bad this season, though I ha'nt seen it myself. However it a'nt more than two rods wide, so I guess you can get across. Just keep, all along, where the cattle have been most, and you can't miss the way."

With these direction we set out. The path was about four inches

ᵍ Probably Bennett Brook.—Ed.

wide, through the dense forest, choked up with undergrowth, and obstructed by logs that had fallen across it. As may well be imagined, five miles by such a road were equivalent to twenty by any other. We crossed the brook, and following the cow-tracks, fortunately took the right turning and found to our infinite satisfaction that the path became a little more distinct and passable than before. Passing over a swampy tract, we saw deer and bear tracks in abundance. Two miles further (which two miles it took us as many hours to accomplish) and we had our first view of the Margalloway—a broad, still river whose sloping banks are, and for centuries will be, clothed with deep forests. We had forgotten the threatened "guzzle," and our very ideas of its nature were somewhat vague and mystified, though the Captain had been at great pains to explain it. But now we came upon it and our doubts were set at rest. A kind of muddy creek, very deep and dirty, extended from the river directly across the path. It was, as the Captain said, about two rods wide, with muddy and slippery banks and no earthly means of crossing but two slender poles, laid one from each bank and resting on a floating log in the middle. On the opposite bank, however, lay a heap of logs with their ends in the water, and bearing to the careless eye an appearance of tolerable solidity. With a commendable spirit of prudence, I induced Dan to make the first attempt. He cut him a long pole to steady himself, and, adding two or three additional supports to the frail bridge, essayed to cross. He planted his pole firmly in the mud and leaned hard against it, but he was not a foot from shore before the bridge began to sink, inch by inch. Daniel's ponderous frame was too much for it and, wherever he stepped, down sunk logs, poles, and branches, and resting place for his foot he had none. Dan got flurried. He splashed here and there, lost his balance, gave a leap in desperation at the treacherous pier of logs on the other side, they tilted up, and in plunged Dan, floundering among the fragments of the demolished bridge and sputtering the dirty water from his mouth. He gained the bank and shook himself like a dog. "Ha! Ha! Ha!" laughed I from one side. "Haw! Haw! Haw!" responded he from the other. "Now let's see you cross," said Dan. I accordingly rearranged the bridge with his assistance and succeeded in getting over, though wet to the knees.

We at length came to a log house with a small clearing about it, where dwell a famous hunter in those parts, one Mr. Bennet[t][25]; a man strong and hardy and handsome, moreover, though I never saw an Indian darker than exposure had made his features. He should like nothing better than to go, he said, but he was in the midst of his haying and could not think of leaving home. "I know who will go with you, though. There's Joshua Lumber [Lombard][26]—he's got a boat and a team of oxen to drag it round the falls." "Where does Joshua Lumber live?" "Just at the foot of the falls, about five miles from here." Bennet's son paddled us over the river, for the path to Lumber's was on the other side; and passing a log cabin or two, we arrived in due time at that sturdy farmer's abode. His house was the last but one on the river, Captain Wilson[27] holding a "clearing" a mile further up—all above as far as the Canada settlements is one vast forest varied, as yet, with not the slightest trace of man's hand, unless it be the remains of the hunter's encampment. Lumber's habitation, like all in these parts, was of logs. He was blessed with a wife and a number of stout boys to whose charge he confided the farm during his absence. His place is situated just within the borders of Maine. A high and picturesque mountain rises on the west, with summits some rounded, some steep and broken. The river flows at its base through fertile plains which Lumber's industry has cleared of timber and covered with a growth of grain and grass. Asesquoss [Aziscoos] is the name of the mountain.[h]

As an initiation into the mode of life which we were about to enter upon, we determined to spend the night in the forest. Accordingly we repaired thither, built a fire, and arranged our camp. Soon we received a visit from Lumber and his sons, and with them came another man whom by his speech I discovered to be an Indian, for our fire cast but a dubious light on the assembly. This Indian [Jerome],[28] who was a nephew of Anantz and an excellent hunter, said that he was going on a hunting expedition up the river in the course of a few days. Thinking that his services might be useful, I appointed a place thirty miles up the river where he should meet us, and where we might engage him to guide us through the forest to

[h] If to the west, this must have been Halfmoon Mountain. Aziscoos is to the east.— Ed.

Canada, in case we should prefer that course to returning the way we had come.

Aug. 4th, Wednesday. Early in the morning, a light skiff, built after the fashion of a birch canoe and weighing scarce more, was placed on a sledge and drawn up the portage by a team of oxen. The length of the portage was three miles and so encumbered was it with logs and fallen trees that the axe had to be employed more than once to open a way. "Considerable of an enterprise, sir," said the farmer when his oxen at length stood panting on the bank of the river above the rapids. Here lay the canoe of Jerome, the Indian, ready for his hunting expedition.

Our boat needed some repairs after its rough passage, but in the course of half an hour we were embarked and on our way up the river. Our stock of provisions was exceedingly limited. Six pounds of bread, some salt, and some butter were all we had; but there was a certainty of procuring fish and a chance of meeting larger game. The Indian, moreover, had a large stock of dried moose-meat concealed near the place where we were to meet him. After half an hour's paddling, we reached the mouth of a cold stream which entered the river; and here we got a dinner of trout, the chief drawback to the pleasure of fishing being that the flies bit infinitely more than the fish. After a paddle of an hour or two more, we stopped; and cutting down wood, built a fire and made a tolerable dinner of our fish. Then resuming our course, we kept on until dark, when we stopped, hauled the boat on shore, cleared a space of a few yards in the forest, built a roaring fire, got ready a scanty supper, and prepared to spend the night as comfortably as circumstances would allow. Our bed was a heap of spruce boughs and our fire warmed the cold night air. Several trees were cut down to maintain the blaze and our camp being of [on] a bank elevated far above the river, there was little apprehension from the cold. Soon the moon came up and glistened on the still river and half lighted the black forest. An owl, disturbed by the glare of our fire, sent forth a long wild cry from the depths of the woods and was answered by the shrill bark of some other habitant of the forest. Thus far, the river bank has been clothed with huge trees and the summits of considerable mountains appeared on the right and left; but tomorrow we pass "the meadows," a flat and marshy tract of ground covered with low bushes through which the stream runs in a winding course for many miles. We have paddled today eighteen miles. Along the banks, moose and bear tracks have appeared in abundance—not so, unfortunately, the animals themselves.

Thursday, Aug. 5th. We resumed our journey but our rate of proceeding was slow, for, by reason of the bends of the river, five miles by water were equivalent to one in a direct line. The stream began to grow shallow, too, and the current swift—so much so that the united force of paddles and poles was barely sufficient, in some places, to propel the boat. We often ran aground on shallows or among rocks, and were obliged to get out into the water to lighten our bark. Once we were stopped by a huge barricade of timber, over which we lifted the boat by main force. The bites of the flies were intolerable, so we made a fire of rotten wood in our frying pan, and, placing it in the bow of the boat, its smoke prevented any further annoyance from that source. We could get no trout today and were obliged to rest content with a dinner of chubs, of which we took some very fine ones. We passed the meadows at length, and again our way was through the forest, and a most wild and beautiful appearance did the river shores present. From the high banks huge old pines stooped forward over the water, the moss hanging from their aged branches, and behind rose a wall of foliage, green and thick, with no space or opening which the eye could penetrate. The river was not here, as some miles below, an expanse of still deep water, but came down over a rocky and gravelly bed in a swift current and some times broke in cascades—a change which, how much soever it might improve the effect of the scene, was of no advantage to the navigation. However, we reached our destination at last. This was the fork of the river, where, branching to the right and left, it preserves on the one side its original title and, on the other, takes that of the "Little Margalloway."[i] This was the place we had appointed to meet

[i] Probably the place where the western branch of the Magalloway leads to the New Hampshire line and the eastern to Parmachenee Lake and thence to the Boundary Mountains.—Ed.

the Indian and where he was to appear at sunrise the next day. We made our camp—this time with a little more care, for Lumber erected a shed of boughs as a protection against the dews. We procured a mess of most magnificent trout, none of them being less than a foot in length, though this is an unfavorable season for them; supped, and went to sleep. Our camp was on the tongue of land between the two streams, and the tumbling of the water was no ways unfavorable to repose. As usual, our chief annoyance was from flies

and mosquitoes, of which the latter swarmed in numbers unprecedented, but their attacks were as nothing in comparison with that of clouds of black flies—animals not much larger than the head of a pin, but inflicting a wound twice as large as themselves and assaulting with such eagerness that nothing but being in the midst of a thick smoke will keep them off. They seemed to take a special liking to me, and I was bitten to such a degree that I am now—nearly four days after—covered with their wounds as if I had the small-pox. There is another cursed race, yet smaller, denominated from their microscopic dimensions "no-see-ems." Their bite is like the prick of a needle, but not half so endurable, and they insinuate themselves through pantaloons, stockings, and everything else.

We slept in spite of them. Morning was on the point of breaking when a shout sounded from the river, Jerome's canoe touched the shore, and in a moment he was amongst us. He had seen a moose, he said, as he came up, had fired at and, he believed, wounded her, and he would go down in the morning to see if he could find her. He wrapped him[self] in his blanket, head and all, and in two minutes was fast asleep. Well he might be, for he had been paddling since nine o'clock of the morning before.

Friday, Aug. 6th. Our bread had almost failed and, still worse, we were unprovided with blankets; we therefore abandoned our half-formed intention of going on to Canada,[j] and determined to return by the way we had come. My chief object in coming so far was merely to have a taste of the half-savage kind of life necessary to be led, and to see the wilderness where it was as yet uninvaded by the hand of man. I had had some hope of shooting a moose; but that hope seemed doomed to be disappointed, although, had we kept on, there was a very considerable chance of finding them. Slade, however, became utterly discouraged and refused to proceed; and this alone would have prevented me, even if there had been no other obstacles. We breakfasted, cleared out the boat, and began our return voyage, the Indian having set out before us, whirling down the swift current like a bubble in his bark canoe. Our descent was nothing compared to our ascent. The mist was rising from the river, and the scenes we had passed the day before with toil and difficulty bore an appearance twice as inviting, now that we were borne by them with no effort.

The canoe was quickly out of sight. We had gone about five miles when a sudden splash into the water arrested our attention, and we saw a young moose, far in front, leap from the bank and wade the river. He ascended the opposite shore, shook the water from his flanks, and disappeared in the woods. I dropped my paddle, cocked my gun, and stood in the prow of the boat. We bore down swiftly and silently to the spot where he had disappeared, but there was no trace of him but the broad tracks which marked the place where he had left the water. A bend in the river prevented our seeing farther on. An instant after we heard another plunge. The snap of a gun missing fire followed, and, sweeping round the bend, we saw a large moose on the point of climbing the bank, while Jerome stood on the

---

[j] By way of the eastern branch, Lake Megantic, and the Chaudière; or by the western branch, Salmon River, and the St. Francis.—Ed.

opposite shore hastily and eagerly picking the lock of his gun. The bank was steep, and the moose stood half way up, nearly hidden in the bushes. I took a quick aim at the back, fired, and the moose tumbled into the river with her spine severed by my bullet. Jerome had fired at her the night before and wounded her in the lower part of the belly. He had just tracked her by means of his dog; she had leaped into the river and he had aimed at her as she was wading across; but, his gun missing fire, she had gained the shore and was attempting to ascend the bank when we approached. The poor beast lay an instant in the water and then, with a convulsive effort, staggered to her feet and stood in the river where it was about a foot deep. Jerome aimed at her head, fired, and missed altogether. I reloaded and, aiming at the eye, struck the head just below the root of the ear. Still the moose stood motionless. Jerome took a long aim and fired again. He hit her fair and full between the eyes. For an instant she did not move; then her body declined slowly to one side and she fell, gave a short plunge, and lay dead on the bottom. Being a female, she had no horns, but her body was larger than a horse's. Each siezed a leg and she was drawn to shore. Jerome shouldered the huge dead trunk of a tree, brought it from the forest, chopped it up, and kindled a fire to keep off the flies. He and Lumber then flayed and cut her up—a process which occupied an hour or more; and then we got under way again, taking with us as much of the meat as we had occasion for. Jerome stayed behind to load his canoe with the rest.

We stopped at our camp of the first night, and, finding our fire still smouldering, we rekindled it and cooked a dinner of moose meat. Getting again under way, we reached our starting place at the head of the rapids half an hour before sunset, having paddled almost unceasingly since early morning and travelled, by the river, a distance of more than thirty miles. We walked to Lumber's and, though he offered beds, preferred the fresh hay of his barn to the chance of what we might encounter in the shape of log-cabin sheets.

Saturday, Aug. 7th. We determined, if the thing was practicable, to reach Colebrook today, although the distance by road was forty miles. Leaving Lumber's an hour before sunrise, at half an hour after we were at Bennet's, where we hired a light skiff and paddled down the river for Brag's—a distance by water of ten miles. We reached the settlement at about half past ten; devoured a monstrous breakfast, for which we paid the enormous sum of nine-pence; and began our journey across the state to Colebrook. Now it so happened that that breakfast, our first civilized meal for some days, relished so extremely well that we both demolished several pounds of the pie, cake, and bread of which it consisted, and, in addition, imbibed

Sketched from the summit of one of the mountains of the Dixville Notch, representing the appearance of the cliffs opposite.

about a quart and a half of rich milk apiece. In consequence, we found ourselves more disposed to lie down and go to sleep than to continue our journey, and Slade became absolutely sick. A freezing-cold bath in a mountain stream effectually expelled my laziness, and relieved him to such a degree that he was enabled to continue his walk; and in the course of half an hour every evil symptom had vanished. It was long past noon when we entered the "Dixville Notch," and the scene appeared to much greater advantage on entering from the west than when seen from the opposite side. The road, which has been constructed within a few weeks, adds greatly to its effect. It is a causeway strongly built of stone against the side of the steep precipices which on the one hand rise abruptly from it, while on the other a shallow ravine, the bed of a winter torrent, is interposed between the road and the crags which overlook it.

These, steep as they are, afford in their crevices root-hold for large trees and a thick growth of saplings which, over-shadowing the road, make with the rocks above a beautiful perspective to one entering the pass. Further on, the rocks rise higher and fire has stripped them of their woods, so that in the heart of the defile nothing meets the eye but the tall pinnacles shooting upward

abruptly and with black and fire-scorched rocks scattered about their bases. Long after nightfall we reached Colebrook, having travelled thirty miles on foot and paddled ten miles!

Sunday, Aug. 8th. After our recent exertions, we were glad of a day of rest. My chief occupations have been sleeping and writing my journal for the preceding week.

This sketch is very inaccurate, but it may give some idea of our course. Leaving Colebrook, we reached in one day Brag's settlement, marked *1*, near the junction of the Margalloway and the Androscoggin. The distance is twenty-two [fifteen] miles, the road passing through the Dixville Notch. Thence to the foot of the rapids, though barely fifteen miles, occupied the greater part of another day. It was here that the memorable adventure of the "guzzle"[k] befel. The boat having been drawn round the rapids, we proceeded up the stream and reached at night the point marked *2*—the place of our encampment. Our camp of the next night was at *3*, and from this place we commenced our return the next morning. Just below *2* is the deserted camp of an old Indian, named Mettallic,[29] who lived here many years and subsisted by hunting, but, being striken blind by a disease, he was found on the bank in a starving state by a hunter.

Monday, Aug. 9th. The imperative necessity of my clothes undergoing a cleansing operation detained us, although most unwilling, at Colebrook. The day was dull and rainy; books were few—entertaining ones none at all; and the writing of a letter or two was my chief defence against an unwonted attack of blue-devils. Tomorrow we set out, on foot, for Lancaster.

Tuesday, Aug. 10th, Lancaster. Today we first turned our footsteps homeward. For myself, I am loth to abandon so soon the excitements and enjoyments of the few past weeks, though many of them have been purchased with "toil and sweat." My pilgrimage, however, must come to an end, and next Saturday will find me at home. I regard this journey but "as the beginning of greater things" and as merely prefatory to longer wanderings.

We left Colebrook early this morning and travelled fifteen miles down the valley of the Connecticut. Stopping to lunch at a little tavern, a couple of barouches drove up to the door; and, to my no small gratification, they were freighted with Dr. Jackson and his assistants. They were going on to Colebrook, but remained an hour and a half at the tavern, which space was occupied, most satisfac-

[k] Probably the "guzzle" was the outlet of Round and Long ponds.—Ed.

torily to me, in conversation upon backwoods matters. Among other kindness, Mr. Williams offered me the use of the note-book of his journies of last year, in which he has preserved a considerable number of Indian legends taken from the lips of Anantz, who is well versed in the traditions of his tribe. I shall certainly avail myself of his offer. Taking a waggon at this place, we proceeded to Lancaster, through the towns of Stratford, Northumberland, &c. Lancaster is thirty-five miles from Colebrook. We passed on our way a mountain of very peculiar appearance, situated, I believe, in the township of Stark. Avalanches had laid bare its sides and exposed a surface of white, glistening rock, which, with the black stains and fissures and, here and there, the stunted verdure which relieves it, affords a strange contrast to the forest-covered mountains around it. As through the greater part of the valley of the Connecticut, the level and beautiful meadows through which the river flows are shut in by parallel ranges of hills, some high and craggy—all wild and beautiful in their appearance. Distant mountains of considerable elevation overlook Lancaster on the east.

Wednesday, Aug. 11th, Littleton. Left Lancaster at two this afternoon— at 4 tomorrow morning leave Littleton for Windsor.

Windsor, Friday [Thursday], Aug. 12th. Leaving Littleton at 4, we reached Hallowell [Haverhill] at 10—a beautiful ride, especially the latter part. Thence we proceeded to Hanover, and thence to Windsor, where I now am, and where I deem it expedient to retire immediately to bed, since I must be off at two in the morning. Ascutney Mountain overhangs the village.

Boston, Saturday [Friday], Aug. 13th. Starting at two this morning from Windsor, I reached Nashua in time for the last afternoon train, and in two hours found myself in Boston[30] after an absence of a month. And a joyous month it has been, though one somewhat toilsome— may I soon pass another as pleasantly.

Windsor, Friday. Aug. 12th. Leaving Littleton at 4, we reached Hallowell at 10 — a beautiful ride, especially the latter part. Thence we proceeded to Hanover, and thence to Windsor, where I now am, and where I deem it expedient to retire immediately to bed, since I must be off at two in the morning. Ascutney mountain overhangs the village.

Boston. Saturday. Aug 13th. Starting at two this morning from Windsor, I reached Nashua in time for the last afternoon train, and in two hours found myself in Boston after an absence of a month. And a joyous month it has been, though one somewhat toilsome — may I soon pass another as pleasantly.

F. P.

*Facsimile of Final Page
of the 1841 Journal*

1842 Journal

Lake George & Lake Champlain

Green Mountains, Eastern Townships

White Mountains & Maine

Introduction

WEARY of books after his sophomore year at Harvard, and acting on his lifelong conviction that "For the student there is, in its season, no better place than the saddle, and no better companion than the rifle or the oar," Parkman set off on another expedition as soon as his summer vacation of 1842 began. He had enlisted Henry Orne White, who was in the class above him at Harvard, as a companion for the strenuous journey he proposed to make. Starting from Albany, he planned to proceed northward by Fort Edward and the battlefields of the Seven Years' War about Lake George and Lake Champlain; then to follow the Canadian boundary eastward across northern Vermont and New Hampshire, returning by way of Mt. Katahdin in Maine. The itinerary was clearly designed to gratify both the student and the lover of the wilderness, for acquaintance with the classic invasion route of the French and Indian War was essential to Parkman's studies, while the final part of the trip would take him through frontier or untouched forest regions. It was a daring effort for an eighteen-year-old, and it is clear from Parkman's lively account that he rejoiced in the dangers and hardships which he encountered. It is worth noting that on this journey, as on that of the previous summer and others still to be made, Parkman wore out his companions, who lacked his almost fanatical zeal for hardening himself and for experiencing the same primitive living conditions as his historical heroes had known. In later years Parkman was to pay dearly in ill-health for trying the flesh so sorely in his youth.

The journal is primarily a spirited account of adventure, which displays Parkman's precocious ability as a writer, particularly in the brilliant descriptions of nature. But it also affords some interesting historical insights in its pictures of Albany, Schenectady, and Saratoga Springs a century ago; in its careful account of the ruins of Fort

William Henry and Ticonderoga, the old English and French outposts on the lakes; and notably in its record of life along the Canadian border when war between the great neighbors of North America was not unthinkable. In fact, when Parkman passed back and forth across the boundary, a dispute over a considerable section of northern New Hampshire was just dying down, after the now forgotten incident of the Indian Stream Republic. On the American side of the border, Parkman, with the mark of Harvard on him, was suspected of being a British agent. On the Canadian side, he found small garrisons established in the frontier towns. But the essential thinness of the tension is evidenced by the charming incident of the singing of "America" with the refrain of "God Save the Queen" by a Yankee landlord presiding over the company in a Canadian inn. At this period the Eastern Townships of Quebec were of distinctly New England character in aspect and in population, and even today they remain a transition ground between New England and New France. Then there are also vivid glimpses of the religious and political ferments at work along the frontier, Millerism and Jacksonian democracy, and of the rude life of the settlers who were gnawing away at the wilderness through which Major Robert Rogers' Rangers had fought their way home after the attack on the St. Francis Indians in 1759.

Forced by his companion's lack of funds and enthusiasm to abandon the plan of returning by way of Mt. Katahdin—first explored by white men only five years before—Parkman consoled himself with the little less ambitious project of cutting across the wilderness from the Connecticut Lakes to the headwaters of the Magalloway, and thence retracing his route of the previous summer. This enterprise— even today not one to be lightly undertaken—he succeeded in accomplishing with considerable toil and hardship and some real danger; and then concluded his summer's outing by passing quickly homeward through his beloved White Mountains.

The journal is clearly written, chiefly in ink but with some passages in pencil, in a 6⅜ by 7¾ copybook with marbled paper covers. The latter part of the journal, describing the trip down the Magalloway, supplied much of the material for a *Harper's* article, "Exploring the Magalloway" (November 1864—XXIX, 735-41).

1842

July 15th, *[18]42*, *Albany*. Left Boston this morning at half past six, for this place, where I am now happily arrived, it being the longest day's journey I ever made. For all that, I would rather have come thirty miles by stage than the whole distance by railroad, for of all methods of progressing, that by steam is incomparably the most disgusting.[1] We were whisked by Worcester and all the other inter-mediate towns, and reached Springfield by noon, where White[2] ran off to see his sister, and I staid and took "refreshment" in a little room at the end of the car-house, where about thirty people were standing around a table in the shape of a horse-shoe, eating and drinking in lugubrious silence. The train got in motion again, and passed the Connecticut. Its shores made a perspective of high, woody hills, closed in the distance by the haughty outline of Mount Tom. The view from the railroad-bridge was noble, or rather would have been so, had not the Company taken care to erect a parapet on both sides, which served the double purpose of intercepting the view, and driving all the sparks into the eyes of the passengers. A few miles farther, and we came upon the little river Agawam [Westfield]; and an hour after, high mountains began to rise before us. We dashed by them; dodged under their cliffs; whirled round their bases; only seeing so much as to make us wish to see more,[a] and more than half-blinded meanwhile by showers of red hot sparks which poured in at the open windows like a hail storm. I have scarcely ever seen a wilder and more picturesque country. We caught tantalizing glimpses of glittering streams and waterfalls, rocks and mountains, woods and lakes, and before we could rub our scorched eyes to look again, the scene was left miles behind. A place called Chester Factory, where we stopped five minutes, is beautifully situated among encircling moun-

[a] This wish was gratified in 1844. Cf. the Boston & Berkshire Journal.—Ed.

tains which rise like an amphitheatre around it, to the height of many hundred feet, wooded to the summit. It almost resembled New Hampshire scenery. I learned the names of some of the mountains— Pontoosac—Bear—Becket—The Summit [Washington]—the last being the highest. The road here is ascending for a considerable distance through the townships of North Becket, Hinsdale, &c. The whole is a succession of beautiful scenes. The Irishmen who worked on the road made a most praiseworthy selection of places for their shanties, which many of them are wise enough to occupy still. Three or four of these outlandish cabins, ranged along the banks of a stream flowing through a woody glen extending back among the hills, made with their turf walls and slant roofs a most picturesque addition to the scene. We crossed the boundary line to Chatham, the first New York village. The country was as level as that about Boston. We passed through Kinderhook and Schodack—or however else it is spelled—and at half past six saw the Hudson, moping dismally between its banks under a cloudy sky, with a steamboat solemnly digging its way through the leaden waters. In five minutes the spires and dirt of Albany rose in sight on the opposite shore. We crossed in a steamboat and entered the old city, which, indeed, impressed us at once with its antiquity by the most ancient and fish-like smell which saluted our shrinking nostrils, the instant we set foot on the wharf. We have put up at the Eagle Hotel—a good house. Nevertheless, we are both eager to leave cities behind us.

July 16th, Caldwell [Lake George]. This morning we left Albany— which I devoutly hope I may never see again—in the cars, for Saratoga. My plan of going up the river to Ft. Edward[3] I had to abandon, for it was impracticable—no boat beyond Troy. Railroad the worst I was ever on; the country flat and dull; the weather dismal. The Catskills appeared in the distance. After passing the inclined plane and riding a couple of hours we reached the valley of the Mohawk and Schenectady. I was prepared for something filthy in the last mentioned venerable town, but for nothing quite so disgusting as the reality. Canal docks, full of stinking water, superannuated rotten canal boats, and dirty children and pigs paddling about, formed the foreground of the delicious picture, while in the rear was a mass of (of) tumbling houses and sheds, bursting open in all directions; green with antiquity, dampness, and lack of paint. Each house had its peculiar dunghill, with the group of reposing hogs. In short, London itself could exhibit nothing much nastier.[4] In crossing the main street, indeed, things wore an appearance which might be called decent. The car-house here is enormous. Five or six trains were on the point of starting for the north, south, east, and west; and the brood of railroads and taverns swarmed about the place like bees. We cleared the babel at last, passed Union College,[5] another tract of monotonous country, Ballston, and finally reached Saratoga, having travelled latterly at the astonishing rate of about seven miles an hour. "Caldwell stage ready!" We got our baggage on board, and I found time to enter one or two of the huge hotels.[6] After perambulating the entries filled with sleek waiters and sneaking fops, dashing through the columned porticoes and enclosures, drinking some of the water and spitting it out again in high disgust, I sprang onto the stage, cursing Saratoga and all New York. With an unmitigated temper, I journeyed to Glen's Falls, and here my wrath mounted higher yet, at the sight of that noble cataract almost concealed under a huge awkward bridge, thrown directly across it, with the addition of a dam above, and about twenty mills of various kinds. Add to all, that the current was choked by masses of drift logs above and below, and that a dirty village lined the banks of the river on both sides; and some idea may possibly be formed of the way in which the New Yorkers have bedevilled Glen's. Still the water comes down over the marble ledges in foam and fury, and the roar completely drowns the clatter of the machinery. I left the stage and ran down to the bed of the river to the rocks at the foot of the falls. Two little boys volunteered to show me the "caverns," which may be reached dry-shod when the stream is low. I followed them down amid the din and spray to a little hole in the rock which led to a place a good deal like the Swallows' Cave, and squeezed in after them. "This is Cooper's Cave, sir; where he went and hid the two ladies." They evidently took the story in *The Last of the Mohicans*[7] for Gospel. They led the way to the larger cave, and one of them ran down to the edge of the water which boiled most savagely past the opening. "This is Hawkeye's Cave: here's where he shot an Indian." "No, he didn't either," squalled the other, "it was higher up on the rocks." "I tell you it wasn't." "I tell you it was." I put an end to the controversy with two cents.

Dined at the tavern, and rode on. Country dreary as before; the driver one of the best of his genus I ever met. He regaled me as we rode on with stories of his adventures with deer, skunks, and passengers. A mountain heaved up against the sky some distance before us, with a number of smaller hills stretching away on each hand, all wood-crowned to the top. Away on the right rose the Green Mts., dimly seen through the haze, and scarcely distinguishable from the blue clouds that lay upon them. Between was a country of half cultivated fields, tottering houses, and forests of dwarf pines and scrub oaks. But as we drew near, the mountain in front assumed a wilder and a loftier aspect. Crags started from its woody sides and leaned over a deep valley below. "What mountain is that?" "That 'ere is French Mounting"—the scene of one of the most desperate and memorable battles[8] in the Old French War. As we passed down the valley, the mountain rose above the forest half a mile on out right, while a hill on the left, close to the road, formed the other side. The trees flanked the road on both sides. In a little opening in her woods, a cavity in the ground, with a pile of stones at each end, marked the spot where was buried that accomplished warrior and gentleman, Colonel Williams,[9] whose bones, however, have since been removed. Farther on is the rock on the right where he was shot, having mounted it on the look-out—an event which decided the day; the Indians and English broke and fled at once. Still farther on is the scene of the third tragedy of that day, when the victorious French, having been in their turn, by a piece of great good luck, beaten by the valorous Johnson[10] at his entrenchment by the lake, were met at this place on their retreat by McGinnis,[11] and almost cut to pieces. Bloody Pond,[12] a little, slimy, dark sheet of stagnant water, covered with weeds and pond-lilies and shadowed by the gloomy forest around it, is the place where hundreds of dead bodies were flung after the battle, and where the bones still lie. A few miles farther, and Lake George lay before us, the mountains and water confused and indistinct in the mist. We rode into Caldwell, took supper—a boat— and then a bed.

July 17th, Caldwell. The tavern is full of fashionable New Yorkers— all of a piece. Henry and myself both look like the Old Nick, and are evidently looked upon in a manner corresponding. I went this morning to see William Henry.[13] The old fort is much larger than I had thought; the earthen mounds cover many acres. It stood on the southwest extremity of the lake close by the water. The enterprising genius of (of) the inhabitants has made a road directly through the ruins, and turned bastion, moat, and glacis into a flourishing cornfield, so that the spot so celebrated in our colonial history is now scarcely to be distinguished. Large trees are growing on the untouched parts, especially on the embankment along the lake shore. In the rear, a hundred or two yards distant, is a gloomy wood of pines, where the lines of Montcalm[14] can easily be traced. A little behind these lines is the burying place of the French who fell during that memorable siege. The marks of a thousand graves can be seen among the trees, which, of course, have sprung up since. Most of them have been opened, and bones and skulls dug up in great numbers. A range of mountains towers above this fine forest—Cobble Mt.—the Prospect, &c., the haunt of bears and rattle-snakes. The ruins of Ft. George[15] are on a low hill of lime-stone a short distance southeast of William Henry—of stone, and in much better preservation than the other, for they are under the special protection of Mr. Caldwell,[16] the owner of the village; but they have no historical associations connected with them. I noticed some curious marks of recent digging in William Henry and asked an explanation of an old fellow who was hoeing corn in a field close by. He said that some fools had come up the lake with a wizard and a divining rod to dig for money in the ruins.[17] They went at midnight for many successive nights and dug till day light. I undertook to climb the Prospect—three miles high, without a path. I guided myself by the sun and summits of the mountains, and got to the top almost suffocated with heat and thirst. The view embraced the whole lake as far as Ty [Ticonderoga]. All was hazy and indistinct, only the general features of the scene could be distinguished in the dull atmosphere. The lake seemed like a huge river, winding among mountains. Came down, dined, and went to church. The church is a minute edifice, with belfry and bell exactly like a little school-house. It might hold easily about sixty. About thirty were present—countrymen; cute, sly, sunburnt slaves of Mammon; maidens of sixty and of sixteen; the former desperately ugly, with black bonnets, frilled caps, peaked noses and chins, and an aspect diabolically prim and saturnine; the latter for the most part remarkably pretty and delicate. For a long time the numerous congregation sat in a pious silence, waiting for the minister. At last he came, dodged into a little door behind the pulpit, and presently reappeared and took his place, arrayed in a white surplice with black facing. He was very young, and *Yankee ploughboy* was stamped on every feature. Judge of my astonishment when he began to read the Episcopal service in voice so clear and manner so appropriate that I have never heard better even in Boston. He read the passage in Exodus—quite appropriate to the place—beginning "the Lord is a man of war." In his sermon, which was polished and even elegant, every figure was taken from warfare. One of Montcalm's lines ran northwest of the tavern toward the mountains.[18] Two or three years ago, in digging for some purpose, a great quantity of deer, bear, and moose bones were found here, with arrows and hatchets, which the tavern keeper thinks mark the place of some Indian feast. The spikes and timbers of sunken vessels may be seen in strong sunlight, when the water is still, at the bottom of the lake, along the southern beach. Abercrombie [Abercromby] sunk his boats here.[19] There are remains of batteries[20] on French Mt. and the mountain north of it, I suppose to command the road from Ft. Edward. This evening visited the French graves. I write this at camp, July 18th. Just turned over my ink-bottle and spilt all the ink.

July 18th, Camp at Diamond Island. Set out this morning in an excellent boat, hired at Caldwell. The sun rose over the mountains like a fiery ball of copper—portending direful heat. The lake was still as glass; the air to the last degree sultry and oppressive. Rowed to the western side and kept under the banks, which were rocky and covered with birch, spruce, cypress, and other trees. We landed occasionally, and fished as we went along. About ten o'clock stretched across Middle Bay and got bread, pork, and potatoes at a farm house, with which and our fish we regaled ourselves at a place half-way down the Bay. Here I wrote my journal for yesterday; we slept an hour or two on the ground, bathed, and read Goldsmith, which Henry brought in his knapsack. At three we proceeded to explore the bay to its bottom, returned, made for Diamond Island, which is now uninhabited, prepared our camp, and went to sleep.

July 19th. I woke this morning about as weak and spiritless as well could be. All enterprise and activity was fairly gone; how I cannot tell, but I cursed the weather as the most probable cause. Such has been the case with me, to a greater or less degree, for the last three or four weeks. Rowed today along the eastern shore. Explored several beautiful bays, in one of which was a curious cave in the rock. Heat suffocating. The water of the lake is equal to most spring water, and we drank it in great quantities. The scenery thus far, though extremely fine, had disappointed me, probably on account of the extravagant ideas I had formed of it; but now it grew continually more imposing. A strong south wind, too, sprang up and raised the glassy flat surface of the lake into waves, and, in part, dissipated the mists that hung over all the mountains. The boat began to pitch and plunge with an enlivening motion, and the motion in the air strengthened and invigorated us. We dashed through the water at a rapid rate. At last we saw a little white flag fluttering among the trees, by way of sign to a tavern. We landed, dined, and set out again. The wind almost blew a gale. The little boat was borne up and down with such violence that we judged best to keep near the shore, so as to be able to get our baggage in case of an overturn. White sat in the stern grunting a German song, about as intelligible to me as to him, while I rowed. We reached what in the War-time was Cankasky [Northwest] Bay, close to the Narrows. Here the storm grew so furious that we landed at the point of the bay—the extremity of Tongue Mt. The lake plunged and foamed like the ocean. At this point it is full of islands and flanked by noble mountains. This is the scene of the canoe-chase in *The Last of the Mohicans*.[21] While White had gone off shooting, I swam across the strait to one of the islands, from which the view down the lake was the finest water-scene I ever saw. It was a perspective of mountains towering above the narrow sheet filled with islands, against which the white breakers were now fiercely dashing. But everything was obscured with mist. When the wind became less violent we rowed to an island in the middle, where we are now encamped.

Wednesday, July 20th. Entered the Narrows this morning, and rowed among all the islands and along all the shores. White trailed a line behind the boat, by which means he caught a large bass. Scenery noble, but mists still on the mountains. Passed along the rocky and precipitous shore of Tongue Mt.; stopped and fished, and caught so many that we flung several dozen away. About 11 o'clock landed on a little island, built a fire and prepared a dinner, White officiating as cook with considerable skill. We rowed down the lake again, and soon cleared the Narrows. On our right rose the ridges of Black Mt., the loftiest summit on the lake. We stopped at a log cabin at its base, where an old man of eighty was splitting shingles under a shed, surrounded by a group of women and children who, with becoming modesty, fled at our approach. The old man lost no time in informing us that he did not belong there, but had only come to work for the family. We went up to the house—one of the most wretched cabins I every saw—inhabited by two families, French and American. Shepherd,[b] the American, was the most deformed abortion I ever set eyes on—his lip split up to the nose and his mouth twisted round the wrong way, so that he spoke from the side of his face, instead of the front, and that in such a sputtering mumbling style that he was perfectly unintelligible. We returned to the old man, who talked politics with great fury, and with more knowledge than I believe falls to the lot of many a state representative. He seasoned his discourse with stories—one about Ethan Allen[22] was exceedingly characteristic, but scarcely to be put in writing.

We left him and kept down the lake, with a fierce wind sweeping down after us, and driving the mists before it. The water was a dark glistening blue, with lines of foam on the crests of the waves; huge shadows of clouds coursed along the mountains. The little islands would be lighted at one instant by a stream of sunshine falling on them and almost making their black pines transparent, and the next moment they would be suddenly darkened and all around be glittering with a sudden burst of light from the opening clouds. We passed under Black Mt., whose precipices and shaggy woods wore a very savage and impressive aspect in that peculiar weather, and kept

[b]Known as the "King of Black Mountain," according to a note on the end paper of the journal.—Ed.

down the lake seven miles to Sabbath Day Pt. High and steep mountains flanked the lake the whole way. In front, at some distance, they
seemed to slope gradually away, and a low green point, with an
ancient dingy house upon it closed the perspective. This was Sabbath
Day Pt., the famous landing place of many a huge army.[23] We
noticed two abrupt mountains on our left, and steering under them,
found them the most savage and warlike precipices we had yet seen.
One impended over the lake, like the stooping wall of an old castle;
its top was fringed with trees, which seemed bushes, from the height,
and great fragments of broken rock were piled around its base. We
ran our boat on the beach of Sabbath Day Pt. and asked lodging at
the house. An old woman, after a multitude of guesses and calculations, guessed as how she could accommodate us with a supper and
a bed, though she couldn't say nohow how we should like it, seeing
as how she war'nt used to visitors. The house was an old, rickety,
dingy shingle palace, with a potatoe garden in front, hogs perambulating the outhouses, and a group of old men and women engaged in
earnest conversation in the tumble-down portico. The chief figure
was an old grey-haired man, tall and spare as a skeleton, who was
giving some advice to a chubby old lady about her corns.

"Well, now," said the old lady, "I declare they hurt me mighty
bad."

"I'll give you something to cure them right off."

"What is it? I hope it a'nt snails. I always hated snails since I was
a baby, but I've heered say they are better for corns nor nothing else
at all," etc., etc.

The old man was a revolutionary pensioner, Captain Patchin[24] by
name, and stout-hearted, hale, and clever by nature. He is the owner
of the place, but the house is occupied by another family—old man,
old woman, and a numerous progeny of youthful giants and ogresses;
but the whole "calculate on" removing to Illinois in the fall. There
were visitors of the family, also, the most conspicuous of whom was
a little Canadian Frenchman[25] with his family, who professed himself a mighty adept at angling, but whose pretensions we found on
trial greatly above his merits. The whose household presently
gathered under the old portico, where stories of Revolutionary
campaigns, rattlesnakes, deadly beasts, and deadly diseases flew

from mouth to mouth with awful rapidity. After a few rifle trials with the aforesaid youthful giants, we took supper, and went on the lake after bass, with the Frenchman in our boat, and the young men following in their own. We had good success—Henry and I caught a dozen apiece, some of very large size, while the vainglorious French-man had to be content with one wretched perch. The Captain tonight sent his dogs to the mountains, in the care of a neighbor of his, in hopes that a deer may be roused and driven to the lake in the morning. One of the children is playing with the tail of a rattle-snake, killed last night by one of the men in the middle of the road.

Thursday, 21ˢᵗ. Fished for bass off-shore with rifle and fowling piece ready, in case the deer should take to the lake. But we waited in vain. It turned out afterwards that the hound had proved unmanageable and refused to follow the scent. We caught fish enough, landed, and with Myrtle Bailey, one of the young Brobdignagians, a simple, goodnatured, strong-handed, grinning son of the plough, set out on a rattle-snake hunt on the mountain back of the Point. Here was the summer den of a swarm of these beasts, who thence infested the whole country. Myrtle told us that they went to their winter den in autumn; then repaired to their summer den in spring, where they educated their children; which parental office being discharged, the[y] scattered at large over the rocks. We climbed through tangled woods and steep sunscorched ledges till we came to the edge of a lofty precipice which towers above the lake. We looked down upon piles of confused rocks and forests of blasted and stunted trees along the foot of the cliff and washed by the lake on the other side. Some crows were wheeling and cawing over the tree tops, looking like black beetles from the height above. Steadying myself by putting one arm round a gnarled tree I leaned from the precipice and dis-charged "Satan"ᵉ into the gulf. The crows ceased their cawing and took themselves off with all speed. We soon reached a still higher point, which commanded the noblest view of the lake I had yet seen. It stretched north and south between its mountains, visible for two thirds of its length, its waters glistening in the sun, dotted with a

---

ᵉ Parkman's rifle, which was named, after the custom of the pioneers who per-sonalized the weapon so vital to their lives.—Ed.

hundred green islands. As it wound down through the huge valley, it seemed like a still clear stream in the bottom of a deep glen, rather than a lake. The waters dwindled to nothing in comparison to the towering mountains that environed them. There would be no finer place of gentlemen's seats than this, but now, for the most part, it is occupied by a race of boors about as uncouth, mean, and stupid as the hogs they seem chiefly to delight in. The captain's household is an exception.

We found the den, but no snakes—they had already dispersed. We looked long and anxiously among the rocks, but in vain, and we had to descend. Near this Mt. is another—mentioned before—still more steep and rocky, called Buck Mt. from the exploit of a hunted deer, many years ago, who being hard pressed on the top by hunters, leaped from the precipice for the lake, but fell whirling upon the rocks at the bottom and sprinkled them with his blood for rods around. Afternoon: fished again—evening: fished again, and caught a very large bass—all in company of Myrtle, whose luck not satisfying him, he cursed the "darned cursed fish" in most fervent style.

Friday, 22nd. Left old Patchin's this morning, he having previously exhorted me to come and buy his place, which he says I may have for $5,000!! A strong south wind compelled us to run towards Ty. We rowed six miles down the lake—mountains less high than before—lake broad—in front lay a confused mass of precipitous mountains, apparently stretching across and barring the passage. On the left was a hamlet at the foot of a range of hills, for which we steered in order to put a letter into the post office, which we knew to be there. We broke an oar when within about half a mile, and paddled to shore with great difficulty through a considerable surf which was dashing against the beach like the waves of the ocean. We found the post office a neat little tavern kept by one Garfield,[26] entitled the Judge. He referred us to a carpenter who promised to make an oar forthwith, and worked six hours upon it, an interval which I spent chiefly in wandering through the country. I followed the course of a rocky brook which came down a valley, with a little road running along its side, with an occasional cabin, or mill, or narrow clearing breaking upon the forest. One old mill stood by the roadside where the stream tumbled in a broken line of foam over a mass of rock into a basin beneath, above which the building stood. Fantastic rocks, crowned with trees and shrubs, leaned above the basin and darkened the whirling waters below, while the dripping logs and walls of the mill on the other side, and the high rock and waterfall in front, gave a sort of picturesque aspect to the place that I never hoped to see the companion of any Yankee edifice. Going on farthur, I found other mills in abundance, and at last one which stood on the top of a steep descent of rock, flanked by the woods, down the surface of which the water came gliding in a thread so small that I wondered what had become of the stream I had seen so large before. Listening, I heard the heavy plunging of water, apparently from under ground. I looked all about, and could see no channel; but the noise grew louder as I approached the woods on the left. I forced my way among the trees and came to the edge of a ravine not ten feet wide but so deep that, leaning over, I could distinguish nothing but dark moss-grown rocks, while the noise of the water came up from the gulf with an appalling din. I went to the foot of the rocks and found the place where the water came glancing furiously out from the shelter of rocks and bushes; and following this guide by means of fallen logs and timbers, entered what seemed the mouth of a damp gloomy cavern. The rocky walls of the ravine rose on each side some sixty or seventy feet, dripping with continual moisture. When I had got a little farther on, I could see a mass of rocks piled up in front, with the water tumbling over it in a sheet of foam. The cliffs leaning towards each other over head and the bushes that projected from them rendered the place almost dark, though here and there the jagged rocks were illumined by a faint stream of sunshine. Just above the cataract could be seen the old green timbers and wheels of a mill, built across the ravine. The whole very much resembled the Flume at Franconia.

Returned to Garfield's and found there Mr. Gibbs with his wife, the "vocalist." Presently the man appeared with the oar finished. White undertook to pay him with a Naumkeag Bank[27] bill—the only bills he had. "Don't know nothing about that money: wait till Garfield comes and he'll tell whether it's genuine or not." "There's the paper," said I, "look and see." He looked—all was right. "Well,

A View of Ticonderoga
(Coverdale Collection No. 2250)

are you satisfied?" "How do I know but what that 'ere bill is counterfeit? It has a sort of counterfeit look about it to my eyes. Deacon, what do you say to it?" The deacon put on his spectacles, held the bill to the light, turned it this way and that, tasted of it, and finally pronounced that, according to his calculation, it was good. But the carpenter was not contented: "Bijah, you're a judge of bills; what do you think?" Bijah, after a long examination, gave as his opinion that it was counterfeit. All parties were beginning to wax wroth when the judge entered and decided that the bill was good.

We pushed from the beach and steered down the lake, passed some islands, and beheld in front of us two grim mountains standing guard over a narrow strait of dark water between. Both were of solid granite, rising sheer from the lake, with a (a) few stunted trees thinly clothing their nakedness. Behind each, stretched away a long train of inferior mountains, like satellites of some gloomy despot. One of these mountains was the noted Rogers' Slide;[28] the other, almost as famous, Anthony's Nose, Jr. Both had witnessed, in their day, the passage of twenty vast armies in the strait between; and there was not an echo on either but had answered to the crack of rifles and screams of dying men. We skirted the base of the Nose—for which sentimental designation I could find no manner of reason— till we arrived opposite the perpendicular front of his savage neighbor. About a mile of water was between. We ran the boat ashore on a shelving rock, and looked for a camping place among the precipices. We found to our surprise, at the side of a steep rock amid a growth of cedars and hemlocks, a little enclosure of logs, like a diminutive log cabin without a roof. We made beds in it of hemlock boughs— there was just space enough—brought up our baggage and guns, eat what supper we had, and essayed to go asleep. But we might as well have slept under a showerbath of melted iron. In that deep sheltered spot, bugs, mosquitoes, and "no-see-ems" swarmed innumerable. Our nets protected us from mosquitoes only. A million red-hot needles were gouged into hands, faces, everywhere. White cursed the woods and me for leading him into such a scrape. I laughed at the bugs and him as long as I could, but at last my philosophy gave way, and the utmost point of my self-command was to suffer in silence. It grew dark, and the wind came rushing along the side of the mountain and stirring the leaves of the trees over our head with a lulling sound, and we were well tired with the labor of the day; so we fell at last into a sort of inquiet and half-conscious doze, ever and anon interrupted by a muttered grumble or a motion to scratch some severely affected part. Late in the night, I was awaked from this blissful state by sounds rather startling in that solitude—the loud voices and shouts of men close by. I sat up and listened, but the moaning of the wind and the dash of the water against the shore prevented my distinguishing a syllable, until there came, louder than the rest: "Now then, G——d damn it, pull for your life—every stroke helps." In an instant it flashed across my bewildered brain that some scoundrels were making off with our boat; and I got clear of my blanket and ran down to the shore, first shaking White to wake him. All I could see through the darkness was that our boat was safe and that another was drawn up beside it, when a man sprang up suddenly from the grass with a startled curse, and demanded who I was. We made mutual explanations. He had tried to run up the lake from Ty, with a companion in another boat, but his strength had failed against a strong contrary wind and he had landed, leaving his friend, who had a less distance to go, to keep on.

The wind drove the bugs from the shore and made it a much more comfortable resting-place; so thither we adjourned, and spread our blankets near the ragamuffin boatman. We built a little fire, and our new friend and White enjoyed a social pipe together. As the light fell on his matted hair; his grisly unshorn countenance, haggard with drinking; and his tattered and patched clothes; and then again flared high up on the cliffs and savage trees, and streamed across the water, I thought that even that shore had seldom seen a more outlandish group—we in our blankets, he in his rags. He told us that the camp where we had been sleeping was made by a man last summer, who lived here for the purpose of fishing. "He was a sort of a villain-like character," said our acquaintance, "he went and stole fish off my grounds, damn him; and then again he killed his own son right down here in this place. The old man got drunk, and said he would have the boy over to this camp, and so he got him in his old boat with him, though the boy's mother cried about it, and said she'd keep him at home, and the boy himself felt afeared to go. Well, the old fellow was

so far gone that when he got to the landing-place—there, just where
your boat is drawed up on the rock—that he forget he had his son
with him, and ran his boat agin the rock and tumbled himself out
of it in such style, that she overset, and pitched the boy into the deep
water. The instant the old man heard his son holler, it sobered him
up in no time, but he nor the boy neither couldn't swim a mile, and
so he stood on the rock and see'd him drown, and then came over and
told the folks of it in the morning. That 'ere cured him of his
tricks for one while, but within a week or two he has been up to
them agin, and I ketched him on my fish grounds last Sunday—may
I be d——d if I didn't dress him."

With this dismal legend did our new friend beguile the hours of
the night-watch. At length we all fell asleep, and did not wake till
day. The ragamuffin said he was hungry, on which we gave him a
piece of bread, got all things on board our boat, and set out again
for Patchin's, where we had left some linen to be washed. This
morning was the most toilsome we had passed. The wind was dead
against us; the waves ran with a violence I had never seen before
except on the ocean. It required the full force of both arms to hold
the boat on her course. If we slackened our efforts for a single
moment, she would spin round and drive backwards. We had about
twelve miles to row under these agreeable auspices. "Well," said
White, "you call this fun, do you? To be eaten by bugs all night and
work against head winds all day isn't according to my taste, whatever
you may think of it."

"Are you going to back out?" said I. "Back out, yes; when I get
into a bad scrape, I back out of it as quick as I can"—and so he went
on with marvellous volubility to recount his grievances. Lake George
he called a "scrubby looking place"—said there was no fishing in
it—he hated camping, and would have no more of it—he wouldn't
live so for another week to save his life, etc., etc.

Verily, what is one man's meat is another man's poison. What
troubles me more than his treachery to our plans is his want of cash,
which will make it absolutely necessary to abandon our plan of
descending through Maine. His scruples I trust to overcome in time.

We reached Patchin's at last, and were welcomed by the noble
old veteran as cordially as if we were his children. We dined, and sat

in his portico, listening to his stories. He is eighty-six. Three years ago he danced with great applause at a country party, and still his activity and muscular strength are fully equal to those of most men in the prime of life. He must once have been extremely handsome; even now his features are full and regular, and when he tells his stories he always sets his hat on one side of his head, and looks the very picture of an old warrior. He was several times prisoner. Once, when in Quebec, an English officer asked him, as he tells the story, "'What's your name?'" "'Patchin.'" "'What, Hell-Hound Patchin!' says he."

At another time an officer struck him without any provocation but that of his being a rebel. Patchin sprang on him and choked him till he fainted, in the streets of Quebec. He served in the Indian campaigns of Butler[29] and Brant[30] about Ft. Stanwix[31]—at the recovery of Ft. Ann[e][32] after it was taken by Burgoyne—was present when Sir John Johnson[33] fled from the Mohawk with his property, and tells how narrowly that tory made his escape from the pursuing party on Champlain. He wants us to come back and hear more of his stories.

We left him and his family and ran down the lake again, bathed at an island, and, White still continuing contumacious, I left him at Garfield's, and proceeded to camp by myself at an island two or three miles off. I hauled the boat on shore, and prepared to wash my pantaloons—an operation I could commit to no one else, since I should have to wander breechless in the interim. I put the breeks in the water to the windward of the island, and, having suitably pounded them down with stones, left them to the operation of the waves while I made ready my camp. Presently taking them out and wringing them, I strung them on a tree hard by to dry, wrapped myself in my blanket and laid down. I read a book of White's as long as I could see. Two boats passed by me as I lay, and the occupants turned a wondering gaze upon me, especially one old lady in green spectacles whom her son was rowing down the lake. I slept comfortably, and in the morning went back to Garfield's, where I found White, Gibbs, and his wife. The Judge was hospitable and kind, and we instantly planned a fishing party for the next day. Today being Sunday, I have staid at home for the most part, written letters, journal, etc. The family are essentially "genteel" in the true sense of the word: the Judge a gentleman, his wife a lady, both polite by nature. The lady has a pretty flower garden—with no sunflowers in it. There is an old Irish gardener, whose department is managed in a most exemplary manner, and who has spent half the afternoon in expounding the superiority of the shamrock over the rose and the thistle. In short the whole establishment is to the dwellings around it what Mr. Cushing's[34] place is to a common farm.

Monday, 25 July. Breakfasted at nine and went shooting with Gibbs —the ostensible object being a robin pie, the true one our own amusement. We made a great destruction among the small birds. The weapon I carried was used in the Revolution by Garfield's father. It was six feet long, slender, small bore, light breech of polished oak, flint lock. It had sent many a fatal charge of buckshot. In the afternoon went fishing with Gibbs and White and witnessed the arrival of the great Nabob, Mr. Caldwell,[35] the founder and owner of the village of that name, who comes here on a long promised visit in a little barge of his own, with flags at prow and stern, and a huge box of wines for his private refreshment. Ask anybody here what kind of a man Mr. Caldwell is, and he will answer with a shrug of the shoulders, or if he is unusually delicate or cautious, it will be, "Oh, he is a very good sort of a man," or else, in the emphatic tone of one defending an accused person, "He is a very clever man, sir, a very clever man." But the truth is that he is a consummate tyrant and fool. He refused to patronize the steamboat unless it was called after his name, and fired a salute on approaching the village, whenever he was present, which is accordingly done. It is impossible to get any favor from him without the humblest deference. He treats the townsmen, his vassals, with favor or the contrary according as they yield him due reverence. Tonight the report of a piece from his boat gave the signal of his approach. Patrick, the Irishman, stood on the beach with the Judge's best gun and answered with a salute, for so it must be, or the great man would be displeased. Somehow or other, the Judge himself, though I believe him as sensible a man as I ever met, seems to regard his humble roof as honored by the mighty presence. Caldwell is of course reported vastly rich, as perhaps he is, but he got all his property from his father, an Irish emigrant who built himself a fortune by trading at Albany.

We were to have gone towards Ticonderoga tonight, but an easterly storm with rain prevents us and compels us to remain here, and sleep under a roof.

Tuesday, July 26ᵗʰ. The great man and his retinue occupied every nook and corner of the little tavern. Two of his satellites were quartered in the same room with us, and entertained us all night with snorings so diversified and so powerful that I wished myself at camp in spite of the storm. Garfield has a very good rifle, which he wanted to "swap" for mine. As his has some important advantages over mine, especially in size of bore, and is only inferior to it in roughness of mounting and in being rather worn by use, I agreed to make a trial with him, which occupied half the morning and showed no marked superiority in either gun. I therefore declined the "swap." Left Garfield's at noon and rowed down to Ticonderoga. Passed close under Rogers' Slide, whose bare perpendicular sheets of granite, with their deep gullies and weather stains and the stunted shrubs in their crevices, present as dismal and savage an aspect as I ever saw, except at the White Mts. Found the steamboat at her wharf at the outlet of the lake and were welcomed on board by old Dick[36] whose acquaintance we made at Caldwell, who now composed her whole crew, the rest being seated under a tree on shore. Dick showed us his rattlesnakes again and told us how a fellow once stole them, shut up in their box, mistaking the rattling for the sound of some valuable piece of machinery; but when he examined his prize and found the truth of the case, he dropped the box in the woods and ran for his life. We consigned our boat to the captain, to be carried back to Caldwell, and got on a stage we found at the wharf which carried us to the village of Ty. It is a despicable manufacturing place, straggling and irregular—mills, houses, and heaps of lumber— situated in a broad valley with the outlet of Lake George running through the middle—a succession of fierce rapids, with each its saw-mill. I bespoke me here a pair of breeches of a paddy tailor, who asked me if I did not work on board the steamboat, a question which aggravated me not a little. I asked a fellow the way to the fort. "Well," said he, "I've heerd of such a place, seems to me, but I never seen it, and couldn't tell ye where it be." "You must be an idiot," thought I; but I found his case by no means singular. At last I got

the direction, and walked about two miles before I saw the remains
of a high earthen parapet with a ditch running through a piece of
woods for a great distance. This, I suppose, was the place where the
French beat off Abercrombie's army.[37] Further on, in a great plain
scantily covered with wood, were breastworks and ditches in abundance running in all directions, which I took for the work of
Amherst's besieging army.[38] Still further, were two or three square
redoubts. At length, mounting a little hill, a cluster of gray ruined
walls, like an old chateau, with mounds of earth and heaps of stone
about them, appeared crowning an eminence in front.[39] When I
reached them, I was astonished at the extent of the ruins. Thousands
of men might have encamped in the area. All around, were ditches
of such depth that it would be death to jump down, with walls of
massonry sixty feet high. Ty stands on a promontary, with Champlain on one side and the outlet of Lake George on the other; his
cannon commanded the passage completely. At the very extremity
is the oldest fort of the fortress—a huge mass of masonry with walls
sinking sheer down to the two lakes. All kinds of weeds and vines are
clambering over them. The senseless blockheads in the neighborhood
have stolen tons upon tons of the stone to build their walls and houses
of—may they meet their reward.

Wednesday, 27ᵗʰ. In Yankee land again, thank heaven. Left Ty this
noon—after going over the ruins again—in one of the great Champlain steamboats,[40] and reached Burlington at night. Visited the
college.[41] It was term time and the students were lounging about the
ugly buildings or making abortive attempts at revelry in their rooms.
The air was full of their diabolical attempts at song. We decided that
they were all green, and went back, drawing comparisons by the way
between the University of Vermont and old Harvard.

Thursday, 28ᵗʰ. Left Burlington this morning, knapsack on back, for
Canada. Saw the falls of Onion [Winooski] River—ruined by dams;
passed the villages of Essex and Jericho. Far on our left front rose the
peak of the Camel's Hump, the highest in Vt. A long line of wild
mountains bounded the horizon. In the midst of them, directly
before us, was Mansfield Mt., second only to the Camel's Hump in

height.[42] Passing the village of Underhill, we descended into a little woody glen, near the road, with a rocky stream running through it, where we consigned ourselves to repose, having walked about 16 miles. Late in the afternoon we started again, and journeyed on several miles, White making by the way several abortive attempts to shoot birds and squirrels. The country was rather hilly, tolerably cultivated near the road, but covered with woods elsewhere. On a hill before us stretched a line of forest, remarkably dense and lofty, and over the tree-tops and among the boughs dozens of crows were wheeling about, croaking in hoarse concert. Ascending this hill, we found ourselves going down into a deep valley on the other side, flanked by barren rocky hills, with flocks of sheep perambulating among the rocks and stunted trees. In front of us was a noble spectacle of mountains, with an intervening country of low hills, forests, and cultivated fields. We turned an angle, and descended into another valley. Mansfield Mt. appeared through an opening on the right, and on the left was a succession of high rolling hills, one behind the other, all covered with forests, with the sinking sun blazing among the trees on the summit of the most distant, and flinging streams of light and shadow over the whole. We followed the road through a deep wood, and when we emerged from it, the village of Cambridge lay before us, twenty-five miles from Burlington. We stopped here for the night. At the supper table was an old farmer who seemed determined to find out all about us and asked, among other little matters, who we were, where we came from, and where we were going. Wrath kept me silent, but White answered his questions, upon which the old fellow, looking fixedly at us, said he should think that whoever we were, we had some kind of prospects to look forward to. The desired explanation not coming from us, he turned to me and asked me if I was not an Indian! I assured him that I was not, on which he coolly shook his head and said that he made it a principle never to contradict any man. He did not consider it any disgrace, for his part, to be an Indian: he had knowed Indians well edicated, afore now. He was very far from meaning to offend. He proved, after all, a fine old fellow; his sins being all of ignorance. Far from being offended, I favored his belief, for the joke's sake, and he firmly believes us both to contain a large share of Indian blood. He invited us to his house, if we passed "his way." We have been taken, on this journey, for people of almost every nation on earth, but this is a consummation we hardly expected.

Friday, 28[9]ᵗʰ. From Cambridge we walked on to Johnson. A fellow in a waggon pulled up as we passed and inquired if we did not belong to the British army—apparently in earnest. The Lamoil[l]e River crossed the road several times. Coming to some deep woods, we were astounded by a confusion of shrieks and cries from them; and approaching, half a dozen hawks, at least, flew off in different directions among the trees. We saw the remains of several of their victims scattered among the rocks and decayed trunks. Yesterday a hawk flew over us, chased and harassed by five or six kingbirds, who would pull his feathers, squall in his ears, and dodge whenever he turned on them. The hawk seemed in high dudgeon.

At Johnson we took the stage for Stanstead, in Canada. The "stage" was a broken-down carryall, into which six passengers with luggage were stowed, and the thing set in motion—under the auspicious influences of two sick horses—over a road of diabolical roughness. By mountain, lake, and stream, we lumbered and wriggled along, the way being made about twice as grievous by a passenger, sick, apparently, of consumption, who could not bear fast riding. He was going home under the protection of his sister—a pretty woman of twenty-five, who seemed all-accomplished, having been, as she said, a traveller all her days, and never down-hearted whatever turned up. She was lively and talkative, though she had been watching the night before, and her country phrases sounded very gracefully from her lips. We rode through a wild and mountainous country. Cliffs of hundreds of feet would sometimes hang over the road. Now and then, there would be a spot among the wooded hills which had just been cleared and burnt, and lay in all the dismal deformity of charred trunks and stumps. Stopped for the night at Troy, near Lake Memphramagog. At supper with us was a girl of sixteen or seventeen; a pretty, innocent little thing, too timid to speak above a whisper. She kept her great black eyes always turned downwards.

Saturday, July 30ᵗʰ, Stanstead, Canada. Resumed our journey this morning in the same "stage." A furious unintermitting rain. The air was full of mists, rolling along the hills, and entangled among the trees. Every mountain was hidden among clouds. We passed through tracts of half-burnt forests, steaming and smoking; some blasted trunks standing upright, others prostrate among charred trunks and tangled underwood, all looking supernaturally dismal through mist and rain. Here and there a dripping and miserable log house, dimly seen, would break the monotony of the forest. The road was made up of "corduroy," rocks, and water. One of the horses came down on a hill side, and we had all to get out in the rain. At last we saw Lake Memphramagog—a direful composition of great sheets of leaden water, scarce distinguishable from the fogs that enveloped it, and a border of melancholy trees which stood apparently lamenting and pouring forth copious tears above it. All nature was in a fit of the blue-devils. At length, ten miles farther on, we passed the line and entered the town of Stanstead, under the same agreeable auspices. The place is large, with several handsome churches. There was nothing in particular to distinguish it from a flourishing Yankee town till we pulled up at the tavern, where were two or three British soldiers, in their undress, standing in the porch. There were thirteen of them, with a cornet, quartered at the house, as there now are in all the border villages.[43] They were good-looking fellows, civil enough; natives of the province. They were gathered round a fire in the barroom, smoking and telling stories, or else indulging in a little blackguardism and knocking one another about the room. They invited us to drink with them, and the liquor being mead—the house is temperance—we consented. They have just clubbed to buy a barrel of cider.

Sunday, July 31st. Last night we were kept awake by the din of bugles and drums with which the soldiers were regaling themselves in the entry, singing and dancing meanwhile. This morning rainy and dismal. Soldiers and all gathered round the stove in the barroom. Their conversation was about as decent and their jokes as good as those of a convocation of Harvard students. They started a conspiracy, headed by the corporal, for making their cornet—who detests smoking—a slave of his pipe; an object to attain which various ingenious expedients were proposed. I went to their roll call, and then to church, dined and wrote letters, ate supper and walked out, the weather clearing up. Our driver of yesterday told us some stories of smuggling. Chase,[44] the landlord, asked us to hear some private psalm singing, in his kitchen. We went and found Mrs. C., her daughter, son, and another youth with a mouth like a gaping oyster seated along a table with their psalm books before them, humming, coughing, and *do–ra–me*–ing preparatory to the commencement. The cornet, who painfully professed himself fond of music, with a few of his soldiers, were in the room; the family stood up behind the singers, except Chase himself, who established himself in front to dictate and pronounce judgment. They sang well, especially the son. With every pause the old man—a downright puritan— would criticize the performance; and the unfortunate cornet declare that it was very good music indeed. They finished—having previously been reinforced by a long-faced individual, apparently a deacon,—with the tune of "America," singing, in order to satisfy all the auditors, the stanzas of the republican song, and adding to each one "God save the Queen." The cornet succeeded in retiring before the end, but his men seemed to like it and crowded into the room.

Monday, August 1st. Chase had promised to get us a waggon to advance us on our journey. He had it ready quarter before seven and we set out to seek Indian Stream and the Ma(r)galloway, that being now our destination, seeing that we are unable to go to Mt. Ktaadin [Katahdin]. Chase drove us as far as the town of Barnston, through Stanstead Plain, a very level and fertile country. He says that he should think Stanstead contained 6,000 inhabitants. Dismissing him and his waggon at Barnston—where four or five more soldiers are stationed—we set out on foot for Canaan, which promised land some told us was twenty miles distant, while others reckoned it thirty. The road for a few miles was good, but we were soon compelled to leave it and take a path through the woods. A beautiful river— smooth and rapid—ran across the road under a bridge of logs, between forest-covered banks. Not far from Stanstead, we had crossed a furious stream, answering to the sentimental designation of the Nigger River. We had walked but a few miles when the clouds settled on the hills and it began to rain. We went to a log cabin for shelter. The "old man" was frank and hospitable like all his genus I ever met, and the "old woman"—a damsel of twenty two, who sat combing her hair in the corner—extremely sprightly and talkative. She seemed somewhat moved at heart by the doctrines of Miller,[45] whose apostles are at work all along the Vermont frontier. We abused that holy man to our content and, the rain ceasing, left the cabin. High rolling hills bounded the horizon, all covered with an ocean of forest. The clouds hung heavy upon them, but would break every instant and admit a stream of sunshine, which would pass across the great carpet of woods, illuminate it in spots for an instant, and then give place to the black shadows of the clouds. Soon after leaving this place, we entered the afore-mentioned path through the woods. Now and then there would be a clearing with its charred stumps, its boundary of frowning woods, and its log cabin; but, for the most part, the forest was in its original state. The average depth of the mud in the path was one foot. Scarce a ray of sunlight ever reached there through the thick boughs overhead. The streams that ran through the wood had no bridges, and most of them seemed to have preferred the artificial channel afforded by our path to the one they had worked for themselves among the mossy stones and decayed trunks of the forest. So we had to wade in deep water about two-thirds of the way. Of course, we were soon covered with mud to the eyes. It was not long, however, before we emerged upon a broader path—one practicable to a stout waggon. This, too, led through a dense forest. We stopped at a log cabin at three o'clock and asked for dinner. A decent one was given us. During the process of eating, the "girls" were working at the spinning wheel and giggling among themselves, the boys sat stiff and upright in their chairs—homemade —and contemplated us with great attention. "How far to the next clearing?" we asked. "Eight mile!" and a long eight miles it was to us—a dismal slough of despond the whole way—mud to the knees. But the path was a singularly wild and impressive one—cut through a wilderness. Huge trees flanked and arched it—maple, pine, cedar, cypress, and a thousand others; bending over it, and intertwined with one another, two high walls of foliage and wooden columns. Below, a fringe of high bushes along the path hid the base of the trunks; but, looking through, the ground was hid with matted masses of green mossy logs, and heaps of rot, with a tangled undergrowth, all wet with the moisture that never leaves a forest like this. The day was showery, with occasional glimpses of the sun; so that we were alternately wet and dry. Late in the afternoon we reached a clearing, with a couple of cabins. Two men were mounting their horses to ride through the woods. We gave the accustomed shake of the hand, etc., walked through another two miles of forest, and came to another clearing, of an aspect so wild and picturesque that a painter might have won the credit of being an astounding genius by only copying things as they were. At the farthur end of this clearing was a stream, swift and cold, into which we walked in order to wash off the superfluous dirt. Thence, passing various dwellings, and holding various colloquies with the inmates, we reached Canaan, and a good tavern. The landlord has quartered [us] in his hall—large as a barn. Canaan is a microscopic village, the houses scattered through a valley among low mountains, all covered with forest. We saw here the Connecticut for the first time—rapid and full of rocks and foam. We follow its banks tomorrow.

Tuesday. Weather still cold and blustering. Thick clouds all over the sky. Set out after breakfast for the Connecticut Lake, twenty miles distant. The road ran along the river, about as good as a cart-track through the woods about Boston, and shadowed by the boughs of the trees. The Connecticut went roaring along on our right. When we had gone about two miles White found he had lost his powder-flask, and had to go back and look for it, an accident which detained us an hour and more. We passed several houses, cabins and others. At one where we stopped for a drink and a talk—for the men regularly turned out and shouted to us as we passed—I rested my rifle against a hogshead standing by a pump trough. A sudden jar knocked it down. It fell so that the muzzle struck with great force upon the trough. I picked it up and walked on, without imagining that it had been much hurt, till some way further, when I found the stock split, the breech-pin broke short off, and other damage done which made the gun almost useless. This was worse than anything that could have happened, short of the loss of our cash, but we determined to keep on to the Margalloway still, and make shift as we could. White seems to have lost his apathy and is now quite ready to proceed. Reports of the Margalloway trout have inflamed him. The road was still hilly, narrow, and, [a] great part of the way, flanked by woods. The valley of the river looked, as it always does, rich and fertile, but the hills and mountains around presented one broad unbroken expanse of forest, made the more sombre by the deep shadows of the clouds. In the afternoon, we reached a hill top and a vast panorama of mountains and forests lay before us. A glistening spot of water, some miles to the north, girt with mountains which sloped down to it from all sides with a smooth and gradual descent, was Lake Connecticut. As far as we could see, one mountain of peculiar form rose above the rest which we afterwards learned was the Camel's Hump [Rump Mt.]. Passing a river with rapids and a saw-mill, at the end of the day we reached the lake, where are two houses, Barn[e]s's[46] and Abbot's.[47] There are steep rapids at the outlet, with a mill, of course. We went to Abbot's house, and asked for lodging and a supper. Abbot, a stout, round shouldered, frank-looking man, was in his hay-field. I inquired of him for a guide to lead us across to the Margalloway, and he at once said that he would go himself, first confessing that he had never been before, and did not know the country in that direction. This was nothing to the purpose. A compass was guide enough. I hired him for a dollar a day.

We went in to supper, which was served in rough style, but had the virtue of cleanliness, as did the whole place—children excepted. There were some eight or ten imps of both sexes, the youngest called Henry Harrison, whence I divined that Abbot was a Whig.[48] There was a schoolmistress from Canaan in the house—plain, but of decent manners and sensible. Abbot was a rough-hewn piece of timber enough, but his wife was a perfect barbarian, as far as the entire absence of all manners can make one, but both were equally open and hospitable. Henry tried the polite, but I judged it best to do at Rome as the Romans do, and I believe got along best. We spent that evening about their enormous cavern of a fire place, whence a blazing fire gleamed on rows of suspended stockings, the spinning wheel, the churn, the bed, and walls covered with an array of piled up cheeses, plates, milkpails, and clothes; all clean and all in order; while the older children were dodging about the furniture of the crowded room and the younger ones venting precocious snorings from a box under the bed. Abbot soon began to rail against Tyler,[49] etc.; then diverged to stories, which we kept going among us, the little school-mistress taking her part, till a pretty late hour, when we were shown to a good bed in the opposite room. Abbot says that one of his relatives, Kenfield by name, fought at William Henry, and, at the massacre, seeing an Indian about to strip a fallen officer, caught him, raised him in his arms, and dashed him to the ground with such violence as to make him senseless.[50] Our host greatly exults in the bodily strength for which his family have been eminent—he himself no way dishonors his race in that respect. These settlements are of old date,[51] but have hardly increased at all for many years.

Wednesday. We devoted today to loafing about the place. White and I went out in an old "dug out" of Barns's on the lake, but caught no fish. The season is unfavorable, but we afterwards caught a few large trout at the foot of the rapids. There is in this lake and in Memphramagog a fish I have never seen, called the lunge.[52] There are moose, bear, and wolves on the mountains; and a beaver has long dwelt, spite of trap, in Indian Stream above the dam we passed two miles before we reached the lake. We lived in backwoods style today—sugarless tea for dinner—water drank from a mug common to all the company, etc. We liked it—I did, at least. Abbot sat cobbling his shoe against his projected expedition towards evening, but as I came up he turned round and remarked that he was not a disciple of St. Crispin[d] but only an occasional follower. As I was marvelling at this unexpected display of erudition, his wife thrust her head from the door, and exclaimed, "Here, supper's ready. Where's that other man gone to?" We accepted the elegant invitation and walked in, where Abbot astonished us still more by comparing the democrat levellers to Procrustes, who wished to reduce all men to the same dimensions by his iron bedstead. All this was while he was squatting on his homemade chair, one leg cocked into the air, shirt-sleeves rolled up to his elbows, bushy hair straggling over his eyes, and eating meanwhile as if his life depended on his efforts. I have since found that he has read a vast amount of history, ancient and modern, and various

[d] Patron saint of cobblers.—Ed.

other things—all fact, however; for fiction, he says, he cannot bear. When twenty-five—he is now thirty-six—he defended himself against a good lawyer in a court, and won his case, his opponent confessing himself outmatched by Abbot's general knowledge and quick memory.

Thursday. Started this morning to strike the Little Margalloway. We proceeded first toward the north, with a path for the first few miles. It soon failed us, and we had to force our way through tangled woods. At about ten o'clock we reached the west bank of the Second Lake. Connecticut is a string of three lakes, on the first of which Abbot's house and all the other settlements are. At this place we met an unexpected delay. The raft, on which we were to have crossed, had broke loose from the bank and gone over the rapids down to the first lake. There was nothing for it but to build another, an operation which took up two hours. We paddled over at last, the mountains which lay between us and the promised river heaving up, ridge over ridge, before us, covered with an unbroken and pathless forest, never trod except by hunters. We landed on this dreary shore— White tumbling over into the water in the attempt—shouldered our packs, and taking a southeast direction by the compass, plunged into the woods. Ten thousand decayed logs scattered here and there, piled one on other, a thick growth of strong and tangled under- wood, rocks, fallen trees, gullies, made the forest almost impassable. It was a constant straining of muscle and sinew. Boughs slapped us in the face, swarms of flies stung us; we trod on spots apparently solid and sank to the thighs in masses of rotten timber. White had hurt his foot the day before and constantly lagged behind, so that we had to wait for him every minute, the prey of torturing flies. At length the ascent of the first mountain made the way still more laborious. When at length we reached the top, we could see nothing on account of the thick growth of trees. We passed through a singular piece of boggy ground, of an oblong shape, enclosed in a fringe of cedars, rising one above the other, all hung with tassels of white moss. There was another place, partially open, near the summit. As we passed it, a large buck sprang from the ground, and leaped with long bounds down the mountain, before my rifle was at my shoulder. We

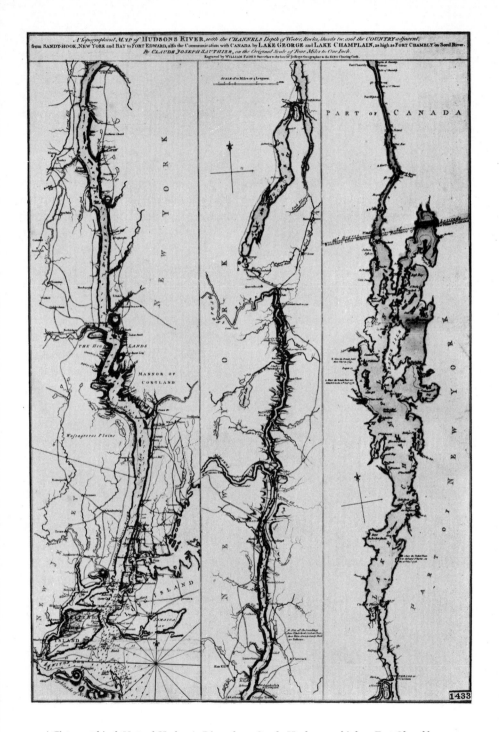

A Topographical Map of Hudson's River from Sandy Hook . . . as high as Fort Chambly, 1776
Engraved map by William Faden after Claude Joseph Sauthier
(Coverdale Collection No. 1433)

heard him crashing the boughs far below. In this spot were several springs of clear, cold water, in broad cup-shaped hollows in the ground, which had probably attracted the deer. We went down the mountain and found a little stream flowing through the valley at the bottom. Both Abbot and myself were for proceeding, but White said he could not go on on account of his foot; so we found a convenient spot and encamped. It was by the stream, flowing half-concealed beneath brushwood and fallen trees, in a thick growth of firs, spruces, and birches. We made a fire, and proceeded to cook our supper. We had brought with us seven pounds of bread, six and a half of rice, and a quantity of butter. We had beside about an ounce of tea, and salt, of course.[e]

We made our fire in the middle of the grove, cut spruce boughs for a bed, lay down on our blankets, and with our knives speedily made way with a mess of rice placed on a broad piece of birch bark amongst us. Then we heaped new wood on the fire, and lay down again, cooled by a gentle rain which just now began to fall. The fire blazed up a column of bright flame, and flung its light deep into the recesses of the woods. In the morning we breakfasted on rice, bread, and tea without sugar and cream, and then—Friday—prepared to resume our course. Abbot led the way, forcing himself with might and main through the bushes and trees, with us following behind. He carried White's blanket, for White professed himself unable, on account of his lame leg. The direction was southeast by compass, up the declivity of the second mountain. White was eternally grumbling and lagging behind. We had to wait for him every few minutes. The guide cursed him to his face, and said he never knew a fellow of so little pluck. At length, after some hours of tedious labor, we stood on the summit, and saw—nothing. The trees crowded round us so dense and thick that our view was confined to a circle of about a rod around, and a few little patches of cloudy sky above; but by climbing to the top of a tall maple, a noble prospect of mountain and wilderness lay before us. Far off rose the Margalloway Mountain, with a sea of smaller hills about it, all pale and indistinct in mist. Lake Connecticut glisten(en)ed among them like a surface of polished silver. Right beneath us was the valley of [Dead] Diamond Stream.

[e] "Written at Camp, without shelter, during a shower of rain."—F.P.

A line of steep and lofty bluffs marked its course, for the river itself was buried too deep among mountains to be visible. In front, close to us, heaved up a long ridge of mountains sloping away to the left down to the Margalloway.

We set the compass and found the river lay still to the southeast of us. We came down, and pursued that course again. We soon began to ascend [descend] the mountain on the side opposite that which we had ascended. The way was rough and precipitous. White lagged more and more, and provoked Abbot and myself beyond measure. After journeying many hours in this painful style, we heard the plunging of waters in a valley below us, and joyfully turned towards the sound. It grew louder and louder. In five minutes more we emerged from the gloomy forest and stood in the rocky bed of a wild stream that came down in a succession of rapids and falls over broad shelves of granite. Just then the sun came out from the clouds and lit up the long avenue of trees that followed the course of the stream, and made the water sparkle and glisten in welcome contrast to the sombre shades we had just left. We had struck a branch of the Little Margalloway. White's lameness seemed mysteriously to leave him; he siezed his fishing tackle and rushed up and down the rocks, pulling a trout from every deep hole and the foot of every waterfall. I soon followed his example. Abbot built a fire by the bank and cooked our fish. We made a plentiful dinner, and then began to follow downward the course of the stream. At first, it was a matter of no difficulty. We could walk well enough down the channel without wading much above the knees in any place, but soon the brooks that poured in from the mountains on all sides increased the depth of the water, so that we had to betake ourselves to the woods again. Four miles below where we struck it, the river was navigable for a canoe; a mile further, and we heard the loud plunging of a fall. We found a ledge of some four feet high stretched across the river, with the water tumbling over it into a deep basin of dark waters. On the right bank, close to the fall, were traces of an old encampment. Night was coming on, so we determined to establish ourselves here, though we had hoped to have reached the forks of the Margalloway, the place where its two branches meet, and where Slade[f] and I made our

[f] Daniel Denison Slade, Parkman's companion in 1841.—Ed.

last camp a year ago.ᵍ In the middle of the fall there was a rock, to which we waded and caught in ten minutes a dozen of trout averaging a foot in length. We built our fire, split open the fish, broiled them on forked sticks, boiled some rice, made some tea, and supped in very luxurious style. We lay down on our beds of spruce boughs and the monotonous plunge of the falls quickly lulled us to sleep.ʰ

Saturday, Aug. 5[6]ᵗʰ. The morning opened with a grand council. How were we to get down the river? Abbot could make a raft, thought he could make a spruce canoe, and was certain that he could make a log one. I told him to make a log one. We roused White from the spruce boughs where he persisted in snoring, in spite of our momentous discussion, and then prepared and ate our breakfast. White went to fishing. Abbot shouldered his axe, and he and I went off together for a suitable pine tree to make our canoe of. He found one to his satisfaction on the other side of the stream, some distance down. I built him a fire to "smudge" the flies, waded back across the stream, and as I ascended the farther bank heard the thundering crash of the falling pine behind me, bellowing over the wilderness, and rolling in echoes far up the mountains. I went back to camp, where White had again betaken himself to his diversion of snoring, took my broken rifle and set out on an exploring expedition to find the basin where the two branches of the Margalloway unite, which I knew could not be far distant. I waded a considerable distance down stream in the water, which varied in depth from the knees to the waist, but finding this method of progression somewhat unpleasing, I took to the woods, forced my way through them in a southerly direction for half a mile, and found at last the object of my search. The old place, though in the midst of a howling wilderness, looked to me quite like home. It was the spot which had listened to Slade's lugubrious lamentations, the extreme point of my last year's pilgrimage; the place where Jeromeⁱ had joined our party; and to crown all, it was scarce five miles distant from the scene of that

---

ᵍ See 1841 Journal, p. 29.—Ed.

ʰ *"Friday, Aug. 5th.* Saw three moose-yards of last winter—known by the marks of teeth on the young trees and by the heaps of dung in every direction.—F.P."

ⁱ Parkman's Indian guide in the preceding year.—Ed.

astounding exploit of knocking over the wounded moose. There lay the great black basin of dull waters, girt with its fringe of forests, but the appearance of things was altered since I had seen it before. The basin was fuller, the water blacker and deeper. Some hunter—Jerome, we found afterwards—had visited it since Slade and I had been there and made a good camping place of split boards. Two or three vessels of birch bark, a setting pole, and a fishing pole were scattered around. There was a fragrance of rotten fish in the atmosphere which told that the visit had not been many months back. I sat down, dipped a cup of water from the basin, took a biscuit from my pocket, and made a most comfortable luncheon. I took Jerome's pole, went to fishing, and in an hour caught large trout enough for several meals for our whole party. As I went back to camp, I found that Abbot was not at work on his canoe. While I was marvelling at this, I stumbled upon a half-finished sp[r]uce canoe, which Abbot had set about making, having found the pine tree, which he had cut down for his log boat, rotten. I was not much pleased at this change of plan: nevertheless, as the thing was begun I lent him [such] assistance as I could, so that by nightfall we had finished something which had the semblance of a canoe, but, owing chiefly to haste and want of tools, had such a precarious and doubtful aspect that White christened it the *Forlorn Hope*. We put it into the water. It leaked. We took it out and stuffed the seams with pounded spruce bark, chewed spruce gum, and bits of cloth. It still leaked, but we hoped it would do, with diligent baling; so, fastening it to the bank, we cooked our supper, rolled ourselves in our blankets, and went to sleep before the fire.

Sunday, Aug. 6[7]th. We were obliged perforce to adopt the sailor's maxim, "No Sunday off soundings," for our provisions were in a fair way of failing, and starvation in the wilderness is not a pleasant prospect to look forward to. So we prepared the last meal we were to take at the Rapids of the Little Margalloway. White, acting as chief cook, arranged the trout on forked sticks before the fire. Abbot filled his little copper kettle with water, and boiled some rice, which being poured into a tin dish and suitably buttered, made way for the tea which was afterwards boiled in the same kettle. The dish was set amongst us, the trout piled on a piece of birch bark close by, and the kettle of tea steamed on the other side. We soon demolished the repast, one item, at least, of which would have been considered an extreme luxury at the breakfast table of the richest man in Boston. I mean the Margalloway trout, which are the noblest in appearance and the most delicious in taste I ever knew. After breakfast we packed our luggage, and proceeded to make the dubious experiment of the canoe. All were embarked; White in the middle to bale, Abbot at the stern, I in the prow. "Push off." The canoe glided with a quiet and gentle motion down the swift stream, between the tall walls of forest on each side, but soon the ripple and tumbling of a rapid appeared in front and the hour of trial came. She quivered and shook as she entered the disturbed waters; at last there was a little grating sound. She had struck upon the stones at the bottom, but the peril was past; the water grew smooth and deep again, and again we floated quietly and prosperously down in the shadows of the woods. At last another rapid came. She entered it, grated heavily over the stones, and struck hard against a large one before her. The water spouted in like a stream from a pump. It would not do. The experiment was an utter failure. We left Abbot with the canoe to conduct that and the baggage as [best] he could down to the basin, and waded to shore ourselves, to walk there through the woods. We had not gone quarter of a mile when "Hallo, here" came from the river. "What's the matter now?" shouted we in return. "The canoe's burst all to pieces!" Sure enough, we found it so. Abbot stood in the middle of a rapid, up to the knees, holding our baggage aloft to keep it dry, while the miserable remnant of the demolished vessel was leisurely taking its way down the current. We pushed through the woods towards the basin, deliberating what to do next. Abbot was sure he could make a raft which would carry us down to the settle-ments, and yet draw so little water as to pass the "rips" in safety. The navigation would indeed be slow with such a machine, but it could be made in an hour or two, and this would more than counter-balance the want of speed. The river was high; the plan seemed eligible, and we proceeded to execute it. Meanwhile it began to rain furiously. We walked into the water to our waists and held the timbers in place while Abbot withed them together. Jerome's camp was demolished to furnish materials, his setting poles and birch-bark vessels appropriated to our use. After about two hours of aquatic exertion, during which we were wet equally by the rain above and the river beneath, the raft was finished. Owing to the badness of the timber, it drew twice as much water as we expected. We pushed from shore in a deluge of rain. Like its luckless predecessor, the raft passed the first rapid in safety, only venting a groan or two as its logs encountered the stones beneath. The rapids in the main river were, of course, much deeper than those of the Little Margalloway, above the basin, where the canoe had met its fate. When it came on the second rapid, the machine seemed to shiver in direful expectancy of its approaching destruction. Presently it grunted loud and dolefully. We set our poles and pushed it into the deepest part. For a while it bumped and blundered downward; at length there was a heavy shock, a crash, a boiling and rushing of many waters. The river spouted up between the logs. We were fixed irrecoverably aground. The water coursed savagely by us, and broke over the end of the raft, but it could not be moved. The result of this second experiment was more dismal than of the first. We were in the middle of the river; the trees on both shores loomed gloomily through rain and mist, and a volume of boiling and roaring waves rolled between. However, there being no remedy, we walked in and, by dint of considerable struggling, waded safe to the western bank, where I directed Abbot to try no more experiments but to work on a log canoe till he had finished it. He accordingly felled another tree, while we were, with great difficulty on account of the rain, building a fire. Abbot worked with great perseverance and skill. Before night, his canoe was nearly hewed out. We plied him with tea to keep his spirits up, relieved him of the cooking and all his other duties, so that his task was accomplished in what seemed an incredibly short time. That afternoon I went back to the basin to get fish for the public benefit. At night the rain, which had ceased for awhile, began to pour afresh. We put up White's blanket, which was wet, for a tent and, spreading mine on the ground beneath, made a great fire before it, ate our supper and lay down. As soon as we were quiet, the continual dropping and plashing of rain through the forest had a sound singularly melancholy and impressive. White dropped asleep, after his established custom on all occasions; but Abbot and myself, both of us wet to the skin, chose to lay and talk before the fire till past midnight. Our guide is a remarkably intelligent fellow; has astonishing information for one of his condition; is resolute and as independent as the wind. Unluckily, he is rather too conscious of his superiority in these respects, and likes too well to talk of his own achievements. He is coarse and matter-of-fact to a hopeless extremity, self-willed and self-confident as the devil; if any one would get respect or attention from him, he must meet him on his own ground in this matter. He is very talkative. I learned more from his conversation about the manners and customs of the semi-barbarians he lives among, than I could have done from a month's living among them. That night in the rain, leagues from the dwellings of men, was a very pleasant one. We slept a few hours towards day; and rose before it was fairly light, he to finish the canoe, we to prepare breakfast. We launched the boat soon after, embarked, and paddled down stream. Dull leaden clouds covered all the sky. The rain fell heavily and steadily. We determined to reach the settlements, if possible, that night; and accordingly we paddled continually all day, only stopping, about noon, to eat our last biscuit. White paddled lazily and unskilfully, and showed much of that kind of resignation which consists in abandoning one's self to fate, instead of fighting with it. Abbot gave him something more than hints of what he thought of him; and when I proceeded, in a truly Christian spirit, to bestow a little friendly advice and exhortation, that he should be up and doing, he flung down his paddle, wrapped himself in his blanket, and sat down listlessly in the bottom of the canoe. As night approached, we began to feel rather uncomfortable at the notion of spending it in the open air at such a time. At length we saw, on the left bank, a camp built of logs for the use of "loggers." We went ashore. The place was dry, the roof being slant and thatched waterproof, with a hole at one side to let out the smoke of the fire. A cart path led from the place towards the settlements, which we knew could not be far distant. In a desperate hope of reaching them that way, we left the certain to pursue the uncertain good. We walked and ran, with our heavy packs and guns, about a mile along the wretched path, which seemed only to lead us deeper into the wilderness. Wading through bogs, stumbling over logs, pitching into

gullies, bruising our skins, running against trees, but still hurrying
on, we came at last to where the path divided into three; and following the best, we came to other ramifications, till the path seem[ed]
almost to disappear and we to be buried in a trackless wilderness.
This was a pretty condition of things for a stormy night. It was too
evident that the roads we had been following were the work of a
party of enterprising loggers, none of them leading, as we had
thought possible, to the settlements, but [rather to] the depths of
dismal swamps, where the best timber grew. There was still, however,
one little path which seemed of older date than the rest, and which,
that no stone might be left unturned, we resolved to follow. It
was getting dark fast. What was done must be done at once. We
dashed on at almost a run. The trees overhead made the way about
as dark as midnight; and the roaring of wind, the beating of rain,
and the creaking of boughs shut our ears against all ordinary sounds.
At all events, it was without much warning that we all plunged up
to our necks into a gulf of muddy water that, swollen suddenly by
the storm, was slowly eddying along through the forest in the channel
which, the day before, held a little brook. As we scrambled up the
bank, after this delightful immersion, we thought of warm taverns,
hot suppers, soft beds, and brandy and water. But none of these
desirable comforts awaited us. We took the best course the circumstances permitted and retraced our way to the logging camp. Fortunately I had secured my matches in a tin case, and this in my
water-proof knapsack, so that we were able to build a fire with the
aid of some dry birch bark we found in the hut. The floor was covered
with clean straw which made us beds. We built a furious fire, which
burned down one side of the hut and might have burned the rest,
had not the logs been well soaked in rain. Hanging our superfluous
clothing to dry, we laid down in the rest and slept comfortably all
night.

*Tuesday, Aug. 8[9]*ᵗʰ. We did not rise till late this morning, so comfortable was our bed of straw. We found our clothes dry and our
limbs active and pliant with the steam which filled the hut. We had
eaten nothing of any consequence since the morning before. Now
we got ready our last mess of rice, boiled all our tea, seasoned the

breakfast with all the butter we had left, and made a very fair and satisfactory meal. When we got out of the hut, we found the forest about us glittering in the morning sun with the rain drops of last night; mists floated above the river and among the trees; the clouds that half covered the sky were light and thin and promised to scatter soon. We could hear, in the stillness of the morning, the rumbling of the distant rapids. We baled the water from our canoe and pushed it from the shore. After paddling about three miles down stream, the hoarse sound of the falls growing louder every instant, we saw before us the line of white foam, stretched across the river, which marked their commencement, and turning towards the bank, found the true pathway to the settlements. A walk of an hour brought us to them. The old logging camp, where we passed the night, was not more than six miles distant from them, so that [it] is not impossible that we might have reached them the night before, had we been lucky enough to have chosen the right turning in the labyrinth. The first man we met was the Indian Jerome, who was cleaning a moose-hide in a field. He shook hands with me very fervently, probably expecting a donation for old acquaintance' sake, but the rascal was disappointed. Jerome is an outcast from his tribe for various misdeeds, too many and too gross to particularize. White, after muttering a salutation which Jerome did not hear, and half extending a hand which Jerome did not see—or pretended not to—stood fixed in awe and abhorrence at the sinister look of the fellow's face, the diabolical size of his mouth, the snaky glittering of his deep-set eyes, the hollowness of his cheeks, and the black marks dissipation has made on his countenance. Jerome is an admirable hunter. He killed more than twenty moose this spring.

We next proceeded to the familiar cabin of my old guide Lombard, or as they all pronounce it about here, Lumber. His wife was in the house and gave us quite a cordial welcome. I asked her to get us some luncheon, and we demolished a miraculous quantity of her bread, milk, and cheese. I found the "old man" at work on the road—which needed it—at quarter of a mile's distance. He was as dirty, big, rough, ogre-like, and hearty as ever. He and a train of his sons went back with me to the house, where he took down from the rafters, amongst suspended stockings, yarn, bladders, etc., the ears of the moose I shot when with him last year. He said he had kept them a whole month in his chimney to dry, and meant to send them to Boston by the first opportunity he had, but such opportunities are not of very frequent occurrence on the Margalloway. I pocketed the valuable relics.

We next followed the "road"—so called by courtesy—down the river towards Capt. Brag[g]'s, where we meant to spend the night. Meanwhile the weather had changed. "Old Esquoss" [Aziscoos], and all the other mountains that flank the valley, stood out in dismal relief against black clouds. Thunder began to grumble and mutter. At length the storm burst over some of the more distant peaks, and the descending rain shut them from sight, like a grey curtain drawn before them. The clouds seemed satisfied with this ebbullition of wrath. They broke, the sun streamed through them, and we hoped to spend that day at least in a dry skin. At last we came to a place where it is necessary to cross the river. There is no regular means of so doing, so that passengers have to depend on the mercy of the farmer who occupies the log-house on the opposite side. We shouted for a boat at the extent of our lungs. No reply. We called the man by name. Presently a voice was heard—"A'nt got no boat—the boy's gone down the river with it arter a schoolmistress." No sooner was this sentence uttered, than White quietly seated himself on the bank in helpless resignation. We had flattered ourselves that now we had reached the settlements our difficulties were over, but here was no contemptible one in the outset. I ran back about a mile to the last cabin we had passed—no boat there. When I returned, I found the indefatigable Abbot looking among the trees for timber to make a raft, but everything seemed to oppose us—all the wood was so heavy as scarcely to float. We now roused White from his torpor and told him that if he had any spunk left in him, he would swim the river and apply for help at some houses we could see lower down the river. He made a flat refusal, but being suitably reviled, and accused of cowardice, want of spirit, etc., etc., etc., at length reluctantly consented. Abbot made him a little raft, of such wood as he could find, to put his clothes on and push before him. We saw him climb the opposite bank, and then set about preparing another resource in case this one should fail. We had already put all the baggage on another little raft, made by Abbot; and, maddened at White's long absence, were stripping ourselves to swim across with it; when Bennet[t], the owner of the house opposite, came down to the bank and called to us to search a little muddy creek near to us, where he said there might possibly be a boat hid. We did so, and found a broken log canoe, in which we embarked and contrived to keep afloat, by constant baling, till we got to the other side. After some time, White made his appearance, bringing with him a tall, long-faced fellow who had a boat, but was afraid to let it to us for fear we should not pay. We quieted his apprehensions on this score by liberal promises, so that at last he agreed to row us down the river to Capt. Brag's— ten miles—for a dollar. The late rains had made the path through the woods by land perfectly impracticable. We set out. The weight of the party sunk the gunnel of the little skiff to within an inch of the water. Mr. Hibbard, of whom we hired the boat, had declared that he hated to go, that he was a delicate man who always took cold when he was wet, and would not stir on any account if he thought another shower was coming. Abbot rolled his eyes learnedly over the firmament. "No, sir," said he, "it won't rain tonight. When you see a white streak in the clouds like that 'ere over the mountain, it's a sure sign of no rain for twenty-four hours." In spite of the white streak, there was a perfect certainty of a furious shower, if black lowering clouds and muttering thunder are any signs; but Abbot's sage remark closed Hibbard's mouth.

Beside the pair of oars, we all paddled, except White. The boat made rapid progress. We had gone about a mile, and there was a long reach of river stretching before us, when the forked flash sprang out from a huge black pile of clouds, and forth burst the thunder like a battery of ten thousand cannon. Then came a deep hoarse sound, apparently from the furthest depths of the forest. It grew louder and louder, nearer and nearer, till down came a deluge of rain on us that seemed as if it would beat our skiff and us to the bottom. Even the sound of the thunder peals seemed stifled in the dismal hissing and roaring of this portable cataract. It fell with such violence that the whole surface of the river was white. Our view was confined to a few rods round us. The wall of trees on each side could only be seen dimly and indistinctly, as if in the night. Feeling somewhat uncomfortable, we ran the boat ashore and waited in the woods till the first fury had past, and then drove down the river in double quick time towards our destination. There was a long line of dead pines, rising up high above the other trees, and flinging their knotted and twisted arms in such fantastic style through the mist and rain that they looked like so many tall imps of the devil, stationed there on purpose to plague and torment us. In about two hours, straining our eyes through the vapors, we saw a line of white objects in front of us, rising, sinking, approaching, falling back, and apparently performing a sort of ghostly dance across the river. These were the waves dashing against the rocks, at the head of the rapids of the Androscoggin, and spouting into the air as they struck. We moored our boat at the head of the portage, siezed our baggage, and ran, waded, plunged, and crawled, through mud, water, and slime, till we got to Brag's and dashed pell mell into his kitchen, inundating it plentifully. Mrs. Brag was full of commiseration. We were soon steaming before a huge fire; half an hour after, eating a hot supper; and half an hour after that, comfortably in bed, listening to the impotent malice of the rain as it beat on the windows. The delicate Hibbard preferred to sleep on a buffalo [robe] before the fire.

*Wednesday, Aug. 9[10]*ᵗʰ. Left Brag's this morning to walk to Colebrook. I had to carry about thirty pounds weight, including my blanket which, having covered White's shoulders through all the storms of yesterday, had become saturated with moisture; and as he had neglected to take any measures for drying it, it was about as heavy, when rolled up, as a log of hard wood. Abbot carried his for him. The day was overcast and showery. When we had got about six miles, we overtook an old fellow in a waggon, who was jolting along over stones, logs, gullies, and all other impediments towards Colebrook. White got in with him and rode the rest of the way, Abbot and I going on together, first committing the baggage to his care, except my knapsack, which I chose to keep with me. We soon entered the Notch. Its appearance is much finer when seen from this side than from the other. There you see nothing but bare cliffs, rising all around you and shutting out everything else, but here a host of green trees spring from every crevice, overhang the road, and half conceal the crags on each hand, and in a ravine on your left a little brook comes down in a succession of foaming waterfalls. We reached Colebrook early in the afternoon, having walked twenty-two miles. Abbot had previously taken a by-road which led to the north, and we saw no more of him.

Thursday, Aug. 10[11]ᵗʰ. Stayed at Colebrook today, for want of means to get off. In the villanous little hole of a tavern there, there is never anything stirring to break the dismal monotony. Every day is a Sunday. There may be a whole week without any customer. Everything is scrupulously neat, the old lady starched and precise and, of course, grossly stupid. There is no fishing or sporting of any kind about the place. She had some old magazines in the house which she hunted up for us, and these were about our only amusement for the whole day.

Friday, Aug. 11[12]ᵗʰ. The stage came by this morning from Canaan. It is called a stage, but is in reality a milk-cart. We got in. At noon we reached Lancaster, where White stopped, being reduced to his last quarter of a dollar, to see his uncle and borrow the needful of him. I kept on to Littleton; where I now am.

Saturday, Aug. 12[13]ᵗʰ. Started for home by way of Plymouth. Riding down through the Franconia Notch, the mountains—rolled up, heads and all, in their blankets of mists—the lake, the martial countenance of the Old Man, and all the other familiar objects of that noble pass seemed to press me to stay in a manner that nothing but necessity enabled me to resist. All but the scenery, however, is changed since I was last here. Oakes[53] has left the tavern at the village, which Fifield has taken, having abandoned his last year's stand at the Notch House, which is now empty. The drunken scoundrel Gurnsey[54] has surrendered his house to one Knight(s),[55] and remains a sort of useless fixture on the premises. With an accommodating driver and a pleasant party of ladies and gentlemen—one of the former exceedingly handsome, romantic, and spirited—we rode on towards Plymouth and got there late at night. There was a general on board, a man of exalted character and vast political influence which he exercised on the righteous side of radical democracy, fiercely maintaining that ninepence was better than a million dollars, insomuch that the possessor of the first is invariably a good man and contented with his lot, while the owner of the last is always a grasping, avaricious child of the devil. When the general alighted at his own tavern, he saluted the first loafer who met him at the door as "major"; the next but one was "colonel," while our driver answered to the title of "captain."

Sunday, Aug. 13[14][th], *Plymouth.* Went this morning to church where a toothless old scarecrow, who had been a preacher twenty-five years ago, mumbled a sermon which nobody could hear. A sentence here and there reached my ears, and seemed to indicate something worthy a better delivery. A son of Deacon Punchard[56] is the settled Congregational minister here. Walked, after church in the afternoon, to see Livermore's Falls, where the Pemigewasset tumbles over a mass of combined mill dams and granite rocks in a furious "burst of yellow foam."

1843 Notebook

Lake George, Montreal, Quebec

White Mountains & Maine

Introduction

THIS was really the first of Parkman's long series of journeys for historical research. The excursions of the two previous summers were largely pleasure trips, though coupled with the love of adventure and of the wilderness which inspired these arduous expeditions was the historian's desire to experience for himself the life led by his heroes. In attempting to match the hardihood of those bold pioneers, and to strengthen a constitution none too robust by nature, Parkman had damaged his health to such a degree that this journey of 1843, except for a few active days in the White Mountains, was perforce that of a student rather than that of a man of action. His ill-health, mirrored in the incompleteness, terseness, and bad temper of this notebook as opposed to the joyous detail of the earlier journals, was such that his family sent him abroad soon after his return to Boston from this journey, rather than back to Harvard for his senior year.

The cryptic quality of this notebook is tantalizing, for here Parkman records his first impressions of the chief scenes of his history, the places which he was later to make celebrated by his spirited accounts of the events that brought the little-known settlements of colonial North America into the European eye. In the Hudson and Mohawk valleys he sought out oral tradition of Sir William Johnson, that wild Irish baronet who ruled the Iroquois for England; of the old Dutch settlers who founded Albany and Schenectady when New York was New Holland, and left their imprint lastingly on the land; of Joseph Brant, that most civilized of Mohawks, who was educated by Eleazar Wheelock, the founder of Dartmouth College, entertained by Boswell, painted by Romney, and commissioned a colonel in the British Army for his services to the king. At Lake George, Parkman wandered again over the much disputed battleground which he had first visited the previous summer, and was to enjoy revisiting until his death fifty years later. At Montreal he had his first contact with the French Catholicism which played so great a role in the history he planned to write. "Roman" institutions and "popish" customs were strange to the young Puritan son of a Boston Unitarian divine, and it is clear that he took more pleasure in his first sight of British regulars and of the forts which defended the much traveled invasion route of the Richelieu and Champlain valleys. At Quebec he was stirred by the old walls—not old enough, however, to have witnessed the actions he was to immortalize—and by the monuments to the great generals whose deeds he was to chronicle forty years later in *Montcalm and Wolfe*, perhaps the greatest single link in his chain of histories.

Always a Yankee, with the true home of his heart somewhere in the wilderness of the White Mountains, Parkman then left the strange new land of Quebec behind him and revisited the scenes of his travels during the two previous summers. This time, however, he was in search of historical information rather than adventure; and so he pumped the old tavern keepers, the antiquarian lawyers, and the garrulous stage drivers of the region, noting down the rich store of legends with which the White Hills abound. His notes proved useful for *A Half-Century of Conflict*, published in 1892. As always, Parkman liked the land rather better than the people; and his notes on the caverns in Crawford Notch and on his horseback excursion to the summit of Mt. Washington are free from the patronizing superiority which characterizes his accounts of fellow travelers. And constantly he jotted down the titles of standard works on colonial and frontier history which might serve his purpose—a necessary method in an age when the compilation of a bibliography demanded more reliance on hearsay than on reference work.

Returning briefly to Boston, he soon set off again with his sister Caroline for Maine, where she was to visit friends and he was to study the Penobscot Indians, the last remnants of the savage population of New England. At the reservation near Bangor he eagerly questioned the Indians about their ancient customs and traditions; but found the most talkative far more concerned with the urban delights of Boston than with the "out of date" ways of his forebears, who had once taken Mohawk scalps. Parkman's failure to gain here much firsthand acquaintance with savage life drove him two years later to visit the Great Lakes, and then in the following year to make the greatest of his journeys, the Oregon Trail trip.

The incomplete record of this summer's journey is found in a small maroon leather notebook, measuring $2\frac{1}{2}$ by 4 inches, written in pencil on both sides of the page with many abbreviations and omissions of punctuation because of the smallness of the page. The writing is fairly clear.

1843

Giles F. Yates,[1] Esq., Schenectady—"The best of Am[erican] Antiquarians"—that is, with an extensive knowledge of the colonial hist. of N.Y.

Rev. Mr. Williams[2]—Schenectady

Kerney—Clergyman—Clermont,[3] Columbia county, N.Y. A grand nephew of Sir W. Johnson.

The Germans of the Mohawk know much of Sir William and family. About Fonda, especially.[4]

The gent. who told me the preceding told me also what follows. He was a man of most extensive and minute information on similar topics.

His ancestor's house, together with one other, were all that escaped the Schenectady burning—for this reason: His ancestor, an old Dutchman, saved a Jesuit priest whom the Mohawks were about to burn at their "burning place" near Schenectady. The priest was secretly packed in a hogshead, boated down to Albany, and thence sent home to Canada. The old man accounted to the Mohawks for his escape by the priest's omnipotent art, magic. This priest accompanied the war party, and protected the house.[5]

The grandfather-in-law of this gent. was saved when at the stake by Brant.[6] He made the Masonic sign. Brant was a Mason, and so interfered.

As for the "burning place,"[7] he said he had dug there, and found a fragment of a skull and some bones.

Lake George. On a little hill, by a pine tree, near Ft. George,[8] I saw a flat rough stone with an inscription as follows "1776 Here lies Stephen Hodges" and more unreadable. Other apparent graves are near.

Close by, on a fresh ploughed [field], a boy with me found a buck-shot and a coin about the size of a 50 ct. piece. I myself picked up a musket ball and a copper coin.

Montreal—Friday. Visited the nunnery of the *Soeurs Grises.*[9] Hospital for invalids. School for children. Patients hideous to look upon—nuns worse. Buildings of the same rough grey stone generally used here. Large—with dismal courts and flanking walls—long passages, rough but neat—a chapel with altars and confessional, and hung with pictures and a piece of the true cross in an ornamental frame. The school rooms and hospital were hung likewise with pictures, etc., and over each door was the name of a saint. A host of pauper children, in a huge room—unpainted—sang a French hymn, looking like so many diminutive washerwomen. We visited the cathedral[10]—visited it again in the morning and saw the service—elevation of the host, etc., priests in abundance.

Two regiments are in town—71st Highlanders[11] and the 89.[12] A part of the 43rd [13] are on the island a short way off.

At St. John's is a small fort and barrack.[14] At I(s)le-aux-Noix a strong and admirable establishment.[15]

"Hope Gate,"[16] Quebec, is defended something in this manner:

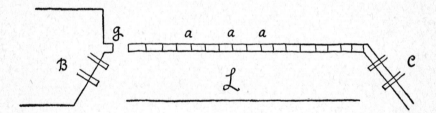

G—Gate. B—Blockhouse, stone below, with loops for musketry—wood above, and portholes for two cannons commanding the street. L—which is a precipice on one side. *a a a*—loop[hole]s all along the walls. C—two more guns on the wall, also commanding the street. The whole struck me as precisely resembling the *description* of the place where Montgomery[17] was killed.[a]

---

[a] "It does not resemble the reality."—F.P.

Wolfe and Montcalm. Inscription on their monument[18]: "Mortem virtus communem famam historia monumentum posteritas dedit."[b] "Here died Wolfe victorious."[19]

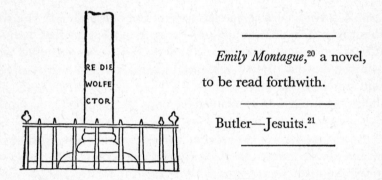

Emily Montague,[20] a novel, to be read forthwith.

Butler—Jesuits.[21]

Saturday night rode up from old Crawford's,[22] starting at sunset. The whole scenery, at that hour, especially about the entrance of the Notch, wild and exciting to the highest degree.

Old Abel tells me that *he* is the "first of the Crawfords." Settled in a log cabin about fifty-five years ago where Fabyan's now is, having got a grant from the state. Ethan Crawford[23] has returned from Guildhall and occupies Dennison's[24] near Fabyan's. Saw a dog at the old man's which had its face dismally swollen from a battle with a porcupine. Also an amusing couple in the shape of a little thin cadaverous youth, called Joshua Waterhouse, and his bride, a pretty, lively, tall damsel—both from Portland, and both stamped "Yankee." Went fishing with them, the lady volunteering her company, which was sufficiently agreeable. She spoke of a young lady who had been at Tom's a day before as "Sarah Thornton," and her mother as "Miss Thornton."

This delicate little flower, whatever it be, I place here in memory of the grimmest, dismalest den on earth, where it grew among moist precipices and rotting logs.[c]

I write at the bottom of a den more savage yet than the last. Turn

---

[b] "Valor gave them a common death; history a common fame; posterity a common monument."—Ed.

[c] A flower, resembling a violet, was here pressed in the notebook.—Ed.

to the left, as you approach Crawford's, enter a gateway of rock, and you will reach two dens that look like the very bottom of Hell. Nothing but great piles of damp mossy rocks, rotten timber, huge black cliffs fencing you in, with trees stretching across from their edges. A stream is plunging somewhere under ground, and breaking out into a black pool among the moss. Behind is a great heap of rocks where you descended. In front a steep descent, choked with fallen timber, and such a tangled mass of vegetation that a bear could scarce get through.

These ferns shall be a memento.[d]

Edifying specimens of humanity are staying here at Tom Crawford's.[25] Two botanists, each styled "Dr.," tall long-legged fellows, go about with tin cases and press boards all over the rocks. They actually reached the top of one of the Notch Mts. today, though one of them nearly killed himself in the attempt, and, as he elegantly remarked, "got sick as a horse, and puked." He stretched his ungainly person on the parlor sofa tonight, grunting with fatigue, and occasionally assisting a sentimental lady who was journalizing and arranging flowers, somewhat as follows: "Here—that ain't the way to press"—"That's the Coribla Em [?]" "I don't know what that is— let's look"—struggling with a groan into an erect position, etc.

Also mineralogists in abundance—tough broad-shouldered men, apparently schoolmasters.

Two pedestrians from Maine arrived last night, one of whom had gone three years ago as lieutenant in the Aroostook expedition.[26]

Rode up to the mountain on Monday morning alone, starting at six and getting back just too late for the stage—so that Crawford had to take me on in a waggon. Was about six hours gone. Laid down, thrust my head into the Lake of the Clouds, and drank a copious supplement to a gill of brandy wherewith I had previously regaled myself. My horse fell twice. Had a glorious time of it.

A man named Russel[l][27] carried me in a waggon from Bethlehem, discoursing deeply all the subjects of religion. Meeting a minister in another waggon, Russel pulled up and they began a conversation

[d] Pressed in notebook.—Ed.

about a debt due from one to another. My companion pronounced the minister a "loud one" and expressed great admiration of him.

Green Mt. Boys[28]

Have spent two very agreeable days at Franconia Notch at the house kept by Knapp.[29] He is a very good fellow. Have hunted, speared fish, etc. Coming to Plymouth, had a driver who expressed, in a very sensible manner, an enthusiastic admiration for the scenery of his route—a perfect phenomenon in his way. In other respects, too, he was an admirable fellow. He always, he said, "felt a kind of comfort as he rode through the Notch."

Stopped at Senter [Center] Harbor.[30] Saw, at the lawyer's, quite a collection of Indian relics—gouges, pestles, arrowheads, etc., found in the neighborhood. They told me of Indian graves about 4 miles off. The "mineral spring," on Ossipee hills, was evidently a place of resort.

M.S. *Wars of Canada*—C. F. Hoffman[31] knows.

Hoffman's *Wild Scenes in Forest and Prairie, Winter in the West*, etc.

Barstow's *New Hampshire*,[32] Dunlap's *N. York*,[33] Whiton.[34]

From Senter Harbor to Fryeburg; spent Sunday, and visited the Pond. Paugus's[35] gun, so-called, is shown at the Academy. Went back to C[onway]—thence to the Mountains again, stopping at Old Abel's. Found there a pedestrian named Wells. I heard downstairs a tremendous noise of tongues and found this gent. reading aloud from the *Northern Traveller*[36] and catechizing Old Crawford, usurping all the talk to himself, and making noise enough for a dozen. This done, he read us a piece in the newspaper. He had been something of a traveller, loved to talk of his experiences, and assumed the chief command: "Now, Mr. Crawford, we are all rather tired with our hard day's work and, if you please, we will retire to our rooms. What do you say, gentlemen, shall we protract our sitting?"

Mr. Stedman and Mr. King[37] are here.

Stayed a day or two, and rode on to Ethan's to spend the night. Mrs. C[rawford] soon produced her history of her husband's adventures, etc.—a manuscript which she means to publish.[38] Nash and Sawyer,[39] she says, discovered the Notch in their attempt to find a road from Upper Coos southward. They received the grant of land in consequence, on certain conditions. Her description of the Willey catastrophe is excellent. She tells, roughly and simply enough, but very well nevertheless, various characteristic stories of the early settlers. Her grandfather, Mr. Rosebrook,[40] settled before the war at the site of Colebrook—near 80 miles from settlements. Ethan's original seat was by the "Giant's Grave," where his house was burnt.

On the night of the slide, their situation was tremendous. In the morning, their fields were flooded, all the bridges for a score and more of miles swept away, great part of their roads torn up—and a bright unclouded sun showed the extent of the desolation. In the still morning they heard the waters pouring from the mountains. Ethan carried an impatient traveller across the swollen Amonoosuck, and left him to find his way to the Notch. He struggled on to the Willey House—found it empty. The children's beds had been slept in—the others had not. The house was started from its foundation and fallen in. The horses were dead—the oxen still alive, and he found an axe and released them. This done, he crept into one of the beds and slept till morning, hoping the family had escaped to old Crawford's. A dog of Willey's, which at first refused him admission, was his only companion.

Next day he found they were not at the old man's, and he passed on carrying the news to Bartlett and Conway. The neighbors and the relatives of the Willeys assembled—a dog pointed out the first body—the flies moving about the drift timber, the rest. The night after the traveller had left, when several people had assembled, Ethan C., who was there and anxious to get back to his own house, probably on account of his own loss, groped his way up the Notch in the darkness, though the road was ruined.[41]

Captivity of Mrs. Johnson,[42] Windsor, Vt., 1807. A book worth getting. Frontier Life in '54, etc.

Riding down to Conway, met Mr. Stephen Meserve[43] in the stage. He told the following particulars relative to the Willeys. On the alarm, he brought his dogs to the Notch at the desire of Willey's brother. They searched all the morning in vain, but on their suspending their efforts and assembling in front of the house, the dogs did not follow, but lay down by a heap of logs, rocks, etc. An old hunter was of the party and exclaimed "that means something." They went to where the dogs lay, and observed flies passing and repassing about the drift timber. Looking closer, a hand appeared clenched tight round a bough, and soon the naked body of a man was drawn out. The avalanche had torn away every shred of his clothes. The dogs no sooner saw it than they whined—then turned and ran the whole way back to Meserve's house in Bartlett. The other bodies were got out by means of the flies.

Riding from Conway to Dover, old Mr. Willey,[44] father to the sufferer, was in the stage with his daughter. He was more than eighty, had served in the Rev[olution]. He was suffering from a cancer in the lip, and was going to Nashua to get it cured.

He and his daughter gave the true version of the Nancy's Brook story. Old Colonel Whipple,[45] some 60 yrs. since, hired her and a young man to take charge of his house in Jefferson, hoping that they would be content to remain there as settlers on his grant—perhaps he thought of matrimonial results, to hold them closer. They "courted," in fact, but next year Whipple came up there with a party, and found his two settlers, though satisfied with each other, very loath to remain in the wilderness. He agreed to take both back with him. He however broke his word and left the girl, who was perfidiously deserted by her lover. The party went down through the Notch. The love-stricken girl was in despair. The few neighbors could not restrain her from setting out in pursuit, though it was winter. She did so; reach[ed] Whipple's deserted camp, at the site of Tom Crawford's, struggled through the Notch, and died near the Brook.

The Colonel was a close old fellow, so honest, however, that he kept a bag of half-cents to make change. He was disliked by the settlers on his grant. He once refused them corn when they were starving, and they took it by boring a hole in the floor of his granary, and letting it leak out into bags. They dressed as Indians and came round his house to frighten him; so that he took to the woods in terror.

He [was] captured in earnest, during the latter part of the Rev., at his Jefferson house by a party of English, Tories, and Indians. He managed to get permission to go to a back room for some clothes, squeezed through the window, and escaped.

The driver of the same stage told me of large eagles on Squam Lake which he saw sieze a lamb (see Jos[s]elyn).[46] Also he pointed out a brook in Ossipee(?) where he said Lovel [Lovewell][47] had ambushed some Indians, and mentioned the Pond in Wakefield which goes by his name, from a fight of his there.

Robert Southey had in his possession the whole of Wolfe's correspondence.[48]

Having started afresh, with C[aroline],[49] reached Gardiner, where I left her and proceeded to Bangor. Rode in a waggon behind the stage, which was full, in company with a stupid young downeaster who had been in the coasting and logging business, and was now going to recover a lost trunk. Broke the axle and had some trouble. Cursed my companion, and told him to run for help. Nothing moved his stolidity. He walked off at a snail's pace, in spite of my exhortations to "fly round." Got righted, left waggon, and went on in the stage to B., the downeaster forgetting his trunk. A miserable old wretch of a speculator and an ex-ship captain were my companions.

Went over to see the Indians.[50] One of them says he thinks there are about 400 in all, but many are gone away. Saw François and others—some squaws extremely good looking, with their clubbed hair and red leggins. Two fellows paddled me a mile or two up the river. The Indians use the genuine wampum. I saw a collar of it— said to be worth $6—round a squaw's neck.

There are a number of loggers in their red shirts seated in the bar; some of them have been to see "The Lord's Supper."[51] One expressed his disapprobation of the character of the exhibition as follows: "G——d d——n it, I should like to take that fellow by the nape of the neck, and pitch him into the road. He's no right to serve that 'ere up for a show in that way."

Bought some wampum of F.'s squaw, which he says he bought

from the Caughnawagas[52] near Montreal, 25 yrs. ago. It is however sometimes made by the whites in Canada.

I mentioned the Mohawks. "You no 'fraid Mohawks?" asked François' brother. "We 'fraid. They bad Indian—look too cross." Whereupon François began the following story, which he told with some excitement, mixing up the name of Castine[53] with it in a way I did not understand. Several hundred "Mohogs" (as he called it) came upon the Penob. and took prisoners and killed a large number. Many of the old prisoners were burnt—the young thrust upon sticks which were stuck in the ground. Soon after the Mohogs were famine stricken. Fifteen P. prisoners were left who volunteered to go out and hunt. The M.'s consented. The P.'s brought in plenty of game, feasted their enemies till they were overpowered with repletion, then fell upon them and killed all but one, whose ears and hand they cut off and sent him home.[54]

A fellow named Mitchell, whom I met in old Nicolas' house (his son), seemed to be a perfect adept in all the vices of cities. He showed me an advertisement of a firm in Boston, printed like a bank-bill. I asked him what he meant to do with it. "Me make some Indian take him—spose he don't know nothin'! Spose me have two, three in my wallet, then they think him bank bill—I get good credit."

He said he liked the city, and talked learnedly about the mysteries of Ann Street, appealing to me if his reasonings were not correct. He was much more practicable in conversation than most of them. It would have been hard to cheat him, with his quick observation and cunning.

He tells me that wampum is made of the sea clam, called *cohog*. The French Canadians, as well as the Indians, make it.

Speaking of the change in the manners of Indians, he says: "What use fight—take scalp—no do any good. Spose me kill snake—no get nothing at all. Spose um kill man, they no get anything."

François says he is glad Indians have left off fighting; "ought to be peaceable," he says. Even hunting, he added, is getting out of date, on account of the loggers, and the Indians are now farmers.

European Journal
1843–1844

Introduction

THE GRAND TOUR was an accepted part of every well-to-do young American's education in the mid-nineteenth century; and when Parkman's health showed signs of collapse under the rigorous regime of Harvard in his senior year, and under the Spartan extracurricular life that he had set for himself, nothing was more natural than that his family should send him to Europe. A sea voyage was the sovereign remedy of the day for the nervous exhaustion which was his chief symptom; and the change of scene and contact with the foreign world might both restore his health and round out his education, so far somewhat unduly provincial in character.

Parkman remained all his life a New Englander of the New Englanders, a Puritan among Puritans. But this early European journey, together with many later trips made both for recreation and for historical research, did much to relieve the provinciality of his environment and heredity, and to give him some understanding of Latin and Catholic civilization, to whose attempt to colonize the New World he devoted his life. Indeed he made a conscious effort, at the age of twenty, to prepare himself for his future work by seeing as much as he could of a world very foreign to that of Boston. It was not mere love of adventure that led him to spend a week in a Roman monastery, but a desire to achieve firsthand knowledge and understanding of the life led by the Catholic priests who played such a great role in the development of New France. In Sicily he visited all the monasteries along the way, "but a more intimate acquaintance with them and their inmates was needful for my purpose. I was led into a convent by the same motives that two years later led me to become domesticated in the lodges of the Sioux Indians at the Rocky Mountains, with the difference that I much preferred the company of the savages to that of the monks." So Parkman wrote nearly half a century later, when he published a revised version of his Roman journal in *Harper's*. But there is a later rationalization and alteration of his youthful motives in this account, for it is clear from the European journal that at this period Parkman was drawn to the Catholicism which was then anathema in Boston. He was in revolt against the arid Unitarianism of his father and the canting Puritanism of his forebears, both systems uncongenial to a temperament that fed on romantic and colorful ideas. In later life Parkman became an agnostic, without ever losing a certain militantly Protestant outlook, but many passages in *The Jesuits* and *The Old Regime* reflect the same attraction to the colorful Catholic tradition and the same conscious resistance to it which are found in the European journal. Parkman, the descendant of a long line of New England divines, was always an anticlerical, and far more anticlerical than he was anti-Catholic. Since one of the vexed questions of Parkman's place as a historian is how far a strongly Protestant writer could understand and appreciate the essential role of Catholicism in New France, this early Roman interlude is of major importance.

The European journal is also a valuable record of the impact of European civilization on a young American of the period. A lover of the past, who distrusted the new notion of democracy and despised the morality of commerce, Parkman found the Old World more to his taste than the New: "Here in this old world, I seem, thank heaven, to be carried half a century backwards in time." He was prepared to dislike the British military, and found to his surprise that he felt more at home with them than with many of his fellow countrymen. This is not inexplicable, for the New England Federalism in which Parkman was bred, and which he largely preserved through a life isolated from the new movements and ideas of his time, is closely akin to English Toryism. This son of the Puritans shared many of the ideas of the Cavaliers. But he was enough of an American to loathe tyranny, and his reaction to the rule of Ferdinand of Naples and of the Austrians in northern Italy anticipates the American sympathy with the revolutions of 1848. This sympathy was very closely akin to that with the Republicans in the Spanish Civil War and with other antifascists of our own time. Parkman's reaction against Austrian tyranny is revealed more fully in his novel *Vassall*

Morton than in this journal, but his lack of sympathy with absolutism is notable, considering the dominance of that system in New France. Then the fact that Parkman was already an able writer, if not a fully qualified historian, makes this youthful record of the Grand Tour more interesting than most; and the journal of a slightly homesick solitary traveler is more self-revealing than most of Parkman's writings, even among these diaries written for his own eye.

The journey was by no means the conventional Grand Tour, which doubtless had little appeal to so energetic a young man as Parkman. He sailed from Boston in November 1843 as the sole passenger on one of the small American merchant barks then so active in the Mediterranean trade. The tedious and rude voyage gave him ample opportunity to recuperate from his nervous exhaustion—reflected in his confusion about dates and his unreasonable impatience at the slow passage—and to jot down vivid descriptions of the sea in full fury, which pleased him so much a dozen years later that he incorporated them almost bodily in *Vassall Morton*. At Gibraltar and Malta he delighted in the pomp and circumstance of British military power, which was to be one major theme in his lifework; but he soon wearied of conventional sightseeing along the beaten path, and so, early in January 1844, he set off on muleback for an arduous tour of Sicily, alone except for an effervescent guide. Here the born historian reveals himself as he marvels over the successive waves of civilization which washed over that strategic island, and as he takes pleasure in tracing the remains of each. Parkman was a romantic, but he had been bred in the classical tradition, as this journal reveals. He was also learning to judge men of a different stamp than his own, to appreciate their foibles, and to sketch the salient elements of their characters with penetrating understanding, if not without the sense of superiority appropriate to a Boston Brahmin. There are evidences of Parkman's enduring Anglo-Saxonism, with its usual condescension to "lesser breeds without the Law."

Having covered Sicily thoroughly, he turned to the Italian mainland, to the home and center of that Catholicism which was so outlandish to a Boston Unitarian and yet so attractive to one whose ideal of life was "a little medieval." Italy rather than France was then the favorite refuge of American expatriates and the goal of tourists who sought European culture at its source; and Parkman encountered many fellow countrymen there. He saw little more of Naples than the average tourist, but after leaving the Kingdom of the Two Sicilies he had uncommon experiences in Rome, thanks largely to his cousin Coolidge Shaw, lately converted to Catholicism and then studying for the priesthood as a member of the Society of Jesus, that Jesuit order which played a major role in Parkman's chosen field of history. Because of the company at Rome of Theodore Parker, that exceedingly learned and most liberal of Unitarian clergymen, Parkman was not completely bowled over by his first real contact with the Catholic Church, but the journal reveals how strongly he was impressed by it; and even the mockeries suggest that he was consciously resisting an influence that he felt was almost too strong for him. Two years later he was still sufficiently concerned with Catholicism to keep up a correspondence about it with his cousin, who had not yet despaired of converting him.

During his Roman stay, this lover of the hills and the wilds wearied of the round of sightseeing among the ruin-dotted lowlands. He fled into the Apennines with his college friend, the painter William Morris Hunt, for a few days of a hardier and simpler life. Then, after the gorgeous pageantry of a Roman Holy Week, it was with eagerness that Parkman left the Papal State and turned northward to the Alps; such eagerness, in fact, that he hurried through the rich old cities of the duchies of Tuscany, Modena, Parma, and Austrian Lombardy with but little regret for the briefness of his stay. Though he was glad to quit Austrian territory and enter a free country, the Alps somewhat disappointed him; he found Lake Como inferior to Lake George and the Splügen Pass hardly more impressive than Crawford Notch. But perhaps these views are best explained by the homesickness that Parkman felt after long months of solitary travel, so evident in the Swiss passages of his journal. He hurried on to Paris, where a knowing uncle showed him the gay capital of Louis Philippe with such thoroughness that no time was left for journalizing—most unfortunately, since a record of this first impact of French civilization on the historian of France's greatest colonial effort would be of absorbing interest. Nothing that he would have been apt to see in the

Paris of that period would have tended to increase his regard for the tradition of absolute monarchy, whose sway in New France he later judged to be one of the main causes of the French disaster. Then Parkman, stricken with colic, short of sleep, and full of worldly wisdom beyond his years as a result of his stay in Paris, crossed the Channel to a Britain already familiar to him from much reading of Dickens and Walter Scott. London both fascinated and repelled him: his were the typical reactions of a young American of the period, who was at once drawn to the civilization which had given birth to his own and irritated by the superior attitude of the English toward transatlantic cousins and all their ways and works. Like many another American, he liked Scotland better than England. The measure of Sir Walter Scott's influence on Parkman is best indicated by the frequent references to the Waverley novels in this journal, and the evident thrill that Parkman experienced in seeing the places whose names had long been familiar to him from his reading. He wandered the border country, visited Edinburgh and Glasgow, regretted that there was no time for the Highlands, and hurried on to Liverpool to catch his ship. Finally there is a vivid account of the voyage home, with its sharp picture of the friction between Americans and Britishers at this period, when relations between the two countries had been strained since 1837 by differences over the New England boundary and the Oregon question. In his delight at being home once more, Parkman did not conclude his journal with any summary of his impressions of Europe, but references in the later journals indicate how keen an observer he had been, and how much this journey had done to free him from provinciality and to make him a citizen of a larger world than that of Boston.

Much material from the European journal went into *Vassall Morton*, the novel with which Parkman distracted his sick mind during 1854-55. For extended discussions of this book, see W. L. Schramm, "Parkman's Novel," *American Literature* (IX, 218-27); and M. Wade, *Francis Parkman*, 328-41. The portion of the journal devoted to Parkman's stay in the Passionist monastery served as the basis of an anonymous article, "A Convent at Rome," in *Harper's* for August 1890 (LXXXI, 448-54).

The European journal is written in ink in two large notebooks:

one, with leather spine and marbled boards, $9\frac{1}{4}$ by $7\frac{1}{2}$ inches, and a second, $8\frac{1}{4}$ by $6\frac{1}{2}$ inches, with purple paper boards, which was purchased in Strasbourg. There is also a small leather pocket memorandum book, of the type that Parkman favored for his travels, which contains penciled notes on the passage from Gibraltar to Malta, and on the Sicilian excursions, as well as fragmentary accounts of its expenses. Its contents are given in the Appendix to this journal.

1843-1844

December [*November*] *16th*, [*18*]*43*. Barque *Nautilus* (Devil of a sea—cabin dark as Hades). Got under weigh from Central Wharf about 10 A.M. of Sunday, Dec. [November] 12th—fine weather, and a noble west wind. Soon after the Pilot left us, we saw the frigate *Cumberland*, coming round a headland, bound for the same destination with us, but she chose to follow a more southerly course, and we soon lost sight of her.

Before long, we were pitched up and down on an execrable swell—the fruit of yesterday's east wind. The barque tossed about like a cork, snorted, spouted the spray all over her deck, and went rushing along like mad in a great chaldron of foam she raised about her. At the same time, it grew cloudy, and the wind became stronger. The sea rose and fell in great masses, green as grass—the wind driving the spray in clouds from their white tops. As I came from the cabin, I beheld, to my great admiration, a huge wall of water piled up in front, into which the vessel was apparently driving her bows; a moment more, and the case was reversed—her bowsprit and half her length rose straight from the waters, and stood relieved against the sky. In consequence of which state of things, I, like a true green-horn, grew sea-sick by the time we were fairly out of sight of land. Accordingly I got into my birth as soon as it was dark, and staid there twelve hours.

When I came on deck in the morning, the weather had changed, nowise for the better. The same short seas were running—the vessel flung herself about in the same villanous style—a great black cavern on one side, and a huge mountain on the other, and a great pile of water rolling after her stern—but the wind had become contrary, and the whole sky was black with clouds. Two or three land birds fluttered about the ship, driven by the wind from shore, which the unfortunates were destined never to see again. I wrapped myself in my cloak, and sprawling on the poop-deck read *The Bible in Spain*.[1] A schooner, with only top-sails set, went scouring past us, before the wind, homeward bound—also, in the afternoon a brig, tossing so that her keel was almost visible. A troop of porpoises went tumbling about us, and I ransacked the vessel in vain for a musket to get a shot at them.

The next morning opened under direful auspices. I came on deck, disconsolate with sea-sickness, when I was straightway saluted by about two hogsheads of water which came dashing over the gunnel, accommodating me with a most unwelcome morning shower-bath. It was showering a compound of snow, sleet, and rain—all was cold, dark, and wretched—the crew enveloped in oil-cloth, looking like drowned rats—the wind dead ahead, and blowing savagely. Foam and spray were spouting over the bows, far up among the sails, and every moment, with a thump, a torrent of water would come against the side, fly up, and innundate the decks. I got an old india-rubber cloak belonging to a former captain, in the stiffened folds of which I enveloped myself to the chin; and, braced in a corner, stood contemplating the crew, listening to the wind, and admiring the savage aspect of the ocean. At length, with a fluttering report, the jib flew to ribbons, and was hauled in. I spent most of the morning in my birth, reasonably miserable with sea-sickness—cogitating, meanwhile, on things human and divine, past, present, and to come. When dinner time came, I heard the captain's invitation to dinner, and staggered to the cabin door, determined to accept it, in spite of fate, when lo! the ship gave a lurch, the plates and the rack which should have secured them slid together from the table, in a general ruin, to the floor. With an execration, the captain grasped the beef and potatoes, and elevated them above his head—while he himself slid down the transom, and joined the medley on the floor. The steward shovelled up the fragments, and we regaled ourselves on the beef and potatoes. When night came, the captain and mate descended to the cabin in great ill humor, the mate swearing that ours was the "wettest craft" he ever sailed in, and declaring he would not embark in her again for the consideration of five dollars added to his wages. This time we contrived to hold the supper on, so that little of it escaped. I tumbled into my birth, but was so flung about from one side to the other that sleeping was not very easy. In the frequent intervals of waking, I listened to the groaning and creaking of timbers, the shouts of the men, the sullen thumps with [which] the seas struck the ship, making her shiver through her whole length, and, immediately after, the shock of the water descending in a torrent on her deck. Meanwhile, the wind howled like a wild beast—and to crown the catalogue of discomforts, my state room was so hot with a fiery stove that I would rather have been in Tartarus. I woke in the morning to another rather dismal day—but the morning after was warm and pleasant, though cloudy, and with the wind ahead. My slight sea-sickness has also left me. Today a brig—English—bore down, as if intending to speak us—but took herself off, without a word.

Saturday, Dec. 19 [*Nov. 18*]*ᵗʰ*. Until today we have been tormented with ceaseless head-winds. The captain especially has chafed incessantly, since this is his first command and he wants a quick passage for his own credit. This morning however was clear, with a respectably prosperous wind. The captain repaired to the cabin and shaved —the first time for a week—by way of celebrating our good fortune; then came up rubbing his chin and smiling with great complacency. A "school" of sperm whales are spouting a few miles off. The fogs of the Grand Banks rest on the horizon in front—but the wind is too good to suffer us to lie to and fish.

Sunday. Driving before a fair wind among the mist and haze along the south edge of the banks. Thousands of gulls, noddies and baglets are skimming over the water. We passed this morning a flock of at least five hundred of the last mentioned birds sitting on the water, filling the whole air with their rank fishy smell. A whale rose last night close to the ship, snorted and puffed for a while, then solemnly turned up his flukes into the air and settled down.

Tuesday. The captain came to my birth this morning with an announcement of another head wind. So here [we] were again, close-hauled, making constant tacks—dodging now to the north, now to the south, without gaining a league in the whole morning. Yesterday the case was different. A breeze, directly aft, carried us over the water at ten miles an hour. The ship with her studding-sails set, looked like a huge bird "predominating over" the ten million gulls that were skimming the ocean all about her.

We have a singular company on board—the three officers, "the passenger," the steward, and six men, viz., a Yankee, a Portugese, a Dane, an Englishman, a Prussian, and an old grey-haired Dutchman, the best sailor in the ship. Of the officers, the captain is a sensible gentlemanly man; the mate has rather more individuality, being, as to his outer man, excessively tall, narrow-shouldered, spindle-shanked, and lantern-jawed—with a complexion like dirty parchment. Mr. Jo[na]than Snow is from Cape Cod, a man of the sea from his youth up. When I first came on board he was evidently inclined to regard me with some dislike, as being *rich*! He constantly sighs forth a wish that he had five thousand dollars; "then ketch me going to sea again, that's all." He is rather given to polemic con-troversies, of which I have held several with him, on the tenets of Baptists, Unitarians, Universalists, Christians, etc., etc.! ! Of course, he imagines that men of his rank in life labor under all sorts of oppressions and injustice at the hand of the rich. Harvard College he regards with peculiar jealousy, as a nurse of aristocracy: "Ah! riches carry the day there, I guess. It's a hard thing to see merit crushed down, just for want of a thousand dollars."

Mr. Hansen, second mate, is the stoutest man on board, and has seen most service, but being, as Mr. Snow remarks, a man of no education, he has not risen very high in the service. He accompanied Wyeth's trapping party[2] to the Rocky Mts., where he was more than once nearly starved and within a hair's breadth of being shot. He speaks with great contempt of Indians, but not with quite so much virulence as I have known from some others of his stamp. He plumes himself on having killed two or three: "Oh, damn it, I'd shoot an Indian quicker than I'd shoot a dog." He is now seated at supper, amusing me and himself with some such discourse as follows:

"I've lost all my appetite, and got a horse's! Here, steward, you nigger, where be yer—fetch along that beef steak. What do [you] call this here? Well, never mind what it be; it goes down damned well, anyhow." Here he sat stuffing a minute or two in silence, with his grisly whiskers close to the table, rolling his eyes, and puffing out his ruddy cheeks. At last pausing, and laying down his knife a moment: "I've knowed the time when I could have ate a Blackfoot Indian, bones and all, and couldn't get a mouthful, noway you could fix it." Then, resuming his labors: "I tell you what, this here agrees with me. It's better than doctor stuff. Some folks are always running after the doctor, and getting sick. Eat—that's the way I do. Well! doctoring is a good thing, just like religion—to them that likes it; but damn the doctors for all me; I sha'nt die," etc., etc.

By treating Mr. Hansen with brandy and water, I have got on very good terms with him, and made him very communicative on the subject of his Oregon experiences. Would that we had a consumptive minister, with his notions of peace, philanthropy, Christian forgiveness, and so forth, on board with us! It would be sport of the first water to set Mr. Hansen talking at him, and see with what grace the holy man would listen to his backwoods ideas of retributive justice and a proper organization of society.

"Shoot him over, and that damn quick, too," is Mr. Hansen's penalty for all serious offences.

Thursday. Yesterday, Captain Fessenden was pluming himself on the remarkably fine weather and smooth seas we have lately had. He had better never have said a word. Last night, I was awakened by the voice of Mr. Snow who came into the cabin roaring after the captain, with an announcement that it was high time to take in sail, for a furious squall was coming up. The captain siezed his clothes and scrambled up stairs. Then followed the shouts, the trampling on deck, the fluttering of canvas;[3] after which sleep was out of the question, such a din did my furniture, trunks, bales, and boxes make, bounding from one side to the other of my state room; and in such an execrable style was I tossed hither and thither in my birth. As soon as it was daybreak I went on deck. Two or three sails were set—the vessel scouring along, leaning over so that her lee gunnel scooped up the water; the water in a foam, and clouds of spray flying over us, frequently as high as the main yard. The spray was driven with such force that it pricked the cheek like needles. I staid on deck two or three hours; when being throuroughly salted, I went down, changed my clothes and read *Don Quixote*, till Mr. Snow appeared at the door with: "You're the man that wants to see a gale of wind, are ye? Now's your chance; only just come up on deck." Accordingly, I went. The wind was yelling and howling in the rigging in a fashion that reminded me of a storm in a Canada forest. The ship was hove-to. One small rag of a topsail set to keep her steady—all the rest was bare poles and black wet cordage. I got hold of a rope by the mizzen mast, and looked about on a scene that it would be perfect folly to attempt to describe—though nothing more, I suppose, than an ordinary gale of wind. The sailors clung, half drowned, to whatever they could lay hold of; for the vessel was, at times, half inverted, and tons of water washed from side to side of her deck. The sea, like the sky, was of a dull gray color. The violence of the wind seemed to beat down the waves, but the sea rose in huge mis-shapen masses, marked with long diverging trains of foam as the wind flew over their surface. As for the usual horizon, it had disappeared—we seemed embedded among moving mountains. Now and then, a towering ridge of waters would heave up to windward, and bear down upon the ship, with a line of tumbling foam crowning it as it rolled on. All held their breath, and clung fast as it approached. It would strike the ship with a crash, and deluge her with water from stem to stern.[4] The wind has not yet abated. It is with much ado that I can brace myself in my seat to write.

Friday. As yesterday was Thanksgiving,[a] I may as well record how *we* fared. Our breakfast was utterly demolished, by the same catastrophe that overtook a former repast—that, namely, of being dashed in ruin upon the floor by an ill-timed lurch of the ship. We dined on a lump of ham, Cuffie being unable to purvey a more sumptuous banquet, because the seas put out the fire in his galley as fast as he kindled it. As for our supper, it was of bread, pork, and onions. Not that this is a fair sample of our bills of fare, which are usually quite as luxurious as any reasonable man need desire.

The gale abated very suddenly at eight o'clock last night. We carried sail all night, and all this forenoon, which was mild and

[a] See below, p. 113.—Ed.

pleasant, though the seas still ran very high. But the wind increased again, sail after sail was taken in, till at twelve it became necessary to heave-to again. Though the weather had been clear all the morning, grey clouds rose, like thunder-tops, all round the horizon and began to overspread the sky. The wind suddenly lulled, but left the waves huge and boisterous as ever; and the ship rose and fell, and was flung to and fro with great violence, but in perfect silence. That low murmuring sound, however, so often spoken of as the prelude of a storm, but which I never happened to hear before, began to growl like stifled thunder. The gale is now on us again. Cuffie, who has made seven voyages to Canton, protests he never saw the like.

Sunday. Night before last was a very bad one. Being rather fatigued by want of rest the preceding night, I slept through the worst of it; yet when I awoke, the booming of the sea was as loud as peals of thunder, for which I at first mistook it. The storm continued through the day—fierce rain-squalls alternating with sunshine. It was a noble sight when at intervals the sun broke out over the savage waste, changing its blackness to a rich blue, almost as dark; while the foam that flew over it seemed like whirling snow-wreaths on the mountains. The wind being fair, we "scud" under fore and fore-top sails, close-reefed—and flew ahead like the very devil—in the early part of the night. At length, we were obliged to lie-to again, lest some of the huge seas which came rolling furiously after us, should overtake us, and sweep the deck clear of everything—men included. We were in fact struck once or twice, in a manner too ominous of what might happen next to be disregarded. The decks were several times buried in water, from which the ship shook herself free with a dismal groaning and shivering. We are now close by the Azores. The gale has subsided. Not a sail nor a spar has been carried away.

Thursday, Nov. 29[30]ᵗʰ. This is, I believe, the true Thanksgiving day after all—and we have fared much more suitably to the occasion than we did a week ago. We have had, for several days, light breezes and calms—an insufferable monotony, relieved only by the circumstance of Mr. Snow's clambering forth on the bowsprit, twining his long legs several times round the martingale; clinging fast with one hand, while with the other he flourished an harpoon and made an abortive attempt to strike some porpoises that were amusing themselves around the bows.

Wednesday, Dec. 6th. We have been tormented for ten days past with a series of accursed head winds. Here we are, within thirty-six hours' sail of Gibraltar, standing alternately north and south, with no prospect of seeing land for many days. The captain is half mad, and walks about swearing to himself in an under tone. Mr. Snow's philosophy has given way—and I never had any. Hansen alone is perfectly indifferent. He sits on deck whistling and talking over his work, without troubling himself about our whereabouts, or caring whether we are in the North Sea or at Cape Horn. The difficulty is to kill time. Recollecting my "whittling" propensities of old, I went to work at manufacturing some indescribable trinket out of a chip, to get rid of the hours till bed-time. Mr. Snow, who had just come down from his watch on deck, stood regarding me for a while with fixed attention. At length: "A phrenologist down to Brewster told me last winter I had a remarkable bump of cur'osity." After pausing a few moments for his hint to take effect, he remarked: "Well, it a'nt polite, I've heard tell, to be asking questions." And so, after another fruitless pause, he retired with unsatisfied "cur'osity" to his birth.

Thursday, Dec 7th. "Day after day; day after day
                   "We stuck, nor breath nor motion,
                   "As idle as a painted ship
                   "Upon a painted ocean."
This has been our enviable situation today. A dead calm—a stupid flapping of sails, and creaking of masts. We lay on deck, watching for hours, with the glasses, a dead fish that floated a short distance off. Mr. Snow is taken sick, and bewails dismally. The captain comes down every now and then into the cabin with: "By George, this is *too* bad! I never see the beat of this! Well, I'll have a smoke anyhow." Then he flings himself along the transom, and lighting his pipe, charged with "pig-tail," fills the cabin with its delicate odors. Breakfast, dinner, and supper are always introduced

nowadays by his exclaiming in a dolorous tone as he sinks into his seat, "By George, this is *too* bad!"

Eleven days ago, we were confident of reaching port in three days! There is a little hope, from some appearances in the sky, that there will be a change tomorrow.

Friday. The ship this morning is proceeding at the rate of about an inch an hour, with her head turned the wrong way! "A head wind and none of it!" groans the captain; "if ever I see the beat of this!" This is but the nucleus of his remarks, so to speak, which he surrounds and adorns with a host of forcible and ornamental forms of expression, which I refrain from recording. We are, however, at last warned of a change impending. The capt. beheld last night in his dreams a woman mounted astride of a white horse; an infallible sign, he says, of a gale.

Saturday. Again a calm! The captain's signs and portents have come to nought. A turtle came up at the ship's side to sleep on the quiet surface, but prudently sank back to the depths just as Mr. Hansen was lowering me by a rope to take him prisoner. A few bonetas splashed about the bows—some "rudder fish" played along side; and a pair of "gar fish" glided about in defiance of all attempts to capture them. Before noon a breeze—a favorable one—sprang up!! It bore us on a hundred miles further, but now has subsided into the old trebly accursed calm.

Monday. We lie here like a log, Gibraltar almost in sight—I could walk the distance in one day—yet not a breath of air for two days past to carry us on.

Tuesday. A light wind today, but dead ahead. More porpoises, and more fruitless attempts at harpooning, on the part of Mr. Snow. I am rapidly growing insane. My chief resource is the conversation of Mr. Hansen, who has humor, volubility, much good feeling; and too much coarse rough manhood in his nature to be often offensive in his speech. Moreover, one man may say a thing, with a very good grace, that would be insufferable from the mouth of another.[b] Witticisms

[b] Several words inked out in text.—Ed.

and stories which, uttered by Snow, would make me turn my back
on the fellow with contempt and disgust, sound well enough in the
frank and bold accents of Hansen.

Evening. We have beat up against the wind into full view of the
Spanish coast. Right and left, from Trafalgar far beyond Cadiz, the
line of rugged and steep bluffs reaches, with here and there a tower
just visible with the glass. But about noon our evil genius becalmed
us again! Late this afternoon I came listlessly on deck; found the
sails flapping against the masts, the sea like glass, and the sky
obscured by thick dull clouds. They looked of an ominous blackness
in the direction of Gibraltar, and, a few miles off, the sea, in the same
quarter, was dark as ink and violently agitated. There was a low
moaning sound, like distant winds, as in fact it was. The blackness on
the water kept approaching nearer and nearer, the noise increased;
then a puff of wind struck our lazy ship, followed by another and
another, till she swung heavily round, and began to rush through the
water. In a moment she was plunging along in full fury. "Now,"
thinks the agonized reader, "we shall get to Gibraltar at last!" Not
at all. The vessel's head was turned south-west. She was running
away from her port! A large "shovel-nosed" shark, whom I imagine
to be an incarnation of the evil spirit that has been persecuting us,
followed in our wake: and thus prosperously are we advancing now,
yet, strange to say, with intervals of perfect calm when the sails
flap as heretofore. *Thirty days from Boston.* Old Worthington[5] promised
that I should see Gibraltar in eighteen, but he is a deacon.

Wednesday. "From grave to gay; from lively to severe," from calm
to tempest. A gale came roaring down the strait at about nine
o'clock, struck us directly in our teeth, and forced us to close-reefed
topsails again. Nevertheless, by diligent tacking and wearing we made
a few miles before morning. When I came on deck, Cape Spartel,
on the African coast, stretched out its lofty and black cliffs close on
the right. Behind it rose, half obscured in vapors, great piles of mountains; all was clouds and darkness but one bright streak of eastern
sky above and behind their summits. The sea tossed angrily, the ship
careering and plunging along like an unbroken blood colt. Now,

we are slowly beating up the strait, in defiance of wind and waves. At times we approach the Spanish coast, bare, rocky, and savage, with many a ruined tower among the crags; then turn away and leave it in mists and darkness behind. The town of Tarifa, renowned for the heroism of Alonzo Guzman,[6] lies about twelve miles in front, and to this point we are straining every effort to attain.

Evening. We have not yet reached Tarifa. Dozens of vessels come past us from Gibraltar, some of them of a most outlandish aspect to my eye.

Thursday. More delay and vexation. The captain has not slept for two nights, and is half worn out by fatigue and anxiety. For myself, I was so exasperated by our continued ill fortune that I could not stay below. We past Tarifa light about midnight—then were driven back four miles by a rain squall. But by nine in the morning, we had fairly entered Gibraltar Bay! "Here we are at last," thought I, and looked up with infinite satisfaction at the warlike rock which rose right above us—with a gray and savage aspect—indented all over with port-holes and scored with zigzag lines of battlements and military roads. At the bottom of the bay appeared a forest of masts. It was now our business to attain that secure haven. "There can be no difficulty there," thought I. Just then, the water at the foot of the mountain was agitated into a violent foam, while a fine spray rose from it like steam from a boiling kettle. In an instant the ship was almost laid on her beam ends by a most savage squall. She righted, to be again struck over. In the course of an hour or two, however, the crew—who worked like dogs—contrived to beat her, in the face of these paroxysms of tempest, about a mile up the bay. Mr. Hansen began to cast the sounding lead to find anchorage. "How deep?" demanded the captain, speaking in the quick tone of an harassed and anxious man. "Can't find no bottom, sir; fourteen fathom of line out." "Well, there must be bottom somewhere," responded the captain, "over with the anchor. By —— I can't stand this longer, nohow." And with a clattering and whirling, down went the anchor.

"How much cable have you let out, Mr. Snow?"

"Whole length, sir. Sixty fathom."

"She holds fast, I suppose."

"Can't tell yet, sir. Don't see how she can help it."

But she did *not* hold fast, and sixty fathoms of chain cable could not reach bottom. This was soon apparent by the rapid drifting of the vessel, toward the opposite shore of the bay. When the captain saw how the case stood, he fairly stamped on the deck with rage and mortification. The crew were set at once to the windlass, to heave the cable in. They could not start it, for two of them have been taken so sick as to be useless. Meanwhile we drifted rapidly towards the shore of Algesiras [Algeciras], opposite Gibraltar. Up went the flag, half mast, in signal of distress. The American frigate *Congress* lay under the rock, and we looked to her for help. Suddenly Mr. Hansen recollected that no boat could legally approach us, as we had not been visited by the health officer. In about an hour, however, a boat was lowered from the frigate, put off towards us, and soon came up with us, with the sailing master of the *Congress*, a midshipman, and twenty men, bringing the health officer with them. This official's examinations were soon concluded in due form, when the man-of-war's-men took us in charge, and brought us to anchor, in about five hours, by the side of their own vessel.

I was heartily tired of the *Nautilus*, and resolved to get on shore if I could before night. The capt. refused to leave his vessel. At last, about dusk, a small sail-boat came alongside with a message from the consul. I told the three rascally Spaniards on board of her to set me on shore, though I had not procured the necessary permit, determining to trust fortune and the consul to aid me in that matter. They said there was scarce time—the signal gun would be fired in half an hour, and the gates be shut. "Do your best," said I, "and I won't complain if you fail." Accordingly the little craft flew through the water, approaching the rock with long tacks, till at last we threaded the labyrinth of feluccas and a host of other strange-looking vessels, and got within ten rods of the mole. Just then the signal gun boomed from the summit of the rock—the gates closed before our eyes. I looked about me and beheld such a throng of miscreants and blackguards that I abandoned the idea that first suggested itself of sleeping in the boat on my baggage till morning. "Turn about, and back to the barque," said I. They set me again on the deck of the

Nautilus, and then the foremost came down into the cabin to settle. "How much do you want?" "*Eight dollars*, sar." I gave him a dollar and a half, which he flung down, but afterwards pocketed. A dollar was the legal price, but new comers must submit to some imposition.

Saturday. Yesterday I came ashore in the barque's boat—landed—got passport signed, and established myself at the "King's Arms." More than fifty men—I speak literally—surrounded me on the mole, arrayed in every variety of dress, jabbering every variety of language, but all entreating to be allowed to carry my baggage. I selected the most decent-looking, who was a slender built fellow, with a sickly countenance. To my utter astonishment he passed a band round my heavy trunks, swung them to his back, and set off at a "dog trot" with them up the steep streets. It needed my swiftest walk to keep pace with him. I dined at the consul's, and spent the day in exploring this singular city—the world in epitome. More of it in future. This morning I set out, in company with a midshipman, the son of Capt. Newton of the *Missouri*, to ride round the bay to the Spanish town of Algesiras. The situation of Gibraltar, as far as my words can describe it, is as follows. A long peninsula of narrow beach projects from [the] Spanish main towards Africa. At its extremity a huge mountain of rock rises, so abrupt and steep that one standing on the summit, more than a thousand feet in the air, could fling a stone down to the peaceful strip of sand below. On the southern side of this rock, where it slopes away to the water, this miracle of a town is built—fenced in on the seaside by tremendous walls, while the rock above is bored full of holes, whence project the muzzles of hundreds of cannon. This strip of sand, bearing Gibraltar on its end, forms a large bay. Algesiras is directly opposite the Rock.

The middy and I passed the British line in a few moments, and found ourselves on genuine Spanish ground. Dirty scoundrels of soldiers, with rusty firelocks, were lolling about some huts by way of guard. A long train of donkeys approached, each hidden under a pair of panniers full of charcoal. They all stopped before the guard house, where every pannier was emptied, to see that no goods were smuggled across the line. I was admiring the vigilance of the raga-muffin soldiery when we beheld a man, mounted on a splendid horse, advancing along the beach towards us. He was a noble looking fellow, arrayed in a richly embroidered dress, wrapped in the huge Spanish cloak; his horse's head, mane, and flanks were hung with tassels and spangles. He carried a carbine slung on his saddle behind him. He was a *contrabandista*—one who practised smuggling in open defiance of the law. A moment after, he was joking and laughing with the officers at the guard-house.

After three or four hours' ride, we approached the town, where more Spanish soldiers were lounging in a group by the roadside. *"Carracho! los Ingleses!"*; with that they set a dog on us; finding this of no avail, they blew their trumpets and shouted to scare our horses. We turned round, and sat laughing at them. *"Carracho! Carracho!"* and one fellow, not satisfied with this Spanish insult, made shift to exclaim "go to Hell!"; whereupon the whole took up the cry in chorus. As we rode through the narrow streets, similar maledictions were showered upon us. Boys followed us, first begging a *cuárto*, and then shouting *"Carracho."* It is a beautiful town—the houses white as snow, with bright green lattices and porticoes—the streets paved with square hewn stone, and without sidewalks. But the noblest sight was the Plaza, or public square, round which stand the public buildings. It was paved with coarse marble; a large and beautiful column rose in the centre, in the midst of a space walled in from the public. All around, by the columns of the cathedral, about the porches of the houses, were stalls of merchants; and beggars in crowds roaring in the name of the Virgin for charity. We left this hospitable town behind, galloped at full speed round the beach, passing lepers by the wayside, soldiers, donkeys, black-eyed women, hedges of aloes and groves of oranges, bare sun-burnt mountains, each crowned with its Moorish tower—vallies even now green as emeralds —and long before the evening guns fired, were within the fortifications again.

Sunday. I entered the cathedral and kneeling with the rest on the pavement, admired the noble architecture of the place; yet it looked more noble still at night, when the shadows of its huge columns and arches left it half in gloom, though a hundred tapers were burning before the shrines.

Sunday is the day to see the motley population of Gibraltar at one glance. Just without the walls is a parade large enough to hold the six regiments stationed here. This evening, according to custom, everybody was thronging up there. I established myself at the foot of a bronze statue of the Defender of Gibraltar[7]—I forget his name[c]— but there he stands towering above the trees and aloes at the summit of a hill above the parade, with the emblematic key in his hand, and with a huge cannon and a mortar on each side of him. Here I had a specimen of every nation on earth, it seemed, around me. A dozen Moors with white turbans and slippered feet lolled one side; Jews by couples in their gaberdines; the Spanish gentleman in his black cloak and sombrero—the Spanish laborer with his red cap hanging on one side of his head—the Spanish blackguard in bespangled tights and embroidered jacket. On benches among the trees officers and soldiers carried on successful love suits; on the parade below English captains were showing forth good horsemanship to the best advantage. The red coats of soldiers appeared everywhere among the trees and in the crowd below. There were women in cloaks of red and black—ladies with the mantilla and followed by the duenna—no needless precaution—and ten thousand more, soldier and civilian, bond and free, man and woman and child. Not the least singular of the group were the little black slaves belonging to the Moors, who were arrayed in a very splendid and outlandish attire; following after their masters like dogs. Bands were stationed on the parade and around a summer house among the trees. The evening gun dissolved the pageant—"God Save the Queen" rose on the air; then the crowd poured through the gates into the town.

I have seen more noble-looking men in this place than ever it was my lot to see before. The Moors, especially, are men of admirable proportions and beauty of features, both set off to the best advantage by their dress. Some of them, from the interior of Barbary, are dark as Negroes; others of a light and florid complexion. The *hamalos* or Arabian Jews who act as porters are extraordinary-looking animals. They are all less than the stature of a woman of moderate dimensions; with a leathery countenance, overgrown with sand-colored beards; a little black scull-cap; broad blue pantaloons, in the

[c] "General Eliot."—F.P.

Turkish style, which reach only to the knee, and expose the calves of their legs, swollen to treble the natural size from the nature of their labor. These fellows stand congregated in groups in the most frequented places, each with a bundle of cords over his shoulder to hold his burden.

The Barbary Jews are very different men, in all except the black scull-cap, and in a certain elongation of visage, made more remarkable by the bushy and grizzly beard. Still another animal is the Jerusalem Jew, specimens of which are rare here.

I got leave, with some difficulty, to see the excavations. They are well worth all the trouble. The solid mountain, on its steepest and boldest side, has been hollowed out into gallereies and great vaulted halls, whence cannon are pointing to all parts of the sea and land, a thousand feet below. I looked down from a porthole; on the beach, the "neutral ground" and the coast of Spain—all were spread out like a map under me. Some soldiers, like black specks of sand, on the plain below, were firing at a mark. The white smoke came from the muzzle of the musket several minutes, as it seemed to me, before the faint report reached us. I dropped a stone from the port-hole. It fell on the sand without once striking the rock in its passage.

From the excavations, I rode along a military road, near the summit of the rock, to the Signal Station. This is an old Moorish tower, with a modern guard-house near it, where a sergeant and six men are stationed. It is in the midst of the mountain—a thirty-two-pounder looks on one side toward the Mediterranean, and a small battery points toward Alge(si)siras on the other. The sergeant gave me a soldier to conduct me to St. Michael's cave. On the way, he gave chace to a young monkey among the rocks, but bruised his shins to no purpose. The rock is peopled with these gentlemen, as well as with a variety of foxes, both under the paternal care of the British government. St. Michael's cave is a vast black gulf, decked with broken stalactites, and filled with the tinkling sound of water dropping from its eaves. It has no bottom—at least none was ever found, though more than one life has been lost among its crags in the attempt. I took leave of the soldier, and followed a narrow path southward; soon reached the extremity of the rock which looks towards the African Mt. Gibil Musa, or as the English call it, Ape's Hill, on account of the baboons with which it swarms. At this point of the road, I noticed an arm-chair, carved, of massive dimensions, out of the rock; facing towards Africa—where, perhaps, the holder of this tremendous fortress might sit and overlook the passage which he commands. Half a mile further, I was on the eastern side of the rock. The path here was frequently hewn through precipices, like roads among the Alps. I saw the white breakers tumbling among the rocks below, but heard not a sound. I emerged at last on a little battlemented platform, among the cliffs. A brass howitzer and a heavy cannon lay there, pointing towards the sea. The whole scene was savage and desolate in the extreme. These grim-looking engines of war were the sole occupants of the loneliness.

I went to a diminutive theatre, in the evening, to see a play performed by the privates of an artillery company.

A "rock scorpion" carried me off to the frigates in the harbor, English and American. The reptile in question was a mixture of Genoese and French blood—spoke both languages fluently, besides English and half a score of others. In no place on earth is the gift of tongues more general than here. About twenty "scorpions"—namely, men born at the Rock—are at present drinking brandy and porter in the public room, and jabbering in twenty different languages.

Look upon this Rock as a phenomenon of nature alone; or only for the miracles of military art which it contains; or for the motley population which inhabit it; or, finally, as the scene of that bloody attack and repulse during our Revolution—in either mode of regarding it, the "Pillar of Hercules" deserves to be considered one of the wonders of the world. I was lounging this morning among the rocks toward the African side, and looking up at the battlements and the black muzzles of cannon that crowned all the highest crags, when a sentinel hastily stopped me, and said I could not pass, for they were blasting rocks in that direction. In fact, some hundred of men were at work to add new strength to a place that now might defy the whole earth.

I got shut out of the town tonight. While I was revolving what was to be done, a Highlander hailed me from the wall, asking if I would like to be admitted. I responded in the affirmative, on which a sergeant came and opened the gate. I owed my good luck to being mistaken for an midshipmen of the *Belvedere*, an English frigate.

Capt. Newton, a noble-looking officer, has just come from Granada, bringing an account which inflames my desire of seeing the place. The *Cumberland* came in yesterday.

Sunday, Dec. —— [*24*]. Got tired of Gibraltar—heard of a government steamer [*Polyphemus*][8] about to sail for Malta—embarked on board of her, abandoning my previous design of penetrating Spain immediately, because the spring will be a season far more favorable for seeing that country. I hired an *hamalo* to carry my baggage to the boat, a distance of half a mile. The little wretch shouldered it all—looking like an Atlas supporting the world—and trotted at a round pace through the streets and onward to the mole, the muscles of his bare legs gathering into solid knots with every step. He was a mass of bone and sinew. The engine snorted—the boat moved from the mole—before night the rock was out of sight. I was prepared for no very agreeable passage, knowing the *hauteur*, approaching to insolence, of a certain class of English naval officers; and was surprised as well as gratified by the polite attentions of Lt. Spark[s], the commander of the boat, with whom I spent about half the night in conversation. Unfortunately, I am the only passenger. Lt. Spark seems resolved that my voyage shall be agreeable notwithstanding—certainly, he spares no pains for my accommodation, opening his library to me—producing an endless variety of wines—doing all he can, in short, to promote my enjoyment.[9]

We have passed Cape de Got and the Sierra Nevada, which looks down on the city of Granada. The coast of Barbary is now in full sight. Today the old man mustered his sailors and marines in the cabin—a large and elegant one—and read the service of the Church, not forgetting a special prayer for the British navy, and the success of the British arms. He knew Sir John Moore,[10] Sir P. Parker,[11] and other heroes of those days—has shaken hands with Blucher[12]—has fought the French by sea and land. Beside his manifold experiences in active life, he has been a great reader—not only of English works, but of all the eminent American authors.

I left Gibraltar with some regret, taking a sorrowful farewell of the consul and his family, and of my friend the midshipman, a frank and spirited fellow, with a relishing spice of the devil in him.

————

Here in this old world, I seem, thank heaven, to be carried about half a century backwards in time. As far as religion is concerned, there are the ceremonies of the Catholic Church; and the English litany, with rough soldiers and sailors making the responses. A becoming horror of dissenters, especially Unitarians, prevails everywhere. No one cants here of the temperance reform, or of systems of diet—eat, drink, and be merry is the motto everywhere, and a stronger and hardier race of men than those round me now never laughed at the doctors. Above all there is no canting of peace. A wholesome system of coercion is manifest in all directions—thirty-two-pounders looking over the bows—piles of balls on deck—muskets and cutlasses hung up below—the red jackets of marines—and the honest prayer that success should crown all these warlike preparations, yesterday responded to by fifty voices. There was none of the new-fangled suspicion that such belligerent petitions might be averse to the spirit of a religion that inculcates peace as its foundation. And I firmly believe that there was as much hearty faith and worship in many of those men as in any feeble consumptive wretch at home, who when smitten on one cheek literally turns the other likewise—instead of manfully kicking the offender into the gutter.

Christmas Day. The crew have had an extra allowance of liquor. A drummer, a fiddler, and a boy with a large iron triangle sit perched on the rail, forward; while the crew, all more or less *elevated*, are dancing below, in a style that would astonish Papanti.[13] The whole deck is alive with merriment. I was talking with a young officer, when the triangle boy, a corpulent jovial-looking youth, came up at the head of a gang of followers, and said, touching his hat, "We've just had the honor to drink your health, sir,"—his companions stood grinning in the rear. The officer took the hint, grinned in his turn, and told them to go down and order a bottle of wine from the steward.

We had an admirable Christmas dinner in the cabin.[14]

Thursday. After a passage of about five days, we reached Malta. The steward waked me, with the announcement that we were in the harbor of Valetta. I came on deck—found the pale yellow walls and battlements of the "*Cité* [*Città*] *Vittoriosa*" rising all round; the harbor filled with shipping, and among the rest several huge British war-vessels, laying black and sullen, with triple tiers of guns, among the smaller craft. I bade adieu to Lt. Sparks and the rest, and went ashore in a species of gondala, multitudes of which were darting hither and thither all over the crowded harbor. Everything about this renowned city is of the same unvaried hue—all yellow except the guns on the batteries and the red-coated sentinels. The bells of St. John's Church were ringing a chime, answered from the remoter parts of the town. I landed, well drenched by a sudden shower. Calling on M. Eyrand, I found that I had the alternative of leaving town that night for Messina, or of waiting ten days. Though sorry to leave so soon a place where so much was to be seen, I had no inclination to stay longer than was enough to satisfy my curiosity. I went to the ancient palace of the knights—the governor occupies it now. The portraits of the grand masters were hung in the long and splendid galleries. In the armory stand the complete panoply and weapons of all the most distinguished of these defenders of Christendom. Banners, warlike trophies, the helmets and breastplates of several hundred men-at-arms of the order, were ranged round the walls. At the head of the hall, surrounded by a forest of weapons, stands the gigantic armor of La Valette[15] himself—a man of tremendous frame, differing in this respect from many of the less renowned brethren of the order, who seem to have been of rather small stature. The English have placed here thirty thousand muskets and other modern arms, in villanous contrast to the ancient weapons of the knights of St. John. A cannon of *ropes*, and some other pieces of artillery as well as armor and weapons, are preserved in memory of the defeat their owners—the Turks—sustained before the walls of this place.

Friday. Late last evening, I made an attempt to see the Church of St. John. It was closed. My servant pommelled the oaken door in vain. He then proceeded to sundry coffee houses in the neighborhood, hoping to find the man who had the doors in charge. Three of [or] four Maltese, all jabbering their bastard Arabic, soon aided in the search. At length the great bell began to roar from the church tower, an unequivocal evidence that somebody was there. "Gu[g]lielmo, Gulielmo," roared my troop of assistants. After a lapse of five minutes Gulielmo descended, and issued from a portal among the columns at one side, summoning me in. All was utter blackness. At length Gulielmo, a tall ghastly individual, lighted a taper—and after a moment's conference with a priest he led the way through a labyrinth of galleries into the church. Meanwhile he had provided every one of my *cortège* with a taper. We passed through a number of chapels, splendidly decorated with pictures and statues, and tombs half-illuminated by the tapers. At length we descended into a lofty vaulted chamber of massive architecture, beneath the pavement of the church. It contained the tombs of the grand-masters. The effigy of La Valette lay on the sarcophagas that contained his bones, in a deep niche. His hands were clasped—his face had an expression of deep devotion—his sword was by his side, and his helmet lay near him. Just opposite was the tomb of one who was a cardinal, and lay there in his pontifical robes, with his sword girt to his side. His hands were crossed on his broad breast. He looked like a gallant soldier, who had done good service to Christianity by dealing death to its enemies. There were more such chambers—all of costly and magnificent workmanship, and peopled with the effigies of dead knights. When we got to the body of the church I could scarcely judge of its dimensions, except by the candles which burned before the numberless altars. They glimmered faintly in the distance like points of light. The low voices of the men with me were reverberated, again and again, from the columns and the roof. Every stone of the pavement bore the name and the arms of a knight who lay below. Leaving reluctantly the church where so many brave men had kneeled to God for his blessing on their matchless enterprises, I got into a boat, and was put on board the Neapolitan steamer *Francesco Primo*, bound for Messina, where I lay an hour or two on deck, listening to the distant music of the English drums and trumpets.

As I lounged about the deck in the morning, utterly unable to hold any intercourse with any one on board except by signs, a sleek-looking fellow came up and accosted me in English. We soon got deep into conversation. My new acquaintance proved to be Guiseppe

Jackson, a Sicilian with an English grandfather, who had been a cook at the Albion, and at Murdoch's tavern[16]—had frequently been to Fresh Pond—knew some of the Cambridge students, and was now on his way to Mr. Marston's in Palermo. I was right glad to see him, cook though he was. He made me a very good interpreter. In the course of our conversation, he made some remark about "the Pope, that fool."

"What," said I, "do you speak so of the Pope? Are you not a Roman Catholic?"

"Ah! I was till I live in America. I was all in the dark—you understand what I say—till I come there. Then my eyes open; I say, dat for the Pope, and his old red cap. Ah! once I was afraid to think of him."

"You are no longer a Catholic: what religion do you believe in now?"

"Oh! no religion in particular."

I congratulated him on so happy a conversion from the error of his ways.

At breakfast—a Mediterranean breakfast of eggs, fruit, and nuts—an old man, of severe countenance and tremendous mustache, sat opposite me. We made various attempts at conversation; as neither understood the other, we had to be satisfied with reiterated bowings, and mutual attentions of various kinds, in which the old man showed himself exceedingly apt and polite. I afterwards found that he was no less a personage than il Principe Statelli, a general of the Sicilian army—but Sicilian *Principes* are apt to be humbugs.

Mount Aetna is smoking vigorously in front of us. We are skirting the shore of Sicily.

We stopped at Syracuse. A hundred boats surrounded us at once; no sooner had we got *pratique*, than we were boarded by a swarm of men, soldiers and civilians, among [whom] were conspicuous several Neapolitan officers, with grizzled moustache and a peculiarly swinish expression of countenance. Meanwhile, there was a burst of music from the town, and about a thousand men filed out from one of the gates, and fringed one of the battlements with a long line of bayonets. Not that this had any connexion with our arrival. In going ashore, a little square-built English looking man, making a low congee,

presented me with a bundle of papers, which proved to be certificates
of his qualifications as a guide to the curiosities of the place. Accordingly, Jack Robinson—for such was his name—and I got into a kind
of ferry boat, and landed on the other side of the bay. Here we proceeded through narrow lanes, lined with aloes and prickly pears,
and alive with green lizzards, till we came to a delapidated convent
of Capuchins. Several of the reverend fathers were gazing from the
turrets and grated windows. Half a mile further brought us into a
wilderness of crags and trees. Jack knocked at a rude door at the
extremity of a low arch hewn into one of the rocks, announcing
himself in a loud voice as "Juan." A cadaverous, hollow-eyed
Sicilian opened it—and we were in the midst of a noble garden of
oranges and almonds and a host of strange unknown plants, and all
shut in by perpendicular crags, near two hundred feet high, overgrown with creeping plants. In some places they would approach
each other, leaving a chasm of but a few yards; then they would
draw apart, and enclose an area of an acre. Here and there among the
shrubbery stood a white, classic-looking cottage, or rather hut; the
inmates—among whom were several very pretty girls—for the most
part engaged in some domestic avocations outside. The place was
full of doves, rooks, and smaller birds.

"For heaven's sake, Jack, what is this?" said I in utter astonishment.

"All made two thousand years ago! You have read of Dionysius'
ear, hey? Well, he try three times before he make it—once down at
the Capuchins'—once here—and once up there, where we go by
and by."

Jack's residence of twenty-three years at Syracuse has greatly
impaired his power of speaking English. I gathered, however, from
his account that the marquis of Somebody turned to good account
the abortive labors of the tyrant in this place by changing his
would-be prison into a garden.

A little further on we came to the true "Ear of Dionysius" of classic
renown.[d] Imagine an area of many acres, shut in by a stupendous

---

[d] "After travelling three months in Italy and Sicily, I have not seen a place more
foreign and outlandish in its aspect than this—it took me by surprise as I saw it, when
just arrived, fresh from America."—F.P.

wall of rock, hewn smoother and more regular than mason work. Dark yawning caves and passages, several by measurement a hundred feet high, lead from this tremendous prison-yard into the rock. One of them is the "ear." We entered, and groped a long distance to the end of it. I remained there, while my guide returned to the mouth. "Jack Robinson," said I in a very low whisper. "Signor Francesco," answered Jack in the same tone. The sound fell on my ear as clear and distinct as if he stood by my side. A man came and fired a pistol. I never heard a clap of thunder so tremendous or so long protracted as the roar that followed. The tearing of a sheet of thin paper was loudly reverberated again and again.

Enough of the ear; we went to the amphitheatres. There are two of them, both hewn out of the solid rock, with subterranean dens and passages for gladiators and wild beasts. It was twilight by this time. Not a tree nor a shrub was to be seen; all was bare white rock, and every rock was hewn—either into a tomb, or an acqueduct, or the foundation of a house. There was a long street, cut into the rock, which was perforated on either hand with tombs, running for rods into the hill. Returning by the larger theatre, I came of a sudden upon a low archway, green with moss, whence a stream came roaring furiously out, and boiling among the stones down into the arena of the deserted theatre. I shut my eyes, and listening to the noise, fully believed myself for the moment among the familiar forests and cataracts of New England—and almost saw the forms and faces associated with them; but when I opened my eyes, there was a filthy Sicilian wench among the rocks with a pitcher on her head, in place of my bright-eyed country women—a rascally Capuchin, instead of a stout woodsman—and there was Mt. Aetna, smoking like a lime-kiln, instead of Mt. Washington.

Next we went to a temple—I believe of Minerva—long since converted into a Christian chapel. A bearded Franciscan, in his brown cowl, led the way with a lamp of the antique form common in the Mediterranean. When he got below the surface of the ground, and showed vault after vault, of a most gloomy and massive architecture, all cold and damp as a cellar; and especially when he pointed out a granite column, to which he said that the monks were bound when condemned to the penance of flaggellation—it would have made a very fair scene for Monk Lewis.[17]

But the catacombs were the most extraordinary exhibition. The same old monk led the way with his lamp for at least quarter of a mile into the bowels of the earth. The passage was narrow and low—multitudes of others branched off on either side. Sometimes there would be a circular chamber a few yards across, with passages running from it in all directions. Jack said that they went through all Catania! I am confident that we must have passed the receptacles for a million of corpses. Some of the tombs were cut deep enough to contain twenty or more. They were empty for the most part, but I picked a bone or two from them.

There is a story of an enthusiastic schoolmaster who, with several of his pupils, got lost in this labyrinth; their remains were not found for years, they had got so deeply entangled in the maze. A subject fit for Dante; and a worthy counterpart to his Hugolino.

More fortunate than the schoolmaster, we got up to the light at last, and made a rush at full speed for the city. A sentry or two challenged us by the way, but Jack had the password. He pointed out a column of a temple of Ceres—a solitary relic—all the rest had fallen and been removed to the city, where I saw them.ᵉ When we were fairly within the gates, I felt myself in a starving state, and told Jack to provide a remedy. Accordingly he bought provisions, "here a little and there a little," as we went along, making his selections with great judgment. Then he introduced me into a cellar, where a crowd of red-capped ragamuffins were jabbering, who made way hastily for "Juan," who seemed well known everywhere. Juan led me to the rear, and spreading his banquet on a table, he drew a pitcher of wine from a cash [cache] and set it before me. It was the juice of the muscatelle grape, which grows here in astonishing abundance.

Jack insisting on showing me his certificates of service in the American Navy; and I being desirous of seeing how the Syracusans lived, I went home with him, and enjoyed the exhibition of his numerous progeny, who were all piled together in bed. This done, we took boat, and went off to the steamer. Jack was so well satisfied with the dollar and a half I gave him for his day's services, that he must needs salute me after the Sicilian style with a kiss on the cheek, which I submitted to. He then departed, kissing his hand as his head

ᵉ "There is a large temple of Minerva in the city, turned into a cathedral."—F.P.

disappeared over the ship's side—the stubborn English temper was well nigh melted away with his long sojourn among the Gentiles. He had been pressed in early youth into the navy—had served both England and America (though the latter, I believe, in the capacity of a washerman). As far as I could see, Jack was an honest man, an exceedingly *rara avis* in these quarters.

Arriving at Messina in the morning, my acquaintance the cook [Guiseppe]—an experienced traveller—was of the greatest service to me. Indeed, without his assistance, my inexperience and ignorance of the language would have put me to serious embarrassment. He showed me how to treat a Sicilian landlord, and to bribe a custom-house officer. I am indebted to him for very excellent accommodations, at a very reasonable price.

Messina, Sunday. I took my station outside one of the gates in the rear of the city, to look at the scum of humanity that came pouring out. All was filth, and age, and ruin—the walls, the tall gateway with its images and inscriptions, the hovels at the top of the wall, and in the ancient suburb, all seemed crumbling to decay. The orange and lemon groves in the ditch of the fortification were dingy and dirty—but away in the distance appeared the summits of the mountains, almost as wild and beautiful as our mountains of New England. I thought of them; and, in the revival of old feelings, half wished myself at home. I soon forgot, however, all but what was before my eyes, in watching the motley array that passed by me. Men and women, literally hung with rags, half hid in dirt, hideous with every imaginable species of deformity, and bearing on their persons a population as numerous as that of Messina itself—these formed the bulk of the throng. Priests, with their black broad-brimmed hats and their long robes—fat and good-looking men—were the next numerous class. They draw life and sustenance from these dregs of humanity—just as tall pig-weed flourishes on a dunghill. Then there were mustachoed soldiers, very different from the stately and sedate soldier of England. There were men bearing holy pictures and images—ladies in swarms, whose profession was stamped on their faces—musicians, with a troop of vagabonds in their rear. All around the gateway were the tables of butchers, fruiterers, confectioners, money changers, boot-blackers, and a throng of dirty men, women, and children. Shouts, yells, and a universal hubbub.[18]

"Dové è [Dov'è] il téatro?" enquired I, with execrable pronounciation, of a short, squalid-looking man at a street corner. "Ah! signor, I am delighted at the meeting with a gentleman of England. I shall have the honor to point out for you the way"—which he did, talking incessantly in this high flown style. "The door of the teater is not open. I think they have postponed the entertainment by the reason of the grand festival of the new year. But I shall have the honor to conduct you to the church where the grand festival is celebrated."

When we got there, I found a sight indeed worth seeing. The cathedral was in a blaze of light from many hundred candles, while all below was a black sea of heads. The priests were chanting, and the incense smoking. Every few moments, there would be a blast of trumpets and a burst of solemn music; at which every one of the thousands there knelt on the pavement, and then rose again with a deep rushing noise, produced by the simultaneous motion of such a multitude.[19]

My new acquaintance kept on talking aloud at my side throughout the whole, in spite of the hard looks of the people near us:

"The decorations of this church are very exceedingly beautiful, but I have seen it honored with a greater number of tapers. The directors of the ceremony are cautious at present. Last year, the fire *took force* on the pictures and ornaments, and the people trod on each other to get out. They trod over the ladies and the women." He said everything with a grin, as if highly amused; rolling up his large lobster eyes to my face, and rubbing the palms of his hands together. "The altar is ornamented with precious stones, which you will observe in the morning."

Here he began to translate into English, for my benefit, the *Te Domine [Deum]* which the priests were chanting. "Do you understand the Latin tongue, sir?" I nodded; at which he immediately repeated about half of one of the eclogues of "Virgilio," with the Italian accent. Some of the people turned round and began to talk with him, looking curiously at me meantime. "These people," he said, "regard it for a very strange thing that you should understand Latin, while you do not know the Italian tongue. They do not consider that they are two different, distinct, languages."

The service concluded with a thundering explosion of fireworks within the galleries, which filled the church with an insufferable smell of gunpowder. "Now we will hasten to go out, previously to the crowd of people." When we got into the street, I questioned this singular character, who told me that his father had taken great pains to let him have a good education. He had been to college, but now he was poor, and could not read his books. "Sir, I ask your pardon, but look at me, and you will see that I am destitute," said he, stripping open his dirty clothes to show that he had no shirt. I asked him what had brought so learned a man to such a pass. He told a story about having an office in the customs, which he had lost by being detected in some dealings with the *contrabandos*. Also he muttered something about his never drinking anything, but only taking a glass of wine with his friend. By this time his grinning mood was gone, and he had worked himself into a crying fit. Lifting his torn hat, he informed me that heaven had sent me to him, to relieve his miseries that night. Having no change with me, I was not tempted to the folly of giving it to him.[20]

Tuesday, Jan. 2nd. This morning I set out on an expedition to see a little of the country, in company with a Spanish gentleman, Don Mateo Lopez,[21] who speaks good English. We hired a carriage together, and got outside the gates by eleven, after some trouble in procuring passports. At night, we reached a little fishing town, called Giardini, not far from Aetna. The weather was beautiful; the atmosphere clear and soft. As for the scenery on the road, it was noble beyond expression. For myself, I never imagined that so much pleasure could be conveyed through the eye. The road was a sucession of beautiful scenes—of mountains and vallies on one side, and the sea on the other—but, as to the people, they are a gang of ragamuffins. The houses of the numberless dirty villages we passed are very low, with tiled roofs, grated windows—if any, at all—and built of stone or land. The narrow streets swarmed with beggars and other vermin; women spinning at the doors; jackasses of diminutive size, tottering under two barrels of water, or a man twice as large as

Joseph Thayendanegea
Portrait in oils of Joseph Brant by George Romney
(Coverdale Collection No. 2383)

themselves; loungers, in their brown capotes, grouped around the
fountains. This capote gives the wearer a most monastic aspect: it
has a hood attached to it, with a peaked crown, which covers the
head and half the face. These disgusting holes of villages only added
zest to the pleasure of the scenery, a pleasure not inferior, and not
unlike that of looking upon the face of a beautiful woman. In many
respects, our own scenery is far beyond it; but I cannot say that I
have ever looked with more delight on any of our New England
mountains and streams than upon these of Sicily. The novelty of the
sight, and the ruined fortresses on the highest crags, add much to
the effect.[22]

At noon of the next day, we reached Catania,[23] a large city, so
old that tradition makes the Cyclops its founders. Since that time,
it has passed through the hands of Greeks, Romans, Saracens, and
Christians, each of whom have left on it some trace of themselves.
Every two or three centuries, Mt. Aetna knocks it to pieces, or floods
it with lava. The Greek and Roman theatre is wholly buried up,
except a few passages which have been excavated. There is a fountain upon which its disagreeable neighbor, in the year 1669, vomited
lava to the depth of sixty feet, but a fountain is a thing of value
here. A patriotic citizen, Prince Boscari, dug through the lava till
he found it. It is now reached by several flights of steps, up which
the women are constantly toiling with jars of water on their heads.
Catania is paved and, in great part, built of lava. It is full of monks,
of all orders. The Benedictines have a noble convent—and a church
by far the finest I have seen. In '69 the lava *came within five yards of
the church wall*, then turned aside without injuring it. On the other
side it came within about three times that distance, and turned aside
in like manner. It appears now like a wall of black stone.

I went to the museum of Prince Boscari, a valuable collection of
antiquities, etc. In the midst of a hall, surrounded by precious fragments of statues and broken pottery, lay the skeleton of a *Chippeway
birch canoe*. I welcomed it as a countryman and an old friend.

I bought some specimens of lava and amber—of a couple of rascals
who asked twice their value, and abated it at once when I refused
to buy.[f]

[f] Six and a half lines, dealing with **Don Mateo Lopez's** nocturnal amusements,
have been inked out here.—Ed.

I went to see an opera of Bellini—a native, I have heard, of Catania. In buying tickets here, you are shown a plan of the theatre, select your seat, which is then crossed off on the paper; and receive a piece of paper like a bank bill with your number inscribed on it.[24] Lopez had a friend waiting for him here—a light-hearted and lively young Spaniard, whose youthful eccentricities sat as easily and gracefully upon him as they did awkwardly upon old Mateo. When we set out on our return, "*il mio amico*," as Lopez called him, was rattling away incessantly, and imitating every dog, hog, or jackass we met.

We had a sort of a *calèche*. Beside the driver, a small boy ran along by our side, or clung behind, ready to do what offices might be required of him. A still smaller one was stowed away in a net, slung between the wheels, where he kept a constant eye on the baggage. The larger one employed himself in tying knots in the horses' tails as he ran along; or he would dart along the road before us, clamber on a wall, and sit till we came by; when he would spring down, with a shout, and run on again.

All around Catania is one great bed of lava. Some spots seem as if sprinkled with the refuse of a furnace: others are covered with vegetation. All the walls, all the houses, and many of the domestic utensils, such as troughs for washing, are of lava. There was an eruption of the mountain two or three weeks ago, by which more than sixty persons were killed or wounded—for, strange to say, the base of this perilous monster is covered with habitations.

At Giarri, a large place where we stopped to rest the horses, we were beset, of course, by beggars. One little rascal, about six years (years) old—whose clothes, if they answered the purposes of warmth, answered no other purpose for which clothing is intended—followed me about for half an hour, like a little dog. I could not muster sternness enough to order him away with effect—and he was too small to kick into the gutter—so he went on, begging for a *carlino* [*carlin*]. At last he began slyly to mock, for my edification, the grave countenance and stately air of Don Mateo; and did it so ludicrously that I stood laughing at him. At this he summoned a larger boy to his side, who hummed a tune, while he danced a sort of hornpipe on the pavement. I could forbear no longer, but gave him a *grano*—

about the third part of a cent. A crowd of loungers had mustered to witness the performance of this mannikin, who was about a foot and a half high. There they stood, in their brown capotes, looking gravely from out of their hoods, at the spectacle of my unparralled generosity, which was a signal for action. I was half stunned with supplications from men, women, and children; and glad, after cursing them a little, to escape into the carriage. Among the rest was a girl, most abominably ugly, who appeared to be a mute. I threw her a large copper coin—the young Spaniard added a couple more, which threw the girl into a perfect frenzy of delight. She danced about among the crowd; flinging both hands into the air—then kissing the coins, and pressing them against her breast; tossing them on the ground before her, and gathering them up again; till her ugly face seemed absolutely good looking with the excess of her pleasure.[25]

The women of this country are not handsome. You see groups of them about the stone door-ways spinning twine, with their hair drawn back in the fashion represented in the portraits of our grand-mothers.

We stopped at night at Giardini.[26] The *padrone* showed us with great complacency the register of his house, which, he said, "con-tained the recommendations of the guests who had honored him with their company." One man's "recommendations" warned all trav-ellers that the *padrone's* beds were full of fleas; another's, that nothing in the house was fit to eat, etc. The unfortunate *padrone* could not read English.

It rained in the morning. The night before had been glorious. I took my last look, I fear, of Aetna, whose immense sides were white with snow and wrapped around with clouds and smoke—the summit was just discernible among the vapors, a volume of white smoke, beautifully tinged by the setting sun slowly rolling from it. This gigantic and portentous mass towers immeasurably above the beautiful mountains that lie around it. If Aetna looked grandly that evening, they were not less beautiful in the evening shadows, with their groves of oranges, and olives, and lemons, and the dark vallies between them.

But in the morning, we could see nothing of Aetna, though we were at its base. The Spaniard and I set out to visit the ancient town of

Taormina, in the mountains above Giardini. We went on mules up a winding path, where the prospect must in clear weather have been noble. We met men, and women, and mules coming down, for Taormina is still inhabited. The chief curiosity of the place is the theatre—in very good preservation. The cicerone who showed it seemed to feel a genuine enthusiasm in his subject. The building must have been very magnificent; Greeks, Romans, and Saracens have held it; but the snails, of which I captured a fine one for a memento, are the only tenants now. Crowning a steep cliff, at an immense height above Taormina, is an old Saracen castle. This country is full of associations—of classic fable—of classic history—and of romance.

Descending—on my part, sorrowfully—we rode on toward Messina. "*Il mio amico*" could not contain the excess of his spirits. Every unfortunate Indian fig plant, with its clumsy broad plates of leaves, felt the weight of his cane, till a plant, a little tougher than the rest, jerked the instrument of destruction out of his hand. The attendant imp picked it up and restored it, but not before a cart wheel had rather impaired its symmetry. We supped together at Messina; and thus ended a most agreeable expedition. I shall not soon forget Catania, with its strange and precarious situation at the foot of the great volcano, which alternately confers blessings on it and menaces it with ruin. Aetna had given it a noble mole of lava, but has since cancelled its own gift, by a second eruption. The revenues of Catania are drawn from the snows of Aetna. Nor shall I forget its origin—back in the darkness of classic fable. The theatre, now buried under the lava, was large enough to contain the whole present population of Catania, about thirty thousand.

The church of the Benedictines is the noblest edifice I have seen. This and others not unlike it have impressed me with new ideas of the Catholic religion. Not exactly, for I reverenced it before as the religion of generations of brave and great men—but now I honor it for itself. They are mistaken who sneer at its ceremonies as a mere mechanical farce: they have a powerful and salutary effect on the mind. Those who have witnessed the services in this Benedictine church, and deny what I say, must either be singularly stupid and insensible by nature, or rendered so by prejudice.

Saturday. I recall what I said of the beauty of the Sicilian women—
so far, at least, as concerns those of high rank. This is a holy day.
They are all abroad, in carriages and on foot. One passed me in the
church of the Capuchin convent, with the black eye, the warm rich
cheek, and the bright glance that belong to southern climates, and
are beautiful beyond all else.

There were grand ceremonies in the cathedral. Five or six noblemen sat on a sort of throne which was covered with crimson silk.
They wore rich black dresses, massive gold chains on their breasts,
and the enormous ruffs of several centuries ago, making them look
as if their heads were screwed down between their shoulders, without
the intervention of a neck. A motley concourse of soldiers and women,
princes and beggars, filled the church.

Sunday. Took leave of the hospitable family of Consul Payson, with
much regret; and went off to the steamer *Palermo*, bound for Palermo.
I found her completely surrounded by boats, wedged close together—
friends were kissing their adieus, and boatmen cursing. The delicacy
of sentiment expressed in the Italian national oath is admirable—
they rival the Spaniards, in that matter—"*Arcades ambo*"; *id est,*
"blackguards both." At length visitors were warned off; the boats
dispersed, scattering from a common centre, in all directions; a man
screamed the names of the passengers, by way of roll-call; and among
the rest the illustrious one of "Signore Park-a-man"; and we got
under weigh. It was late at night. We passed the long array of bright
lights, from the fine buildings along the quay of Messina—could just
discern the mountains behind the town, indistinct in the darkness,
like thunder-clouds—left a long train of phosphoric light behind us,
as we steered down between Scylla and Charybdis—and in half an
hour were fairly out on the Sicilian Sea. The ghost of departed perils
still lingers about the scene of Ulysses' submarine adventures: an
apology for a whirlpool on one side—still bearing the name of
Scylla—and an insignificant shoal on the other. I thought, as we
passed, and the moon made a long stream of light on the water,
that it would [be] an adventure worth encountering, to be cast away in
that place—but my unwonted classical humor was of very short
duration; for, going below, I found a cabin-full of sea-sick wretches,

which attractive spectacle banished all recollection of Virgil and Homer. I was doomed to lie all night, a witness to their evolutions; a situation not many degrees more desirable than being yourself a sufferer.

In the morning we were skirting the bold and wild coast of Sicily, in a drizzling rain. We entered at length the crescent of high mountains that rise around the bay of Palermo. Midway between the horns of this crescent, in a wide hollow between the mountains, lay the city, with its Asiatic towers, and its two hundred thousand inhabitants. Coming to anchor, the sea around us was absolutely *paved* with boats, and the steamer taken by storm. After a hard fight, I rescued my baggage, had it transported over six boats into a seventh, which last was only a rod or two from the out-skirts of the throng—and have it now, happily, safe in the Hotel de France.

Monday, Jan. [*15ᵗʰ*]. Have been a week in Palermo, and seen all the lions, which are numerous—churches, catacombs, and mountains. I hired Guiseppe, the cook, as a servant and a teacher of Italian, which he is said to speak remarkably well. Palermo is under the special protection of a saint, to whom everybody renders the devoutest worship. It is a place as gay as any in Europe—the people moreover have the faculty of being gay on the smallest means. Yesterday, hundreds of tailors and shopkeepers, with an income of an hundred and fifty piastres a year, were lounging about the fountains of the public garden in satin and broadcloth, or prancing along the Marina on horseback among the carriages of the nobles. The nobles themselves do not greatly abound in wealth. As for the ladies, they do well enough before marriage, for the sufficient reason that they are not trusted out of their mothers' sight—but after marriage the case is altered; insomuch that the English residents here pride themselves on keeping wholly aloof from any intercourse with the Sicilians.[27]

The other day, I went up Monte Pellegrino, the dwelling place of the sainted patroness of Palermo. Every year, half the city makes a pilgrimage to the summit of this high mountain, to pay their homage, while the whole valley below is bright with illuminations. The mountain is very precipitous, but a road of solid mason-work has been made, by which its perpendicular side is made accessible without the least difficulty. Our donkeys carried us up in a couple of hours. At the summit, in a great solitude of rocks and snows, we found the shrine of the saint. Santa Rosalia was the niece of William the Good, one of the Sicilian kings. She left the court in a fit of enthusiasm, and climbed to the top of this mountain, where she spent her days in a large grotto in the rock against which the present little church is built. Several centuries after, when a pestilence, wholly unmanageable by the priests, was desolating Palermo, the saint appeared in a dream to a man who inhabited a hut half way down the mountain; telling him where her bones were to be found. Accordingly they were brought from the grotto where she had died; and borne with great ceremonies to the city. The pestilence was instantly arrested.

The priests guided me through the church, into the grotto behind—a huge black den hung with broken stalactites, whence water icy cold was dropping on to the floor. The snow had found its way through a large cleft above; altogether, the habitation of the young saint wore a most sombre and cheerless aspect. The lamps were burning in a remote part of the cavern before her shrine. The priest kneeled before a grating beneath the altar, and motioned me to look in between the bars. Two or three lamps were burning there, but for some time, I could discern nothing else. At length, I could distinguish a beautiful female figure, sculptured in marble, and clothed in a robe of gold, lying with a crucifix in her hand and a scull beside her. The white transparency of the marble showed beautifully in the light of the lamps, and suited well the mild enthusiastic expression of her face. I scarce wondered at the devotion of the Palermitans. Drinking some of the water that trickled from the roof into a stone basin by the side of the altar, I left the grotto, which was as cold and chilling as a New England winter. The priest gave me a rough picture of the saint, to which I retorted with a suitable *buonamano*.[g] After taking a last look at the ancient and moss-grown church, and the black cliffs around it, I left Monte Pellegrino. As we waded through the snow down the mountain, the view of Palermo was noble. The valley was as smooth and level as the ocean, and set between the

[g] Tip.—Ed.

immense circle of snow-covered mountains, as green and bright as an emerald. The city was but a very small part—there were forests of olive-trees, and innumerable gardens, all dotted with white houses, and the palaces of the nobles. It was the king's birthday, and the city was half covered with the smoke of cannon.

The next day, I went to the Capuchin convent, where the holy fathers keep many thousand mummies, in vaulted apartments under ground. I was so edified by the interesting spectacle, that I bought a mass, for fifty cents, and appointed four o'clock the next morning to hear it performed in the sepulchres. Guiseppe waked me, and we sallied forth. Though it wanted more than two hours of daylight, many people were abroad. Fires were burning outside the *caffès* and confectioners', with ragamuffins and *filles de joie* grouped around them for the sake of the warmth. The porter made his appearance at the gate of the convent, and conducted us in, where we found five [or] six of the fathers assembled with lamps, awaiting the coming of the prior. When all was ready, we descended into the tombs. The mummies, each from his niche in the wall, grinned at us diabolically as we passed along. Several large cats, kept there for the benefit of the rats, stared at us with their green eyes, and then tramped off. When we got to the little chapel, the prior put off his coarse Capuchin dress, and arrayed himself in white robes—the curtain was drawn aside from the image of the Virgin behind the altar—the lamps lighted—and the mass performed. When all was over, one of the fathers lighted a torch to show the catacombs by its light. Coffins piled up below—men, shrunk into a mere nothing, but clothed as they used to be above ground, all ranged along the wall on either hand—a row of sculls under the cornices—this made up the spectacle, which was rather disgusting. There were one or two children, just dead, and a few men, flung down in corners, waiting for the drying process. Women are placed here, as well as men. The virgins all wear crowns of silver paper, from beneath which they grin and gape in a most alluring fashion.

I soon cried enough, and returned to the upper air. The morning mass in the church was just begun. One of the monks conducted me to an ancient apartment behind the altar: here the whole convent were kneeling, telling their beads—the faint light, their dark cowls, their beards, and their deep murmurings at their devotions made quite an impressive scene. The little church itself was half full of people, though it was not yet daylight. I looked awhile at the old pictures about the rooms and passages, then bade adieu to the fathers, who thought me mad, and departed.

The Capuchins of Monreale, four miles from Palermo, have a similar burial place. Monreale, however, is chiefly remarkable for the noble church, built in the 12th century, which is attached to the Benedictine monastery. The walls of this church are covered with mosaics representing scripture history. The monastery is a very large one. All the monks are sons, I believe, of noblemen; as is also the case with the Benedictines of Catania. Monreale is famous, moreover, for the rapacity of its inhabitants, who consider a stranger fair game. Some fellow(s) brought me specimens of the mosaic, picked from the wall of the church, which was undergoing repairs. I gave him twice their value, which he returned and demanded more. I pocketed what I had given him, and ordered the coachman to drive on, whereupon the crowd who had assembled set up a yell, and followed us with maledictions for quarter of a mile.

Palermo is full of beautiful fountains—water-gods—horses—serpents—fishes—every imaginable variety of figure—pouring forth the pure water of the mountains, into basins full of gold fish, or over rocks of marble covered with a growth of water-plants. Sometimes a group of water-nymphs are seen sporting together, flinging the water at each other.

The city is very regularly laid out. Two large streets cross at right angles in the centre, where is a little square, called the Quat[t]ro Cantoni, ornamented with four fountains.

I have just returned from a ride on a donkey—horses are not to be had here—about the neighborhood of the city. Guiseppe first led the way to an ancient and delapidated church at the foot of one of the mountains; a place carefully preserved in memory of the Sicilian Vespers.[28] The man, who lived in a sort of hovel under its foundations, had not the key. He led the way, however, up some narrow and broken stairs to a window just below the e[a]ves, from which I had a fair view down into the church—deserted, sombre, and filled with dust and decay. The slightest whisper, where I stood, was reverberated among the arches. There were two or three good pictures—a broken altar—and innumerable cobwebs. In the mountain behind this church is a grotto filled with fossil bones, which Guiseppe and the man said were the remains of giants. Doctors disagree as to the nature of these bones—some will have it that they are veritable fossils, others say that the cave was the receptacle where the animals killed in the Greek and Roman amphitheatres were flung.

Thence we proceeded to the convent of Santa Maria de Gesu. I went up to a little stone building on the summit of a rock, where was an image of the Virgin, with flowers placed before it, and an inscription promising forty days' indulgence to whoever should say three paters in that place. Without availing myself of this opportunity, I lay down in the sun on the wall, and gazed at the magnificent view of the valley of Palermo and the mountains behind. After riding about the valley all day, we returned to the city.

Tuesday. I saw today a review of several thousand Neapolitan conscripts, the only species of troops in Sicily. Ferdinand[29] sends his Neapolitans here, and keeps his Sicilians in Naples. The latter are not conscripts, but serve voluntarily. The fellows I saw were almost all slight and feeble-looking men. Many of them, in fact, were mere boys. Some of the battalions fired well, but none of the manoeuvres were executed with the precision and unity of the English soldiers. I remembered that the Neapolitans were the only nation of whom Napoleon could not make soldiers.

Wednesday. I have just arranged an expedition to Girgenti, at the southern point of the island. Travelling in Sicily is no joke, especially at this season. I engaged a man named Luigi to furnish three mules—supplies of provisions—cooking apparatus—an attendant—and thus to pilot me round the island, paying himself all tavern reckonings and *buonamano's*. For this I am to give him four dollars a day. I thus avoid all hazard of being imposed upon, or robbed, for I shall have scarce any money with me. Luigi is perfectly familiar with the island; has, moreover, the reputation of an honest man, notwithstanding which I follow Mr. Marston's advice in making him sign a written agreement. I have laid it down as an inviolable rule to look on everybody here as a rascal of the first water, till he has shown himself by undeniable evidence to be an honest man.

Guiseppe has been with me as a servant of late. The chief fault with him was his continually stopping to kiss some of his acquaintances in the street. He seems to know everybody—understands perfectly how to cheat everybody—has astonishing promptness and readiness for all kinds of service. "It is 'trange, Mist'r Park-a-man," he modestly remarked the other day, "that I cannot go nowhere, but what all the people seem to like-a me, and be good friends with me." He is vain as a turkey cock—dresses infinitely better than I ever did. He is a great coward, trembling continually with fear of robbers in all our rides. The Sicilian robbers, by the way, are a great humbug. When I engaged Guiseppe, I offered him half a dollar a day for wages. "No, Mist'r Park-a-man, I no take-a wages at all. When you go away, you make-a me a present, just as much as you like; then I feel more better." So I told him I would "make-a" him a present of half a dollar a day; which I did—a mode of remuneration more suited to Guiseppe's self-importance.

Thursday. Jan. 18th. All this morning Luigi Rannesi was in a fever-heat of preparation. I told him to be ready at two; he came to me at 12, announcing that all was ready; that he had engaged mules at Marineo, and that the carriage was at the door to take us there. I was not prepared for such promptitude. After some delay, I got ready, too, and we set out. Luigi, a diminutive Sicilian with a thin brown face and an air of alertness about every inch of him, began to jabber Italian with such volubility that I could not understand a word. He must needs exhibit every article of the provisions he had got ready for the journey, extolling the qualities of each—and they deserved all his praises—and always ended by pounding himself on the breast, rolling up his eyes, and exclaiming, "Do you think Luigi loves money? No! Luigi loves honor!" and then launching forth into interminable eulogiums of the country we were going to see, and the adventures we should meet there. We stopped at night at Marineo, where Luigi provided a most sumptuous dinner; talked and gesticulated, half frenzied because he found I could not understand half he said; then siezed my hand, which he dutifully kissed, and left me to my meditations. He reappeared, however, bringing a decanter of wine, and a large book of antiquities which he had brought for me to read.[30] All this was at his own expense. The terms of his bargain bound him to nothing else than to keep me alive on the road.

Early in the morning, we left Marineo—a fair sample of a Sicilian village. A group of little square, tiled-roofed, stone houses crowded close together on the side of a mountain; a castle on the eminence above, green and beautiful mountains rising everywhere around, without a tree or a shrub.[31]

We rode all day over a country of mountains, stopping at noon at a solitary inn to find some maccaroni. As we were on the point of setting out, the usual number of beggars beset us—among the most respectable was a blind fiddler and his boy, who scraped a tune on two broken violins. Luigi became excited; tumbled himself from his mule, and began a dance in a most amateur-like style to the music, in the midst of the ring of beggars. We stopped at night at a large and dirty village called Lercara [Lacara], where nothing but fleas were to be had in the enormous stone albergo.[32]

There was a storm all night. In the morning, the wind swept as cold and raw over the mountains as on a November day at home. The hazy softness of the scenery was gone—all was dark and bleak. We rode along in company with two muleteers, jabbering their unintelligible Sicilian. Some *contadini*, or field laborers, at work told us that the road had broken away in front; so we turned across the fields—which every traveller for a year or two will probably be obliged to do. After fording a stream, wading through an abyss of mud for several miles, and climbing a hill, we found an ancient pathway of stone along the side of a mountain. A headlong muddy stream was tumbling among the olives below us. The stones of the pathway were worn through with age, and kicked far and wide over the hillside by the passage of some hundred generations of mules. We soon came to the mud again; then another bridgeless stream, and another and another. One of them with its broad bed of stones—the shrunken stream rippling down in the centre—reminded me of the streams of New England—but a glance at the bare and cultivated hills—at the olive-trees in the vallies, and aloes and Indian-figs ranged along the

bank, and clustered thick about the old grey house of *contadini* near
the landing—was enough to dispel the illusion. The mountains closed
thicker around us—grew wilder and higher, too. The weather became
dark and gloomy. My mule fell and nearly flung me from the saddle—
an accident which warned me to be cautious, as the miserable path
frequently ran along the edge of hills where a fall would be followed
by a tumble of some hundred feet into a little rocky torrent at the
bottom. At length, as we were crossing a bridge at the top of [a] narrow
gorge of very high and abrupt mountains, a violent wind suddenly
came down the passage, bending the long tufted grass on the lower
declivities—the precursor of a heavy rain-storm. But as we got out
of this place we saw the cathedral dome and the tiled roofs of Castel
Termini in a hollow of the mountains, far in front. After riding an
hour over a stony hill-side, where our mules were nearly knocked
over by the wind, we got into the ancient path, worn deep into the
rock, which led up to the town. A noble diorama of stormy mountains lay on the left.

Luigi is a great antiquarian. He rakes up ancient money at every
village as he goes along. His antiquarian skill is a passport to intro-
duce him anywhere, to the nobles and princes—who are not always,
however, such dignified personages as would appear from their
titles. I went with him to-night to the house of a judge, who produced
a bottle of *rosolio* and showed me a grotto in his garden, which he
had stuck all over with specimens of the Sicily minerals. I then went
with him to a *conversazione*, where some dozen people were playing
cards. They looked at the *signore Americano*, as the judge introduced
me to them, with great curiosity, and at last left their game and
clustered round me, very curious to know something of the place I
came from. I talked to them for some time in a most original style
of Italian; but getting tired of being lionized in such a manner, I
bade them good night and went back to the *albergo*. One of them, an
officer of gendarmes, a Greek by blood, tried to talk to me in his own
language, but made an entire failure. He was a broad shouldered
and athletic fellow, remarkably intelligent and well informed. I told
him I came from Boston, on which he asked me if it was not near
Charlesto[w]n—a miracle of information for a Sicilian, with whom,
as I have had occasion to observe, America from Greenland to Cape

Horn is all the same thing. He came from one of those detached Greek villages of which there are several in Sicily, established about two centuries ago [by] fugitives from the north of Greece.[33]

At the door of the inn I saw, for the first time, the national vehicle of Sicily—the *lettiga*. It is a large box, exactly like a sedan, only it is carried by mules instead of men. One strong mule goes before and one behind, while the box swings between two poles in the centre. Each mule wears gaudy trappings about the head, and a dozen large bells fastened to a triangular machine on the back. A man walks alongside, with a pole like a fishing rod to guide the mules, and another follows behind with a sumpter mule. After this fashion they proceed along paths that would break the legs of any horse in five minutes. You can hear the rattling of the bells among the mountains half a mile off.

The country inns of Sicily are notorious. This one of Castel Termini was a fair sample, though in point of dirt, fleas, etc., it fell far short of some others.[34] A Sicilian *albergo* is an ancient gloomy building of stone, like all the rest; they usually have a little sign; or at least a branch of a tree stuck at the door, by way of indicating their public character; but to look up at their half decayed walls, and the small square windows thinly distributed over the front, you would take them for dungeons. Enter, and you stumble down a stone step into the kitchen—a spacious cavern, dark as Tartarus, with a floor of earth, and seldom any windows. Water jars, harness, and outlandish-looking utensils are scattered about. Groups of idlers are crouching in the corner over a brazier of charcoal, and crucifixes and images with little lamps burning before them are hung about the walls. Close adjoining are large stone apartments for mules and asses, who have usually separate accommodations in the *albergos*, though in the private house a corner of the family room, usually the cleanest, is assigned them. Ask for *ap[p]artamenti*, and a woman leads you up a broken flight of stone steps to a room floored with a kind of cement. There is one window—one strongly secured door—a holy picture on the wall and a bed full of fleas. You can seldom get anything to eat, unless it be maccaroni. This is an inn of the interior. The others are better. I speak from the experience of three nights, and I solemnly aver that the picture is not over-colored.

I have forgotten a prominent feature of the establishment—the beggars. A decrepid beast, covered with dirt, unshaven, with bleared gummy eyes, and covered all but the face in a rotten capote, thrusts a rosary into your face, and whines out of his withered throat a petition for alms. All about the door stand groups of idlers, enveloped in the same capotes, staring and conversing listlessly. This capote covers the face exactly like the hoods of mail you see in the old editions of Tasso and Ariosto—but the face of a Sicilian is anything but martial or knightly.

Such being our nocturnal accommodations, we were glad enough to be among the mountains again. The morning was beautiful. The mule track was in many places literally paved with alabastar. We passed huge rocks of this mineral—and troughs hewn out of it, for refreshing the mules, wherever a spring came out of the hill-side. About noon we approached a deep valley, whence we heard in the stillness the loud tumbling of water—a moment after we saw a wide stream running through the meadows below us, which were covered with hundreds of the long-horned cattle of Sicily. At the height where we stood, the faint sound of their bells was like the tinkling of a brook. Descending to the river, we found waiting under the bank two men, naked below the waist. Their handsome and muscular limbs were tanned as dark as their faces by many days of exposure. Both were noble specimens of flesh and blood. One of them led the foremost mule—the other followed behind, as we crossed the ford.

The mountains around this place were very high and rich in vegetation. The sun lay on them hot and sultry—there was a haziness in the air that softened their asperities, and threw an air of quiet and drowsieness over the landscape. We soon came to a village [Carminia] on the side of a mountain. All the houses were plastered with a grey cement of gypsum—everything wore the same grey hue. As we rode up the steep street, the women were sitting in the hot sun on heaps of stone outside their doors, arranging their hair, or nursing their children; some lay stretched at full length in the sun asleep. Many were pretty—all wore the appearance of full health and vigor. They seemed like the women of earlier times—the partners of the primeval inhabitants of Sicily of whom the pastoral poets speak. On the opposite side of the valley another village lay basking in the sun, the yellow palace of its proprietor conspicuous above the grey square houses of his tenants.

I went to visit the famous sulphur works not far from these places. In the shaft I entered, the rock was solid sulphur—scarce any mixture of foreign ingredient. As we rode away, a noble prospect of volcanic mountains lay off on our right. Soon after the mule-track became a good road. A carriage from Caltanizetta passed us, belonging to some English travellers[h] who had made a wide detour for the sake of a road. We saw at last the battlements and church spires of Girgenti, crowning a high hill before us, and had occasional glimpses of the sea through the vallies. Approaching the hill, we found a deep and shadowed valley intervening. Luigi left the road and descended into it by a wretched mule-track. Flocks of goats passed on the road above us—mules and asses, loaded with their panniers, came down from the city. One of his fits of enthusiasm had taken possession of Luigi. He began to lash his mule and drive him along over mud and rocks at such a rate that I thought him mad, till he told me that it was necessary—*per bisogno*—to get to Girgenti before the Englishmen. "*Cor(r)ag[g]io*, my brave mule! *Corragio, signore*," he shouted, "we shall be the victors!" At that, he drove full speed up the steep hill toward the gate. Nothing would stop him. He leaped over ditches—scrambled through mud and stones, shouting "*corragio*" at the top of his lungs. At last an insuperable gulley brought him up short. He clapped his hand to his forehead, exclaiming "*Santissima Maria*" in a tone of wrath and despair—then recovered his spirits and dashed off in another direction. We succeeded. When we got to the top the carriage was quarter of a mile off, and Luigi shouted "*Vittoria!*" as he rode into the gate, as much elated as if [he] had accomplished some great achievement. It was a *festa* day. All the people in the crowded streets and in the little square wore white caps. They were a hardy and athletic race—their faces, their short strong necks, their broad and prominent chests, were all burnt to a dark ruddy brown. There is a strange difference in the physical character of the people in the different parts of Sicily; nor in this alone—costumes, habits, manners, domestic utensils, everything in short varies as you go from town to town. In some places, the women ride astride like men; in others, they have a kind of side-saddle. In one little village almost all the

[h] Named Dawson, according to Parkman's pocket notebook.—Ed.

women were exceedingly pretty, though dark as Indians. Their black hair was arranged with great neatness and care in a peculiar fashion which attracted my notice at once, since in every other place I had seen the hair was not arranged at all—and the less said or seen of it the better.[35]

Between Girgenti and the sea is the site of the ancient Agrigentum. Standing on the town wall, you can look down on immense fertile hills and plains, amid which appear the ruins of five or six temples, standing together along an abrupt ridge of land, which in one direction formed the boundary of the ancient city. I went down to the ruins, with a cicerone, of course, to plague me by his chattering. I saw all the temples—I admired and wondered, but was not exactly overpowered by enthusiasm. I bought a book to describe them; a task I leave to the more classically disposed, feeling little inclination to it myself.

Luigi brings me pockets-full of ancient money, and seems greatly astonished at my indifference. As for himself, he is rabid. He dodges into every house and shop, inquiring for *antica moneta*, stops *contadini* at work with the same question; he has scraped together an enormous bagful for which he pays scarce anything, perfectly familiar as he is with its true value, and with the *costumi del paese*, as he says, the customs of the country. His enthusiasm embraces every object, far and wide. He raves of love on the road—tells how he eloped with his wife—sings love songs; then falls into the martial vein; shouts *corragio*; defies the wind, rain, and torrents. He enters into all my plans with the most fervid zeal, leaving me nothing to do. Every night he comes up stairs, bringing all kinds of dresses and utensils of the people for me to look at. Sometimes he comes in with a handful of old coins, telling me with a chuckle that he had bought them for *pochissimo*; kissing them repeatedly in the exaltation of a good bargain. I have lived most sumptuously ever since I have been with him. He puts the whole inn into a ferment—rakes the town to find the best of everything—and waits on table with an eulogium of every dish. "Ah, *signore*," he repeats, "do you think Luigi loves money? No, Luigi loves honor." He has something to give to every beggar he meets. In short the fellow is a jewel, and shall be my particular friend henceforward.

I went with him to the house of a signor Politi, who is fairly rampant with antiquarian zeal, and deeply enamored moreover of the fine arts. The studio of this virtuoso presented a formidable display of old pictures, plaster casts, vases, fragments of statues, and a confused medley of indescribables. He was sitting at his easel copying a Madonna of Gu[i]do. Luigi pulled off his hat with great respect, advanced, and drawing an antique cameo from the multitudinous folds of his handkerchief presented it as *un picc(i)olo complimento* to signore. The virtuoso examined it through his spectacles, expressed his approval, and coolly pocketed it, leaving me in equal admiration at Luigi's making a *complimento* of such value, and at Politi's cavalier-like style of accepting it. The mystery was soon solved—it was like Turkish or Indian presents: Luigi expected as a matter of course a *complimento* in return. In fact, he retired with a handkerchief-full of antiquities. He told me he always carried something with him, *per fare un complimento* to the *signori* who honored him with their acquaintance. He knows everybody from princes to beggars.

At the English consul's, I met a blind traveller, a Mr. Hol(e)man,[36] who has been over Liberia, New Holland, and other remote regions, for the most part alone, and written seven volumes of his travels. Travelling, he told me, was a passion with him. He could not sit at home. I walked home with him through the streets, admiring his indomitable energy. I saw him the next morning sitting on his mule, with the guide he had hired—his strong frame, his manly English face, his grey beard and mustaches, and his sightless eyeballs gave him a noble appearance in the crowd of wondering Sicilians about him.

From Girgenti our course lay westward to a village called Mont' Allegro. A wretched muletrack again; a wilderness of mountains with scarce an inhabitant. There was one broad valley covered with a growth of the *jumara*—a plant of which baskets and ropes are made. It was a dark and gloomy day. Down in the bottom of the valley a herd of oxen were grazing—there was a *contadino's* hut of reeds on one of the abrupt hills near by. It was like the lodge of an Indian— the cattle were like a herd of buffalo; I could have thought myself on the prairies. But as we passed by the herd, there stood the herds-man in his shaggy breeches of goatskin, leaning on his staff—gazing at us through his tangled hair and unshorn beard. His savage dogs, wild as himself, growled loudly as we rode by. The American frontier could show no such a group.

Before night, Mont' Allegro lay before us, among mountains of alabastar, with a wide green meadow between; and a grove of orange trees at the skirts of the close compacted group of houses. A ruined Saracenic castle, and an assemblage of ancient dwellings, crowns the summit of one of the highest of the mountains. It rises before me now, as I write in the window of the *albergo*, the white rock contrasting beautifully with the thick, growth of Indian fig that springs from every crevice, from top to bottom. It is a quiet and beautiful evening. The capoted idlers in the street are talking and laughing and looking up at the stranger—the same beings that their fathers were before them centuries ago. The town is built and paved with alabastar.

Luigi came up in the evening, to hold *un discorso* with me, according to his custom. He was in his usual state of excitement. He takes a glass of wine in his hand; "*Viva l'onore, signorino mio!*" rolling up his eyes and flourishing his hands, "*Viva Bacco; viva Dio; viva il console Americano!*" and so on, the finale being a siezure and kissing of my hand; after which he enquires if I shall want him, looks about to see that all is right, kisses my hand again, and goes off.

I picked up in the morning fine specimens of alabastar—and afterwards of agates in the beds of the streams. We reached at night the city of Sciacca, handsomely drenched by a shower. In the morning I rode up the mountain behind the city to visit the convent of St. Carlogero at the summit, where are the celebrated vapor baths which Diodorus speaks of, said to have been arranged by D[a]edalus. After circling about the whitewashed walls of the convent, we entered a little dirty den for the accommodation of mules, from whence we saw the refectioner, through an opening at the head of some stone steps, cooking maccaroni for the fathers, over some little charcoal furnaces. He came down at our call, shook down his tucked-up robes, pulled his cowl over his head, and led the way to the baths. There was an immense cavern in the rock, under the walls of the convent, closed with a strong wooden door. The monk opened it, and immediately a volume of vapor came rolling out, so warm and pleasant that it was hard to leave it, though it drenched you to the skin as effectually as a shower of rain. I undressed in a sort of barn, provided for that purpose hard by, and sat quarter of an hour in the cavern on the stone benches of Dedalus. The consequence was a most profuse perspiration. There was a roaring in the remote parts of the cavern like a hidden cataract. The monk afterwards showed me a hole in side of the mountain, where a similar steam issued, with a still louder noise. When I paid the monk the usual *buonamano*, I found the holy man had cheated me by giving false money in change. The view of Sciacca on a hill by the sea, with its white battlements, its church domes, and the ruined castle of Count Perolla,[37] was very fine—its hot and sunscorched appearance was relieved by the groves of olives spreading up the sides of the hill, and over all the country.

One of Luigi's dignified acquaintances in this place was the Marchese Giacomo, a nobleman of great wealth, and a determined virtuoso. Luigi called on him with an offering of coins, and returned with an invitation to his *signore* to visit the marchese and see his pictures. He had a most admirable picture gallery—among the rest was an original of Guido. He kindly invited me to dine with him, but Luigi's care had supplied me a plentiful meal already. So much for one specimen of a Sicilian nobleman; I saw one or two more of nearly the same stamp at a *conversazione*. The next morning, I found Luigi at the *albergo* sitting over a bottle of wine with a large, fat, sleepy-looking man, in rather a dingy coat, whom on my entering, he slapped on the shoulder—"*Ecco, signore, mio amico il barone; un brav' uomo,*" etc., running on with a long string of praises of "his friend the baron," at which this extraordinary specimen of a noble kept shaking his large head in modest denial. The baron brought us a melon and some fine nuts as a present, which he did not disdain to place on the table himself. While our mules were saddling, I went with Luigi to see the domestic establishment of his friend. It was a large and reasonably clean house—some women were spinning in a spacious outer room, where some hens were cackling about the floor. The baroness received me in the inner room—the bed room. She was a stout rosy damsel, with good physical womanhood about her, and much beauty, though not over refined. She blushed, as though not used to entertaining strangers. Five or six holy pictures and little wax images with lamps burning before them were about the room. Luigi took down one picture of Santa Maria, the patroness of Sciacca, which he piously kissed and put into his pocket, observing that now we should have good weather till we got to Palermo. The baroness got me another, by way of making assurance doubly sure. Thus armed against fate we rode away. I was rather inclined to suspect a little humbug about the baron and his establishment, till I got to Palermo and I found by inquiry that noblemen of his description were very common in Sicily.

The weather was fine—the country to me uninteresting, since, though fertile, it was one great plain, on which the January sunbeams fell like scorching fire. The mules sunk to the knees in mud. The *contadini* were at work in the rich fields, slowly plodding after their long-horned cattle, sleepily holding on to the tail of their clumsy ploughs. These ploughs are worthy of all admiration, as partaking of the simplicity of primitive times. Iron seldom enters into their construction. They scratch up a little groove in the ground, without turning over the sod. The men were noble fellows; with gigantic busts, and massive limbs, and a wild untaught look. They wore the shaggy breeches of goatskin that make the people of this part of the island look like so many Robinson Crusoes.

Early in the afternoon, we approached the ruins of Selinantium [Selinus] over the fields where the Carthagenian besieging army had been encamped. The largest temple is of Jupiter—one column is standing; the rest have been levelled by the Carthaginians or by earthquakes. The stone is not of good quality, but a grey limestone, full of fossils—the relics of a yet remoter antiquity. How these sculptured rocks could have been transported is the great mystery to me, as to everyone else. The Sicilians will have it that these are houses of the giants; they may well be puzzled, since the national method of transporting building-stone is to tie it to the back of a jackass. Luigi laid a cloth on one of the flat stones, and spread a needlessly luxurious dinner of cold sole, oranges, almonds, wine, etc., which I disposed of—after which we proceeded to Castrovetrano [Castelvetrano].

The way was enlivened by the edifying singularities of the muleteer Michele, who walked along talking without intermission for an hour together, though no one listened or replied. He interrupted his discourse only to belabor his mule, and curse him in Sicilian. When we came to a steep place, he would take a firm hold of the beast's tail with one hand, while he belabored him with a rope's end that he held in the other—and thus they would scramble up together. Where the mud was more than a foot deep, Michele would place both hands on the mule's rump, and vault, with a sort of grunt, upon his back; wiggle himself about for a while to find a comfortable seat, and then burst forth with some holy canticle in praise of a saint.

Just after leaving the ruins of Selinantium, we were struggling along in the mud of a lane between rows of cork-trees and aloes, when Michele suddenly set up a yowling like a tom-cat—stopped in the midst of a note to expostulate with his mule—and then proceeded in a more dismal tone than before. Luigi clapped his hands, and shouted, "*Bravo! compare Michele; bellissima!*" at which the gratified Michele redoubled his exertions, and squalled at the top of his throat, putting his hand to the side of his mouth to increase the volume of sound. A young *contadino*, who was wading along on an ass at a little distance behind, was siezed with a fit of emulation, and set up a counter howl to one of the airs peculiar to the *contadini*. I cried "*bravo!*" to this new vocalist, while Luigi cried "*bella!*" and "*bellissima!*" to the exertions of Michele. Michele jogged along on his mule, the tassel of his woolen cap flapping; while Luigi twisted himself in his saddle to see how I relished the entertainment, remarking with a grin: "*Canta Michele!*" ("Michele is singing!")

In spite of the protection of Santissima Maria, a cold storm came up this morning, under the benign influences of which we issued from the gate of Castrovetrano. Four miles' ride brought us to the quarries of Campo Bello, whence was taken the stone of which the temples of Selinantium were built. It is a most extraordinary place. About the base of a little hill, near an old plantation of olive trees, are lying fragments of columns cut from the rock thousands of years ago. Further on are others completely carved, but not yet severed from the mother rock. The process of cutting them out was this. A circle, of the same diameter with the column wanted, was marked out on the flat rock. The workmen then hewed down into the rock, around this circle, until the column was long enough, when it was cut off and drawn out, leaving an orifice like a well. There were some where the circle had just been traced—others where the column was standing ready to be drawn out of the hole—others where the hole was empty, and the column was rolled down to the foot of the hill.

At Mazzara, I saw the effigy of Count Ruggeiri [Ruggiero][i] riding over the prostrate Saracens. His tomb was in the church, but the fathers being at table, I was much disappointed in being able to see nothing but this effigy on the wall outside. Departed in a hard rain—there is a gloomy satisfaction in travelling in bad weather, wholly unconnected with the scenery or sight-seeing of any kind—we had enough of it by the time we got to Marsala. I had ridden from sunrise to sunset without food, and felt like a starved wolf.

Marsala, as everybody knows, is famous for its wine. For travellers, there is little to see. The fishermen here wear a hooded capote of brown cloth, ten times coarser and thicker than a Mackinaw blanket, and accommodating itself to the person about as well as a garment of sheet iron. It is turnished with arms which project on each side like the flappers of a seal, giving the wearers, who are naturally a stout broad-shouldered race, a most gigantic appearance. The broad-shouldered fishermen, with their ruddy visages staring listlessly out of their formidable garments—the restless priests, with their large three-cornered hats—the nun-like women, enveloped in their black mantles from head to foot—the passage of mules and asses, shouldering their way through the throng—the squalls of criers and dealers at the street corners—make altogether a lively and amusing scene in the streets of this place.

Marsala was the ancient Sibylum. I saw the reputed tomb of the Cumaean Sybil, under the Church of St. John.

The rocky ground around Marsala is pierced thick with narrow passages and large subterranean chambers for an immense distance. These caverns were made by the removal of stone for building the city. They are the dens of ruffians and the scum of humanity. Many of the Sicilian cities have similar asylums for their rascals.

Morning. A gloomy and sullen day. We were riding past an old house of *contadini*, when Luigi suddenly reined back his mule upon mine, uttering in a whisper of consternation, *"Santissima Maria!"* I

[i] Roger of Sicily.—Ed.

looked at him, and saw that the natural ruddy brown of his thin face was changed to a most cadaverous yellow. I asked him what was the matter. He made no answer, but shouted aloud for Michele— who was a little way behind, among the trees—and then began to cross himself and mutter prayers. I could see nothing except a man with a gun, walking away from the road toward a group of a dozen *contadini*, who were standing in front of the shattered house. We had left them far behind before Luigi was so far recovered as to tell me that a man had pointed a gun at him from the bushes, but had desisted when he saw Michele. He added that next to the mountains around Palermo, this place was the most notorious for robbers in all Sicily. I do not for a moment imagine that the fellow intended us bodily harm—nothing is more likely than that he meant to exact a contribution from us—nothing more unlikely than that he meant to revive the nearly exploded custom of shooting a man first and robbing him afterwards. A simple robbery would be thought little of, while this last summary process would set the gendarmes on the tracks of the perpetrators.

We had lost the path, and got throuroughly wet through, before we reached Trapani. The fortifications of this place are tremendous. A soldier of the custom-house stopped us at the gate; a *carlin(o)* mollified him and he let us pass. We found an admirable *albergo*, and an excellent dinner.

I went out towards evening to a little gate that opened on the rocks by the sea. Some Neapolitan soldiers were standing there, looking at the breakers as they rolled in against the rock, sending the spray as high as the roofs of the houses. One of them, in answer to my inquiries, pointed out the reef of Asinello, just discernible through the mists, at half a mile's distance. This was the rock where [A]Eneas placed the green bough, when he held games in this place in honor of his father.[38] In another direction was the rock of Malo Consiglio, where the Sicilian Vespers were planned. The waves were breaking in white foam over its whole extent.

The renowned Mt. Eryx—now Mt. St. Giuliano—rises behind Trapani, next to Etna the highest mountain in Sicily. I went to the top to visit the ruined shrine of Venus—founded by Eryx—enriched by Eneas—resorted to by the old Sicanians, and in later times by the Romans. I found a walled city of six thousand inhabitants at the top. The narrow streets were almost deserted. The wind came through them as cold and sharp as on a January day at home; the citizens were wrapped in endless folds of cloth and goat skin. After traversing its whole extent, I came to the wide ditch of an old castle that stood a little above the city, over the site of the temple. The castle itself is tumbling to decay, and disgraced into a prison for captive robbers. Of the temple, there is nothing but a well and a fragment of a foundation. The scenery from this place was, however, charming beyond measure. There was a fine view, among the rest of Trapani, sweeping out into the sea in the form of a sickle, whence its ancient name, Drepanon [Drepanum]. Here Saturn dropped his sickle, after his surgical operation upon his father—or, according to the other story, here Ceres lost hers as she went to look for Proserpine. On this mountain, Hercules slew Eryx, and here was the tomb of Anchises. In after times, when Roman pilgrims came to pay their homage at the temple of their favorite goddess, a thousand fair and kind priestesses waited to welcome them. I was not so fortunate. A few crest-fallen robbers shewed me about the ruined and dingy fortress.

Descending, I stopped at the church of the famous Madonna of Trapani. A monk led me through the sacristy, and a series of chapels and passages, into the holy of holies, at the very heart of the enormous edifice. It was almost dark. Great lamps of silver swung from the roof; shadowy columns of marble, and the glittering decorations of the splendid altar were just discernible. The muleteer and guide went down on their knees, while the monk lighted the candles, drew aside the curtains, and displayed the holy image. Two angels of marble, in robes of silver, held rich lamps on either hand of the figure, which was covered from head to foot with a profusion of jewels, coral ornaments, and gold and silver watches. The effect of this little chapel, with its faint light and its magnificent decorations, was very striking. It was not at all increased by the drawing of the curtain and the revelation of the mystery behind. The lips, cheeks, and eyes of this statue were painted—an execrable practice, which ruins some of the best statues I have seen in churches.

From Trapani we rode towards the north. Met by the way a dead *contadino* riding on a mule, to which he was bound in such a manner that the body retained a position nearly upright, while the head fell forward upon the chest. The fellow was in his working dress—a remarkably large and powerful man. He was probably the victim of some quarrel. The men who rode with him seemed inclined to consider the affair as a good joke.

At twenty miles from Trapani, Luigi and I turned from the road to see the ruins of Segesta. We rode for nearly two hours over solitary and pathless hills. Two or three gigantic bulls, grazing the short reeds in the bed of a marshy brook, were the only tenants of this solitude. We entered a valley between two very abrupt mountains. The high grass swept our faces as we passed through it. Emerging, we were in the midst of an amphitheatre of high and solitary mountains. Before us on a little eminence was the temple of Segesta—the relic of a city as old as the Trojan War, and afterwards noted for its riches and its misfortunes. Agathocles[39] destroyed it, because it refused him tribute; put to death its men by torture, cut away the breasts of its women, and sold its children as slaves. He left not a wall standing, except this temple and a theatre too massive to be destroyed. I have seen nothing in art so striking and majestic as this solitary temple. Its situation apart, none of the temples of Girgenti can compare with it. Standing, as it does, a monument of the fate that overtook its builders, and in the midst of a scene so sublime by nature, the effect of its noble architecture is immeasurably increased. The city was on the mountain above. Its green side seems now more thickly spread with stones than those of its neighbors; but there is nothing to mark at a distance that a great city once stood there. Look more closely, and you find fragments of beautifully sculptured marble columns, and numberless wells filled up with stone when the city was destroyed. The theatre is at the end of the mountain, in excellent preservation.

It was near sunset when we descended from the mountain to find our way to the city. After fording a rocky stream at the bottom of the valley, we came upon the path. The attempt would be useless, or I would try to convey some idea of the scenery of this spot; it was certainly beyond any conceptions of the strongest imagination, whatever snarling cynics may say about the delusions of fancy creating beauties that never have existence. In the midst of it, a large cross, freshly cut in the bark of an olive tree, marked the scene of a recent murder. Just at sunset, we caught a parting glimpse of the melancholy temple of Segesta, standing alone among its mountains—a landscape of unmatched sublimity and beauty. I turned from it reluctantly, and rode up to the dark and dirty city.

The next day, nothing particular occurred but another ducking. We stopped at night at Partinico, a dirty village, which looked wretched and dismal in the dull rain that had set in. The *albergo* was like a deserted castle. I finished my dinner, ordered a brazier of charcoal which had no effect whatever on the atmosphere of the enormous stone-paved chamber. Placing the table in the centre, with the fire underneath, I went to work to study Italian in order to kill time. About nine o'clock the oil failed in my miserable little earthenware lamp, and I went out to order a new supply. I groped my way through two or three chambers—some damp cold passages, with a taper stuck against the wall, but saw nothing and heard nothing of inhabitants. I beat against a door with both fists till the old house echoed again—I shouted at the top of my lungs. A dead silence above and below! I groped down a flight of stone steps, till I was brought up by a strong door that evidently led to the outer air, and was secured with a number of wooden bars. I renewed my explorations above, and was rewarded at last by the sight of a light glimmering through the chink of a door. Five or six gendarmes were drinking wine within. One of them pointed out to me the lurking place of the people of the house—an enormous, cave-like kitchen, which was only to be reached by wading through the mud of the yard. About a dozen travellers were crouching here and there over braziers of charcoal, or lying on wooden benches, wrapped in cloaks. Luigi sat on a stone bench, eating maccaroni. He sprang up, the instant he saw me enter, and in half a minute the lamp was replenished.

There was a thunder-storm that night. In the morning, every mountain was white with snow. The gendarmes led out their horses, slung their carbines at their thighs, and rode off—the best looking soldiers I have seen in Sicily. We followed them, after Luigi had fought a hard battle with the landlady about the price of the lodging, and I had denied a contribution to the money-box of saint somebody, which was handed me as I was mounting. How much of the money thus received goes to the saint, may admit of some question.

An hour's ride brought us into the heart of the mountains. Meanwhile a furious snow-storm began, while we were riding up a very narrow pass between parallel mountains, by a road cut along the side of one of them. The snow obscured the summits of the mountains over our heads and the valley beneath us, where strong winds were whirling about the drifts, giving us an occasional glimpse of a muddy torrent tumbling with a loud roar among the rocks below. The snow-storm was accompanied by dull heavy peals of thunder, a novel circumstance to me. The passage was very much contracted as we approached its head. We saw there the waters of the torrent, descending in one fall from an immense rock into the gulf we had been passing. Though the passage was several miles long, we had not met a single man by the way. As we approached a little stone house, I asked Luigi what it was, but he turned round with an anxious countenance, and put his finger to his lips. We passed the place of his suspicions without interruption. Luigi drew forth and kissed his Santissima Maria di Sciacca, who, however she may have treated us in the matter of weather, certainly preserved us, as Luigi insisted, from the *briganti*. I thought to myself that I little deserved such celestial aid, as I had used my picture to light my lamp the night before. An hour more, and the broad flat valley of Palermo lay below us, green among the white mountains around it.

We turned off to the left, and after a long ride came to the monastery of San Martino, in a wild and sublime situation among mountains. The Benedictines here are all of noble blood. Everything is on a scale of magnificence and luxury—pictures, fountains, the church, the chapels, the library, the interminable galleries of the enormous building. There are no tawdry ornaments; everything is in good taste—but for ascetic privations, and mortification of the flesh, look elsewhere than at San Martino. The fathers were at table. I was served with a dinner of lampreys, and other delicacies, which a prince might have envied. There is a preserve of wild game, a formidable establishment of cooks and scullions, a beautiful *conversazione*, and billiard rooms, for the diversion of the pious devotees.

In a palace-like hall below the surface of the ground, sustained by columns and arches of the rich marbles of Sicily and lighted from above, is a noble statue of San Martino. He is a young soldier on horseback, with as little savor of the saint about him as any of his votaries in this luxurious monastery.

I have seen my last of Sicily. I bade adieu to Luigi, who insisted on my receiving a number of valuable ancient coins, and would have given me an hundred if I had let him have his own way—took leave of the Marstons and Gardiners—had my baggage carried on board the *Palmero* by three *fac[c]hini*, and followed it myself. An old monk was on board, among the crowd of nobles and exquisites, with the cord of St. Francis holding his tattered rags together. He had a little contribution box in his hand, and was gliding about in a crouching posture, with his cap in his hand, begging for his patron's benefit. He would look up into the faces of an inattentive group, with a humble and supplicating countenance, just like a starved dog expecting a piece of meat at a dinner table. A pleasant voyage and perfect safety was to be the reward of all who dropped a *grano* into the box. My heart was moved with compassion towards the old fellow, he looked so humble and so miserable. I tried to catch his eye to give him something—but my unwonted feeling of benevolence toward a Sicilian beggar was destined to bear no fruit—for just then all visitors were warned off. The old monk tumbled himself over the side into the boat of a charitable *fachino*.

The next morning the famous Bay of Naples looked wretched and dismal enough, under the influences of an easterly storm, through which Vesuvius was just visible. I went to the Hotel de Rome, an excellent house, with a restaurant beneath where you get and pay for precisely what you want, an arrangement far better than a table d'hote.

I spent the first day at the Royal Museum, where I could not determine which I liked best, the "Hercules Farnese," or the "Venus" of Praxiteles. This morning, I went to Pozzuoli in a *calèche*. Just after leaving the city, you see houses cut out, like artificial caves, in the natural rock. Not much further on, the road itself enters the rock, under which it runs for a great distance. The opening at the extremity seems like a mere point of light. This Grotto of Posilippo, as it is called, is very lofty, and wide enough to serve as one of the chief thoroughfares of Naples. It is as dark as Tartarus, and excessively damp and cold. The lamps that are kept constantly burning at intervals along the walls are a mere mockery of light. The shouts of drivers, and the heavy rolling of wheels down in this den, make a tremendous uproar, reverberated as they are by the rock above.

At Pozzuoli I selected a cicerone from fifty who beset me in the dirty street. I rode on the back of a donkey down to Lake Avernus, which lies shut in by high hills on every side; yet there was nothing very impressive or terrific about the infernal lake. Close to the bank is the Grotto of the Cumaean Sybil. The deep passages were filled with the smoke of torches, and the walls were blackened with soot. The deepest parts—the baths and chamber of the Sybil—were covered with water through which a man carried me on his back. The Sybil had a particularly modest piece of sculpture over the arch of one of her apartments. Coming to the upper air, I paid the three fellows who showed the cave what was justly due to them—they of course made a great outcry and demanded more, returning me what I had given them. They would not desist from their importunities till I brought my cane to bear a part in the conversation, which dispersed them for a while. As I rode along by the lake, I heard them coming again. This time, they brought for sale pieces of mosaic, and little bronze amulets worn by the Roman ladies, of the same delicate description as that which I had admired in the cave of the Sybil. I could only rid myself of their importunities by resorting a second time to the same summary measures. These fellows fear a cane as much as a thieving dog does.

I made the usual circuit about Baiae and Cumae, looking at all the temples. At the former place I stopped at a little *albergo*, where I got a bottle of the Falernian wine—whether the same that Horace used to drink, I cannot say, but the grape grew in the same spot. I saw Solfatara, too—a place I have long wished to visit, and which somewhat disappointed my expectations. It is the crater of an extinct volcano. The bottom is composed of a volcanic soil, with here and there an opening whence steam and sulphurous fumes issue with a roaring sound. About these orifices every stone and stick is encrusted with little crystals of sulphur. The ground sounds hollow when stamped upon. The hills around, which formed the wall of the ancient crater, are beautifully green and fertile. At every place the *custode* demands a *buonamano*, and invariably grumbles and follows begging after you, how much soever you may give him. Moreover, a troop of boys and men follow you with "antiquities"—which are manufactured in great profusion at Naples. Add to this, the beggars, most of whom pretend to be mutes, and make horrible noises in their throats to convince you of it—the boys who will wipe a spot of mud off your donkey's back, and then demand a *carline* for the service— and your insatiable cicerone—add together all these, and you have a sum of petty vexations, enough to damp any man's zeal for explor- ing classical localities. Fortunately I never had much to lose. I would go farther for one look into the crater of Vesuvius than to see all the ruined temples in Italy.

Among the most curious of the "sights" of today were Nero's vapor-baths—not unlike those of Sciacca, except that they consist of very long and narrow passages in the rock instead of one large cave. Seated in the entrance was a miserably emaciated old man, who stripped off his shirt, exposing his bare ribs and gaunt arms, and after lighting a torch, led the way down into one of the passages. It was so intensely hot that I told him to go back to the fresh air. When he came into the upper cave, he panted like a dog, while the perspira- tion ran in streams from his body. He reeled about unsteadily, and then sat down exhausted in a corner.

Friday. I went to the Lake d'Agnano, passing again through the Grotto of Posilippo. After visiting the minor lions of the place, I asked for the keeper of the Grotto del Cane, which is just on the bank. At length a fat surly old fellow, with a red cap, came slowly along, followed by two dogs. He showed none of the sharkish prompt- ness of the other cicerones. Something had displeased him, for he was growling and swearing to himself. He said not a word when he saw me; but calling the two unhappy dogs, he made fast a cord round the neck of each, and waddled off sulkily to the cave, dragging them after him. Arrived at the cave, he bundled one of them up, holding him by all the four feet in one hand, while, with the other, he opened the door. The dog gasped and writhed about for a while, and then lay motionless, on which the old fellow drew him out by the hind leg, and tossed him on the grass. He soon recovered, ran back to the cave, smelt a little of the gas, snuffled in disgust, and ran to join his companion in demolishing a crust of bread which a boy had thrown down.

After this I went to Virgil's tomb, on the hill of Posilippo. I met a laughable adventure here. Like a genuine tourist, I thought I would take away a memento of the poet, and seeing a bush which from its position had escaped the violating hands of former travellers, I determined to get a branch of it. The tomb stands at the edge of a rock about two hundred feet high above the street; this bush was on the side of the cliff just outside an opening in the back part of the tomb. There was a stout iron bar to hold on by—no man of ordinary nerve and muscular strength would have the slightest cause of apprehension. So I told the cicerone to hold my cloak, grasped the bar, leaned from the opening, and got hold of the plant, which I was about to secure when I heard a simultaneous shout from both guides, who sprang upon me and siezed me fast.[40] I looked round at them. Both were pale as ghosts, with their mouths wide open, and eyes staring out of their heads. I asked them what the devil was the matter—they replied by siezing me by the arms and shoulders and pulling me away from the hole. I got free of them by a sudden effort, but they sprang at me again, and began to roar for help. "Oh, come this way, signore! come this way; you must not go there." I was a good deal vexed, but could not help laughing at being mistaken for a madman. I thought I would try a little intimidation, so aimed a blow with my fist at the nearest fellow's face. They dodged off a moment, but returned to the charge with faces doubly earnest and anxious, and pinioned me from behind. "Oh, signore!" they said, "we don't want money; only come up with us to the gate." I saw the folly of contending with the idea that had got possession of them, so told them I would go. Thus I went out from Virgil's tomb a prisoner. I thought my quiet compliance would have allayed their fears a little—no such thing; nothing would do but I must mount with them to the garden gate above. Half way up appeared a gang of men, rushing in hot haste to secure the madman. They were soon about me, when confiding in their numbers they loosened my arms. I was resolved not to lose my relic of Virgil, so despatched a boy to pluck a leaf from the door of the tomb, since the men would on no account suffer me to go myself. I got this memento of my adventure, and departed. I had some little suspicion that all this terror of my guides was counterfeited in order to give them a chance to pick my pockets; but all my money was safe.

I met at the house of Mr. Rogers, Mr. Theodore Parker,[41] and Mr. Farnum, from Philadelphia. I had already met Mr. Parker at the Hotel de Rome. Yesterday we went up Vesuvius together. "What stock in trade for an orthodox minister!" exclaimed Mr. Parker. The mountain is unusually active now. We stood on the edge of the great crater, which is three or four miles round and more than a thousand feet deep. In the midst of it, a great cone of lava rose up, from the top of which came smoke and fire, and every moment it would throw up showers of lava [a] quarter of a mile into the air, with a loud bellowing and an occasional shock like the report of a cannon within the mountain. The abyss that we were looking into was half filled with smoke and fumes of sulphur, which the wind drove down into it from the crater of the little mountain in the midst. The bottom was a crust of lava, full of cracks through which the liquid fire underneath was visible. What with the dismal bellowings of the mountain, the volumes of smoke, and the obscurity of the tremendous gulf below us, it was, as Mr. Parker intimated, a lively picture of Hell. We stood for a while, watching the melted lava whirling up into the air, and falling over the black sides of the cone, whose edges were continually crumbling and falling down into the crater. The grumblings and reports down in the bowels of the mountain grew louder and louder; the puffs of smoke came out thicker and thicker; till at length Mr. P. and I could endure it no longer, but determined to have a nearer view of the monster. So we scrambled down into the great crater. The bottom was so hot that it scorched our shoes. We set our canes on fire by thrusting them down into the cracks. There were numberless fissures and holes where brimstone fumes came up with a suffocating stench. We went as near as we safely could to the little mountain in the middle, which appeared at times like a fountain, flinging up showers of fire from a mouth many rods in diameter. At times, a sudden wind would come, whirling the smoke of this infernal outlet down to where we stood; which compelled us to make a prompt retreat, or else to hold the head in a crevice of the lava pavement, to avoid being suffocated. Our guides went quite near to the base of the cone, dodging the falling lava with great activity. Some of these melted masses must have weighed a ton. As they fell, they spread out over a large surface. The guide would make a sudden dash at them, detach a small portion with a pole, which he carried to a safe distance and then stamped by pressing a copper coin into it. After a while, Mr. P. and I took our part in the exercise, and secured several trophies. The floor of the great crater, on which we stood, had been a sea of melted lava only three days before.

We got some of the famous Lachrymae Christi wine at a house half way down. We reached Naples at three, where the outskirts of the town were deserted, with the exception of a few miserable old men and women sitting in the doorways. It was Sunday—the great day of the Carnival.[42] King Ferdinand, however, sets his face against the carnival, which for several years has been a mere nothing at Naples. This year, in consideration of the distress of tradesmen, he has consented, much against his inclination, to make a fool of himself. This was the day appointed for a grand masked procession, in which the king and his ministers were to pelt his subjects with sugar-plums, and be pelted in return. There was a great crowd, as we entered a square upon the Toledo—the main street of Naples. While we were slowly driving through it, the head of the procession appeared. First came a dragon about fifty feet long, with his back just visible above the throng of heads, as if he was swimming in the water. He was drawn by a long train of horses. Five or six masked noblemen were on his back, pelting the crowd and the people in the galleries of the houses on each side. Then came a sort of car, full of bears, cats, and monkeys, all flinging sugar-plums. The horses of this vehicle were appropriately ridden by jackasses. Then came a long train of carriages, which we joined. The crowd was enormous. The Toledo was one wide river of heads, the procession slowly moving down on one side and returning on the other. Along the middle, a line of dragoons sat motionless, with drawn swords, on their horses. Mrs. P. was hit on the nose by a formidable sugar-plum, flung by a vigorous hand from one of the balconies. She was in great trouble, but there was no such thing as retreat. We got our full share. Mr. Farnum's dignity was disturbed—Mr. Parker had a glass of his spectacles broken—I alone escaped uninjured. At length the royal carriage appeared. Ferdinand—a gigantic man, taller and heavier than any of his subjects—was flinging sugar-plums with hearty good will, like all the rest. As they passed our carriage, the royal family greeted us with a broadside, which completed Mrs. Parker's discomposure. They threw genuine sugar-plums—the others were quite uneatable. The king wore a black silk dress which covered him from head to foot. His face was protected by a wire mask. He carried a brass machine in his hand to fling sugar-plums with. His uncle, his mother, his wife, and all his chief noblemen soon appeared, all protected by masks.

The procession passed several times up and down the Toledo, with occasional stoppages. One of these happened when the king's carriage was not far before us, while directly over against it, on the other side of the street, was a triumphal car full of noblemen. Instantly there began a battle. Ferdinand and the princes sent volley after volley against their opponents, who returned it with interest. The crowd set up a roar, and made a rush for the spoils. There was a genuine battle for the sugar-plums that fell between the two carriages—pushing, scrambling, shouting, yelling, "confusion worse confounded"; till the dignified combatants thought proper to separate.

The theatre of San Carlo here is one of the largest and finest in Europe. I liked better, however, some little boxes, scarce large enough for a hundred people, which are scattered thick along the quay, and in some of the inferior squares of the city. In these places you may see the performances of a character peculiar to the kingdom of Naples, called Pulcinella. I went tonight to the Teatro Sebeto—an establishment consisting of a pit, eight boxes, and a gallery where none but men sit. The piece was a deep tragedy, full of love, jealousy, and murder; dungeons, trap-doors, etc. Pulcinella here assumed the character of a pilgrim. He always wears a black vizard which covers his face as far as the end of his nose, leaving the lower part bare. His entrée, which was in the midst of the most tragic part, was greeted by a loud laugh. The father of the distressed lady was busy in bemoaning his afflictions on his knees, with hands clasped. Pulcinella kneeled down a little behind him, and caracatured all his motions most ludicrously. In the next scene, the distracted husband, whose lady has proved unfaithful, encounters the pilgrim and makes at him with drawn sword, taking him for the betrayer of his beloved. Pulcinella meets him with his pilgrim's staff, which he brandishes at him in a most laughable manner, turning into ridicule all his anger and distress. The audience roar with delight, but do not applaud. Pulcinella then has a scene to himself with two girls, each of whom falls in love with him, and treat[s] him to sugar-plums. Some of his evolutions are very particularly indecent. After this, he did not appear again. Tragedy resumed her reign undisturbed. After the death of the heroine, the curtain rose again for a dance, performed by several persons, who chased each other about the stage, beating each other with straps of leather, in time to the music.

Punch and Judy may be seen at any time on the quay. There are also jugglers, etc., in great abundance. Outside of all these establishments stands a soldier, with musket and bayonet, to preserve order. A whole company kept guard last night, in the porch of the theatre San Carlo, while as many more were distributed inside. Ferdinand has some fine-looking Swiss troops. There was a grand masked ball at S. Carlo last night.

I saw a funeral procession in the Toledo this afternoon. First came a large number of men in white robes, with white broad-brimmed hats, and white cloth covering their faces. The coffin, covered with gilding, was borne next, on a machine covered with gold and tinsel. Then followed a concourse of men in dingy black dresses, each of whom bore a little banner with a death's head. A soldier walked a short distance before the procession.

The men in white belonged to the company of penitents, who wish to expiate some sin they have committed. They are paid by the friends of the deceased. The money all goes to the treasury of the company. The men in black came from the king's poor-house, which contains six thousand paupers. These mourners are selected by the officers of the establishment, who receive the money. The funeral I saw was that of a man of high rank. From this downward, there is every grade of splendor and meanness, ending in the exit of some wretched *lazzaroni* who is put into a wheelbarrow and pitched head foremost into one of the pits of the Campo Santo. In some parts of Sicily, the poor are rammed by main force into a little square box, which is carried by two men to the common burial ground outside the city gates.

About sunset this evening, there was a great mustering of soldiers in the square in front of the royal palace. Among the rest, a fine body of cavalry came down the street; and some companies of the king's guard, selected for their great stature and fine appearance. There was a body of Swiss in their white uniforms. The whole open space between the elegant buildings of the square was soon filled by the soldiery and the crowd of lazy Neapolitans. It was a fine sight, as the sunlight fell on the bayonets and the helmets of the cavalry. All this was merely the preparation for a repetition of the sugar-plum farce of Sunday. It was a poor affair. I got well powdered with sugar plums, but the sight was hardly worth seeing.

The Toledo is a noble street. Every hour of the day, it is thronged with a dense crowd of men and women of every kind and degree. Carriages and carts drive along at full speed with a noise that would split the head of a nervous man. The shops are small, but elegant, and open on the street. Priests and monks, in every variety of dress— troops of military scholars, in cocked hats—straggling soldiers, mustachoed to the eyes—women in very neat and beautiful cos- tumes—criers of various commodities—and a host of well dressed men of all nations, together make up the crowd that swarms night and day in this street. The houses are very high and elegant. There are no sidewalks; woe to the absent man—he will be knocked down and run over twenty times a day, and have his pocket picked a hundred. A gayer and livelier scene could scarce be imagined.

The remoter and most obscure parts of this great city are quite as interesting. Here you may see an endless variety of costumes of the women, almost all beautiful and neat. There is something par- ticularly attractive about these women, who are seldom, however, handsome, properly speaking—but there is the devil in their bright faces and full rounded forms. Each town in the environs has its peculiar costume.

I saw Pompeii yesterday. From the nature of most of the utensils found there—which are of coarse workmanship, not unlike the pottery used here at this day—I was prepared to find a mean and sordid village. Not so, however. Many of the private houses were palaces. The temples were elegant pieces of architecture—so was the forum and the amphitheatre. We visited Herculaneum on our return. It is scarce worth seeing after Pompeii.

Pulcinella is a most original character. His ridicule does not spare the hero and heroine themselves. In a terrific scene of encantation and sorcery which I saw today, Pulcinella pretended at first to be very much frightened, but siezed an opportunity to knock over Death himself, who was rising out of a fiery pit to sieze him. He kicked a sultan in the face. He is always present in every tragic or pathetic scene, turning the whole to ridicule by his ludicrous caricatures or his affected sympathy. He is always planning tricks to get his best friends into a scrape.

I saw him today represented by a puppet about two feet high at a little theatre on the quay, where I bought a box for two cents and a half. There was a pit that held thirty people; an orchestra of a violin and a flageolet; and one tier of five or six boxes. Everything was well encrusted with dirt. Above the stage, which a man might cross at two strides, was the classic inscription, very instructive to the audience, "*ridendo discitur.*"[j] Another similar establishment had the following words on its roof, which was likewise embellished [with] a view of Mt. Olympus—"*castigat ridendo mores.*"[k] Most of these little theatres are open several times a day. A man stands at the door, making the loud squeaking noise which the showmen use as the voice of Punch and Judy. This invitation is accepted by vagrant *lazzaroni*, sailors and their inamoratas, idle children and so on, who fill the place in a few minutes. The violin and flute keep them quiet till all are assembled—when the doors are closed, and the piece performed in a most business-like manner. The theatre is then

[j] "Learn by laughter."—Ed.
[k] "Correct evil ways by laughter."—Ed.

cleared, and opened again after a little breathing time is allowed to the actors. Outside of these places, Punch and Judy are screaming night and day to a ragged but picturesque crowd gathered around; beside a dozen other shows of all descriptions. Here, too, are fruit-sellers, and dealers in some very strange articles of food, which I could not master philosophy enough to taste.

There is a quarter of the city inhabited exclusively by three thousand ladies whom the policy and morality of Ferdinand keeps close prisoners—a place very edifying and curious to look at. There is another quarter, known as the "Old Town," where the streets are seldom more than ten feet wide, and often not half so large, though the ancient stone houses rise to six and eight stories. Here are shops of all kinds—small taverns—wine stands—and an endless swarm of dirty but picturesque men, women, and children. Long and low arches, so dark that lamps are kept burning there all day, connect the different parts of these streets, or lead out to the quay. Sometimes there is a wide street, or a little square, completely filled with a noisy and restless crowd of fruit- and fish-dealers, and idlers. The fruit is spread on the ground, or piled up on painted stands—the seller, man or woman, never ceases from yelling and screaming at the full stretch of lungs. There is an infinite variety of costume—from the cloak, the peaked hat, and the tight breeches of the Calabrian, to the cowl, cord, and sandals of the Franciscan friar. Near an old church, in this quarter of the city, is the square where Ma(r)saniello[43] raised his revolt—now occupied chiefly by a ragged army of dealers in cloth and old iron.

I saw, in a little "show" on the quay, a number of canary-birds who would fire cannons, pretend to be dead, come to life at the word of command; drag each other in carriages; and perform a number of other feats of the same kind. Admission, two *grani*; audience, soldiers, sailors, and *lazzaroni*, which last word means nothing more than a lazy dirty lounger about the streets.

On Saturday I left Naples for Rome in the diligence, with Mr. and Mrs. Parker. Coming to a little hill a mile from the city, the six consumptive horses attached to the ponderous machine were utterly unable to drag it up, though the postillions spattered and swore *cazzo*, and kicked their gigantic boots against the gaunt ribs of the miserable beasts, and lashed till they split their livery jackets. In vain a dozen ragamuffins tugged at the wheels—nothing would move us, till the horses were taken out and a train of oxen substituted. Then, indeed, we got slowly under weigh, when *crack* went something below—a jounce followed—a scream from Mrs. Parker—and then there was another stand-still. We had broken one of the springs. The conductor and postillions, after swearing and jabbering a full half hour, resolved to return to Naples. We did so; and got refitted in the course of three hours, when we sallied out again—came to another pause at the bottom of another hill—sent for more horses—after which we proceeded prosperously enough.

A little after midnight the summons of the conductor to alight and have our baggage searched, warned us that we(re were) were passing the dominions of King Ferdinand, and entering those of His Holiness the Pope. We rubbed our eyes, groaned, and followed our baggage to the custom house. There sat three or four officials, each of whom demanded a handsome bribe—and when this vexatious business was finished, the *facchini*, or porters, came thronging before the windows with lanterns, demanding a *buonamano*, while the postillions screamed for a *bottiglia* in the rear. This road is notorious above most others for custom-house exactions. An American, jealous of his rights as a traveller, refused a few days since to satisfy their illegal demands. His trunk was broken open in a moment, and searched to the very bottom, especial care being taken to tear and soil everything as much as possible.

When I woke at sunrise, we were passing the Pontine Marshes. It was a clear cool morning—the wide flat meadows around were white with dew; the ranges of mountains in the distance—Soracte and the rest—were enveloped in a transparent veil of mists, and hung with half-illumined clouds, dissipating slowly as the sun rose upon them.

The people in the villages were a striking contrast to the Neapolitans in dress, features, and manner. They stood gazing solemnly at us, with no trace of the gaity and vivacity of their southern neighbors. The women wore a most picturesque costume. Dozens of them passed us riding astride their donkeys, like men. At length we got a glimpse of St. Peter's. On every side of us were remains of temples, aqueducts, and tombs—Mr. Parker became inspired, and spouted Cicero and Virgil. Three young Romans followed us for a mile, running along in their rags, with their dingy peaked hats in their hands, constantly exclaiming in a wailing tone: "*Eccelenz[a], eccelenz! Povero miserabile, molto (di) fame!*"—"Your eccelency, your eccelency, I am a poor miserable devil, very hungry!"

Mrs. Parker, a pretty, timid, gentle little woman, was full of curiosity to know everything and see everything. She studied every ruin as we went along in the guide book, while Mr. P. was wrapped in his own meditations. We found a "centurion," as Mr. Parker called him, mounted at the gate, ready to escort us. We passed through the grand and imposing streets of the new city, with the soldier following behind. Mrs. Parker made a sudden exclamation "Oh, only look here: *do* tell me what this is!" Her husband burst out with rather an untheological interjection, and caught me by the shoulder, "The Coliseum!" But we had only time to look up at a mountain of gigantic arches, piled one on the other, when we were buried in the narrow streets below. The hotels were all crowded. We were fortunate enough to find rooms, but some English travellers walked the streets all night.

Monday. Today is one of the great days of the Carnival. Mr. P., with his lady and myself, went in a carriage to see the "show." The streets were crowded with maskers of all description, in carriage and on foot. A blast of trumpets from the end of the Corso was the signal for all the carriages to draw up to one side and the crowd to divide, to make way for a column of the Pope's soldiers. First came the Sappers, with beards and mustache that fell over their chests, shaggy bear-skin caps, and leather aprons. Each carried a broad axe over his shoulder, and his musket slung at his back. They were savage and martial-looking fellows. A long train of soldiers followed, with a body of cavalry bringing up the rear. So much for the Pope's summary measures for preserving order. After this, the Carnival began in earnest.

It was not the solemn sugar-plum foolery of Naples, but foolery entered into with right heartiness and goodwill. There were Devils of every description, from the imp of two feet high to a six-foot monster with horns, hoofs, and tail, and a female friend on each arm. There were harlequins with wooden swords, or with bladders tied to poles—which they beat over the heads of all they met—Pulcinellas, and an endless variety of nondescripts. Some of the carriages were triumphal cars gayly ornamented—full of maskers, men and girls, in spangled dresses. Instead of sugar-plums, they flung flowers at one another. Some of the women wore wire masks or little vizards, which left the lower part of the face bare; many, however, had no covering at all to their faces. Few had any regular beauty of features, but there was an expression of heart and spirit, and a loftiness, beside, which did not shame their birth. They flung their flowers at you with the freest and most graceful action imaginable. To battle with flowers against a laughing and conscious face—showering your ammunition thick as the carriage slowly passes the balcony— then straining your eyes to catch the last glance of the black-eyed witch and the last wave of her hand as the crowd closes around her— all this is no contemptible amusement.

The inferior class of women walked in the street, very prettily dressed in a laced jacket and a white frock that came an inch below the knee. Some were disguised as boys—some wore fierce mustache which set off well enough their spirited faces. Hundreds of men were shouting round the carriages with flowers for sale. Thus it went on for hours, till the report of a cannon gave the signal for clearing the Corso for the horse-race.

I saw Pulcinella at the theatre in the evening, in great perfection. He is *not*, then, peculiar to Naples, as somebody told me he was.

Tuesday. The last day of the Carnival[44]—a concentration of all its frolics. The Corso and the squares and streets for a great distance round were crowded with carriages and maskers again. The Corso is a noble street, of a most grand and solemn architecture, befitting Rome. Today it had little of its usual air of stately magnificence. Every window and balcony was filled with people, and hung with rich crimson hangings. The crowd shouted, laughed, and danced with redoubled vigor. The cannon fired at length. The carriages withdrew down the side streets, leaving the Corso a long perspective of gaudily attired houses and palaces, with a restless throng of fluttering plumes and spangled dresses from end to end. A body of troops marched into it again, dividing the throng to right and left, constantly dropping its rear files for sentinels as it had passed along, so that when it reached the end of the street, it had dissolved away to nothing. There was a clear space down the centre, and the people crowded on each side.

The horses were to start from the upper end of the Corso, where it expands into a square, surrounded by fine palaces and churches. The people sat on raised benches on each side of this square; a strong rope was stretched across the upper end, to restrain the horses till the signal should be given. Near this, under a canopy, sat the officers of the state.

At length a body of dragoons rode in, circling around the space, while their officer made his obeisance before the seats of the senate. They then passed out. There was a yell from the crowd without, and the horses were brought in, each by two grooms, snorting and plunging with terror. They had leaden balls, set round with needles, hung against their sides, to spur them as they ran, which they do without riders. There were large sheets of thin metal and gilded paper tied to their manes and backs. For a moment, there was an active struggle between the grooms and the frightened horses—then at a signal, down went the rope, and the horses sprang away at full speed down the Corso. The yells of the people passed down the street along with them, growing more and more faint, till they were lost entirely.

It was now almost dark. When I went back to the Corso, the street seemed on fire through its whole length, to the very roofs of the houses. The carriages had returned; the crowd were as active as a swarm of bees; thousands of wax torches were tossed about, extinguished and lighted again. This is the game with which Carnival concludes. Everybody carries a torch which he tries to keep burning, while he extinguishes his neighbor's. Flapping of handkerchiefs, flinging of flowers, blowing, and twenty other means were used to put out the lights. At every successful attempt, the man shouted: "*Senza moccolo*." These sounds mingled into one roar which filled the street. The light of the torches glaring on the gayly dressed figures in the carriages and balconies, and then suddenly extinguished—the glittering forms of the maskers, leaping into the air to preserve their own light, or put out that of another—the shrill cries of the girls, who fought like little Amazons, and had strong arms, as I can testify —made altogether an appropriate finale to the Carnival.

There was a masked ball in the evening, where I could see nothing worth noticing.

So much for my classic "first impressions" of Rome! Yesterday was the 22nd of Feb.—the birthday of Washington. The Americans here must needs get up a dinner, with speeches, toasts, etc. It was like a visit home. There they sat, slight, rather pale and thin men, not like beef-fed and ruddy Englishmen; very quiet and apparently timid; speaking low to the waiters instead of roaring in the imperative tone of John Bull. There was not a shadow of that boisterous and haughty confidence of manner that you see among Englishmen— in fact most of them seemed a little green. A General Dix[45] presided and made a speech about the repudiation; the consul, Mr. Green[e][46] made another excellent speech—so did Dr. Howe.[47] Mr. Conrade of Virginia gave us a most characteristic specimen of American eloquence, and toasted "Washington and Cincinatus! Patrick Henry and Cicero!"

There are numbers of American artists here, some of them fine fellows. In fact, it (it) is some consolation, after looking at the thin faces, narrow shoulders, and awkward attitudes of the "Yankees," to remember that in genius, enterprise, and courage—nay, in bodily strength—they are a full match for the sneering Englishmen. Would that they bore themselves more boldly and confidently. But a time will come when they may meet Europeans on an equal footing.

Feb. 27th. A weary week of lionizing. I would not give a damn for all the churches and ruins in Rome—at least such are my sentiments at present. There is unbounded sublimity in the Coliseum by moonlight—that cannot be denied; St. Peter's, too, is a miracle in its way; but I would give them all for one ride on horseback among the Ap(p)en[n]ines. This driving all day, from morning till night, for a fortnight at a time, from church to church and ruin to ruin, keeping an account in a book of those that you have seen and those that you have not seen—it is worse than seeing nothing, and is very appropriately designated here "going through the mill." I met a self-satisfied philosopher, one Mr. Smith, at Palermo, who denied the existence of any such faculty as the imagination, and looked with great contempt on those who could find pleasure in such a childish amusement as looking at "old stones." "Don't tell me about your Tarpeian rock. I've seen it, and what's more, the feller wanted I should give him half a dollar for taking me there. 'Now look here!,' says I, 'do you s'pose I'm going to pay you for showing me this old pile of stones? I can see better rocks than this any day, for nothing; so clear out!' I'll tell you the way I do," continued Mr. Smith; "I don't go and *look* and *stare* as some people do when I get inside of a church, but I pace off the length and breadth, and then set it down on paper. Then, you see, I've got something that will keep!"[1]

I never thought, when I listened to these remarks of Mr. S. in Mr. Marston's parlor at Palermo, that I should ever feel any sympathy with him; but a week of lionizing has convinced me of the contrary. But I hope to go back among the mountains in a few days.

Yesterday I found a crowd of people in the Coliseum, attending the company of penitents, who were clothed in a dirt-colored robe, with cap and vizard of the same, and were parading from one to the other of the fourteen little chapels that stand around the arena. A cross-bearer, two lantern-bearers, and a priest led the procession. At every chapel, they kneeled; and a prayer for deliverance from certain evils was made by the priest, and followed by chants from the penitents and the crowd of people around.

A Virginian named St. Ives,[48] lately converted to Catholicism, has been trying to convert me, along with some of the Jesuits here. He has abandoned the attempt in disgust, telling me that I have not logic enough in me to be convinced of anything, to which I replied by cursing logic and logicians.

I have now been three or four weeks in Rome—have been presented to his Holiness the Pope—have visited churches, convents,

---

[1] "Mr. Smith was an upstart speculator from New York, about five feet high, and three inches broad—gulled and befooled at all hands, but fortunately about to depart this life, for he was in consumption."—F.P.

Mr. Smith and his methods of sightseeing provide the materials of Chapter XXVIII of *Vassall Morton*, pp. 162-66.—Ed.

cemeteries, catacombs, common sewers including the Cloaca Maxima, and ten thousand works of art. This will I say of Rome—that a place on every account more interesting—and which has a more vivifying and quickening influence on the faculties—could not be found on the face of the earth—or at least I should not wish to go to it, if it could.

It is as startling to a "son of Harvard" to see the astounding learning of these Jesuit fathers, and the appalling readiness and rapidity with [which] they pour forth their interminable streams of argument, as it would be to a Yankee parson to witness his whole congregation, with church, pulpit, and all, shut up within one of the great columns which support the dome of St. Peter's—a thing which might assuredly be done.

The Catholics here boast that their church never stood at so high and happy a point as now—converts are pouring in—wisdom and sanctity abound. There is an artist here, Overbeck,[49] from Germany, who is a man of wonderful genius. I visited his studio today. His works are scarce more than sketches with a pencil—but every face may be an hour's study, and speaks plainer than words the character of its author's mind: mild, earnest, and devout to enthusiasm. All his subjects are scriptural.

I went down to the Cloaca Maxima, which venerable common sewer still retains its ancient name, and still discharges its ancient office—as it has done for three thousand years, since Tullus Hostilius built it. The temples of Rome are turned into cattle-houses, or burnt into lime—the Forum has been a cow yard—but the Cloaca Maxima still belches out into the Tiber the accumulated filth of Rome, the only monument of the city that retains unaltered its original character. When the Tiber is high, the whole arch is concealed, but now you can easily see, by descending among some dirty houses and wading down an abyss of mud, a stream about a rod wide and of unexplorable depth slowly creeping along beneath the archway. It is best not to come too near—or scrutinize too closely into the nature of this subterranean river. There is good fishing there. The fish come up, as Juvenal says the pikes did in his day, to feed on the offal. Just below where it discharges into the river, you may see half a dozen or more large scoop-nets, arranged in the manner of a large water-wheel, so as to be turned by the force of the current and dip up any fish that may be swimming by. A fellow sits watching them, smoking his pipe, ready to take out the delicate morsel for the market. There are other flat nets, about twenty feet square, which are lowered into the muddy water horizontally by means of a framework of long poles; and then raised quickly up again, in the desperate hope that a fish may be passing above them. There are another kind of sportsmen about this place, and in fact all along the river, who stand on the bank with a kind of grapple made of the stem and projecting branches of a small tree, cut to a proper length. This contrivance has a long cord attached to it, coiled together on the ground like a whale-line. When they see any piece of drift wood or fragment of brush come floating down stream, they whirl the grapple once or twice round their heads, and send it flying through the air towards the valuable prize. Sometimes three or four are let fly at once for the same miserable branch of a tree—and frequently all miss, for the current runs as it used to when Horacles [Horatius] Cocles and Cloelia swam it.

The other day as I was standing in the entry of the Hotel d'Allemagne, a servant came up to me and said that my brother had been inquiring for me, and was now up stairs with another gentleman. I told him he had mistaken the person. He asked me if I was not Mr. Parkman from America—he was sure that was my name, and he would run and call my brother now. So off he went, leaving me in some curiosity, but not without a suspicion of the truth. Sure enough, John and William Hunt[50] came down stairs, six steps at a time, and had me by the hand in a moment. The last time I had seen them was at Cambridge, when they bade us good-bye at table one morning, as they were about to sail for Europe—of course we were glad enough to meet at Rome. John was grinning from ear to ear at the idea of being taken for my brother. I went round with them to their lodgings, where I enjoyed the gratifying sight of *Peirce on Sound*, and Whately's *Logic*, which John, in an ebullition of Freshman feeling, kicked up against the ceiling. The whole family of the Hunts are here.

We rode to Tivoli—the ancient Tibur—together, the other day, with Mr. P[arker] and his lady in our company. We spent some hours in making the tour of the antiquities on jackasses—saw the villa of [H]Adrian—of Cassius—the modern villa of the dukes of Ferrara, which inspired Tasso, as well it might. Saw the cascades, too; and the temple of Vesta perched on the rock above; also scrambled down into the Grotto of Neptune—in short, finished the whole job, and persuaded the jackasses to carry us back to the village. Here we dined—the whole convoy betook themselves to their carriages, leaving my old classmate [William Hunt] and myself behind to undertake an expedition back into the country, to which I had persuaded him.

Claude Lorraine[51] chose one of the landscapes of Tivoli as the subject of one of his pictures, which I have seen, I think, in the Doria palace. What is strange enough, the finest of the cascades here is artificial—formed, like that of Terni, by turning the course of the stream over the rocks. The Anio is here conducted through a channel of very great length, cut through the heart of a mountain. You can pass from end to end by means of a narrow ledge by the side of the water, which rushes along by your side very swiftly with a loud noise, and emerging to the light, leaps over a precipice some hundred feet high into a deep valley, where it tumbles and foams among the rocks for a while; but, growing calm at length, winds prettily down among the fields and olive plantations at the bottom. Numbers of little cascades come streaming down from the mountain, and from under the arches of Mecaenas' [Maecenas'] villa to join it—so with the town on the heights above, and the Campagna like a dimly seen ocean in front, it makes, just after sunset, a landscape to which Claude Lorraine has not done justice.

We got up an illumination of the subterranean passage of the river—called the Grotto of the Syrens—by having bundles of straw set on fire, and suffered to float down on the stream. The rocks about here are recent calcarious depositions, which sometimes assume very singular forms. One of them, precisely resembling the breast of a woman, was exhibited to us as a veritable relic of Lucretia, the "*putana Romana*"—as our guide informed us she was, a version of the story quite new to us.

When we looked out in the morning and found the mountains white with snow, and the *piazza* below us wet and wretched, and the sky the color of lead, I thought my Sicilian experiences were going to be revived. But we got a couple of asses and a guide, and set out. No sooner were we outside the gate, than the clouds split apart, and scattered in all directions—the sun poured down bright and clear on the country, which looked all the fresher for the last night's storm. The road was full of knots of laughing black-haired girls— now and then a priest on a donkey would come jogging past and greet them with an expression of countenance where the temporal got the better of the spiritual.

We soon left girls and villages behind, and followed the road up the banks of the Anio, a rapid and headlong torrent. Its valley soon grew quite narrow. We came to a village at the top of a rock by the bank, containing a specimen of what our guide called Cyclopean walls, though the masses of stone were square and not polygonal.[52] Further on, we stopped in the yard of the convent of San Cosinato. It stands on the edge of the precipice, which here sinks sheer down hundreds of feet to the river. We roused up a father, who led us down the face of the rock by a zigzag path hewn into it, a work of no little danger and difficulty—the roar of the river alone was enough to startle weak nerves. To our surprise, the whole face of this rough precipice was honeycombed out into sleeping rooms and little chapels; in short, a monastery of Benedictines had burrowed into the rock and lived there. I have heard of hermits thus sequestering themselves, but a whole monastery clinging to the face of a savage precipice, above a stream like the Anio, shows an admirable example of courage and enthusiasm. Over against the rock rises a shaggy and wild mountain, and looking up the stream the valley expands into a scene of wonderful beauty. I carried away a flower as a memento of the gallant monks.

While we were stopping at a dirty *osteria* to regale the asses, Hunt and I had a tub turned bottom-upwards outside and spread our provisions upon it. Very good wine here cost three cents a quart. This *osteria* was a fair specimen of its kind. In a long dirty stone room, some muleteers and others sat drinking at venerable wooden tables—while some mules were refreshing themselves hard by. I waded along through the mud and straw of the floor to the upper end, where some olive-sticks were burning under a huge tower-like chimney. In the recess of this chimney, all round the fire, low stone seats were built; from which you could look up into the black gulf above, and see volumes of smoke lighted by the rays of sunlight that came through the lateral holes where the smoke was to have escaped. A woman discharging the maternal function, two dirty girls, two cats, and several children were grouped around this singular fire-place, all staring at the stranger in silent admiration. An old sportsman, who was drinking a flask of wine, with his dogs at his knee, in one corner, told me that the wolves had lately made an irruption, and carried off eighty sheep. Wild boars also abound here. I have seen them brought into Rome in numbers.

Leaving this place, we rode on toward Subiaco in a perfect amphitheatre of mountains. Those on the right lay in dusky shadow, for the sun was setting behind them; but on the other side the enormous bare rocks were glaring in the light, with their tops still whiter than themselves with the snow. Grey villages, with light smoke hanging over them, were scattered thinly along their sides and summits, a thousand feet in the air. The air was beautifully clear, and the afternoon still as death. Some of the distant Appenines were blue as the sky itself, and peculiarly shadowed in the oblique light.

Men and women were at work, pruning in the vineyards. The forms of the women were full and graceful, and set off to the best advantage by their costume—a tight bodice, namely, usually of a bright red or green. Their headdress is a handkerchief, folded square, and falling down behind.

We came suddenly upon Subiaco. It stood on the top of a detached rocky hill, among the mountains. Goats, cattle, trains of mules and asses, women with jars of water on their heads, old woodsmen with the heavy crooked chopping knife in their girdles and a bundle of faggots on their shoulders were coming down the different pathways from the mountains toward the gate of the town—for it was near sunset. The town was already in shadow, except the castle at the top.

All this was very well; get within the gate and the scene changed. A crowded pile of high and crumbling stone houses—streets so steep that a horse cannot ascend them, and answering the purpose of a common sewer for all the filth of the inhabitants—so narrow, too, that a strip of the red sky could scarce be seen between the tottering roofs—here was Subiaco; and not Subiaco alone, but Italian country towns in general, as far as my observation goes. The women, with their water-jars, were gathered around the town fountain—more were seated about the corners in a little public square, spinning. More still were kneeling, singing vespers, in the church. The men lounged about in red breeches, smoking and staring.

In the morning we passed down through the quarter of the black-smiths, each of whom, covered with dirt and hair, was hammering and filing in a species of narrow den under the houses. Thence, we went up to the mountains. We passed a bridge thrown over a deep and narrow ravine, where the Anio came down from the valley above. It boiled savagely down at the bottom, half obscured by the olive and laurel trees that grew thick in the crevices of the ravine. We rode for a mile up the mountain till we came to a monastery of Benedictines, under an impending rock at the top. The Anio twisted about like a white thread among the rocks directly below. It was cold as winter at that height. The porter was sitting in an old carved chair, with the brass basin under his chair, in the hands of the barber; so I called the sacristan, who showed us over the place. St. Benedict must have had a peculiar taste for wild and lonely situations. They have built the monastery over the cave where he lived from his fifteenth year. One day the devil came to tempt him in the form of a woman: the saint sprang from her embraces and threw himself upon a little thicket of briers that grew close by. They show the briers to this day, still growing in the same place! I was under strong tempta-tion to beg the fathers to let me stay in their monastery a few days—it is as strange in its interior as in its situation. Full of relics of the middle ages—and contains halls and vaults built partly by art, and partly formed by the natural rock. It seems doomed to speedy destruction. There is a deep crack in the cliff above, which leans forward, as if every moment to fall. I asked the fathers why they took no measures to secure it in its place. "Oh," they piously replied, "St. Benedict will see to that!"

Some hours after, when we had scrambled among the Appenines by a miserable mule-path, we came to a little village called Rocca di

San Stephano, where they insist that St. Stephen was stoned to death. Here was scarce a male inhabitant, except the *padrone* of the *osteria*, which consisted of one dirty and crumbling room, with a charcoal fire in the middle. Beside the *padrone*, there was a fat vender of salt and tobacco. The rest of the men were at work in the Roman Campagna, on the lands of the nobles. We spread out provisions by the fire and proceeded to eat, while the *padrone* and his friend looked on in horror and astonishment to see us carve with an old dagger, which was the only good knife we could find at Tivoli. The salt and tobacco man's wonder was still further excited by the tongue we brought with us—he had never seen such a thing, and opened his eyes as wide as his prot[r]uding cheeks would let him. We handed him a piece. He looked at it—smelt of it—laughed a sort of gurgling laugh from the depths of his vitals; then mustered his resolution and ate it. The other man hesitated. He turned his piece over and over, as if it might be poison, which, though it suited us, would not agree with a Christian constitution. He ate half at last, and kept the rest, as he said, to show to his friends.

They asked us if we were "*Inglesi?*" "No." "*Francesi?*" "No"; whereupon they looked doubtingly at each other, as if to say: "They are neither Italians, nor English, nor French—therefore they must be the devil!"

After traversing a great chesnut forest which covered the mountains far and wide, we saw a little village before us, perched on one of the highest peaks. We clambered up the steep pathway. Below and around lay in the sun a vast expanse of mountains, a panorama embracing the sea itself and the villages of the remote interior.

The battlements were ruined—the houses crumbling—the people dirty—but here we found none of the execrable inns of Sicily. The old *padrone* sat smoking at his porch, just within the gateway: off went his hat from his grey head, and with a multitude of Italian congees he ushered us into a large old house, containing long suites of rooms, some tapestried and furnished with ancient beds and chairs—others hung with blackened and dingy pictures. The *padrone* is evidently the great man of the village. Among the pictures are old portraits of knights in armor, priests, cardinals, and monks.

The beggars of Civitella call every stranger a *pittore*, because painters are usually the only visitors of the place. Well may they come, for the situation of Civitella is magnificent. I sat till dark on a square Pelasgian fort, older than the Bible, watching the changes in the scenery as the sun went down. Hunt betook himself to sketching at once.

The old man had a fireplace not unlike a Yankee one. I spent most of the evening trying to illuminate him on the subject of the Indians, about whom he showed a very eager curiosity and asked questions which showed great acuteness and some information. His son, a stout fellow with less thirst for knowledge, stood behind, contenting himself with remarks on the state of the paths. Two or three priests, in their black breeches and three-cornered scrapers, dropped in to see their friend—then came the full storm and rattle of Italian conversation, with the true gesticulations, shrugs, exclamations, and offerings of the snuff-box.

We went next day to Palestrina, the ancient Preneste. Here we examined the Pelasgian walls, and the ruins of the temple of Fortune, with the extraordinary mosaic found there—and here we found another remarkable *albergo*. It was kept by two sisters, one of whom might be about eighteen and the other twenty, and both handsome as the sun. They saw our admiration, which by no means displeased them. We spent the evening before the fire talking with them, though Hunt, who does not speak a word of Italian, kept up his share of the conversation by signs. My Italian was not much better; but the girls were as intelligent as they were handsome, and, I think, as virtuous.

At six in the morning I was awakened by hearing a modest voice below the window pronounce the word, "*Monsieur.*" I looked out and saw our guide standing below, looking patiently and pensively up at the window, like a faithful dog—his invariable custom, for having no means of knowing the exact hour, he usually takes his stand under the window at least an hour before the time we tell him. Taking leave of our handsome hostesses—who looked upon us with some astonishment as natives of a country five thousand miles off— we rode on to Cara. Here our good luck in *albergos* failed us. We found rather a dirty hole, but no match for the inns of Sicily. It was a *trattoria*, or restaurant, and therefore had a public room where a strange group congregated in the evening before the fire. In the corner crouched two or three old crones, like living skeletons. An unshaven country-man sat on one side—fat and silent loungers from the town, with infant mustache—shabby dandies in cloaks—children and dogs, crouching together on the hearth. At a little distance, two or three thin-visaged and savage-looking *contadini* stood erect and motionless in the glare of the fire. Our guide Guiseppe sat drinking wine at the long tables ranged around the barn-like room. He had a very pretty girl to wait on him, who would come from time to time and stoop over the fire, so as to show to the best advantage her classic features and the enormous silver pin in her hair. Hunt and I sat telling each other college stories and recalling college recollections till the people had withdrawn from the room, and left us almost alone, in front of a glowing pile of half consumed embers.

The next day we went to Vellitri [Velletri] where we hired a conveyance to Rome.

Sunday, March—— [*24*] '*44.* There was High Mass at St. Peter's this afternoon. Several thousand people were in the church—hundreds of candles were burning about the altar, which was one blaze of light. By way of guarding the flesh of Christ from the too near approach of the over-pious, a line of Swiss halberdiers was drawn before the shrine, with their black hats, and the bright blades of their weapons rising above the kneeling crowd. The responses sounded through this gigantic church like a moaning of wind. There was previously the usual service in the Capella del Coro—where eunuchs supply the place of women in the choir.

Tuesday. I went off to Albano in the public carriage. In the morn-ing, I got a mule to ride up to the convent of the Passionists, at Rocca di Papa, some miles off. The Passionists are, I believe, the strictest of the orders of monks—wear hair-cloth next the skin—lash their backs with "disciplines" made of little iron chains, and mortify the flesh in various other similar ways. I had some desire to see the mode of life of these holy men, so went to ask permission of the superior to stay in the convent a few days. I bestraddled a gigantic jackass, which no sooner came to the steep part of the road, than he stopped with an expression of quiet determination. The boy cudgelled him in the rear with full force—the beast was immoveable. A man pulled him by the haltar—he grumbled his dissatisfaction and began to pull backwards, upon which I kicked him and beat him till my bones ached. He bore it for awhile—then down went his head and up flew his hind legs into the air, perpendicularly. Then he rubbed against the wall, to scrape my legs, then he reared, then twisted himself about till his head and tail were close together— then began a series of plungings and kickings that came near unseating me. The boy remarked that he was "*molto furioso,*" and ran off for another. This next one proved manageable, and climbed peacefully enough up the mountain; till reaching a wooded height, I saw Lake Albano, black as ink and set deep among the hills. The waters looked deep and sullen, as they lay directly at the foot of the steep hill, far below us. We circled half way round them among the rocks and woods till we came to the convent, which was a very large and ancient building standing alone on the rocky side of the mountain. Within, it was the gloomiest and darkest I have seen. The superior came out of his cell, like a rat out of his hole. I told him what I wanted. He said he was very sorry, etc., but the rules of his order would not allow him to receive me without a permission from his superior at Rome—which fairly defeated my purpose. Mancinelli had told me that no permission was necessary. I remounted the jackass and rode down again, thinking to go to Rome immediately, get the permission, and return next day. But the public carriage had already left Albano, and no other conveyance was to be had except at a most exorbitant price. I therefore walked out to see the Lake of Nemi. It was a most beautiful morning, and the scenery looked the brighter for the rain of the night before. The chesnuts and the elms were just budding—hundreds of spring flowers were scattered about the sides of the hills. Every place was alive with lizzards—most of whom had their tails bitten off in fights with each other. In the bottom of the wooded valley, or ravine, which separates Albano from Aricia, groups of women in their bright red national dress were washing cloths in the brook, and hanging them to dry on the branches of the olive trees.

The Lake of Nemi is like its neighbor of Albano, except that (that) it lies still deeper among the hills, and is much smaller. But when I saw it, the sun poured down bright and hot upon it and the mountains that fence it round, and puffs of wind rippled its surface—it had none of that cold and deadening aspect which Byron attributes to it, but was one of the noblest sights I have seen in Italy. One little village stands half way up one of the mountains—all the rest is a solitude of woods.

I had made my breakfast of a couple of rolls, sitting by one of the fountains by the roadside; and by the time I got back to Albano, felt a little hungry. I saw a sign over a door, "*Locanda del Americano*," which I accepted as an invitation to enter. Neither the hostess, nor any one there, knew the origin of the name of their house—so that whether some enterprising Yankee had once actually set up a *locanda* in Albano, or whether the name was given out of pure love for the Americans, I cannot say. Americans are almost universally liked here, probably as contrasting favorably with the surly and haughty English. Talking with a priest the other day, he asked me of what nation I was—when I told him, he made a low bow and exclaimed, "*Bravo Americano!*"

This place at Albano did not, however, do the nation much credit. Wine and maccaroni were, as usual, all that could be had. Even bread had to be sent for. A dozen laborers were quarrelling over three cents worth of wine, on the question of who was to pay. This was an establishment of the middle class—the greater part are a kind of half-subterranean apartment, set round with large and dirty wine-casks, and furnished with dirtier tables and benches. Here there is a great crowd of ragamuffins, drinking and laughing—but seldom drunk—and usually attended by a very pretty girl. In Albano, nearly every other house has the green bough, or the painted door-post, or the little sign "*Spaccio di vino*"—to indicate that wine is to be sold.

Rome, Friday. Yesterday, I went to the Capuchins for permission to stay there, which was refused peremptorily; but the Passionists[m] told me to come again at night, and they would tell me if I could be admitted. I came as directed, and was shown a room in the middle of the building, which contains hundreds of chambers connected by

[m] "Their convent at Rome, beyond the Coliseum."—F.P.

long and complicated passages, hung with pictures of saints and crucifixes. The monk told me that when the bell rang, I must leave my hat, come out, and join the others—and then, displaying some lives of the saints and other holy works on the table, he left me to my meditations. The room has a hideous bleeding image of Christ, a vessel of holy-water, and a number of holy pictures—a bed—a chair —and a table. Also, hung against the wall, was a "Notice to persons withdrawn from the world for spiritual exercises, to the end that they may derive all possible profit, from their holy seclusion!" The "notice" prohibited going out of the chamber without necessity— prohibited also speaking at any time—or making any noise what- ever—writing, also—and looking out of the window. It enjoined the saying of three Ave Marias, *at least*, at night—also to make your own bed, etc.

"The devil!" thought I. "Here is an adventure!" The secret of my getting in so easily was explained. There were about thirty Italians retired from the world, preparing for the General Con- fession[53]—and even while I was coming to this conclusion, the bell clanged along the passage, and I went out to join the rest. After climbing several dark stairs, and descending others—pulling off their scull-caps to the great images of Christ on the landing places— they got into a little chapel, and after kneeling to the altar, seated themselves. The shutters were closed, and the curtains drawn immediately after—there was a prayer with the responses—and then a sermon of an hour and a half long, in which the monk kept felici- tating himself and his hearers that they were of the genuine church— little thinking that there was a black sheep among his flock. The sermon over, we filed off to our rooms. In five minutes the bell rang again for supper—then we marched off to a *conversazione* in another part of the building—where the injunction of silence was taken off. I told the directing priest that I was a Protestant—he seemed a little startled at first—then insinuated a hope that I might be reclaimed from my damnable heresy, and said that an American had been there before, who had been converted—meaning my acquaintance St. Ives. He then opened a little battery of arguments upon me—after which he left me, saying that a lay brother would make the rounds to wake us before sunrise.

The lay brother came in fact, but not before I had been waked by a howling procession of the Passionists themselves, who passed along about midnight. There was a mass, another prayer, and another endless sermon—soon after which we were summoned to coffee. I observed several of the Italians looking hard at me, as I drank a glass of water instead of coffee on account of my cursed neuralgia. Doubtless they were thinking within themselves, "How that pious man is mortifying the flesh!"

There was an hour's repose allowed—after which came another sermon in the chapel. This over, a bell rang for dinner—which was at eleven in the morning. The hall was on the lower floor—very long, high, and dark—with pannels of oak—and ugly pictures on the walls —narrow oaken tables set all round the sides of the place. The monks were all there, in their black robes, with the emblem of their order on the breast. They had thin scowling faces, as well they might, for their discipline is tremendously strict. Before each was placed an earthen bottle of wine, and a piece of bread, on the bare board. Each drew a cup, a knife, fork, and wooden spoon from a drawer under the table—the attendant lay brothers placed a bowl of singular-looking soup before each, and they eat in lugubrious silence. The superior of the order sat at the upper end of the hall—a large and powerful man, who looked sterner, if possible, than his inferiors. We who sat at another table were differently served—with rice, eggs, fish, and fruit. No one spoke; but from a pulpit above, a monk read at the top of his lungs from a book of religious precepts, in that peculiar drawling tone which the Catholics employ in their exercises. There was, apparently, little fructification in the minds of his hearers. The monks eat and scowled—the lay-men eat, and smiled at each other, exchanging looks of meaning, though not a word passed between them. There were among them men of every age, and of various condition—from the field laborer to the gentleman of good birth. The meal concluded with a prayer and the growling responses of the Passionists—who then filed off through the galleries to their dens, looking like the living originals of the black pictures that hang along the whitewashed walls.

A monk has just been here, trying to convert me, but was not so good a hand at argument, or sophistry, as the Jesuits. I told him that he could do nothing with me; but he persisted, clapping his hand on my knee and exclaiming: "Ah, *figlio*, you will be a good Catholic,

no doub !" There was a queer sort of joviality about him. He kept
offering me his snuff-box; and when he thought he had made a good
hit in argument, he would wink at me with a most comical expression, as if to say: "You see, you can't come round me with your
heresy." He gave over at the ringing of a bell which summoned us
to new readings and lecturings in the chapel, after which we were
turned out into the garden of the convent, where we lounged along
walks shaded with olives and oleanders. Padre Lucca, the directing
priest, talked over matters of faith to me. He was an exception to the
rest of the establishment—plump and well-fed, with a double chin
like a bull-frog, and a most contented and good-humored countenance. As we past the groups of Italians, they took their hats off
and kissed his hand reverently, and then immediately began to joke
and laugh with him as if he was a familiar friend—as I suppose he
was, as I have observed that many of the priests are to their parish-
ioners.

The Coliseum is close to the window of my room, with Rome
behind it—gardens in front, and endless ruins—arches—columns—
walls—and fountains—around. Now—about sunset—a hundred different church bells are ringing in the city, and the dome of St. Peter's
is red in the light of the setting sun. It is a sight that would intoxicate
an antiquary, and is pleasant enough to anybody.

After supper tonight some of the Italians in the *conversazione*
expressed great sympathy for my miserable state of heresy—one of
them, with true charity according to his light, said that he would
pray to the Virgin, who could do all things, to show me the truth.
The whole community assembled to vespers. The dark and crowded
chapel fairly shook with the din of more than a hundred manly voices
chanting the service.

There is nothing gloomy or morose in the religion of these Italians
here; no camp-meeting long faces. They talk and laugh gaily in the
intervals allowed them for conversation; but when the occasion calls
it forth, they speak of religion with an earnestness, as well as a cheerfulness, that shows that it has a hold on their hearts.

Saturday. This morning, among the rest, they went through the
Exercise of the *Via Crucis*, which consists in moving in a body around
the chapel, where are suspended pictures, fourteen in number, repre-

senting different scenes in the passion of Christ. Before each of these, they stop—the priest reads the appropriate prayer, and expressions of contrition from the book, repeats a "Pater Noster," etc.—and so they make the circuit of the whole. I saw the same ceremony on a larger scale in the Coliseum, without knowing what it was.

A thin, hollow-eyed father tried to start my heresy this morning, but was horrified at the enormity of my disbelief; and when I told him that I belonged to a Unitarian family, he rolled up his blood-shot eyes in their black sockets, and stretched his skinny neck out of his cowl, like a turtle basking on a stone in summer. He gave me a little brass medal of the Virgin, with a kind of prayer written on it. This medal he begged me to wear round my neck, and to repeat two or three "Aves" now and then. It was by this means, he said, that Ratisbon the Jew was converted not long since; who, though he wore the medal and repeated the "Aves" merely to get rid of the impor-tunities of a Catholic friend, yet nevertheless was favored with a miraculous vision of the Virgin, whereupon he fell on his knees, and was joined to the number of the Faithful. I told the monk that I would wear the medal, if he wished me to, but should not repeat the "Aves"—so I have it now round my neck, greatly to his satisfaction. Miracles, say all the Catholics here, happen frequently now-a-days. The other day, a man was raised to life who had just died in con-sumption—and now is walking the streets in complete health!

These Italians have come to the seclusion of this convent in order that their minds may not be distracted by contact with the world, and that the religious sentiments may grow up unimpeded, and receive all possible nutriment from the constant exercises in which they are engaged. It is partly, also, with the intention of preparing them for the General Confession. It is only for a few days in the year that any are here. Their "exercises" are characteristic of the Church. The forms of prayer are all written down—they read, repeat, and sing—very little time is allowed them for private examinations and meditations, and even in these they are directed by a printed card hung in each of the rooms and containing a list of the subjects on which they ought to examine themselves—together with a form of contrition to be repeated by them. The sermons and readings are full of pictures of Christ's sufferings, exhortations to virtue, etc., but

contain not a syllable of doctrine. One of the first in the printed list
of questions which the self-examiner is to ask himself, is· "Have I
ever dared to inquire into the mysteries of the Faith?"

Sunday. This is Palm Sunday—the first day of the famous *Settimana
Santa*—the Holy Week. I determined to get out of the convent and
see what was going on. The day and night previous I had worn the
medal, but had no vision of the Virgin—at least of Santissima Maria.[54]
Padre Lucca was unfeignedly sorry to have me go with unimpaired
prospects of damnation. He said he still had hopes of me, and taking
the kindest leave of me, gave me a book of Catholic devotions, which
I shall certainly keep in remembrance of a very excellent man. He
looked at the book I had been reading the night before, and expressed
his approbation. It was a life of Blessed Paul of the Cross, detailing
among other matters how the apostle hated women with a holy
and religious hatred, justly regarding them as types of the devil and
fountains of unbounded evil to the sons of men—and how when
women were near, he never raised his eyes from the ground, but
continually repeated "Pater Nosters" that the malign influence might
be averted.

When I got into the fresh air, I felt rather glad to be free of the
gloomy galleries and cells—which nevertheless contain so much to
be admired. I went to St. Peter's, where thousands of soldiers stood
forming a hollow square, where a procession of bishops, cardinals,
and all the high dignitaries of the Church were moving round in
procession with palm-branches in their hands. The Pope was in the
midst, seated on a species of canopied throne borne on the shoulders
of men, with his Swiss guard round him, one of whom bore a sword
whose blade—six feet long—represented flames of fire.

There was no more of this till the Wednesday after, when *Tenebrae*
was sung in the Capella del Coro at St. Peter's. On the three remaining days of the week, the Church was to celebrate by appropriate
ceremonies the scenes of Christ's passion. On Thursday there was
High Mass in the Sistine Chapel, whence the consecrated bread, or
Christ himself, was borne in solemn procession to the Pauline Chapel,
the other side of the hall, where it was enclosed in a gold box, with

the figure of a lamb upon it. This was to represent the burial of
Christ; or rather, as they maintain, was in fact his burial. The box,
called the Sepulchre, was placed in the midst of the high altar in the
midst of a thousand candles which illuminated the darkened chapel,
and the crowd rushed in and kneeled down before it. The cursing of
Jews, heretics, etc., and the blessing of the people was the next
ceremony. The Pope was borne as before on the shoulders of men to
the window of the Loggia in front of the church—a cardinal came
forward and damned us all in a loud voice, the people taking off
their hats, and most of the heretics imitating them, in ignorance of
the compliment they were receiving. There were several regiments
of the Pope's army drawn up in a hollow square, in the middle of
the Piazza, which was thronged with an endless multitude. Some of
them had brought bags of seeds and other things, which they held
over their heads to receive the benefit of the Pope's blessing. His
Holiness stretched his arms towards them, and immediately the bells
of the city rang by a signal, cannon fired, and then the crowd rushed
at full speed up the steps, and pushed—fighting, scrambling, and
laughing—through the doors to see the Pope wash the feet of thirteen
Pilgrims, in imitation of the humbleness of Christ. I went up immediately to the Sala Regia, where a dense crowd was close wedged on
each side of the lines of soldiers, who kept the passage open for the
Pope to come out. He appeared at last, seated under his canopy,
surrounded by his cardinals, bishops, and the soldiers of his Swiss
guard, who to-day wore a steel helmet and cuirass. The instant he
was gone, the crowd pushed furiously towards the door of the
Loggia, where the Pope was to wait on the Pilgrims at table. The
women screamed and fainted; the men swore. The soldiers stood
composedly leaning on their muskets, unmoveable as statues. The
people most distant would push—but when the[y] found themselves
near the line of mustachoed guards, they recoiled. The door was
thrown open at last, which redoubled the scrambling and cursing.
In the Loggia, which is a lofty and richly decorated hall, a table was
set, adorned with the images of the apostles, and placed so high that
it could be seen above the heads of the crowd. There we stood an
hour—no man could stir an inch—some grew cross—others laughed.
At length there was a loud murmuring, or growling, among the

crowd in the courts and staircases below. It increased every moment
—the crowd in the Loggia grew restless, talked louder, and swayed
to and fro. Cardinals and bishops jumped up on the seats of the table
and stretched out their hands to impose silence. The Swiss, also,
who had stood motionless hitherto at their stations round the hall,
stirred in their corselets, and struck the butt of their halberds on the
floor. At last the pilgrims,[n] dressed in white, filed in and took their
stand before the table. Some looked embarrassed; some tried to keep
from laughing; and others coolly surveyed the crowd. The Pope came
in, surrounded by cardinals and prelates, to make an exhibition of
his humbleness. He held a gold basin to each of the pilgrims, who
pretended to wash his hands in it. They then took their seats. A
cardinal kneeled and presented a dish to the Pope, who passed it to
a pilgrim, who rose and received it, bowing with the profoundest
reverence. When all were served, they began to eat, but apparently
with no great relish. The Pope walked to and fro, with folded hands,
looking as meek as a drowned kitten. He afterwards poured out a
glass of wine apiece for the pilgrims, and then left them. The
Italians seemed to regard the affair as an amusement; indeed one
who stood by me said: "They expect us to feel reverence—it is
impossible."

The soldiers marched to their quarters with reversed arms, in
token of mourning for the death of Christ—to my thinking, one of the
richest ceremonies of the day.

Two public carriages—with fourteen travellers—have been robbed
by the *banditti* between here and Naples, and the travellers in one of
them handsomely whipped with sticks. The reason of an attack so
unusual: a jackass who was coming to Rome with several thousand
francs, thought he would insure his safety on the road by hiring an
escort—so he got *one* gendarme. The robbers heard of it—eight of
them armed to the teeth came down from the mountains—the
gendarme ran for it—the conducter lay down bellowing under the
wheels—while the fellows rifled everything.

I heard it computed that there are forty thousand strangers at
Rome, which must, however, be a great exaggeration. The English

[n] "They were no pilgrims, but priests, intended to represent the apostles."—F.P.

are the most numerous—esteemed and beloved as usual. One of them, standing in St. Peter's before the ceremony yesterday, civilly exclaimed: "How long does this damned Pope expect us to stand here waiting for him?" A priest who spoke English reminded him that since he had come to Rome, it was hoped that he would conform to the usages, or at least refrain from insulting the feelings of those around. The Englishman answered by an insolent stare; then, turning his back, he said: "The English *own* Rome!"

These ceremonies of Holy Week, about which so much is said, would not be worth seeing were it not for the crowd of people they draw together. On Good Friday, they celebrated, by anticipation, the resurrection. I was standing at the door of the Capella del Coro at St. Peter's, when Mancinelli came up and joined me. The choir were singing in a dismal and lugubrious tone—the picture behind the altar was hidden by a veil—the bishop sat with his hands before him, with his mouth pursed down, and his fat face miraculously long—all the priests looked wretched and disconsolate, as if afflicted with some awful disaster. "He is not up yet," whispered Mancinelli to me, in explanation of this dismal appearance of things. But all at once the choir came out with a grand crash—a bell began to ring— two or three cannon were fired from the Castle of St. Angelo—the priests and the bishop rolled up their eyes in an ecstasy—and the curtain was drawn aside from the picture. "He is up now," said Mancinelli. "He is just out of de tomb—now you may see how happy they all look; now de soldiers will not carry their guns upside down any more, because Christ is risen. The damn fools! Now see them all kneel—let us go away."

On Easter Sunday the Pope blessed a huge army assembled in front of the Church, for the second time. That night St. Peter's was illuminated by myriads of candles, disposed over its whole front to the very top of the cross. It was a kind of phosphorescent light— faint and beautiful. At eight o'clock all changed in a moment. Bright fires kindled in a moment over all the church and the collonnade around the piazza. St. Peter's was all at once a glare of light, and cast strong shadows among the dense crowd in front. It was a sight well worth all the rest of Holy Week.

Wolfe's Monument, c. 1830

Water color drawing by Lieutenant Colonel James Pattison Cockburn

(Coverdale Collection No. 343)

On Monday there was an exhibition of fireworks at the castle of St. Angelo, which in grandeur and magnificence more resembled an eruption of Mt. Etna than any artificial illumination I ever saw. This was the end of Holy Week.

The next day I left Rome for Florence, in the diligence—and left it with much regret and a hope to return. A young American named Marquand went with me. After two days and nights we reached Florence. A manly and soldier-like young Irish gentleman,[55] with his sister, and an old Frenchman with a lady to match and two young ladies beside, were the fellow passengers of Marquand and myself in the diligence. One of the Frenchman's convoy was an English girl, very spirited and intelligent and a Catholic—but a few years too old to make converts.

In Florence everything speaks of the middle ages and of the Medici. The Duomo is an enormous Gothic church, dark and gloomy, with stained windows. The Piazza del Granduca is surrounded by dark Gothic palaces, and has in its centre an equestrian statue of Cosmo I, returning from the conquest of Sienna. The picture galleries of the Pitti palace and of the Galleria Reale far surpass any in Rome—but there are few good statues except the "Venus de Medici" and her companions in the Tribune.

A quiet and beautiful place, full of ancient palaces and churches— the Arno dividing it in the middle, with four noble stone bridges thrown across, and a perspective of mountains and woods between the lines of fine buildings, both up and down the stream. No beggars in the streets—the people civil and goodnatured.

Sunday night thousands of people were gathered together in the Piazza Granduca, each with a lottery ticket in his or her hands, waiting for the drawing. The proceeds of this lottery go to the assigning of dowries, of ten dollars each, to poor girls who are in a hurry to get married. The people were excited, but in great good humor. This lottery was in celebration of the approaching marriage of the Grand Duke's daughter with Leopold of Bavaria, which marriage took place to-day in the Duomo. The people were *invited* by a notice at the street corners to hang tapestry from their windows

—accordingly the street glistened with red and green silk. Mr. Payson, American Consul at Messina, whom I was fortunate enough to meet here, was with me in the church. The church was illuminated, and crowded with the scum of Florence—we got wedged in the dirtiest part of it. Mr. P., who is six feet and a quarter high, saw the top of the bride's headdress. I saw nothing but a fat hog of a priest, who stood in his regimentals just within the line of soldiers before me. Before it was over, I got out. The square in front was full. I had scarce got into a breathing place when there was the rush of a signal rocket from the dome of the church; then a tremendous cannonading in the distance; then a stunning crash of musketry from two regiments drawn up close by, followed by a general start and squall from the women. I saw afterwards the bride and bridegroom, as they left the church in their splendid carriage, covered with gilding and liveried servants and drawn by six noble horses.

I went to the studio of Powers[56] the sculptor, a noble looking fellow and a wonderful artist. I have seen Florence—that is, I have had a glance at everything there, but one might stay with pleasure for months. Its peculiar architecture and its romantic situation make it striking enough at first sight, but the interest increases, instead of diminishing. It is impossible to have seen enough of its splendid picture galleries, gardens, and museums. The people, too, are as attentive and obliging as the rest of the Italians—and the town is not infected with cicerones and other beggars. There is, however, one public character, on the stage for these ten years past, who generally astonishes foreigners a little. I was sitting in a *caffè* one morning when I saw a very pretty woman, about twenty-five, with a basket of flowers on her arm, dancing about the sidewalk and distributing her flowers to every decent-looking person she met. She caught my eye fixed on her, and bounded into the *caffè* with a large bunch of flowers, which she fastened into my button hole; laughed, and ran off to repeat the same operation on somebody else. She must once have been extremely handsome—she was very good-looking still; and looked all the better for a most inimitable expression of arch impudence acquired in the course of her flower-dealing speculations, and in the other avocations which no doubt she follows. Her plan is to give flowers to all the strangers she can find, and trust to their generosity for her pay at some future day. She is sure to get twice the value of her flowers—at least if others treat her as well as I did.

On Wednesday I left Florence, unsatisfied but unable to stay longer. After all, I shall not see Granada—at least for some years; thanks to the cursed injury[57] that brought me to Europe: for as I find no great improvement, I judge it best to see what a French doctor can do for me, instead of running about Spain. I called a *facchino* to carry down my baggage to the diligence office for Milan, but was answered: "*Non si puo andare, signore; bisogna aspettare, perchè è morto il nostro primo ministro dello [di] stato.*" While I was wondering what connexion the death of the first minister of state could have with the detention of my baggage, the street before the hotel door was suddenly filled with a dense crowd of people, all scrambling in the direction of the Cathedral, as if some extraordinary sight was to be seen. The throng seemed interminable—the whole length of the street was black with it—even one of the distant bridges of the Arno was covered with men, women, and children. It was late, and the diligence waits for no man; I exhorted the *facchino* to be up and doing —he expanded his hands and shrugged his shoulders, by way of expressing the helplessness of any attempt to make head against such a current; when providentially a large waggon, with two furious horses and a reck[l]ess driver, came up the street, scattering the crowd to right and left and jamming them against the sides of the houses, as it came on like a war-chariot driving through the ranks of a hostile army. The *facchino* saw his chance—made a desperate effort, and siezed the tail of the waggon fast with one hand, while he dragged his little cart of baggage with the other. Thus we got in good time to the office. I bade adieu to Mr. and Mrs. Payson, who with their daughter have just arrived from Messina, and of whose usual kindness to strangers I have certainly had my full share.

The diligence was full of Frenchmen. In one day and one night we got to Bologna. Here, in the yard of the office, among the soldiers and other officials who stood with folded arms listlessly staring at the strangers, was an animal nearly seven feet high, with a face like a large baboon. His motions, too, exactly resembled a large monkey's.

He bounded about, swinging himself up and down the diligence, tossing about heavy trunks and bales as if they were feathers, with his long muscular arms. He kept his eyes rolling about in his head, glancing at everything in the yard with an expression of infinite alacrity and anxiety; and whenever he saw anything that met his disapproval, he would jump to rectify it, with a sort of angry chattering in his throat. He was a deaf mute. I wanted my passport to be taken from the police, and applied for that purpose to the conductor of the diligence, who referred me to this human baboon. I protested against the employment of such a negotiator, but the conductor assured me that all would be safe in his hands. The animal stood by, meanwhile, attempting to express, by horrible contortions of his features, his sense of responsibility; and kept pressing his enormous skinny hand upon his heart. I gave him the commission—and in fact, when I entered the yard next morning, the first object I met was the mute bounding with a loud chattering towards me, with the passport in his hand. He took off his hat most gracefully when I gave him two *pauls* for his trouble.

Bologna is a strange-looking place. Here is none of the gaiety, the noise, the rush, and the endless variety of picturesque costume you see at Naples. The people walk gravely about their business—those of them that have any business. The streets seem, by comparison with the cities of Southern Italy, quite deserted—but the architecture is beautiful. Every sidewalk is beneath an elegant portico, supported by rows of columns—often of marble—which run the whole length of the streets and make a very fine appearance, especially when these long collonnades are lighted in the evening.

The Church of St. Petronio—a very ancient and very large Gothic building—is famous as having been the scene of Charles V's coronation. The roof is supported by innumerable lofty and slender columns—every side chapel has a splendid stained window, which sheds its peculiar light over the church. The scutcheons of noble houses—the tombs of nobles—the relics of saints—and a number of ancient pictures and effigies, give the old church an air of feudal times. The piazza in front wears an aspect in accordance with the dingy walls and heavy massive arches of the old palaces about it, and the high tower of Asinelli rising above the houses a short way off.

The next day, getting under weigh again, we passed through the duchy of Modena, and met the Duke in his carriage. In the city of Modena, I found an Italian translation of *The Last of the Mohicans*. I have seen translations of nearly all Cooper's novels, here and in Sicily.

We next entered the duchy of Parma. At the city, the diligence was to make a stay of some hours. I went out in search of a dinner, and enquired of a man, who was sitting at his shop door, if he could direct me to a *trattoria*, or restaurant. "*Signore*," he replied, "come with me, and I will show you the best *trattoria* in Parma." Passing a street or two, he opened a little door which led into a black entry, whence another smaller door conducted to a flight of stone steps. I stumbled down these steps and found myself in a twilight den with a mud floor, where a charcoal fire was burning in a corner, and two dirty blackguards were devouring something at an oak table such as you see in the lowest *osterias* and wineshops. Some hens and a few disgusting children were wandering about the floor. The *padrone*, a lubberly fellow with a red cap, emerged from a dark corner. "Would your excellency like dinner? Please step this way, and I will have it ready in a moment." On occasions of necessity, I can eat anything that a dog can, but I had no mind to banquet gratuitously on dirt; so, telling the *padrone* that his establishment was not to my taste, I went off, leaving him growling in the rear. An old soldier, who sat in a doorway with his fatigue-cap on one side of his shaggy head while he smoked his pipe and twirled his grey mustache, pointed out to me a very decent place, where I found a respectable dinner.

This finished, I proceeded to look at the town, and picked up a man who walked around with me through the whole. Among the rest I visited the beautiful garden of the Duke, which was filled with the song of birds and cooled and shaded by fountains and high trees —a most agreeable contrast to the dirt and hubbub of the city. The troops were mustering and the bands playing in the court-yards of the Duke's palace. The hall was brilliantly lighted, and centries walked to and fro within. A part of his guard were stationed at the ancient and massive gateway of the palace-yard—some talked listlessly—some slept seated on the benches—others lay stretched at full length, to get rid of time till their turn of duty should come.

Feeling inclined to imitate their example, I went to the diligence and slept there, till the harnessing of the horses and the arrival of the other passengers waked me. At ten in the evening we left Parma.

At five in the morning we were at Piacenza. Here we stopped an hour or two. Here again the striking difference between the towns of Northern and Southern Italy was manifested. The people looked as grave and solemn as the brick fronts of the palaces and churches. The town was just bestirring itself. Well dressed men were thronging to the *caffès* for breakfast—the shops were being opened, and the market people coming in with their produce. Tall *contadini* were driving flocks of goats about the street, stopping and milking one into a little tin measure whenever some housekeeper or the servant of some *caffè* came out to demand *latte fresca*.

There was an amusing concourse of market people in the public piazza, before the lofty front of the old government palace. Cheeses, meat, butter, eggs, and piles of live hens, tied neck and heels as you see them in Canada, were spread in every direction over the pavement, surrounded by sellers and purchasers, both apparently half asleep. At a little distance were two long lines of women and men, each with a basket of eggs in hand, standing immoveable with an expression of patient resignation, waiting for a purchaser. The men were little shrivelled farmers, in breeches and broad hats, with staffs in their hands and dickeys standing up erect, like diminutive Englishmen. High above this motley swarm of helpless humanity rose the statue of some great lord of the Farnese family, seated on horseback, holding his truncheon of command as if at the head of an army; and looking as if one act of his single will, or one movement of his armed hand, would be enough to annihilate the whole swarm of poor devils below him.

The fish market was under the arches, and in the enclosures of the palace. Here were gigantic eels fresh taken from the Po; pike, crawfish, and bull-frogs. These last looked exceedingly delicate, with their pantaloons taken off, and their heart and liver folded between their forepaws.

We crossed the Po by a wretched bridge of boats, and entered Lombardy and the domains of Austria. The black eagle of Austria was painted above the guard-house on the further bank, where a dozen sullen-looking soldiers loitered about. There was a barrack of them near the custom house, w[h]ere we must stop an hour and a half to be searched, and to pay the fellows for doing it. After that, we rode all day through a beautiful and fertile country, passing through Lodi, the scene of Bonaparte's victory, till at night we entered Milan, saturated with dust.

Sunday, April 21ˢᵗ. The Milan Cathedral is worthy of Rome—I like it as well as St. Peter's. Milan has a forum, an amphitheatre, and a noble triumphal arch, the last two commenced by Napoleon when he was here. I went to the top of the arch, and looking to the north, saw what seemed light streaks of cloud high in the air. As I looked at them, the idea crossed me: "Possibly they may be the Alps themselves!"—yet I thought it very unlikely they could be seen on a sultry and hazy day like this, at such a distance. I watched them for a long time—they did not change position or figure, yet to my eye— not unpracticed in observing mountains—they looked more and more like thin clouds. I inquired of a man what they were—they were in fact the Alps! He pointed out the different peaks, and the situation of the various passes. The Splügen, the highest and wildest of all, and which I mean to pass, lay hidden in black piles of clouds that rose between it and the inferior mountains around the Lake of Como.

This Triumphal Arch was designed by Napoleon as the termination of his road of the Simplon. Curse him and his roads; he should have left the Alps alone. I will steer clear of him. The country about here looks like anything but the neighbor of such a wilderness of mountains; it is as flat as the ocean, and green with rich vegetation. The forum and the Place of Arms are thickly studded with lime and horsechesnut trees, just budding in the warm spring weather; and the ditches below the ramparts of the city are bordered by elms and weeping willows. The Simplon itself, a wide level road running straight northward for the mountains, is flanked by a double line of fine trees. The whole plain of Milan is bright and beautiful in this spring weather.

As for the city, it is well enough. The people are different in appearance, in manners, in language, and in habits from the Southern Italians. The women are all out sunning themselves; whole flights of them came out of the cathedral, with little black veils flung over their heads, and mass-books in their hands. Their faces and figures are round and rich—of the fiery black eye of Rome I have seen nothing; their eyes are blue and soft, and have rather a drowsy meek expression, and they *look* excessively modest.

This morning when the whole city was quiet, the shops shut in honor of Sunday, the people issuing from the cathedral, gentlemen walking listlessly about, and porters and *contadini* sitting idle at the edge of the sidewalks, there was a group of gentlemen taking their coffee under awnings in front of each of the *caffès* in the piazza before the cathedral. This vagabond way of breakfasting and seeing the world at the same time is very agreeable. There is no place where you can be more independent than in one of these cities—when you are hungry, there is always a restaurant and a dinner at a moment's notice—when you are thirsty, there is always a *caffè* at hand. If you are sleepy, your room awaits you—a dozen sneaking waiters are ready at your bidding, and glide about like shadows to do what you may require, in hope of your shilling when you go away. But give me Ethan Crawford, or even Tom,[58] in place of the whole race of waiters and *garçons*. I would ask their pardon for putting them in the same sentence, if they were here.

Leonardo de Vinci's "Last Supper" is here—in the refectory of a suppressed convent—but miserably injured, or rather destroyed, by the damps of three centuries and a half. An old man who has charge of the place told me that he was at the Bridge of Lodi, and was a sergeant at Marengo.

A funeral procession filed into the cathedral, each priest, layman, woman, and child with an enormous wax candle in hand. The noble chapel, at the left extremity of the transept, was hung with black for the occasion; the coffin was placed in the midst; and the ceremonies were performed. The priests seemed not fairly awake—one fat bull-frog of a fellow would growl out of his throat his portion of the holy psalmody, interrupting himself in some interesting conversation with his neighbor, and resuming it again as soon as the religious office was performed. Another would gape and yawn in the midst of his musical performances—another would walk about looking at the people, or the coffin, or the kneeling women, singing meanwhile with the most supreme indifference and content on his fat countenance. I could imagine the subject of their conversation, as they walked out in a double file, leaving the coffin to the care of the proper officials, after they had grunted a concluding anthem over it: "Well, we've fixed this fellow's soul for him. It was a nasty job; but it's over now. Come, won't you take something to drink?"

I used to like priests, and take my hat off and make a low bow, half in sport and half in earnest, whenever I met them—but I have got to despise the fellows. Yet I have met admirable men among them; and have always been treated by them all with the utmost civility and attention. Civility is almost universal among these Italians—farther south, it is manifested in gesticulations, takings-off of the hat, bowings, and reiterated exclamations of *"padrone,"* which is equivalent to "your servant, sir." Here it is shown rather in deeds than in words; thank a man for any favor—he does not scrape and flourish, and say *"padrone"*—he only smiles quietly and replies *"niente fatto."*

I asked a man the way to one of the palaces this morning—nothing would satisfy him, but to go with me the whole way, which was a full mile, and when I thanked him, it was *"niente fatto"*—"I have done nothing." A ragged man with one eye knocked out, who guided me for quarter of an hour through the intricate streets, was quite angry when I offered him a *zwanziger.*

I met Marquand in a picture gallery, and was not sorry to find an acquaintance and countryman, where I supposed I was alone. We went up to the roof of the cathedral together—and saw Milan, with every street laid open to view, and the whole current of population that was circulating through them, like the skinned specimens of anatomy in the Florentine museum. Palaces, churches, and arches, and league upon league of the flat surrounding country intersected by roads, all converging to the city—all seemed to lay directly beneath. As for the church, sixty-four hundred statues, large as life, adorn its sides, roof, and the countless marble spires that rise all around you, like the masts of vessels in a crowded harbor. Thirty-six hundred statues are still to be placed in their stations—10,000 in all. All is white marble—carved everywhere into fruit and flowers.

We next went under the church to see the tomb of St. Carlo Bor[r]omeo—the richest tomb, so they told us, in the world. The coffin is of pure rock chrystal (from the Alps!) set in silver, and adorned with sixty little images of solid silver. The saint lies embalmed within, as plainly visible as if nothing intervened—clothed in his pontificals, with golden images—the votive offerings of princes—crucifixes of emeralds, and other splendid ornaments arranged about his body—à la Indian. The chapel is completely encased in silver, wrought to represent the events of the saint's life. I write on the Lake of Como, with three women, a boy, and four men looking over my shoulder, but they cannot read English.

I wrote the above as the lake steamer lay waiting for her passengers, as time has become a valuable commodity to me. This morning I had just time to give one parting glance at the cathedral, which, like St. Peter's, improves on acquaintance—but not to the same degree. It requires some imagination and some grasp of mind to fully comprehend St. Peter's, and great study, and, in my case, a strong effort beside. For there is no point where more than half of the church can be seen—the rest must be imagined. Not one in ten who visit St. Peter's thinks of the domes and the chapels that are hidden from his sight—they look at the great dome and the central nave, and omit to take the rest—all that lies behind the columns and between the arches—into account. But in the Milan Cathedral, you can embrace all at a glance—yet with every visit, the beauty and majesty of its hundred and sixty marble columns, of its rich tombs, its carvings, the rich fret-work of the roof and dome, and of the windows painted [with] the histories of saints, strike you with a stronger effect.

Milan has a sort of counterpart of Pulcinella, called Gerolamo; but I believe that he appears at one theatre only, which is christened after him Teatro Gerolamo. I saw an exhibition of wax figures, among which was one of a dead Christ, covered by a sheet which the showman lifted away with great respect. The spectators, who consisted of five or six young men, immediately took their hats off.

Yet, in spite of their respect for the subject on which the artist had exercised his skill, they did not refrain from making comments on the execution of the figure.

I am now at the little village of Colico, on the north extremity of the Lake of Como. Some Swiss, Bohemians, and Tyrolese are singing at the top of their voices over their wine in the room below.

I have seen nothing at home or abroad more beautiful than this lake. It reminds me of Lake George—the same extent, the same figure, the same chrystal purity of waters, the same wild and beautiful mountains on either side. But the comparison will not go farther. Here are a hundred palaces and villages scattered along the water's edge, and up the declivities. There is none of that shaggy, untamed aspect in the mountains—no piles of rocks grown over with stunted bushes, or half-decayed logs fallen along the shore. There are none of those little islands, covered with rough and mossgrown pine trees, which give a certain savage character to the beauties of Lake George. All here is like a finished picture: even the wildest rocks seem softened in the air of Italy. Give me Lake George, and the smell of the pine and fir! But now I am at the foot of the Splügen, and the Alps all around, covered with snow, their sharp summits just losing the red tinge of the evening. Not long since the lake was all in a glow; but now it is like a sheet of lead, and the western mountains have become dark as night. The path I have chosen is by far the sublimest and most savage of all; and it is little frequented. Tomorrow I shall be where I have wished to be for years.

Andeer. A village just beyond the pass, in the midst of the mountains. The Splügen itself disappointed me—scarce any part of it was superior to the Notch of the White Mountains,° which the lower parts of it greatly resemble. We were from two in the morning till four in the afternoon in getting across. Among the glaciers and endless snows at the summit it was impossible for any carriage to pass; so the horses were taken out at the Austrian government house near the top, and fastened each to a small sled. Two of the sleds carried the baggage—the other two held myself and the other

° Crawford Notch.—Ed.

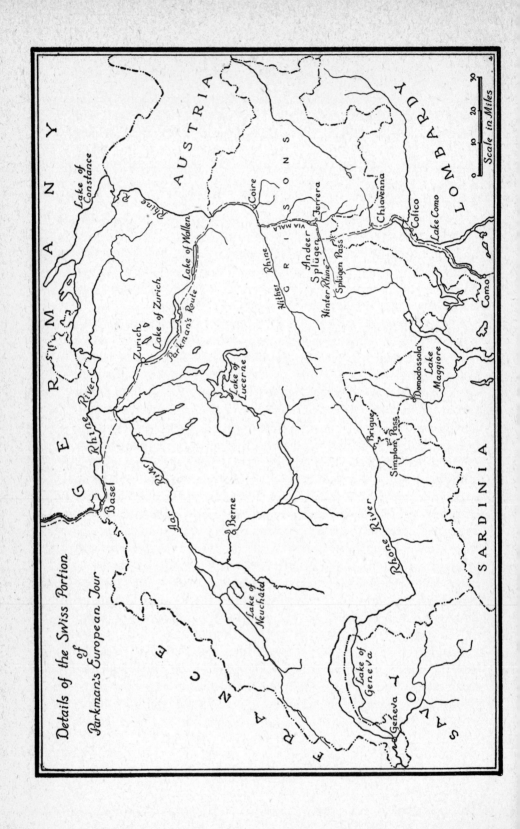

Details of the Swiss Portion
of
Parkman's European Tour

Scale in Miles

GERMANY

AUSTRIA

LOMBARDY

SARDINIA

SAVOY

FRANCE

Lake of Constance

Rhine River

Basel

Aar River

Berne

Lake of Neuchâtel

Lake of Geneva

Geneva

Rhone River

Simplon Pass

Brigue

Domodossola

Lake Maggiore

Como

Lake Como

Colico

Chiavenna

Splügen Pass

Winter Rhine

Splügen

Andeer

Ferrera

VIA MALA

Coire

Hither Rhine

GRISONS

Lake of Wallen

Parkman's Route

Lake of Zurich

Zurich

Rhine R.

Lake of Lucerne

traveller. The snow was fifteen or twenty feet deep in some places, and the horses waded and plunged through it as they might. The baggage was turned over two or three times, but no other accident occurred, though the horses dashed head foremost, with the sledge at their heels, down the steep descents. In fact, there is no difficulty whatever, even at this season, in making the passage; and as for the danger from avalanches—no one has been hurt by them these five years. The view was desolate and grand—one expanse of white glistening snow covering all but the pointed pinnacles at the summits, and the ragged forests of the black pine that reached up the lower declivities. Yet, as I said, I was disappointed. The road itself is so enormously high that it brings you near to the mountains' peaks, and diminishes the effect of their elevation.

But my disappointment ceased the moment we had passed the mountain. In a valley at the bottom was the village of Splügen—a contrast to the formal groups of stone houses that make up the Italian villages. It seemed like home, as we emerged from the forests of spruce and fir that covered the sides of the steep gorge where the road ran, to see before us great piles of lumber, and a wooden saw-mill, and the banks of the Rhine. The bridge, too, was of wood—so were the houses, though their projecting eaves gave them a far more pictur-esque aspect than belongs to a New England mountain village. The Rhine was a headlong torrent, which ran swiftly down the little valley to enter the woods and rocks again, not far below. The lower declivities of the mountains that completely surrounded this village were blackened by the heavy growth of spruce and pine, but above these woods rose gigantic peaks white with snow, that glistened with a brightness painful to the eye. In two hours we were at Andeer—a place not less wildly situated, and reached by a road winding through a succession of most savage ravines close by the Rhine, which foams and roars among the rocks and fir trees like an imprisoned wild beast.

I stopped here, and will stay here several days. Nothing could sur-pass the utter savageness of the scenery that you find by tracing up some of the little streams that pour down on all sides to join the Rhine; not a trace of human hand—it is as wild as the back-forests at home. The mountains too, wear the same aspect. There is one valley where a large stream comes down to join the main river, a mile from Andeer. Last night I followed it for a mile or two, back into the mountains—not Cooper himself could do it justice. The river was a hundred feet below, in a ravine, where it lashed from side to side and bounded sometimes in a fall of fifty or sixty feet—the green headlong water, the white foam, and the spray just visible through the boughs of the distorted pines that leaned over the abyss. There was in one place a peasant's hut of logs, but it seemed only to increase the sublime effect of the wilderness. I got down to the bed of the river, and leaped out to some rocks near the centre. It was nearly dark—long after sunset. What with the deafening thunder of the stream—the gloom that began to involve the shaggy branches of the yellow pines that leaned nearly across the gulf, and the stiff and upright spruces that sprang from every crevice of the rock—what with this and the savage aspect of the rocks, which were black and dripping with the spray—there was something almost appalling in the place. Above the tops of the trees, rose mountains like ours of New England, covered with fir trees wherever one could cling in the crevices of the steep cliffs. And in another direction the more distant peaks were white with snow, which retained its glistening brightness long after the moon had begun to cast a shadow.

Here was a change, with a vengeance, from the Italian beauties of the Lake of Como! I sat on the rock, fancying myself again in the American woods with an Indian companion—but as I rose to go away the hellish beating of my heart warned me that no more such expeditions were in store for me—for the present, at least—but if I do not sleep by the camp-fire again, it shall be no fault of mine.

This morning, as I got half asleep into the post-carriage at Colico, I was saluted by a *buon[o] giorno* by a small voice from a dark corner, where I discovered, by groping about, a fine boy of thirteen or fourteen, with great promise of muscles yet undeveloped. He was a young Swiss who spoke Italian; so I began to talk with him. He spoke in a frank and bold manner. I asked him if he did not mean to be a soldier. He said he should have to, for all the Swiss were obliged to serve from the age of eighteen to twenty-four[p]; but he meant to be

---

[p] "He was mistaken—the Swiss military system resembles ours."—F.P.

an officer, because he was noble. The conductor at this moment brought a lantern to the window, which showed a handsome, Quentin Durward-like boy, but clothed in rough homespun and clouted shoes that did not look much like nobility—and reminded me of Quentin's pretensions. He had not heard of America, and inquired with great curiosity how far it was, and how long the term of military service was. I told him the period that we are expected to be in readiness, which astonished him exceedingly. "*Corpo di Bacco! Piu di quarant' anni (di) militare! Ma quell' è bello! Piu di quarant' anni (di) militare!*" He said he was a Calvinist, and that all of his religion were considered as devils—"*come diavoli*"—by the people around. He fell asleep at last, and did not wake till we stopped at Chiavenna, when he jumped up, shook himself, took his stick, and walked off to the mountains.q

Thursday. I spent the day yesterday in the Valley of Ferrara, one of the wildest and loneliest in the Alps, and accessible only by a bad foot-path. The river comes down at the bottom, which the sun scarcely ever touches. The mountains rise on each side many thousand feet, broken into crags and precipices, with streams falling down them in all directions, scattering into white mists before they reach the bottom. The spruce trees are sprinkled all over the cliffs, wherever there is a crevice to cling in; some gigantic pines stoop across the river, and fairly seem to quiver with the tremendous roar of the water.[59] All is solitary, and still as death except the noise of the river; yet you cannot sit on one of those rocks, and watch the green and furious water glancing between the trunks and branches below, without fancying that you hear sounds and voices about you. I never knew a place so haunted by "those airy tongues that syllable men's names."

This village of Andeer stands by the [Hinter] Rhine, in a valley where the mountains draw apart and leave a large space of fertile fields and gentle declivities. As you descend from the road to Splügen, Andeer looks almost like an American country village. There are

q This entry refers to an incident of Parkman's passage from Lake Como over the Splügen Pass—Ed.

barns and small houses of wood—roofed with boards, flat stones, and shingles; and, sprinkled among them, large square white houses with green blinds, which look at a distance like the buildings of a New England village. They are of stone, however, but plastered over and whitewashed. There are low walls to these villages; the little Calvinist meeting-house, something like one of ours, stands on an eminence in the midst. Beside Andeer, half a dozen others are scattered about the valley, down by the river or high up on the slopes of the mountains. You see a line of dingy wooden houses, with eaves projecting two or three feet, on almost all those declivities which the mountain forms at its base, before it rises into cliffs and inaccessible precipices. The women are all out at work in the fields, manuring them with wooden forks. Would to Heaven our women did the same, if it could make them as strong and hardy.

They speak here a German dialect, and have German faces—and here, for the first time I felt the helplessness of being without any medium of communication. A tall, stout, ruddy-cheeked mountain girl, who presided at the inn in the absence of the landlord, came up to know my commands. I tried Italian. She understood not a word; but in her zeal to serve me kept sputtering German, as if she thought to make it intelligible by repetition; so, to convince her of her mistake, I entertained her with long speeches in English, to which she listened with eyes and mouth wide open. Sometimes a bright gleam would shoot across her face, as a word similar to one of her own language struck her ear. This suggested an expedient; so I began to pronounce the English names of all the things I wanted, using all the synonyms I could think of. I thus managed to make out a very good meal, though the items of it were decided by the accidental coincidence of their names with the Swiss. When the *padrone* returned, I found that he spoke Italian, and there was an end of my difficulties for the present. The second day of my stay at Andeer, I spent in the Via Mala, a place by nature more savagely wild than the Valley of Ferrara; but not so solitary, as it is the sole outlet by which Andeer and its neighboring villages communicate with the rest of the world. But here paper fails me, and I must buy another volume!—if I can find one in Strasburg.

Strasburg, May '44. The Via Mala is a cleft in the mountains, which divides them for a mile, leaving the opposing cliffs bare and raw, as if a wedge had been driven in to split them asunder. Here the Rhine gets out from the mountains; but must force its way through a ravine, or crack, about a foot wide and, of course, immensely deep. The road that leads from the valley must take the same course, and crosses again and again the bed of the torrent, as if searching to find some means of extricating itself from the pass. Standing on one of the bridges, you may see the Rhine like a white narrow ribbon in the bottom of the dark gully, a hundred and fifty feet below. Sometimes it is buried entirely among the rocks, but you can hear its dead roaring noise; and when, after half a mile of such imprisonment, it escapes at last, it is all in a white foam. Torrents, and little streams turned all to mist as they descend from that immense height, come down the cliffs on each side to join it. Where the sun can strike them, you always see a rainbow among the scattered spray half-way down the mountain.

Four days ago I took the diligence from Andeer, and passed through this place on the way to Coire. I never left any place with more regret than these mountains. Descending into the wider valleys of the Grisons, the scenery was not less magnificent, though of a different character. At Coire, the capital of the Canton, I was reminded that I was no longer in Italy. A servant stood at the head of the stairs in the large inn there, welcoming each guest with a "good night," and ushering him into a large, low, wooden apartment, where some thirty men and women were smoking, eating, or lounging at the tables and benches. Boys stood ready to receive hats and cloaks; and waiters attended on each newcomer to know what he would have. All was ease, good-nature, and equality. The old Germans and Swiss grunted over their beer-pots, and puffed at their pipes. The young ones laughed with the servant girls. A Frenchman gulped down his bowlful of soup—sprang to the window when he heard the postillion's horn—bounded back to finish one more tumbler of wine—and then siezing his cane, dashed out in hot haste. A prim, strutting, little German student stalked to the window to watch him; pipe in hand and a complacent grin on his face; then turned to discourse in a half patronizing, half gallant way with the girl.[60]

Departed next morning for Zurich, and early in the forenoon reached the head of the Lake of Wallenstadt [Walen See]. Of the people by the way, some were Catholic, some Protestant; some spoke the German, and some the *lingua romancia*, a compound of several languages. It was a dark and cloudy day. The mountains around the lake were piles of abrupt precipices, whose tops were hidden in the clouds, and whose sides seemed alive with the numberless streams that came pouring down to the lake. Some were trickling lines of water, marking the face of the cliffs with a long dark stain; others were headlong cataracts, spouting from some cave high up among the clouds, and tumbling down the mountain, full of savage life. Others still seemed like ribbons waving in the wind from the top of a precipice. The lake itself is a black and narrow strip of water, shut close in by these tremendous rocks. The puffings of the steamboat were hoarsely reverberated from the precipices. When we reached the foot of the lake, all was bright and clear again, in seeming accordance with the change of the scenery; for I was to see no more of the Alps.

The Germans lighted their pipes with their flint and steel, and, stretching out their legs and unbuttoning their coats, disposed themselves to take their ease. Here was none of the painful dignity which an Englishman thinks it incumbent upon him to assume throughout his travels—no knee-pans aching with the strain of tight strapped pantaloons—no neck half-severed by the remorseless edge of a starched dicky.

Here began again something of Italian softness on the features of the scenery—or so at least it seemed, by contrast with the passages of the Splügen. All was cultivation and fruitfulness. The picturesque wooden cottages were more lively embellishments of the scene than the formal stone houses of Italy. But the white and neat houses of the wealthier republicans, surrounded by apple orchards and green meadows dotted by dandelions, made me fancy myself at home. Still more, when, having passed the Lake of Zurich, we approached at nightfall the town of that name. Here I could have believed myself entering an ambitious New England village—the same intermingling of white houses with blossomming apple and pear trees—the same grass-plots and wooden fences—nay, at intervals, the same old dingy barns of rough boards.

Zurich is a beautiful town; clean and neat, with all that air of newness and fresh paint that Dickens attributes to Boston.[61] Here I found myself brought to a stop, because, by the mistake of a servant, my passport had been visèd for Zurich alone, instead of Zurich and Basle. The diligence was to go in an hour. I went to the police office. Three old women were sweeping it out; and the pipes of the absent functionaries hung in a row between the windows. Remembering, however, that I was now in a republic and no longer in an Austrian state, I thought I would go on at all events, and take the chance of interruption. My passport was not even demanded of me.

In the cabriolet of the diligence were two German gentlemen, one of whom spoke several languages and English among the rest, so that I enjoyed the novelty of a companion. Waking in the morning, the sky was covered with lowering moist clouds. The glasses of the windows, too, streamed with the breath of the sleepers. It was a flat and cultivated country. Basle was just visible in front over the shoulder of the postillion. One of the Germans had shrunk down to a confused pile of legs arms and head, which latter member was tumbled over on one side, with the mouth wide open. My polyglot friend sat bolt upright in his corner, sleeping with an expression of savage determination on his mustache and compressed under lip.

At the diligence office in Basle I was nonplussed. I could not make the fat stupid-looking fellows who surrounded me understand what I wanted to be done; when the German gentleman politely offerred himself as interpreter. I went to the splendid Hotel (or rather palace) of the Three Kings, where I found a waiter who spoke a little English.

Here in Basle you find none of the palaces, and none of the dirt, of an Italian city. No soldiers, except those of the garrison of the citadel and of the gendarmerie; no beggars; no spies in the cafés; no vexatious questionings of suspicious officials; no anxious scrutiny into passports, or rummagings of baggage. The people walk about the quiet streets with solemnity on their faces, and pipes in their mouths. Fat, ruddy female faces are seen at all the windows of the steep-roofed houses, where an arrangement of mirrors enables them to see what passes below, without seeming to be on the watch.

It was Sunday, and all the shops were shut. Groups were walking quietly to church, each with a hymn-book in hand; the women arrayed in their best, with their hair braided into two long ropes behind, to which ribbons of a yard in length were attached. This ingenious contrivance, streaming out behind, gave them a most whimsical appearance. The meeting-house was large and square, and its high roof was sustained by a number of fine columns. The women occupied pews by themselves, in the middle; the men had each a kind of little stall, around the sides. The parson sailed in, in all the dignity of Geneva bands and gown, clambered into his pulpit, and with a scowling countenance opened the services. They resembled ours, with the addition of a disagreeable accompaniment to the sermon, in the shape of a man who made the rounds of the church with a bag tied to the end of a stick, in which he received the contributions of the congregation while the parson was holding forth above.

The Catholic Church holds its head scarce so high as at Rome. I saw the people coming out from mass—a stream of ugly, contented, and healthy visages. You did not see, as at Rome, a poor devil in rags, bursting with diseases and a walking menagerie of fleas, kneeling before an altar that shines with massive gold and silver, and dipping his shrivelled fingers into a font of holy water carved most exquisitely out of the richest marbles. The rough beams of this church were plainly visible—two dingy candlesticks, and some bunches of flowers, were the richest decorations of the altar—and the holy water was contained in a common copper kettle. But the people were strong, ruddy, and clean: the women looked like Amazons (though not amazonian in the etymological sense).

The Rhine divides Basle in the midst. Not the furious torrent I saw among the forests and precipices of the Rhinewald, but a broad, deep stream, whose waters make a loud rushing sound with their headlong current. The suburbs of the city are sprinkled thick with houses and orchards. Gardens are down in the ditch of the fortifications, and lime and horsechesnut trees grow on the ramparts. The fields are the resort of the people on Sunday evenings, when they come out to walk about—look at the rifle-shooting—or regale themselves on bread and cheese at benches placed outside the little inns of the suburbs. The rifle of this country is a formidable piece, carrying a ball of about twenty to the pound! Some of the German troops here in Strasburg carry them, with a short sword contrived to fit to the muzzle, by way of bayonet. After staying a day at Basle, I took the railway for Strasburg.

Passing a number of German towns, with their steep roofs half-buried in trees and the spire of the Minster rising from the midst—we got by noon to our destination. Here I staid a day, though Strasburg is an uninteresting place, with little to see; then got into the diligence for Paris. About ten o'clock, I was roused from sleep by a deafening sound of laughing, proceeding from a woman's lungs of very unusual capacities. I found that my fellow passenger had got out from the coupé, and that the conductor had introduced two women in his place. I fell back into my corner and went to sleep again; but not so soundly but that I could hear for hours an occasional remark made in the hoarse grunting voice of an old woman, and always responded to by the same shrill peal of laughter from her companion. When day dawned, I looked with some curiosity to see who my fellow travellers might be. One of them looked like a superannuated baboon, except that she had a pair of grey mustache and a large frilled cap, which gave her such a whimsical look that I burst into a laugh. The other was about thirty—a most luxuriant specimen of womanhood. She must have weighed some three hundred pounds, though she was exceedingly well proportioned, and her features handsome. I soon, however, lost the company of this edifying pair, who got out at Nancy.

The journey to Paris occupies two days. Yesterday morning, looking from the window, I saw an ocean of housetops stretching literally to the very horizon. We entered the gate, but rode for nearly an hour through the streets before we reached the diligence office. Then I went to the Tuilleries, the Palais Royal, the Boulevard des Italiens, and the Place Vendome. "Let envious Englishmen sneer as they will," I thought, "this *is* the Athens of Modern Europe!"

I had called on my uncle, and found him not at home. He called on me with the same fortune, but left a note directing me to be at a celebrated café at a certain time, where he was to be distinguished by a white handkerchief in his hand. I found him there, and went with him to a ball at the Champs Elysées (Mabille).[62]

Bo[u]logne, May 16th. I have been a fortnight in Paris, and seen it as well as it can be seen in a fortnight. Under peculiarly favorable circumstances, too; for it was the great season of balls and gaieties, and I had a guide, moreover, who knows Paris from top to bottom— within and without. I like to see a thing done thouroughly. If a man has a mind to make a fool or a vagabond of himself, he can do it admirably in Paris; whereof I have seen many instances. If a man has a mind to amuse himself, there is no place like it on earth; diversions of every character, form, and degree waiting for him at every step; let him taste them—then get into the diligence and ride away—or stay, and go to the devil. You find there the same amuse-ments variously seasoned to suit different tastes; if you have a fancy for the poetic and romantic, you can have that; but if you want to make an absolute beast of yourself, without varnish or gilding, it can be done to most admirable perfection.

I came to Bologne today; and am waiting for the boat to take me across to England. This is a dull and stupid town. The white cliffs are full in view on the horizon; but, being afflicted with a colic, I do not feel in a romantic mood; and I also hear the dinner-bell. Before midnight, however, I shall be in the "mother country."

London, May 18th. I approached the shores of England in a most shameful fashion. The night was dark and gloomy. Nothing was to be seen on deck but the phosphorescence on the black water, and the sparks from the chimney of the little steamer. The wind came up the straits of Dover as cold as a January northwester. I gaped, went down below, and in half a minute was sound asleep on a sofa. Two or three hours after, the captain shouted in my ear: "We are here, sir! Been here half an hour." "Here? Where is here?" said I in entire bewilderment. "Folkestone harbor, sir." The cabin lights were half burnt out, and the passengers all gone. I got up and reeled off like a drunken man to the hotel, where I went asleep again.

The next day I took the railroad for London. Heavy grey clouds seemed to rest on the very tree-tops. A tremendous wind was blowing, with an occasional puff of sleet and fine rain, sending a chill into our very bones. The passengers' noses turned blue—nobody spoke a word —two or three pulled out respirators from their pockets—and all crouched down together in the open cars, and drew cloaks and shawls close about them. Our northeasters may do their worst; they cannot match that wind.

When I got to London, I thought I had been there before. There, in flesh and blood, was the whole host of characters that figure in *Pickwick*. Every species of cockney was abroad in the dark and dingy-looking streets, all walking with their heads stuck forwards, their noses turned up, their chin pointing down, their knee joints shaking, as they shuffled along with a gait perfectly ludicrous but indescribable. The hackney coachmen and cabmen, with their peculiar phraseology; the walking advertisements, in the shape of a boy completely hidden between two placards; and a hundred others seemed so many incarnations of Dickens' characters. A strange contrast to Paris! The cities are no more alike than the "dining room" of London and the elegant restaurant of Paris—the one being a quiet, dingy establishment where each guest is put into a box, and supplied with porter, beef, potatoes, and plum-pudding. Red-faced old gentlemen of three hundred weight mix their "brandy go" and read the *Times*. In Paris the tables are set in elegant galleries and saloons, and among the trees and flowers of a garden; and here resort coats cut by the first tailors and bonnets of the latest mode, whose occupants regale their delicate tastes on the lightest and most delicious viands. The waiters spring from table to table as noiselessly as shadows, prompt at the slightest sign; a lady, elegantly attired, sits within an arbor to preside over the whole. Dine at these places—then go to a London "dining room"—swill porter and devour roast beef!

The Haymarket Theatre—a little place, very plain and simple, and scarce larger than our departed Tremont. Not like the great theatres of Rome and Naples, or the still larger La Scala at Parma. Very unlike, too, the splendid opera house at Paris, where the richness of the decorations, the beauty of the architecture, and the excellence of the performances are only equalled by the extravagance of the prices. They gave us enough of it, certainly, at the Haymarket.

The performances lasted from half past 7 till midnight. Such admirable acting I never saw before. Charles Matthews[63] was the star; and appeared in a piece of his own, in which he took occasion to vent several sarcasms against American repudiation.[64] But the drama is at its last gasp. The Haymarket alone, among all its companions, preserves unaltered its ancient character—the rest are turned to opera houses.

I went immediately to Catlin's "Indian Gallery."[65] It is in the Egyptian Hall, Picadilly. There was a crowd around the door; servants in livery waiting; men with handbills of the exhibition for sale; cabmen, boys, and pickpockets. I was rejoicing in Mr. Catlin's success, when the true point of attraction caught my eye in the shape of a full-length portrait of Major Tom Thumb,[66] the celebrated American dwarf, who it seems occupies the "Indian Gallery" for the present. I paid my shilling and went in. The little wretch was singing "Yankee Doodle" with a voice like a smothered mouse, and prancing about on a table, à la Jeffrey Hudson,[67] with a wooden sword in his hand. A great crowd of cockneys and gentlemen and ladies were contemplating his evolutions—but [as] for the "Indian Gallery," its glory had departed; it had evidently ceased to be a lion. The portraits of the chiefs, dusty and faded, hung round the walls, and above were a few hunting shirts, and a bundle or two of arrows; but the rich and invaluable collection I had seen in Boston had disappeared, and no one thought of looking at the poor remains of that great collection that were hung about the walls. Catlin had done right. He would not suffer the fruits of his six years' labor and danger to rot in the dampness to gratify a few miserable cockneys—so has packed up the best part of his trophies.

St. Paul's, which the English ridiculously compare to St. Peter's, is without exception the dirtiest and gloomiest church I have been in yet. I went up to the ball at the top of the cupola, whence the prospect is certainly a most wonderful one. I have been on mountains whence nothing could be seen but unbroken forests stretching in every direction to the horizon, and I enjoyed the sight—but to look down from St. Paul's and see tiled roofs and steeples, half hid in smoke and mist—a filthy river covered with craft running through the midst; and to hear the incessant hum and to smell the coal smoke that pollutes the air—all this is very curious and amusing for a while, but I would scarce trouble myself to look again. All was dirty and foul; the air was chilly and charged with fog and sleet, though it is the genial month of May. The smoke, that you could see streaming in the wind from ten thousand earthen chimney-pots, mingled with the vapors and obscured the prospect like a veil. It was an indistinct but limitless panorama. The taller church-spires alone rose above the cloud into a comparatively clear atmosphere; and they could be seen faintly, far off on the horizon, to show how far this wilderness of houses reached. "Now," thought I, "I have under my eye the greatest collection of blockheads and rascals, the greatest horde of pimps, prostitutes, and bullies that the earth can show." And straightway all the child's-book associations of London rose before me: the Lord Mayor's show "all so grand," and the host of narrow, stupid, beef-eating civic functionaries, and the unmatched absurdities and self-conceit of cockneyism. "Was there ever such a cursed hole?" I thought as I looked down on the smoky prospect.

You are shown a large stone vaulted room, covered with cobwebs and smoke-dust, where hang, already rotten and half dropping from their staffs, the flags that were borne at Nelson's funeral.

Walk out in the evening, and keep a yard or two behind some wretched clerk, who with nose elevated in the air, elbows stuck out at right angles, and the pewter knob of his cane playing upon his under lip, is straddling his bow legs over the sidewalk with a most majestic air. Get behind him, and you see his dignity greatly disturbed. First he glances over one of his narrow shoulders—then over the other—then he edges off to the other side of the walk, and turns his vacant lobster eyes full upon you—then he passes his hand over his coat-tail—and finally he draws forth from his pocket the object of all this solicitude in the shape of a venerable and ragged cotton handkerchief, which he holds in his hand to keep it out of harm's way. I have been thus taken for a pickpocket more than a dozen times tonight—not the less so for being respectably dressed, for these gentry are the most dashing men on the Strand.

There is an interesting mixture of vulgarity and helplessness in the swarm of ugly faces you see in the streets—meagre, feeble, ill-proportioned, or not proportioned at all, the blockheads must needs put on a game air and affect the "man of the world" in their small way. I have not met one handsome woman yet, though I have certainly walked more than fifty miles since I have been here, and have kept my eyes open. To be sure, the weather has been raw and chill enough to keep beauty at home. Elsewhere Englishmen are tall, strong, and manly; here the crowd that swarms through the streets are like the outcasts of a hospital.

I spent seven or eight days in London. On the eighth day I went up the river to Richmond in a steamboat, with a true cockney pleasure party on board whose evolutions were very entertaining. The day before, while I was in Westminster Abbey—which, by the way, is the most interesting church I ever was in—a man came up and enquired if my name was not Parkman, saying that a gentleman wished to speak to me. I did not know that I had a single acquaintance in London, and was rather astonished at finding George Atkinson[68] standing among the tombs. He was just imported by steamboat from America. He informed me, to my great surprise and admiration, that he and I had just become uncles when he left home. He went with me to visit the "industrious fleas" (not the exhibition which goes by that name in Paris!) and we made the circuit of half a dozen exhibitions together. He went with me to Richmond the next day. The river scenery of this place is beautiful—so are the fields and villages you pass on your return by land. By a miracle, the day was fine. The carriages of the nobility thronged about Hyde Park. Regent Street swarmed with thousands of people, and was filled with a heavy, stunning din from the wheels of carts, omnibusses, cabs, and carriages, careering along in both directions at full speed, but without confusion or accident. But the Strand at night is the most characteristic scene in London. The sidewalks are crowded with as dense and active a throng as in the day-time—more than half of whom are women on their nightly perambulations. The glare from the shops makes all as bright as sunlight. A watchman stands in his cloak at every corner. Strong bodies of the police are continually marching in order to and fro, with loaded clubs hung at their sides.

I got into the cars one night—having sent my trunks to Liverpool—and found myself in the morning at Darlington, nearly three hundred miles distant. Thence I took stage for Carlisle, famous in Border story; having had some trouble in negotiating a passage from the difficulty in understanding the damnable dialect of Yorkshire. It was not long before we passed the veritable Dotheboys Hall of Dickens, exactly answering to his description in appearance, in situation, in all things. It is deserted utterly—*Nicholas Nickleby* ruined not this establishment alone, but many other schools with which the vicinity abounds, though some of these latter were in no way objectionable.

It was not long before we passed another spot far more interesting. As we rode out of one of the little stone villages of the country, I saw a large ruined castle on a high rock above a clear swift stream, shaded from the sun by beautifully wooded banks. The old coachman saw me looking earnestly at it, so twisted round his broad red face and pointing with the butt of his whip, said "Yon's old Barnard Castle, sir, and yon's the Tees." I burst out with an oath at being so unexpectedly introduced to the scenery of Scott's *Rokeby*. A gentleman who had joined us at the village gave me an account of the present proprietors, and said that he was connected with the family of the former owners.

We dined at Penrith—resumed journey—saw off to our left the Cumberland hills, enclosing among them the valley of St. John, the renowned "Lakes," and the home of Wordsworth. An old farmer who had wandered over them all, out of a very unusual admiration of the picturesque, gave enthusiastic descriptions of their beauties—then launched into the subject of their geological formation, whence he diverged to geology in general—then followed a discussion on chemistry—then on metaphysics and religion—then on the breeding of cattle. By this time the old fellow had reached his house, and scrambling down, lifted his dingy hat off his white eyebrows to salute us, while we rode on to Carlisle.

I went away at four in the morning for Abbotsford. We were in the region where one thinks of nothing but of Scott, and of the themes which he has rendered so familiar to the whole world. The Cheviot [Teviot River] was on our right—the Teviot [Cheviot] hills before us. The wind came down from them raw and cold, and the whole sky was obscured with stormy clouds. I thought, as we left the town, of the burden of one of his ballads, "The sun shines fair on Carlisle walls." It was little applicable now. The ancient fortification looked [as] sullen and cheerless as tottering battlements and black crumbling walls, beneath a sky as dark and cold as themselves, could make it. I was prepared for storms and a gloomy day, but soon the clouds parted and the sun broke out clear over the landscape. The dark heathery sides of Teviot [Cheviot]—the numberless bright, rapid streams that came from the different glens, and the woods of ash, larch, and birch that followed their course, and grew on the steeper declivities of the hills—never could have appeared to more advantage. Esk and Liddel, Yarrow, the Teviot, Minto Crag, Ettrick Forest, Branksome Castle—these and more likewise we passed before we reached the Tweed, and saw Abbotsford on its banks among the forests planted by Scott himself. I left my luggage at the inn at Galashiels, telling the landlord that I was going away, and might return at night, or might not. I visited Abbotsford, Melrose, and Dryburgh—and consider the day better spent than the whole four months I was in Sicily and Italy. I slept at Melrose, and returned to Galashiels in the morning.

Three days was all the time I had to spare for these places; but rising at six and going to bed at ten, and being on my legs during the whole interval, I managed to see almost every spot of note for eight or ten miles round. I found a little stone cottage down by the Tweed, not far from Abbotsford, where an old woman told me that, "if I wad be pleased to walk in," she could show me a room where she was accustomed to receive gentlemen in the salmon-fishing season. I came back to the house at night, and found she had arranged the room and built a fire for me, and sent for a fishing-rod and lines. The old lady had only been in [the] place about twelve years, but well remembered Sir Walter's return from the Continent and his funeral. She saw him in the carriage as they were bringing him to Abbotsford after his landing. "He was an awful dull and heavy lookin' mon, to be sic a grand writer," she said.

I asked her if she had any books in the house, on which she brought out of a closet a Testament bound up with *The Psalms of David, done into English verse, for the service of the Scottish Kirk*—also a volume of the sermons of the Reverend Simeon McCabb. She then produced a bottle of whisky, remarking, "Mayhap it wad mak ye sleep better." I rose at daylight, and fished in the Tweed for two hours, following it far up among the hills.

I like the Scotch—I like the country and everything in it. The Liverpool packet will not wait, or I should stay long here, and take a trout from every "burnie" in the Cheviot[s]. The scenery has been grossly belied by Irving and others—it is wild and beautiful—I have seen none more so. There is wood enough along the margins of the streams (which are as transparent as our own)—the tops of the hills alone are bare. The country abounds in game—pheasants, moor cock, curlew, and rabbits.

I returned to headquarters at Galashiels just in time for the Edinburgh coach; and got to the city at night, where the fine situation and magnificent architecture of the "Modern Athens" very much surprised me. The view from Calton Hill is, to my thinking, the only city view I ever saw that deserves to be called sublime. There is an amusing contrast between the old and new town—the region of the Grassmarket, and that of Moray Place and Princes Street. In point of architecture, the new town surpasses Regent Street—in point of neatness and quiet, it would be an insult to Edinburgh to make any comparison. But the old town makes the finest appearance, taken in the mass, in spite of the dirt and squalor you find there on close examination. Stand on Princes Street and look across the gulf that separates the two quarters, you see the opposite hill-side crowded with a dense mass of venerable buildings, from six to ten or twelve stories high. In this region are all the spots famous in the history of the town, and in the romances of Scott. The Castle rises, on the top of a craggy hill, far above the rest.

Sir Walter Scott is everywhere. His name is in everybody's lips, and associates itself with every spot around this place. I ask the name of such a street—such a mountain, or island, or cottage, or piece of woods—the words of the reply have been familiar to me as my own name for the last six years. The old booksellers here have all seen him—many of them had dealings with him—all speak of him alike. One of them yesterday showed me a letter written by Scott while he was collecting the *Minstrelsy*, saying that he had bought it for a great price because he was determined to have some memento of Sir Walter. They are erecting a magnificent monument to his memory on Princes Street; the more needed since his grave at Dryburgh has not even a stone to mark it.

The gentleman who showed me Scott's letter, showed me also one of Burns', or rather a fragment of one, of a very edifying nature. It was addressed to a married lady, and in a style most poetically persuasive, yet frank and bold. The end, where the enamoured poet had probably stated more clearly what he had been driving at all along, was torn off by the son of the lady. This son must have been a blockhead or a madman. He in some way got the letter into his possession, and had no scruples in selling it to a stranger, though his mother's name is written out at full upon it.

I walked up Arthur's Seat, passing the spot where Jea(n)nie Dean[s] had her interview with her sister's seducer,[69] and, when I arrived at the top, looking down on the site of her father's cottage. Under the crags here is the place where Scott and James Ballantyne[70] used to sit when boys, and read and make romances together. Edinburgh, half wrapped in smoke, lies many hundred feet below, seen beyond the ragged projecting edge of Salisbury Crag, the castle rising obscurely in the extreme distance.

In the castle are the regalia of Scotland—the crown, sword, sceptre, and jewels—the first worn by Robert the Bruce and all who succeeded him till Charles II's time. They were hidden from the light for many years. The soldier pointed out the heavy oaken chest where they lay concealed, until the Scottish nation should have forgotten its ancient independence and become content under its "annexation" to England. I remembered the scene just after the opening of the chest, when a party of *literati* and ladies were looking at these insignia of ancient glory, and one frivolous fellow lifted the crown to place it on the head of a simpering young lady. "No, by God!" exclaimed Scott, who stood by. The man blushed like scarlet and laid the crown down. There is a power in a little profanity, when it comes from a moved spirit, and is not affected, like the oaths of a consumptive apprentice with a cigar in his mouth, who lisps "Hell and Damnation" because he thinks it sounds manly.

Saw the house, just above the Canongate, where John Knox lived and preached. Even now, an image of him is stuck at the corner, in the very act of holding forth. This the people hold in great reverence. A scurvy-looking population they are. The old stone houses of High St. rise story above story to a stupendous height above them, looking more ancient and venerable than the Castle Rock. Their grey attic windows and dingy eaves look the very personifications of antiquity. The dwellings of nobles were there once, where now you find squalling town-cats and yelling children, old hags with frilled caps, ruffian men, and young ladies to correspond. Walk out of High Street to the top of Calton Hill and here you may see a magnificent specimen of *new* Edinburgh. It was designed to erect the Pantheon of Athens on this commanding height—but the men of modern Athens were too ambitious. Their funds gave out; but not till a foundation was laid, and a row of beautiful columns erected. There they stand yet; enough to display the magnificence of the design, and to excite regret that it could not be fully realised. Holyrood Palace still contains Queen Mary's bed, and specimens of tapestry worked by her hand. All is arranged as when she inhabited the room. The fatal supper-room is shown, where she sat at table with Rizzio and her guests on the night when her favorite was murdered. Darneley's armor is lying on the table. The stain of Rizzio's blood can still be seen in the floor near the door of her audience hall, where the body was found. She had a partition of wood put up, to keep the place from her sight.

The great hall of the palace, where the portraits of the Scottish kings are placed, is a gloomy and sombre room with wainscotting of some dark wood. The last of the many royal entertainments of which it has been the scene, was, I think, those balls given by the Pretender, at which Waverley acquitted himself so well.[71]

Edinburgh, altogether, is a most interesting place—not so Glasgow, where I spent a day. There is nothing there that I could find worth looking at except the Tolbooth, celebrated in *Rob Roy*. I saw in Edinburgh, by the way, the opera of *Rob Roy*, in which Mackay personated Baillie Nicol Jarvie. This performer, I think, was the original Baillie, to whom Scott sent a present and a compliment; certainly his performance was far superior to any of the rest.

The vicinity of Glasgow to the Highlands is particularly tantalising to one who has not time to go there. The steamer sailed for Liverpool on the evening of the day when I arrived. She had on board about a hundred passengers, beside seventy or eighty cattle, and a large flock of sheep. They all were taken sea-sick in the course of the voyage, and made a most curious but pitiable spectacle. I enquired for my birth, which the steward pointed out to me, and I immediately went to sleep. About midnight I heard somebody speaking to me; opened my eyes, and saw a tall thin broad-shouldered Sawney,[r] with a particularly sneaking expression of countenance, standing over me, directing me to get up as I had his birth. I told him he was mistaken, and must not disturb me; and soon dropped asleep again. Shortly after, the fellow returned with the steward, who said he had made a mistake and shown me the wrong birth: so I rolled into the next one, whence I saw Sawney by the light of the Steward's lantern tumbling himself into the one I had left, with a grunt of satisfaction at his victory. He preferred to have the birth he had engaged, though another person had slept in it, to selecting one from three or four other precisely similar which remained vacant close at hand. He spoke no word of thanks or apology, but pointed to a red-headed brat of his who was snoring like a porpoise in a birth below us. Nothing would do but the anxious father must be within arm's reach of his cub.

After a twenty-four hours' voyage, we reached Liverpool late at night. The town looked quite as dismal as I had imagined it; smoky with the chimneys of numberless iron-foundries. I found my trunks had arrived safe from London, and got an order for their delivery from the clerk of Baring Brothers, to whom I had consigned them. This order I gave to a cabman, telling him to bring the luggage to the hotel as soon as possible. He went off in hot haste, but returned in half an hour, saying that the man at the store-house refused to give them up. I was astonished and provoked; but got into the cab to see to the matter in person. When I got to the storehouse, an old

[r] Derogatory term for a Scot.—Ed.

man made his appearance, with a large bunch of keys in his hand, and inflexible obstinacy and stolidity written on his broad countenance. I produced the order, and demanded what induced him to withold the trunks. He turned over the paper three or four times, scrutinizing it in every direction; then returned it, saying doggedly, "Can't let ye have 'em." I asked him what more he would have—there was a written order for them. The old fool wriggled about and dangled his keys in evident trouble, but still replied: "Can't let ye have 'em. 'T would be much as my place is worth." Nothing would shake his stupid honesty—not even my letter of credit on the house, or the card of the Liverpool partner, Mr. Gair, which I had with me. "Oh, he didn't entertain no suspicion—not at all—he dare say all was right—but I couldn't have the trunks without the paper was signed by Mr. Gair himself." I had to send the cabman to the house of this gentleman, who was a good deal vexed at the bull-headed faithfulness of the old man. This is the only instance in the course of my journeyings where I have met with too much honesty. The matter did not end here. I had returned to the hotel, having described the two trunks to the old fellow, and told him that my name was printed on the lid of each, to which he kept replying "Oh, yes, oh, yes; there was two just such trunks in the store-room—he had been watching them for a whole week." So I thought the matter settled at last, and was writing a letter in my room when a porter entered with a box of pine boards eight feet long and four wide, beneath which he could hardly stand. "Here's the other," said the coachman, bringing in one of my trunks. "It's all right now, I s'pose, sir"; and he lifted his hat, for his remuneration. I was too much amused to be angry, and despatched him again to the storehouse, with directions to tell the old man that he was a fool. This time he brought the right trunk, which, being small, had been packed away under a desk for safe-keeping.

I was obliged to remain several days in Liverpool, and lamented the arrangement of the Glasgow steamers, which forced me to throw away, on this disgusting city, time which I might otherwise have spent in the Highlands. I was lucky enough to meet Col. Winchester with his son and Mr. Green whom I had seen at Rome. Green and I, with a young Irish friend of his, went to a *fête* at the Liverpool

Zoological Gardens, where were at least a dozen American ship-captains in the crowd. This crowd had little resemblance to the swarm of young men and grisettes at the corresponding places of entertainment at Paris. Here were other countrymen of mine, in the shape of a black bear, a cougar, and a Canada wild-cat, who were glaring through the bars of their cages in a fury at the rockets and other fire-works.

The Irishman invited us home with him to supper, where we found his brother. Like other Irish gentleman, they had not a particle of English coldness and haughty reserve—all was frankness and cordiality. Supper over, they ordered the "matarials" with which to make a pitcher of Irish punch. Green seasoned it with his dry and humorous stores, in the precise manner of Dan Slade,[72] whom he actually surpasses in stature, being six feet four inches high.

The next day we went on board the *Acadia* by the small steamer hired to take off her passengers. As we sat on deck, contemplating the destined companions of our voyage, messenger after messenger came to Green from his various acquaintances: one brought him a package of newspapers, another a bundle of letters, another a case of presents for friends, each repeating the same formula, "Would Mr. Green oblige Mr. _____ by taking charge of this little parcel?" At last a fellow came down with a large wooden box on his shoulders, full of samples of sugar, alum, salt, etc., and made the same modest request. Green had been growling and swearing for some time, as each successive bundle came in; but when he saw this approaching, he roared out—"Take it away! Pitch it overboard. Don't you see I've got enough to sink the ship alongside of me now!" The porter walked off with the box. Col. Winchester was quite exempt from this species of nuisance; but as we were leaving the wharf, a small active-looking man hastily shouldered through the crowd, siezed his hand, and proffered for his acceptance a thin volume of poems—a production of the donor's deceased wife—which he ventured to hope might afford amusement and consolation to the Colonel during the hours of sea-sickness. The present was understood to be from the daughter of the defunct poetess. A note from her was enclosed in the volume. The Col. showed it to me—the whole composition was extraordinary, but I only remember the conclusion:

". . . we part, I fear, for many months; but that Heaven may bless you and yours, will ever, sir, be the ardent wish of one whose pride it is to enrol herself,

"With respect and affection

"On the long catalogue of your friends

—————— W.——"

We soon got on board of the *Acadia*, and watched the smoky city, half concealed behind a forest of masts. The spectacle was ugly enough; but not uninteresting, as this was the last we were to see of European cities. In two hours more we got under weigh—were saluted from a fort not far down the Mersey, and replied from two brass guns, to the consternation of the ladies.

It was two days before we passed Cape Clear. Head winds, and a sea not smooth. Our sixty-five passengers kept below for the most part, for the sight of dinner had become an abomination. There was nothing but groanings and vociferations, through the long ranges of state-rooms. The poems failed to console the Colonel, who was terribly sick.

There were on board English, Irish, Scotch, French, Germans, and Americans, beside half a dozen Canadians. In a week, the general sickness nearly disappeared. The table is set five times a day, beside which many of the passengers manage to keep eating in the intervals, for anything is to be had when called for—by the terms of the engagement. Those who are disposed for more intellectual enjoyment play cards, or gather round the chimney on the upper deck to dispute on the merits of their respective countries.

The English gather into a knot by themselves. They sit in a group near the captain, discussing the quality of their wine, or talking on military matters, as they are chiefly Canada officers. The "damned Yankees" are scattered everywhere about the tables, and of every grade and character, from gentlemen down to some vulgar and conceited travelling-agent from New York. When evening comes, the din of conversation and laughter begins. Everyone has his punch, his wine, or his porter, and joins a group according to his taste. The Bishop of Newfoundland, who is on his way out, betakes himself to the study of a volume relating to his interesting diocese. The Englishmen gather and talk of their wine again, casting from time to time contemptuous glances over their shoulders at the noisy groups of Americans, Scotch, and Irish. One of them usually retires by himself to the farthest corner of the room, where the tables are quite empty, where he drinks his bottle of wine, neither looking to the right hand nor to the left. He always appears in full dress, with startched dickey erect, threatening to saw his ears off. Occasionally he will honor the Bishop's chaplain with an intimation that his company will be agreeable, and the pair drink the wine together.

In calm weather, when the upper deck is dry, Green comes up with a Scotch plaid round his shoulders and propping his head against the mast, flings out his legs to an incredible distance, and reads the *Mysteries of Paris*—a needless task with him, by the way, for he is tolerably initiated into *les vrais Mystères*. Col. W. comes up also, and wrapping himself in his cloak, lies down likewise. His son joins the party. Then merchants, travelling gentlemen, agents—in short a fair representation of the Yankee Nation—gather round and assume the same comfortable but inelegant attitude. Meanwhile the officers have been perambulating the deck, head erect, shoulders back, with a measured tread of dignity, and a look of supreme contempt for all the world. When they approach the Americans, their [there] is a perceptible rising of the chin, and a redoubled stiffness of carriage. Their eyes seem to be bent on vacuity, but they will glance down an instant disdainfully at the variety of uncouth attitudes of the group—then as they turn away, one will curl his lip and whisper to the other. Green bawls out to the Colonel's son: "Billy, you don't understand how to be comfortable. Here, let me show you the way to enjoy yourself like an American and a freeman" —so he lifts one of his long legs up to Billy's head, and reaches the other out to the railing of the deck. "Well, I swow!" says another, "you do things first rate, I calculate, and no mistake. *We* don't live under a despotic government, I guess!"—and this man tries to emulate Green by stretching both feet across his neighbor's lap. "Yes," says the next man, "Freedom's the word—to all but the niggers! I wish we kept those cattle in the north—a good thing to exercise a man on, of a cold morning, and give him an appetite for breakfast. I'd lash mine till they roared again." "I'd roast mine alive," says another, taking out a pen-knife to pick his teeth, "if they didn't behave." "I'd raise a breed for the doctors," adds another, "they sell well, and it don't cost anything to raise them, because the thinner the body is, you know, the better it is to dissect."

All this being uttered in a loud voice, the Englishmen could not help hearing. Unlike some of their countrymen, they began at last to "smell a rat"—so, casting a look of disdainful ire on the grave countenances of the Americans, they descended with stately steps, to the lower deck.

I knew a young American in Paris who was possessed with the same hatred against Englishmen which the buccaneer Morgan is said to have felt against Spaniards. Walking with him in the street, if an Englishman happened to pass, his face would change suddenly; he would turn round and follow the man with his eyes, as if he were a mortal enemy. He used to insult them, and play tricks on them, on every occasion. The masked balls, especially, gave him ample opportunities; and he particularly delighted in manoevring to turn them to ridicule before their partners, or to get their partners away from them—and then he would assail them with sneers and jests which would have got him into a scrape at any other place than a masked ball.

On Saturday evening the different nations separate, and remain till late drinking the customary toast of "Sweethearts and Wives." On Sunday the Bishop of Newfoundland preaches us sermons which the meanest Freshman in Harvard ought to have been ashamed to have written. The Bishop (who—with reverence to his lordship be it said— seems not to be gifted with any extraordinary share of common sense, whatever his spiritual gifts may be) takes great delight in lengthening out his precious liturgy as far as possible, repeating the creed, and the prayers for the government and the Royal Family several times. He does not deign to regard the two-thirds of his auditors, who are neither British subjects nor Episcopalians.

His lordship is a great enemy of the Temperance reform, and relates with great satisfaction the story of a pewter mug which was presented him by the "publicans," for preaching a sermon against it. It is a sin, he says, to teach men to do for their worldly interest that which they ought to do purely for the glory of God. It may, he says, produce results apparently good, but it "implants a bad principle"— and the evil effects are at some future day to be made manifest.

One evening we saw an iceberg in the distance. A double watch was set all night, and one or two passengers were nervous enough to sit up in dread of a catastrophe. None occurred; the sea was perfectly calm in the morning, with no ice in sight; the ship moving steadily on at the rate of eleven knots. Hitherto we had made an average course of no more than six knots, on account of the rough sea and constant head winds.

The sea has now been calm for several days. I came on deck this morning[8] and smelt the land breeze; half an hour after, the coast of Nova Scotia was visible, but fogs and cloud soon sank upon it, and shut it from sight. We are now too far distant from any part of the shore to discern it by the ordinary laws of vision; yet you can see distinctly from the deck a long line of high lands, with forests and patches of open soil. As the state of the atmosphere changes, and its refractive power becomes greater or less, this false coast rises higher above the horizon, or sinks down below it.

[8] "*June 17th.*"—F.P.

Appendix

European Notebook

Polyphemus. There is a man on deck, with a face dark as a Negro or mulatto, yet features unlike those races and very powerful—a beetling brow, shaggy with hair, a swelling nostril, black strong beard—and an expression as fierce and savage as I ever saw. He stands with folded arms, a strange contrast to the light hair, florid faces, and military stiffness of the Marines.

Lt. Sp[arks] still nourished a strong dislike against the French—the embers of natural hatred still-born. He expressively calls them "tiger-monkeys."

Speaking of English leniency towards colonists, he mentions, as an instance of forbearance, that the English religion has been *forced* upon none of them, but they have been suffered to enjoy their own.

Christmas Day. The men dancing on deck, to the sound of a drum, a violin, and a fiddle, the musicians perched on the rail. All more or less "excited." A group approached a young midshipman with whom I was talking. "We've had the honor to drink your health, sir," said a fat drummer boy, touching his hat, while his companions were grinning in the rear. The midshipman stop'd a moment, blushed, hesitated, then told them to go and get another bottle of wine from the steward. All are in high enjoyment.

We had an excellent Christmas dinner. The swarthy Maltese officer was, even at table, a butt for his companions, especially the officer who the other day insolently shrugged his shoulders as I past.

After dinner we adjourned to the gun-room and played cards, this quiet personage called the Dr. taking a rather unwilling and indifferent part.

The officer aforementioned was half "slewed," flung the furniture and plates carelessly about, and designated everything as "bloody."

Messina. A broad long street along the water—with stone buildings, many of them exceedingly large and beautiful, on one side—the shops on the other. Shops and stores of all kinds on the ground story of the buildings, all with wide open fronts crowded with merchandise. Splendidly tinselled liquor shops, with here and there a padre for a customer—barber's shops with the row of basins in front—tobacco shops—exchange—cobbler's shops. The broad street full of people. "Boot blacks" waiting for a job at the sides and corners—butchers, fruiterers, money changers thronging around the bases of the columns where an arch opens into the back of the town, exposing a long perspective of narrow crowded streets. Capuchins in their brown garb—priests with their looped-up hats—and embryo priests on a smaller scale. Criers and hawkers; soldiers moustachioed, with the broad white belt across their grey surtouts. Men carrying sacred pictures and images—a madonna or some saint, by the way, is stuck at every corner.

"*Dové è il téatro?*" I enquired of a fellow at the corner of the street. "Ah! *signore*, I am delighted at de meeting with an Englishman. I shall have de honor to show you to the teater. This is the night of the grand festival through the countries of the Catholic religion. . . . Ah! the door of the teater is closed, dey have postponed the entertainment. But I shall have the honor to show you the church where they celebrate at present the grand festival of the new year."

We went there—the cathedral was a blaze of light—all the floor was a black sea of heads—the priests were chanting, and incense burning—a flourish of trumpets—a burst of solemn music, and the throng bowed down as the host was elevated.

"Thee, God, we praise," said my acquaintance who stood at my side, looking up into my face with his large grey eyes—and translating the *Te Domine* for my benefit. "The decorations of this church, sir, are very exceedingly beautiful, but I have seen it honored with a greater number of tapers. They are cautious at present. Last year the fire took force on the pictures and ornaments and the people trod on each other to get out, the women, and the ladies, and the men." All this he said with a grin, as if highly amused, rubbing the palms of his hands together. The people all looked towards us.

"The altar is adorned with precious stones, which you will observe in the morning. Do you understand the Latin tongue, sir?" Then he began to repeat with Italian accent several lines from the eclogues of "Virgilio." Several of the people turned round or talked with him in Italian, looking curiously at me. "Those people," he said, turning to me, "consider it to be for a very strange thing that you should understand Latin, while you are ignorant of Italian. They have not reflected that these are two different languages."

Here, with a crash of fireworks in the galleries, the service concluded. "Now we will hasten out, previously to the rush of the crowd. Take care of your pockets, sir. There are very nimble fingers here."

When we got out, I questioned this singular character. He said his father was in good circumstances, and had taken great pains to give him an education—sending him to college. But now he was poor and had no shirt—"Sir, I ask your pardon, but look here"—and he stripped himself to show the truth of what he said. He could not read his books now, and he had a family at home.

I asked him how he had fallen so low. He told some story about having an office in the customs and being caught dealing with the *contrabandos*—and of drinking a glass of wine with his friends.

By this time he had worked himself up into a crying fit. Lifting up his ragged hat, he said he thought heaven had sent the English gentleman to relieve him—but having nothing less than a dollar, I left him.

Have just arrived at Giardini—stand in the window of the *albergo*—filled with admiration at the singular beauty of the scenery. Had no idea that so much pleasure could be conveyed through the eye.

"Recommendations" at Giardini.

Road to Catania. Etna, in clouds, snow, and smoke. Beggars. Lava. At Catania, visited the convent of the Benedictines which so narrowly escaped destruction in [16]69. The Boscari Museum; and fountain. The Greek theatre. Went in the evening to the opera—one of Bellini's, said to be a native of Catania. Lopez and a young Frenchman my companions, the latter an admirable example of the national liveliness and light-heartedness. In buying pit tickets for the theatre here, you are shown a plan of the theatre—select an unoccupied seat, which is numbered—and a paper ticket given you, corresponding to the number.

Etna had an eruption two or three weeks since—more than sixty killed and wounded.

Sicily is called by Mrs. Starke "the birth place of pastoral poetry"—for Theocritus was buried there. It is well fitted to be.

Returning, were accompanied by a singular looking boy, who ran behind, or clung on, ready to help in emergencies. Everybody here rides mules; the rider often the biggest of the two. The brown capote of the country is worthy of notice. I tasted the Indian fig at Giarri, where we stopped. Beset there by beggars, one of whom, a little boy, trotted after me wherever I went, danced a kind of hornpipe, and made most ludicrous signs and grimaces. Also a mute girl. The old blind beggars by the road-

side the most disgusting. Etna looked most grandly, in clouds and smoke.
The smaller and nearer mts. were a noble spectacle at sunset.

Giardini. Thursday, Jan. 5[4]*th*. The people about here seem chiefly
engaged in weaving, spinning, dying cloth, and fishing. Their plows are
not very unlike the Spanish. They drive their oxen with a rope round the
horns like reins. About the church-porches groups are basking in the sun
and picking vermin from one another's heads.

Every house, as far as I know, has a holy picture, with a lamp before it.
Dined at Mr. Gardiner's. Greatly edified by Mr. B[rown]'s conversation.
The two captains at Mr. Marston's. Silence of Capt. *Emily,* interpreted
into deep thinking and observation; the frankness, good nature, and
heartiness of Capt. *Cecilia,* with his conversation: "Now I can't get along
without tobacco, nohow. Some say it's a nasty trick to be chawing of it
all the time, but I—," etc.

The English invalid gentleman.

The legs, heads, and arms of wax, hung up in the churches—given in
commemoration of vows by the sick afflicted in any of those members.

Mr. Brown—his table talk—his conversations with Miss ———— at the
theatre, explaining the formation of the thighs of women as distinguished
from those of men—making constant *double-entendres*—very plain ones. A
gay bachelor.

The people here paint crosses against such walls as they do not wish
defiled.

Mr. Smith, the invalid, at the Marstons'—his notions of antiquities.

Books and pictures are exposed for sale on the sidewalks—scriveners
sit in the frequented places, ready to write letters. The shops are all open
in front—the signs are carved with images, for the benefit of those who
cannot read. Hosts of foppishly dressed and sickly looking men beset the
streets. The carriages of the nobility, with liveried servants, roll through
the streets. The little painted mule carts—the mule with a high-peaked
and gaudily ornamented saddle—are seen everywhere. Indian figs, corn,
beans, chesnuts, oranges, and sweetmeats are sold at the street corners.
The confectioners usually have a little fountain, in the form of a bird
pouring a small stream of water from its beak.

Giuseppe—his . . . .

Stockings	1	Shirts	5
Dickey	1	Drawers	1
Handks.	4	Towels	2

Village ten miles from Palermo. Some of the people wear leggings of thick fur—and of leather. "*Viva la divina providenza*" inscribed over the wine shops. Mules, asses, and sheep kept in the house.

A Silician Town. A great cluster of square-shaped, tiled-roofed houses, in a hollow among green and beautiful mts.—an old castle on an eminence above—green and cultivated fields around. Enter it and you must pass through narrow and muddy streets; the houses of stone sometimes plastered and whitewashed, with strong grated windows and open doors. Old women sit spinning; ragamuffins lounge in their capotes; mules and ass-carts, soldiers and priests, pass you. Here and there is a fountain, green and mossy, with groups of boys and women filling jars and little casks. Holy pictures and images in niches. The Piazza with its loftier houses—its *albergos*—its throngs of idlers around the provision stalls— and the church with the solemn-looking capoted loungers on its steps.

Village of M[arineo]. Luigi is a diminutive Sicilian, thin and spare, full of shrugs, and gestures, and exclamations. In the carriage he began to talk with the greatest vivacity, gesticulating and rolling his eyes, half frenzied by desire to be intelligible. He has provided a most excellent dinner here, where we stop till tomorrow, when we change the carriage for mules. I went to the house of our muleteer's brother and was treated with nuts. Luigi says he will be my Italian master—talked and gesticulated —kissed my hand—and after arranging all things, went off. He has brought excellent provisions—wine—and a large book of antiquities for me to read.

Staleles: salt-cellars. Greeks: Calabrians.

Friday. Left the town on mules—changed them for a carriage. The scenery very beautiful. Luigi talkative and lively as ever. When we stopped to lunch, a blind man came up and began to play on a violin, accompanied by another. Luigi jumped out and began to dance in a most amateur-like style to the music. An ugly beggar woman, who stood by, tossed her child in time with the musicians, hoping probably to win a *carlin[o]* in consideration of her part in the performance. When we reached a village, we found nothing to eat either in the *albergo* or the town, and had to depend upon Luigi's preparations. A large and dirty village. A floor of earth to my room. Costumes vary in different parts of Sicily, as do dialects. We passed warm baths—great houses for the *contadini*—and straw huts for the same. Luigi found a friend—his "Don Juanino mio." Stone here supplies the place of wood in architecture. Troughs—all of stone. Natural fountains have stone troughs hollowed out of the living rock beneath, for the mules, etc. Flax and grain of various kinds—spinning still the occupation of the women. The black-capoted and staring idlers, grouped around the huge stone stables beneath my room, make a strange appearance.

Morning, La Cara. A throng of men and cattle in the stable below, mules going out with their panniers and their tails knotted; others being equipped.

Began on foot. Walked on over a bad road in company with two muleteers talking their villanous patois, of which I understood not a word. It was like a New England November—the wind came cold and sharp over the mountains. The mules overtook us, and we mounted. We had not gone far, when some *contadini* told us that the road was broken away. We turned back—waded through a vast slough of mud in the bottom of a valley—then followed a narrow and broken pathway of stones along the side of a hill, while a swollen stream roared along among the olive-trees below. After this we found no road at all—or where there was one, it was a gulf of mud. We forded a dozen streams—one of them in its broad bed of stones, with the water rippling in a narrow stream down the centre, closely resembled ours—but the illusion was dispelled by a glance at the bare and smooth hills, with olives and Indian figs, and the stone house of refuge with tiled roofs, not far from the landing place.

My mule did not behave himself. He had a propensity for stumbling in dangerous places—would also turn longing glances at the fair ones of his race, and make a horrible noise meanwhile. When fairly in among the mts., it began to rain. A violent wind, too, sprang up as we crossed a little bridge at the bottom of a narrow gorge, where a stream came down from the mountains.

We soon after saw Castel Termini on the side of a hill in front. After riding an hour over a stony and barren hill-side in the rain and wind, which were excessively cold, we got to the town. The scenery about here might be beautiful in fair weather; it was gloomy and savage then. We approached the town by a path a yard wide—which by the use of ages had become worn deep in the soil so that to a spectator at a distance we should have seemed half buried. The town is a fine one; very clean. The usual crowd collected at the *albergo* to see us. I dined and (and) went out with Luigi, who show'd some antique coins, and a beautiful grotto adorned with Sicilian minerals. A broad-shouldered Greek, a non-commissioned officer in the Neapolitan gendarmes, attempted a conversation in his own language with me, but without success. The judge showed me into a *converzatione* where a dozen or more people were playing cards. They stared at me with great curiosity, and finally left their game and gathered round me in a ring, very curious to know something of the place I came from. I talked as I could with my limited stock of Italian. They asked me what province I came from; I told them Massachusetts, at which they paused in astonishment, and then muttered "*Cattivissima parola!*" The Greek alone succeeded in pronouncing it. I got tired of being an object of curiosity to so many, bade them good night, and went to the inn.

Yankee curiosity is nothing to the curiosity of these people.

Left the inn in the morning and rode over a country of mountains by a mule-track, literally paved with alabastar in some places. Saw a *lettiga*. Approaching a deep valley, we heard the noise of water at the bottom, and saw a wide and turbid stream that we must cross. The broad meadows below us were dotted with hundreds of the long-horned oxen of Sicily, each with a bell round its neck, which sounded at that height like the tinkling of a stream. The mountains lay still in the hot sunshine, softened by a sort of sleepy haze. When we got down to the bank, we found there two men naked from the waist downwards, whose muscular and handsome limbs were tanned as black as their faces by constant exposure. One went before our mules—the other brought up the rear. The water was up to the horses' bellies, but we got through dry. Stopping now and then to water the horses at alabastar troughs cut at the bottom of springs, we reached the village of Carmina at noon. It was excessively hot, and sultry as we entered the town and climbed the steep street. All the houses were plastered up with a gray cement of gypsum—everything was of the same gray hue but the brown roofs. The women sat on stone benches outside their doors, with loose hair and a primitive dress, combing their hair or caressing their children. Some basked at full length on the ground. Many were pretty, though the full vigor and health on their sunburnt cheeks were the chief part of their attractions. All was rude and primitive. Capoted starers and Neapolitan soldiers were congregated in the piazza before the ancient church. Opposite this village—on the other side of the valley—another similar village lay basking in the sun, with the yellow palace of its proprietor conspicuous above the grey houses. There was no *albergo* here. Luigi took possession of a private house, where he produced dinner. Some fellows then guided me to the sulphur mines just back of the village.

As we rode away, we had from the hill-top a glorious spectacle of ———— and mountains. We rode until late in the afternoon, when we saw Girgenti crowning a steep hill in front, and caught glimpses of the sea through the vallies. It was near sunset—the scenes we past were rich and beautiful beyond expression. Flocks of goats were driven past us; mules and asses with their panniers came down from the city. We left the road, and crossing a little mule path, descended into a deep and shadowy valley, on the opposite side of which rose the hill on which the city stands. Luigi was in a great excitement to be there before the Dawsons. "*Corragio,* my brave mule; *corragio, signore,* we shall be victors." He went on driving his mule at full speed up the steep hill; making short cuts; leaping dangerous gullies, in neck or nothing style, till he got to the top; and shouted, "*Vittoria!*" as he rode into the gate, as much elated as if he had accomplished some great enterprise.

"*Ecco mi pronto; sono Luigi! Viva l'onore!*"

The women of Cara—they reminded me of the women of Virgil's ecclogues, the wives of the primitive inhabitants of Italy. There was health and strength and good physical womanhood about them. There were the affections of a Roman—strong and unpolished: some fondled their children; some caressed their husbands; some hugged and kissed pet dogs—fit mates all for the wild foresters and mountaineers of whom the pastoral poets speak.

A Sicilian inn. An old house of stone, like all the rest. A den below, with a mud floor—filled with water jars, harness, stone troughs, and a thousand strange utensils of cookery—all handsomely encrusted with dirt. A dirty image of the Virgin on the wall, with a lamp before it. Dirty loungers crouching over braziers of charcoal—this in the kitchen, all as dark as Tartarus. Close adjoining to it, on the same floor, are great stone apartments for the mules and asses, who in the good inns are usually accomodated with separate apartments, though in private houses a corner of the family room, always the cleanest, is assigned to them. Ask for *apartamenti,* and you are conducted up flights of dilapidated stone steps to a room floored with cement as hard as stone—with plastered walls garnished with a crucifix or a holy picture—one strongly secured window—and a bed whereof you are never allowed to be the sole tenant, for a regiment of fleas is always quartered upon you. The only kind of fire is one of charcoal in a brazier. As to food, it cannot be had. I speak from the experience of three nights, and I solemnly aver that the picture is not over colored.

It is an amusing sight to see the mules and asses go out from their quarters in the morning. The mule I have ridden is young and inexperienced—though a wretched mule, he has sympathy with his kind.

A prominent feature of a *locanda* I have for[gotten]—it is the beggars.

A filthy and wretched beast, all tatters and rags, unshaven, with bleared gummy eyes and a crouching posture, stands covered all but the face in a rotten brown capote at the door—thrusts forth a rosary in your face, and mutters a petition for alms. Some of them have a cylindrical box with an image of the Savior on the cross painted on it, which they hold out to receive your gift. Luigi takes off his hat to the image, but declines any more substantial token of respect. These are professed beggars—only one form of the nuisance. Each man, woman, or child about the place occasionally practices the trade.

Morning, Monday. Visited the old temples of Agrigentum on the hill below Girgenti—tombs, temples, roads, *fascinae*, etc. I had rather see Mt. Washington, notwithstanding dear Miss Prentiss' predictions.

Luigi has provided an excellent dinner—his zeal is most admirable. He comes in: "Ah, *signor*, do you think I love money? No, Luigi loves honor," slapping himself on the breast and rolling up his eyes. He is perfectly rabid with enthusiasm in everything—raves of love on the road— tells stories of his elopement with his wife—sings songs—shouts *"Corragio"* —says, assuming a most heroic attitude on his mule's back, *"Il vento—il [la] neve—il pioggia—li fiume—tutto fa niente, corragio, signore"*; and then breaks out into a song. He is mad after antiquities—comes up to tell me that he can buy *antiqua moneta* at Girgenti for *pochissimo*. He enters into my plans with most fervid zeal, leaving me almost nothing to do. Wherever we stop, he first provides dinner—waits on table with an eulogium on every dish, and a list, daily repeated, of the provisions he has provided— then reappears, bring *molte cose de curiose* in the shape of vases and domestic utensils. I hint at anything to be done—he pounds his breast, and exclaims: *"Ecco mi pronto; sono Luigi!* All is safe under the care of Luigi; do not trouble yourself, *signore*."

This ebullition of zeal in all things is curious enough at times—last night in his fiery charge up the mountain, with his whole soul set on vanquishing the Dawsons. We came to a ditch which he could not pass— he struck his forehead—exclaimed, *"Maria Santissima!"*—then recovering his spirits, roared *"Corragio,"* and dashed off, mad with eagerness, in another direction. This sort of enthusiasm seems common enough here. There is a Signor Politi, half rampant about antiquities—he and Luigi boil over together, and aggravate each other's madness.

Luigi says he always brings with him some antiquities *per fare complimenti* to his acquaintances—for which he receives other *complimenti* in return—an interchange of civilities very characteristic of this excitable

people, with their huggings, kissings, and swearings of eternal friendship.
The blind traveller, Mr. Oldham(?) [Holman].

Went to see Signore Politi—got his antiquities of Sicily and saw the
works of Signore Fennimore Coopero, translated. Visited the Duomo—
gathered curiosities—descended to the port, five miles distant, and thence
proceeded to Mont'Allegro. When half way there, a large town lay
before us among the mts.—Siculiana—built of alabastar; the people were
different in costume from others—some of the women wore their hair
arranged in a very beautiful manner. The occupants of the crowded
doorways were, however, engaged in spinning like the rest. The women
here in Sicily ride astride the mule, like the men.

We proceeded thence by a mule path through a country of rocky and
broken mts., with an occasional view of the sea betwixt them. The
valleys we traversed were full of sheep. Our mules waded frequently to
their knees in mud. Late in the afternoon we saw Mt. Allegro—a village
wildly and beautifully situated at the base of mts. of alabastar—the
summit of one of them, just above, is crowned with a ruined castle and an
assemblage of ancient dwellings. It rises before me now as I write at the
window of the *locanda*—the white rock contrasted with the thick growth
of Indian fig that springs from every crevice, from top to bottom. It is
a quiet and beautiful evening. The usual groups of idlers in the streets are
talking and laughing—the same beings that their fathers were before
them, six centuries ago. The approach to this place, which is almost
surrounded by a belt of orange groves, is over rocks of alabastar, in which
the constant passage of mules and asses has worn a deep narrow channel.

Luigi excited. He sat by the table with a glass of wine, gesticulating,
rolling up his eyes, opening and shutting his mouth: "*Viva l'onore! signorino
mio, viva Bacco—viva Dio—viva il console Americano*"; then he kisses the
buttons of his coat, which have the American eagles; then seizes my hand
and kisses that.

Morning. Picked up beautiful specimans of alabastar. *Afternoon.*—of agates
and jaspers. It rained—the country uninteresting—the mules slipping in
the mud—reached Sciacca, a town of more than 20,000 inhabitants.
Found rooms, after some difficulty.

Morning. At Sciacca are vapor baths—arranged by Dedalus, but now the
property of Santo Carlogio—at the summit of a high mt. a few miles from
town. I rode up there in the morning, came to the convent of the St. at
the top where, circling around the whitewashed wall, we came to a

diminutive stable, where through an opening at the head of a flight of stairs we beheld the refectioner engaged, with gown tucked up, in the operations of his office. He conducted me to the baths—a great cavern under the convent, secured by a strong door. I undressed in an apartment opposite, and staid quarter of an hour in the cavern, where a stream of vapor, with a roaring down in the bowels of the mt. like a waterfall, filled the whole place and brought on a most active perspiration. My cicerone, who staid there, discoursed meanwhile on their antiquity, till I cried enough, made a dash for the room, where he rubbed me down with a towel. Not that the towel was supplied by the fathers. The holy father then led me to a hole in the mt. below, where a similar steam issued, with a still louder noise. The view of Sciacca on the little hill below—with its white battlements, ruined castle, and numerous churches—was very fine. Descending, bought pots and kettles, etc.; saw the castle and the tomb of its ancient master, Ct. P———; the Carmelite church, which was a gift of his to the monks. He was a grandson of Roger, the expeller of the Saracens. The fathers were at dinner—one of them, however, showed me the church, and faintly refused my *bonamano,* as the rules of his order dictated; he took it, however, on my holding it forth again.

Accounts of European Journey

	Drafts
Mr. Sprague	£13 in sovereigns
Mr. Payson	$20 sp. in Spanish dollars
—Do.—	Piasts. 30 in Piastres
Mr. Gardiner	Piasts. 80
Do.	Piasts. 70
Booth and Jean	Psts. 100
Do.	Sp. dolls. 50 in Spanish dlls.
Freeborn	Sp. dls. 60
Do.	Sp. dls. 20
	Sp. dls. 40
Du Fresne	Tus. dls. 100—each Tuscan do.—=Sp. dlls. 1.05
Ulrich	Francs 200
Hottinguer	Francs 1200
Baring Brs.	£ 70.1.6

```
   200                              13
  1200                              70.1.6
  ─────                             ──────
  1400 francs                       £83.1.6

          30  Payson     50
         150  Gardiner   60 ⎫
         100  R.J.J.     20 ⎬ = 120              83
         ───  piastres   40 ⎭                     5
         280            ───                      ───
                        170                      415
                                                 450
    1400 francs                                  500
                                                 ────
    280 piastres                                 1365
    170 Sp. dols.
    83.1.6 £.s.d.
        80
        70
       100
        50
        60
        20
        40
```

Expenditures

Gibralter   £ 6   in sovereigns

Passage to M. £ 13   in sovereigns

Malta and ⎰£ 4   in sovereigns
Syracuse   ⎱Doubl. ½   in 1 quarter and 2 eighth doub.

Messina⎰Doubl. ⅛   in eighth doub.
      ⎱Sp. $ 16   in Spanish dollars
      ⎱Piastres 14

Palermo   ⎰Piastres 96
and journey⎰Sp. $ 4
to Girgenti ⎱Doubl. ¼

Luigi's services began at noon, Thursday, Jan. 18th.

Crucifixes, pictures, images suspended in churches by the sick.

11 piastres to sundries

5
—   Giuseppe
18
20   Luigi

D. 16.75 = 1 1st   Thursday
½D. 8.37½ = ½ 2nd   Luigi   [?]
D. 16.75 = 1 3rd   15½   31C
              4th–8th = 13 pieces   4¼   31   24   5
   3   9th   60   2   7
   3   10th   2   84
   4   11th   62
                           3
                          ——
                          65⅞
                          65.10½

Boston & Berkshire Journal
1844

Introduction

IN THE course of his European travels Parkman had not lost his love for the New England countryside; and as soon as he could get away from home after his return, he made an expedition to the Berkshire Hills in western Massachusetts. The record of this journey is of particular interest, for it shows him observing his country and his people with eyes freshened by European travel. He was awakened to a new appreciation of America; and he liked his land none the less for having seen others. The opening pages of this Berkshire journal offer more of Parkman's conclusions about Europe than the European journal itself. His observations of the New England scene are sharper and more objective than before he went abroad, and they reveal a greater maturity. In short, travel was beginning to make him a citizen of the world.

The journal opens with an account of the Fourth of July celebration at Concord, which is followed by the record of an excursion to Nahant. Then, scrawling a note on the flyleaf of his little notebook that he must be at Cambridge on the third Wednesday of August—for his graduation from Harvard—Parkman set off westward for a few weeks among those Berkshire Hills which had aroused his interest two years before, when he was bound for Lake George. He had historical research in mind, for the region was rich in legends and traditions of its frontier days, which figure considerably in *A Half-Century of Conflict* and *Montcalm and Wolfe;* but Parkman was also anxious to refresh himself with a few weeks of outdoor life. He traveled light, with a knapsack containing "three shirts, two stockings, flannel drawers, fishing apparatus, powder and shot, and *History of B[erkshire]*." Passing westward by Springfield, Cabotville, Chester Factory, and Lee, he came at last to Stockbridge, perhaps the most charming of the old New England towns. Here he gathered a great store of memories from ancient village notables. Then he turned southward to Great Barrington and Mount Washington, the most isolated settlement in Massachusetts; then northward to Lebanon Springs, over the New York line, where he witnessed a mass meeting of the Anti-Rent Rebellion. Finally he came to North Adams and Williamstown, once the frontier outposts of Massachusetts and consequently full of interest to him. He had a long interview with General Epaphras Hoyt, the antiquarian and historian of the French and Indian War; and learned much of Major Robert Rogers, Sir William Johnson, General Israel Putnam, Montcalm, the partisan Marin, Baron Dieskau, and other great figures in his drama. For the rest the notebook is crammed with references to books, magazines, papers, maps, and a long précis of Dieskau's own account of his defeat at Lake George in 1755. History had resumed its unrelenting hold on Parkman.

The record of this journey is contained in a small green leather notebook, 4 by 2½ inches. The penciled writing is badly smudged on the opening and concluding pages, and is sometimes indecipherable. There is much greater use of a personal shorthand, involving many abbreviations, than in any of the earlier journals.[1]

1 8 44

July 4ᵗʰ, [18]44. The Celebration at Concord. The admirable good-humor of the people in the cars, during some very vexatious delays, was remarkable.

Some young men sung songs and amused themselves with jokes, among whom my former schoolmate was conspicuous. In spite of the coldness attributed to the Am[erican] character, he seemed to play the *rowdey* with all his heart, and as if he considered it the height of glory.

The cheerfulness, the spirit of accommodation and politeness, was extraordinary. Perfect order, in the most difficult evolutions of the day. An hundred soldiers would not in Europe have ensured such quiet and unanimity. Some young men exhibited a good deal of humor, and of knowledge, in their observations, and I remembered that this is *our lowest class.* This orderly, enthusiastic, and intelligent body is the nearest approach to the peasantry of Europe. If we have not the courtly polish of the European upper circles, the absence of their stupid and brutal peasantry is a fair offset.

The girls came in throngs to the road as the train passed, to be greeted with cheers. And in Concord, when the procession passed the groups of women in the windows and balconies, there was the same cheering.

I saw two drunken men. One, at the dinner, was immediately pushed out with expressions of vexation and contempt. He made long speeches at the door to the crowd. A tall, thin, black-browed Yankee had pushed him out, and was disposed to assume the bully over him; but finding his position in that capacity rather absurd, he began to change his bullyism into a half-amused air and tone.

"Now, don't ye be provoking me to strike ye," he said, "'cause if I should, I should make a leetle daylight shine through you in no time"—turning with a triumphant consciousness of superiority to the bystanders, to see how they would be amused by his treatment of the drunken man.

An old farmer exhibited a sprightliness not very common among Yankees. He danced about with great activity, giving his advice aloud on all topics in a humorous strain—when the train was coming slowly up, he shouted out: "Fetch a log there, and block the team."

Students of H[arvard] do not on all occasions appear much better than their less favored countrymen, either in point of gentlemanly and *distingué* appearance or in conversation.

The rooms of Jonas and Levi, with their jack-at-all-trades knick-knacks—bugs, pictures, guns, skeletons of fish and mice, etc., etc. Levi's manufacture of wreaths for his sisters and friends. The simplicity and absence of forms—what Englishman would call the *provincialism* of society here. A species of family—admits familiarities which could not be borne elsewhere.

The discussion on Fourierism,[2] etc., of the she-philosophers of W[est] Roxbury. Their speculations, and the whole atmosphere of that haunt of *new philosophy*, were very striking and amusing after seeing the manners of Paris and London—the entertainments and pleasures and the workings of passions which they in their retirement seem scarce to dream of.

Monday, July——. "Old Snow"[3]—his careless abandonment—his tobacco chewing—his admiration of George[4]—his hatreds—his indifference and laziness—his want of foresight—his violent expressions of friendship.

A ship without a rudder—a good fellow, but on the way to wreck and worthlessness.

England has her hedges and her smooth green hills, robed with a spirit of power and worth, strengthened and sanctioned by ages—but give me the rocky hill-side, the shaggy cedar and shrub-oak—the wide reach of uncultivated landscape—the fiery glare of the sun among the evening clouds, fling[ing] over all its wild and ruddy light. All is new—all is rough—no charm of a familiar country.

Fierce savages have roamed like beasts amid its rugged scenery—there was a day of struggle, and they have past away, and a race of indomitable men have supplanted them. The day of struggle was short, yet its scenes of fear and blood are not without a horrid romance; and well does the rugged landscape recall them to mind.

The spring at the granite ledge near Pine Hill. "It's chockfull of animils"—a host of frogs leaped in. "Is the water good?" I asked. "Well, I guess it ain't the best that ever was," etc.

Nahant, July 17ᵗʰ. The company on board the steamboat—difference in silence and intelligence from a cockny party. The man with the model of a bee-hive from Ohio. His dry sarcastic replies. "Why, what hurt do the millers do?" asked a man, with reference to a sort of trap to catch bee-moths.

"Hurt! Why, when they've killed about nine-tenths of the bees in the United States, and spoilt every hive in Ohio state, I should think they might be doing hurt, shouldn't you?"

The travelled fool, setting his name in the bar-book as "————————, *Cosmopolite*."

He finds some improvements here "very creditable to the town"—of which he is a native. He imitates English dress and manners.

The dinner party was various and far from *distingué*.

At Whitney's another class yet of people were assembled—awkward heroes of the counter, bashful boys, and corresponding young ladies—they drive off in waggons to fish. The old fisherman, when I paid him for a rod and declined to take change, simply and gruffly said "thank yer" as he walked off.

———————

59 & 51 Pine St, N. Y.   J. G. W. Shea[5]

———————

"Have your ever seen any about here?"—"No, not about here, I ha'nt." Q. Had he anywhere?

———————

Roland Green,[6] Mansfield—his family have relics of the Indians. House before you come to the R. R., left hand.

———————

The disagreeable, whining manner of some vulgar Yankee girls.

John Norton's Captivity[7]—taken at a fort in Adams, 1746.

"A thousand associations throng on us at their name. The breezes of the Tweed are an atmosphere of poetry and song, chivalry and romance. They kindle the spirit of the enthousiast into flame—the dullest feels that wonder and romance are around him—thus have the deeds and the fancies of ages charmed that spot. And now turn thence to our dark unstoried woods! The poetic spark grows dull and dies, for there is nothing to fan it into life.

"For a thousand ages her trees rose, flourished, and fell. In the autumn the vast continent glared at once with yellow and red and green; and when winter came, the ice of her waters groaned and cracked to the solitudes; and in the spring her savage streams burst their fetters, and bore down the refuse of the wilderness. It was half a world consecrated to the operations of Nature!"

Springfield.   The independent Yankee whom I spoke to about his failure to call me. In Job's language, he "stood right up to it," giving shot for shot. No English cringing.

The landlord—no bowing.

Montague[8]—grape shot dug up.

Cabotville. The Negro family, who sell "refreshments beer & cake." The old man, the boy with the pears and water-melons, and the woman with the money-box.

The landlord of Chester Factory, sitting cross-legged on his chair, took no notice of me as I came in; but on my asking if the landlord was in, he said, "Yes, here I be."

Parties—dances—ministers.

The stage and driver from Ches[ter] Fac[tory]. A fellow with hollow eyes, and peculiar sullenness and discontent on his features. He had travelled all over the State, sometimes driving, and sometimes singing at cows[a]—but usually following his inclinations. Nothing pleased him. He hated the country, the road, and everything else. He had engaged on it for a year, but intended to get away at the first opportunity. He hated hard labor, and set such a value on his services that he refused to be coachman to a southern gent. who offered him $15 when he demanded $25. He intended never to marry, but liked "training with the girls." We past the house of a man who was rich for the country, having about $20,000. "I suppose he likes this place," said the driver, looking up with contemptuous discontent, and giving his horses a switch under the bellies. He says he could be rich in a month, if he chose to try, but he "always wanted to take comfort, and have nothing to think on when even'g came. Working in the day-time was enough for him."

There are occasional dances in the villages. The Methodist ministers are changed every two years. Beside their salary, they receive contributions and presents. The people are in the habit of coming to tea, sending or bringing the materials to the minister's house.

The driver turned to me with a surly envy, and said he guessed I "warn't used to hard labor." The lazy rascal envies all who can live without labor. As we were driving on, I remarked on the beauty of the road. "*Humph!* Wouldn't you like to live here?" I enquired who were the occupants of a certain house. "Paddies"—with exquisite surly indifference. "Where does that road lead?"—"Don't know," in the same tone.

Clark[9]—Watchmaker, West Stockbridge

An American landlord does not trouble himself to welcome his guests. He lets them enter his house, and sits by quite indifferent. He seems rather to consider himself as conferring an obligation in anything that he may do for them.

Lee is full of factory girls. The very devil beset me there. I never

[a] As a cattle drover.—Ed.

suffered so much from certain longings which I resolved not to gratify, and which got me into such a nervous state that I scarcely slept all night.

Stockbridge. Maple and beech have followed the fir of the original growth. The railroad has lessened the value of land by the influx of western produce. These towns never sent produce to Boston and do not now—the expense of the R.R. transportation is too great.

Stockbridge. An old man at the church told me that the original meeting-house where Sergeant[10] preached stood on the green in front. About half a mile off is the site of the church of 1784 where, in the mound on which it was built, were found a number of Indian bodies. An old man, present when the grave was opened, said that they were heaped confusedly together, without instruments of any kind with them. Perhaps they were flung there by the whites after Wolcott's [Talcot's] fight in [King] Philip's War.[11] The Stockbridge Indians had a burying ground, the care of which they consigned, on leaving the place, to old Mr. Partridge,[12] who keeps it carefully for them. It is in the village, and seems to contain a large number of bodies.

The old Negro[13] at the church. He remembered all about the Indians and exchanged recollections with the old man aforesaid. He had been a soldier in W's [Washington's] army. He had four children in the churchyard, he said with a solemn countenance, but "These are my children," he added, stretching his cane over a host of little boys. "Ah, how much we are consarned to fetch them up well and virtuous," etc. He was very philosophical, and every remark carried the old patriarch into lengthy orations on virtue and temperance. He looked on himself as father to all Stockbridge.

Agrippa Hull—the "African Prince."

The "full-blooded Yankee girl," of whom I asked the way to Monument Mt. "She'd been up there going arter the cows." Bold, lively, and talkative. "Would she go and show me the way?" "Well, that *would* be rather curious!"

The group by the road-side—the beautiful girl with her hand in that of the man on horseback, and her friend sitting close by on the bank.

Mrs. Stephen Jones[14]

Went up Monument Mt.

House of Jones.[15] His kindness and obliging disposition. He had two large bowls of ash knots—a beautiful material—made by the Indians. The largest is used only for making wedding-cake. Also a mortar, of a piece of the trunk of a maple, made by the Indians for his grandfather. The pestle was of stone. The conch which was used to call the Indians to church now calls his household to dinner. His brother, Mr. Stephen Jones, is a great geologist, and very talkative. I got of him a chisel and two arrowheads.

Dr. Partridge. The old man was in his laboratory, bedroom, etc. among his old tables, book-cases, etc., with shelves of medicines, and scales suspended hard by. He is about 94,[16] and remembered Williams[17] well, who he describes as a large stout man, who used often to visit his father, and taken him on his knee. And once went out the door and blew a trumpet to amuse him. He says he remembers the face as if he saw it yesterday, especially the swelling of the ruddy cheeks.

His father, Colonel Partridge,[18] was in the service, and despised Abercrombie [Abercromby][19] as a coward. The Dr. remembers seeing a thousand of Abercrombie's Highlanders at Hatfield, or some other town where they were billetted. Abercrombie was always trembling with fear of Indians, and sending out scouts about camp. When Howe[20] fell, Partridge, the Dr. says, was at his side; and his lordship said: "This army has no leader, and is defeated."

On one occasion Abercrombie ordered 800 rangers to be detached. Partridge, or some other officer, drew them up in a cornfield, directing the short men to stand on the hills and the tall ones in the hollows. The British officers were struck with admiration at the uniform height of the men.

When A. was about to sail down the lake, he ordered the rangers to stay behind to protect the embarcation[b]; when it was finished, they received immediate orders to pull forwards to the head of the column. They did so, and left the army behind; stopped at an island where they caught fish and made a meal; and then pulled on to the foot of the lake, keeping under the eastern shore till they reached the outlet. Here they landed, and concealed themselves at its south side. When the army appeared and attempted to land, the French opposed them. The rangers, taking deliberate aim from their ambush, fired on their flank, and in the doctor's expression "killed half the regiment."[c] [21]

Amherst[22] he considers a very different man from A[bercromby]. When he had landed and sat down before Ti[conderoga], he offered a great reward to any spy who should explore the works. Three men at length offered themselves: an Indian, a half breed, and an Irish ranger named Morrison,[23] who died in Stockbridge and from whom the Dr. got the story. Amherst reminded them of the peril of the service, but they resolved to venture; and passing down the outlet in the breech-clouts of Indians, they landed under the walls. Passing on in a violent rain, they found the first sentry in his box. Him the Indian killed and scalped; and directing Morrison to remain there, the other two proceeded. They served another sentry in the same manner, till they arrived to where there was a flag, with another sentry, who was also killed. They then withdrew, and had only reached the beach when they heard the drums beat to relieve the sentinels. Morrison could not run as well as the others; so they siezed hold of him to help him, and dragging him behind, they got into the woods and hid. They soon heard guns fired, as the relief guard came to the first sentry box, followed soon by two other successive discharges, as the other dead bodies were discovered; and they heard noise and firing for some time in the direction of the fort. When they came to camp, the Indian showed the scalp to Amherst, who refused to believe on such evidence that they had gone so far into the works, on which the Indian unfolded from his body the flag which he had taken on killing the third sentry—indisputable evidence. The general

[b] "Partridge used to describe the embarcation as he then witnessed it as superb."—F. P.

[c] "On his father's authority.—F.P."

Major Robert Rogers, 1776
Engraving by Martin Will
(Coverdale Collection No. 2280)

ordered some rum, and promised the reward in the morning. In the night the fort was evacuated. Morrison took credit to himself as the cause, and old Dr. P., admitting his claim, promised him doctoring gratis in consideration of his service to the country.[d]

The Dr. tells some familiar anecdotes of Williams, and says that Kunkapot[24] and some other Indians accompanied him to the war. He remembered nothing of the affair of William Henry.[25]

Great Barrington. On entering the bar-room, an old man with a sunburnt wrinkled face and no teeth, a little straw hat set on one side of his gray head—and who was sitting on a chair leaning his elbows on his knees and straddling his legs apart—thus addressed me: "Hullo! hullo!! What's agoin' on, now? Ye ain't off to the wars aready, be ye? Ther' ain't no war now as I knows on, though there's agoin' to be one afore long, as damned bloody as ever was fit this side o' hell!" He proceeded to inform me that he was an old soldier, and always fought on the side of Liberty. He swore like a trooper at every sentence. He cursed the temperance reform which has run mad all over Berkshire.[26]

Someone speaking of a girl's uncle—"Uncle, is it; uncle ain't the (the) thing. You must look farder up"—and then laughed between his toothless gums. "The' ain't none o' them thing now-a-days, now the temperance folks says you mustn't," remarked a man. "You mustn't," said the old farmer, "G–d d–m you mustn't."

He then began to to speak of some of his neighbors, one of whom he mentioned as "that G–d damnedest sneakingest, nastiest puppy that ever went this side of Hell!" Another he likened to a "sheep's cod dried"; another was "not fit to carry guts to a bear." His features were remarkably bold and well formed, but thoroughly Yankee, as also were his positions. "That d——d rascal's brother," said he, pointing to a man near him, "played me the meanest trick you ever seed," etc. The man was rather amused.

The old Dr. at Stockbridge told me that when Williams went to the war, he told a girl of the village that if she would mourn eleven months for him in case of his death, he would leave her a great part

[d] "Rather doubtful, like the rest of the old man's stories."—F.P.

of his property. The girl replied that she would put on mourning for no one but her husband. It afterwards appeared that she was engaged to a young man of the place.

The Dr. was fond of dwelling on Abercrombie's failings. Once, he says, his father's rangers fired their guns in the woods about camp. "'What, what,' says the general"—thus he tells the story— "'we shall have the Indians on us if you let your men go on so.' 'Your lordship,' says he, 'don't know nothing about our kind of fighting. We fire our guns off for the Indians to hear, and when we see them coming, we shoot 'em!'"

Stopped to get a dinner at a house in Mt. Washington. One was provided, such as it was. The old woman was very kind. Speaking of the difficulty of finding the way to the falls, she said in the peculiar whining tone, "Well, I should think the folks at the house might accommodate a stranger with somebody to show the way." "Well," replied the daughter, "I guess they a'nt got nobody that's big enough."

Bash-a-bish lower Fall [*Bish-Bash Falls*]. A noble spectacle. Rocks covered with pine, maple, yellow birch, and hemlock sweep round in a semi-circular form, the water plunging through a crevice in the middle.

The cliffs stretch away above, thick-set with vegetation—you see but a small patch of sky from the deep gorge. The basin at the foot of the fall is filled with foam, and the stream escapes downward in a deep gulf, full of rocks and shadowed by the trees of the opposite mountain declivity.

An old Indian told Murray° that the word *Taconic*, applied to the mountain, was derived from the following circumstance. A stream of water in the west of Berkshire flows out and forms a pond on a level with its outlet. In the summer the pond grows less by evaporation; and the Indians, imagining that the water had run back into the mountain by the passage whence it issued, called the place "Taconic." The word means "run out and run in" or something similar; and is pronounced "Ta-con-nic."

° See below.—Ed.

Mt. Washington. As I rested by the road, a little boy came up with a kettle full of vinegar in his hand. He said he lived near the head of the falls. But was going to move soon, and go off he did not know where, but "Mr. Jenkins said it was a great ways." I showed him how to fire my gun, which very much pleased [him]. After clambering up the steep path for a mile or more, we reached the top; and the path led on into a very wild and narrow valley, with a house at the foot of it. The brook ran down through the middle, till it flung itself over the cliffs at the foot, some hundred feet down, into the deep gorge we had just come up. The mountains of this little valley were very steep, and drew nearer to each other as we proceeded up the brook. There was a delapidated barn, some old potato fields, etc., but the woods of birch and maple came close down on each side, and all was wild enough. At length a high dam and a mill appeared up stream, and a new log-house on the other side among the pine trees. We came opposite to it, where, though drift-rotten logs enough were laying about, there was no means to pass the stream. A woman[f] came down to the other side and tried to lay a plank across, but without success, so I waded through with the little boy. The woman immediately began to apologize for her bare feet, saying that she had mistaken me for her cousin, and was so glad to see an acquaintance in that place that [she] had "ran right down to see." She showed me her house, which was remarkably neat, with a little sheltered porch before it, and a rude garden fenced with the outside slabs of boards from the mill. There were plenty of ducks and geese about. She did not wish to give me lodging as she was alone, her husband being gone; but she sent "Abel" to the spring for water, killed a duck, and gave me an excellent supper. "I warn't never rich," she said, "but I a'nt always lived in a log hut." The place she stigmatized as a "Hell on earth," which she was going to leave as soon as possible. She described her terror when, sitting alone, she hears the footstep of a man about the house. Once, she says, she thought nothing of it; but now, in that lonely place, it frightens her. A wild cat from the mountains has invested the house, and stolen her ducks and hens. She has seen it; and one night, hearing the hens cackling, she went out, though in great terror, and made a fire to keep it off.

[f] Mrs. Comstock. See below.—Ed.

I went to Mr. Murray's—the other house—to spend the night. His wife was Dutch. He is a broken tradesman. His house is neatly plastered; and he, the picture of ill-health and leanness, sat smoking his pipe, and talking slowly between the whiffs. The room where I slept contained various relics of departed prosperity. A handsomely curtained bed—images and french toys on the mantel. A table with books, vases, pamphlets, and a *basket of cards* upon it. His girls' dresses were hung up around, with a few maps, etc. The furniture, though a little old, evidently belonged to his better days; and these various articles contrasted queerly with the hearth of rough stones, and the rude whitewashed fireplace, filled by way of ornament with pine and hemlock boughs.

Murray is a broken man every way—duns are frequently upon him, Mrs. Comstock says, but he says that he is pleased with that place, because it is *"retired."* He has had enough of company, and wants to be by himself, and his wife echoes his words. "Well," says Mrs. C. in a true woman's strain, "I should think Mrs. Murray might wait till she *feels* what she says, and not pretend to be so Christain like and humble, when we all know she don't like the mounting no more than I do."

I breakfasted with Mrs. C. in the morning, who on my departure refused to take any remuneration, which I was obliged to throw into the form of a gift to her little boy; and took my leave of this very kind and hospitable woman.

The falls from the top of the rock are an extraordinarily fine scene—almost as fine below and seem to me one of the finest scenes in N. E. [New England].

The rainy day—the scene of mountain and vapors from Scott's field at the top of the ascent.

————————

The hearty, horse-swapping, thumping young Dutchman, who would be damned if he cared for anything if he could only swap off his old waggons for Jim Pray's colt.

The crouching, cadaverous, lank old man, with the opium for his rheumatic wife, and the long string of misfortunes.

————————

Mr. Tuttle's private tavern, with the store. His "woman."

————————

Widow Evans, Pownal, near Rev. Grand.

A man at Lebanon Springs, not far from the lower tavern, says that he has some journals of his father, which contain, for what he knows to the contrary, notes of his services in Rogers' Rangers[27] when a young man. The man is grandson of the W[idow] Evans above.

The Patroon's (or the "Patteroon's") tenure is in peril.[28] The tenants refuse to pay rent. I went to Stephentown to see the gathering for resistance. All along the road occurred boards with "Down with the rent"—and flags in the village and the gathering place, which was on a hill at a mean tavern surrounded by a group of houses. The assembly was of the very lowest kind. The barroom full to suffocation, and vilely perfumed. One old man sat and talked for a long time. He had been with Indians, and kept remarking on their good qualities; which remarks were received with great applause. The chief actors were to appear in the disguise of Indians. There was another old fellow who had been with the Indians and kept constantly talking of their friendship for him, perfuming all near with the stench of his filthy, rotten teeth. Another fellow had been at Plattsburg,[29] and distinguished himself by the vileness of his appearance and conversation. Another old fool, with a battered straw hat, and a dirty shirt for his only upper garment, kept retailing his grievances, lashing himself into enthusiasm and exclaiming "Down with the rent!" The "Indians" at length appeared, and went through some meaningless manoevres. A hole in a block of cast iron was charged with powder, and a plug being driven hard into it, it was repeatedly fired. After a while, it was attempted to come to business. A few of the more decent squatted themselves on the bank of grass before the platform erected for the directors, but were listless and inattentive while the directors, who managed the whole affair, nominated deputies from the different districts to arrange the matter. Those loudest in their noise were not of the number on the bank. The voice of the old man with the straw hat could be heard declaiming, and sharply exclaiming, "Down with the rent!" while the rest were eating or watching the clumsy and absurd movements of the "Indians."

The other towns of the Patroon's domain have also revolted; and his feudal tenure, so strangely out of place in America, has probably lived its time.

I have never seen a viler concourse in America.

Captain Edmund Badger,[30] North Adams
W's [William's] Will[31]

Family of Col. Jones[32]

Dr. Robbins—"Pastor of a church in Rochester, Mass."—author of the Address.

The "Hopper." A great mountain rises before me, covered with trees—birch, beech and fir; and near the top and down its sides light vapors are resting among the tree tops—now sinking below them, now rising up and obscuring them; sometimes a line of firs will be relieved against the white cloud, turning nearly black by the contrast. A ridge beyond is black with firs, with a few light green birches dotted among them and a rough, bare avalanche slide. They are stiff and erect all along the top of the ridge.

The clouds rise upward from the forest like smoke from firs below. The shadows of the clouds pass over it—now it is dark and now light—now the brightness is on the wet smooth stones of the slide. The clouds move rapidly overhead, and the weather grows clearer. The stream makes a loud noise below. The hillside where I sit is scattered with the remains of large pines—lying with their branches tangled and twisted together—and numberless dead ones stand erect, burnt about the roots by fire. The living pines above raise their arms out towards the light—opposite the declivity they stand on.

The little brown wren hopping among the fallen pine trees.

Ft. Massachusetts.[33] It stood on wide green meadows, surrounded on every side by hills. The Hoosic on the other, some 6 or 8 hundred yds. distant, with a high forest-covered hill—a ridge of Saddle Mt., I think, beyond. Wooded hills on the other side, sloping down to the meadow, less distant. In front and behind, as I stand, distant, undulating hills. The crows caw loudly among the woods. Under an apple tree is a broken head-stone with a fragment of inscription, where the bones of the officer who was shot—bones now in the W [Williams] college—were found. The bullet was in the spine.

It is a beautiful situation, this fine day.

French hatchets have been found here, beside Indian weapons of stone.

Horse radish planted by the soldiers grows here quite abundantly. I got a hatchet and gouge from Capt. B[adger].

The Irish Priest—with his jovial conversation and hints about a mitre. The surly boy of a driver.

The number of geologists among the old farmers of the country. The country Professor Hopkins,[34] Stephen Jones, Capt. Badger, etc. Geology seems a science of peculiar attraction to this class of people all the world over—witness the old farmer whom I met in England.

Boston Telegraph, Sept 9th, 1824: Col. Williams' legacies.

Capt. E. Badger at North Adams showed me a copy of the will of Col. W.—the final will made at Albany. The original is in the Hampshire [County] offices.

Capt. B., an old member of legislature, a great geologist, has been about with me, discoursing on marble quarries, manufactories, etc., with his old hat pulled down over his eyebrows, his dingy coat hung on his shoulders, and his cane in his hand. He is, of course, practical in all his views of things. He has a number of stones in an old kettle which constitutes his collection. He was very obliging and talkative.

Col. W. had a house in Stockbridge, as appears by the will, but the Capt. says he lived at Deerfield—perhaps he meant Hatfield.[35]

The old Capt. returned tonight, bringing me some little bits of crystal, and a fragment of jasper which he had smoothed on a grindstone. He was much pleased, evidently, at my listening to his geological remarks, which are none of the most profound. He makes some queer assertion, to which I venture to dissent; he then makes some preposterous argument, winking on me with one eye in the triumph of success. An idea once in his head, it monopolises it wholly. Everything is the work of "iron." Every phenomenon is caused by "petunse."

He showed me a common stone in the street, which he said he could at any time polish and get $10 for it.

American Medical Biographies.[36] They will contain a valuable letter from the brother of Col. W.

Stephens [Stevens] writing a hist. of Putnam.[37]

Dr. Williams[38] of Deerfield has letters of Col. W. and his b[rothe]r, the Dr., of the greatest interest.

Moulin } ? [Marin][39]
Molang }

Rogers[40] born at Methuen, Mass.

Father killed while hunting a bear. Rogers himself was a hunter and a wanderer from his youth up.

Old General Hoyt[41]—unquestionable authority—says that a man at Deerfield named Catlin, in the rangers, told him that he was conducting a train of waggons to Abercrombie's army at the lake. Between Ft. Ed[ward] and Bloody Pond, he saw a crow picking the dung in the road, which ran through a low swampy place. He was in front of the wagons, and thinking no danger, thought he would shoot the crow. So bending under the bushes, he crept along the side of the road to get a shot. The crow would not suffer him to approach, but flying up and re-alighting, drew him on some distance from his men, and at length flew away. He was now on a rising ground again, when a tremendous yell and fire of musketry burst forth below him. The train, in the low part of the road, were fired on by a party who did not touch him, although he had passed close to the muzzles of their guns. He immediately escaped to the station at Half-Way Brook, but most of his men were killed.[42]

Stephens [Stevens] at Cambridge has plans of Johnson's and W [Williams'] battle grounds,[43] and a minute account of Montcalm's descent by a Jesuit[44] who accompanied the expedition.

General Hoyt has journals, letters, etc., of great interest, and a *complete unpublished life of Rogers.*

Nil desperandum.

———

Rogers' Rock was the scene of the great winter fight where the two officers were lost on the ice.[45] So says the General.

———

Was Putnam's fight with Molang [Marin] the narrows of S[ou]th Bay (1) or the narrows nearer Whitehall (2)[46]? Hoyt says that an old man found a sword and a gun, much decayed, in a species of cave near the latter place. H. asked for the sword. "It made me a damned good carving knife," said the man, who had cut it in two for this purpose.

———

The two girls on the road from N. Adams. One of them was a mixture of all the mean qualities of her sex, with none of the nobler. She was full of the pettiest envy, spite, jealousy, and malice, singularly impudent and indelicate.

———

"Should have given ye a pie today, but ain't got no *timber* to make 'em."

———

Gen. Hoyt has plans of Montcalm's siege[47]—perhaps also Stephens.

I had a talk of four or five hours with the old General, and took tea with him.

———

Williams' *Hist. of Vermont*[48] and Thompson's hist.[49]

———

Hendrick[50] rode a little pony.

———

Hoyt's *I[ndian] wars*[51]

Gentleman's Magazine—By means of Index

———

Maps: "Province of Quebec according to Proclamation of '63"—Various maps of Canada—"Province of N. E."[52]

Wynnes' B[ritish] Empire in America[53]

Rogers' *Concise Account of North America*[54]—Proposed to be continued by a volume with map. Does such a vol. exist?

State histories

The Contest in America. Relation of the F[rench] & E[nglish] colonies. London, 1757.[55]

Barber's *Hist. and Antiquities of N. E.*[56] contains an account of Dieskau's fight taken from Dwight's *Travels*.[57]

On the border of a swamp—a bright warm afternoon—with my rifle. There is a brisk breeze. The wind involves together the upper boughs of a hickory and a cedar, and the bare blind top of the latter grunts a sound, as if some animal were in the branches.

A high detached rock at the bottom of a shaggy, woody hill at the edge of a swamp. It is half buried among cedars, hickory, saplings, etc. The dry swamp is full of little bushes; and a wood of swamp-maples, rising from among the shrubs and undergrowth border it—bright in the sunlight, while the swamp and the wooded hollow in front are in the shadow of the hill behind. The distant pine-trees on the rising ground in front are also bright, but the shadow has almost reached themselves.

Dwight's *Travels*—account of Gen. Lyman, Vol. 1, Letter XXXI.

Account of and reflexions on Crown Pt. (Vol. 2, p. 447), with other matters of local history through the volumes.

"Two Journies to Lake George," with accounts of its battles (Vol. 3, p. 337, etc.).

"The Iroquois"—with poor list of authorities (Vol. 4, p. 186).

Camp Meeting, Saturday Evening, Aug 24; there will be a steamboat at 10 o'clock.

Mrs. Upham's—one day

4410-4414—Maps of B. & Fr. settlements [17]55

"Carte de l'Amérique Septentrionale"—the French claims. 4415

Fr. Claims in 1720—Map 4416

Br. Claims 1715—4419. This old map has a small colored picture of Niagara, with an inscription remarking "some make this Water Fall be half a league, while others reckon it to be no more than a hundred Fathom." In the foreground a colony of beavers dragging building materials on their tails.

Br. dominions by the treaty of [17]63—4421

Large maps of the N. E. states and other parts of N. America, 1776—4403.

Large maps of Pensylvania in the same volume (?)

Turn over: *Topographie Générale de L'Amérique Septentrionale et Indes Occidentales, ou recueil de toutes les cartes marines ou autres arpentages particuliers et plans de cette Partie de Monde.* Londres, 1768.   No. 4394

Ms. containing invaluable plans and maps and among the rest Braddock—Bat. of Lake George—Bouquet's fights—Little Meadows —Plan of Du Quesne—line of march to its attack—Ticonderoga and Aber.'s [Abercromby's] attack—New York—a small but minute map of the lakes with surrounding country—Shegnekto Bay and Ft. Lawrence—Louisburg—Montreal—Quebec. English attack (several maps)

Murray's *Travels*[58] and novel.

Campaigns of '55-'56. Winslow's MS. journal[59] in Mass. Hist. Soc. Library.

Letters from officers in the State House.[60]

Part of Montcalm letters in England.[61]

Sir W. Johnson papers were at Albany, the possession of a family named Cooper, Sparks thinks, but Stone got them.[62]

Dieskau's letters in Sp[ar]ks'.[63] library.

There is a Jesuit account of Montcalm's descent on W[illiam] H[enry]—the priest was in the expedition.[64]

A pamphlet accompanied the map of the Bat. of Lake George— but Sparks has not been able to find it.[65]

M. W. F. [Monday, Wednesday, Friday] 10–11. Introduction first on Friday

---

The following are notes taken from a Fr. manuscript, supposed to be written by Dieskau when he had returned to France. This is the supposition of Sparks, who copied the MS. from the F[rench] War dept.[66]

Dieskau was to attack *Chouayen* [Oswego] with 4,000 men and 12 cannon. 2,000 had gone to [Fort] Frontenac, where was the rendevous; when news came from Varin,[67] Commissary of Marine at St. John's, that Johnson was within (in) two days' march of Fort Frédéric(k) [Crown Point], with 3,000 men.

The Gov.-General,[68] at this, would have Johnson opposed at all events, though Dieskau urged that, though the news were true, the possession of Ft. Frédéric was by no means the possession of Montreal —for Ft. St. John's and Chambley would remain to be taken, to say nothing of the difficulties of the country. But the Gov.-Gen. was resolved to opp[ose] Johnson—so D. set out, and reaching Ft. Fred., found Varin's story false. He had 3,000 men. At Ft. F., D. learnt that J. was at St. Sacrement [Lake George] with 3,000 also—that he was building a fort to ensure his retreat, and that all his supplies were drawn from Ft. Edward, which he heard was ill fortified, with 500 wretched levies camped round it. He resolved to make himself master of the Ft. and so cut off J.'s supplies. The first day he got to Carillon [Ticonderoga], whence he marched with 1,500 men, leaving the other half of his army, part at Carillon and part at *les deux rochers* [Twin Rocks], to secure a retreat in case of need. He took 8 days' provision for his meditated *coup de main*. The night of the 4th day, he camped in the woods a league from Ft. E[dward]. Here he mustered a council of I's. [Indians] and told them his plan. They demanded time to deliberate it. Two hours after, the Algonquin, Nepissingues [Nipissing], and Abenaki chiefs came and said that, for their part, they were willing, but the Iroquois (300 in number) had refused, and, they being the superior, the other tribes must follow them. He sent for the Iroquois chfs.; [told them] that he only wanted them to make a false attack—the reglrs. and Canadians would fight—they should be safe; but they said they would not attack the E[nglish] on their own ground, refusing absolutely.

He said it was shameful to turn back with nothing done, on which they offered to go against J.'s army, which they said was not on English ground. So at daybreak they marched up the road from Ft. E. in three columns, C[anadian]s. on the right, Inds. left, reglrs. centre.

A prisoner told them that 1,000 men were within half a league. He sent Canadians 300 paces in advance in ambush, keeping reglrs. behind, so that the disposition had the figure of a *cul-de-sac*.

D. thought he should take all the E[nglish].; but some Indians, "more curious than the rest," looked up and saw that the E. had with them "un corps d'Agniere [Agniers]."[69] These told the rest, on which the Iroquois fired in the air to warn the E. The attack then began, but the Iroquois alone would not fight.

They followed the E. to the fort, where the Indians first, and then the Canadians, refused to obey, though D. told them the regs. should bear the brunt of the cannon which so much frightened them. Urging them on, D. was wounded at one moment by two shots in the leg, and one in the knee, exposing himself too much. He fell near a tree and was helped behind it by Montreuil,[70] second in command, whom D. ordered to take the command and, if necessary, to order a retreat, but to send two men to take care of him. M. left him reluctantly, and soon sent 2 Canadians. One was shot and fell across D.'s legs, the other went to find assistance—but soon D. heard the retreat beating, but saw nothing, being in a hollow place with his back against a tree. Half an hour after, he saw a soldier aiming at him from behind a tree, close before him; to whom he signed not to fire, but was shot through the body. The sold. leaped out, exclaiming in F. "*Rendez-vous!*" D. demanded why he fired at a wounded wretch like him. The s. said he might have pistols—and that he was a F. deserter—deserted 10 yrs. before. Others came up and D. was carried to J.'s tent.

Indians soon came rushing in, frantically demanding D. to be burnt, but J. pacified them and sent them off, telling D. that he was safe.

The I.'s came again with the same demand, but J. pacified them, and they gave their hands to D. D. wished to go to another tent, but J. said he must wait till the I.'s were asleep as they would fall on him. He went to a Col.'s tent with a guard of 50 men. An Indian came in, in the night, apparently unarmed, and the sentinel let him pass, but he drew a sword from under his cloak and would have killed D., had not the Col. sprung between.

9 days after, D. was sent to Albany to the house of Johnson, and 4 weeks after to New York.

A letter of Dieskau to Doriel[71] at Montreal:

Of D[ieskau]'s original army 700 were regulars, 1,600 Canadiens, 700 Indians—in all, 3,000. He had all along suspected the Iroquois of the Sault and of the deux Montagnes—300 in all.

27th August one Boileau, Canadian, told him that 3,000 E. were camped near the house of Lydius, where a fort was begun.[72]

The Abenakis brought him a prisoner, who told him that 500 men were at Edward, the main army at Lydius' house. He took with him 600 Indians, 600 Canadians, and 200 regulars.

He was to have reached and attacked Edward on the 4th night, but the Iroquois guides misled him and brought him to the road a league off, too late.

Here he took a courier and some prisoners.

Marching toward the lake, his scouts told him of W.'s [Williams'] detachment—a prisoner confirmed the news. "1,000 men or more, going to the succor of the fort."

He ordered his savages to be ready to take them *behind*.

The Iroquois at the left treasonably showed themselves.

D. wished to enter the camp pell mell. But the Iroquois gathered together, and would not advance; the Abenakis followed their example; and the Canadians were discouraged.

The regulars were almost all killed.

———————

Turner's Falls
Indian Orchard Falls, Springfield
Leyden Glen
Cascade in Leverett
Bash-pish Falls, Mt. Washington, ascend the rock above the upper Fall.
Gorge and Falls in Royalston
Road from Will[iamstown] through New Ashford

Saddle Mt. & the Hopper, Williamstown Bridge, N. A. [North Adams].

Monument Mt.

Town of Mt. Washington, by way of Egremont, Bashapish falls.

Sugar-Loaf Mt, Deerfield. Bloody Brook (from Williamston to Hancock "an interesting excursion")

Westfield River following the Pontoosuc turnpike

The defile of Deerfield River between Shelburne and Conway[g]

Analysis of C. Disignate Introduc.: America in a state of transition. Her original state—her present—England's present—we look to the future, her future—no romance of warlike achievement—all peace and utilitarianism—Indian wars—even now.

The child's journey, his associations—true elements of the romantic —but age dispels the fanciful illusion—too close a view. The heroes of our old wars, the farmers, etc., of our day. Matter of fact, universally prevalent. The traveller's attempt to find a hero. Abandons America in despair.

Every possible thing done to ruin the face of nature—but unsucessful. Instance.

The traveller in Europe. Art, nature, history combine.

In America Art has done her best to destroy nature, association nothing. Her former state. Her present matter of fact aspects illustrated.

The battle ground of the North—her history—her matter of fact struggles.

Essentials of poetical war-fare. The Spanish guerrilla—the revolutionary soldier.

Obscure recesses of other countries contain men untouched by civilization—the Welsh—the Highlander—the American backwoodsman.

Traveller abandons the search for the poetical.

America's remaining beauty. Her wildness. Her associations—the scenes that encounter the traveller.

Lake George and its heroes.

[g] Evidently Parkman listed in advance of his excursion the beauty spots of central and western Massachusetts.—Ed.

Old Northwest Journal
& Pontiac Notes
1844-45

Introduction

THIS notebook is something of a grab bag, with a curiously assorted collection of contents which mirrors Parkman's diverse interests at this period. References to historical books and documents predominate; then there are brief sketches of Parkman's forays and excursions when the Dane Law School (forerunner of the Harvard Law School) weighed too heavily upon him. There are vivid bits of autobiography concerning the misunderstood lover, amusingly irreverent accounts of Millerite and Fourierite meetings, and thumbnail pictures of various Bostonians and Harvard men. These sketches of character and incident were part of Parkman's apprenticeship to the writer's trade, and they are sharp and promising. The main portion of the notebook is an account of a journey to the Old Northwest in July and August 1845, a research trip centered on Pontiac's conspiracy, the subject of Parkman's first historical work, published six years later.

The aim of Parkman's *History of the Conspiracy of Pontiac* was "to portray the American forest and the American Indian at the moment when both received their final doom," as the author put it in his preface. The British conquest of Canada in 1759-60 upset the balance of power in America. "Could the French have maintained their ground, the ruin of the Indian tribes might long have been postponed; but the victory of Quebec was the signal for their swift decline. Thenceforth they were destined to melt and vanish before the advancing waves of Anglo-American power, which now rolled westward unchecked and unopposed. They saw the danger, and, led by a great and daring champion, struggled fiercely to avoid it." This champion was Pontiac, chief of the Ottawas, one of the greatest of Indians, who almost brought about a great coalition of all the tribes against the whites. Since his mother was an Ojibwa, he was able to form by 1755 a loose confederacy of the Ottawas, Ojibwas, and Potawatomies. He was an ally of the French, and probably saw service with them at Braddock's defeat in 1755 and at Quebec in 1759. He knew that the policy of the British, who were interested in settlement and hence in exterminating or driving out the Indians, was very different from that of the fur-trading French, who made allies and converts of the savages. After the conquest of Canada, the French traders and hunters of the Great Lakes encouraged the uneasy Indians with vague promises of help from France if they would war against the English. In the winter of 1762-63 Pontiac organized a simultaneous assault on all the British outposts from Fort Niagara to Mackinaw on the Lakes, and from Fort Presqu'ile down along the Alleghany frontier. Though the main attacks on Fort Pitt and Detroit failed in the summer of 1763, nearly every minor fort was captured, and the English suffered great losses in men and property. Then the great conspiracy petered out, as one tribe after another was forced to make treaties with the English. Pontiac himself made peace in 1766, through the efforts of Sir William Johnson. Two years later he was murdered at Cahokia near St. Louis by an Indian who had been bribed by an English trader.

Parkman's journey in search of Pontiac material took him first to New York and Philadelphia, and then, with Simon Stevens as his guide, to the old Alleghany frontier: Lancaster, Harrisburg, Williamsport, Trout Run; then north to Buffalo by Tioga Creek, and Seneca Lake, and then along the Great Lakes to Detroit, Mackinaw, and Sault Ste. Marie—the focal points of the Old Northwest. Lieutenant Henry Whiting showed Parkman about Mackinaw, the strategic center of the Lakes, and introduced him to Robert Stuart, the fur trader of Astoria fame. At the Soo, in the absence of the Indian agent H. R. Schoolcraft, Parkman checked that authority's statements with missionary, trader, and savage. He continued on to Palmer (St. Clair), Michigan, to sift six trunks of papers belonging to Lieutenant McDougall, Pontiac's prisoner during the siege of Detroit. On his return trip he crossed over into Canada to seek out descendants of Baby and Campeau, the early French traders at Detroit; and then went back down Lake Erie, taking careful topographical notes as he went. At Niagara he stopped to inspect the battle sites and to marvel at the cataract, and then continued eastward by train, stopping at Onondaga to visit the home of the Five Nations. After fruitless attempts to elicit historical information through gifts of cheap cigars to the stolid descendants of the Iroquois, he continued on down the Mohawk Valley, the scene of many a border fray. Reaching the Hudson, he returned to Boston by way of the steamer from New York, just in time for the Commencement festivities at Harvard. The trip had added much to Parkman's historical lore, and notably had given him a fuller acquaintance with the Indians than he had previously had.

The journal indicates Parkman's state of mind at this period. At his father's insistence he was studying law under Judges Story and Greenleaf; for it was one of the three professions open to a Boston gentleman of his position, and he had no inclination toward medicine or the ministry. Indeed, he had none toward the law; but since his father refused to take his literary ambitions seriously, it was the least of three evils, since it left him some leisure to pursue his own chosen path. Most of his energy was devoted to historical studies, and references to this avocation far outnumber legal notes in his notebooks of this period. There is a despairing note in this one that "according to Burke, more Blackstones were sold in the Colonies than in England," which indicates how unwilling an apprentice Parkman was to the law. His discontent and frustration are echoed in the ruthless sketches of friends, companions, and casual acquaintances. Parkman was dissatisfied with his own life and hence had little use for his fellows. Only the few purple passages devoted to nature are free of the acid which flowed all too freely from his pen at this period, and at least one of these is haunted by a brooding melancholy.

The accounts, reckoned to the last half-cent, which fill a good portion of this notebook, are given in the appendix. They indicate how little capital was involved in Parkman's historical investigations, and how his money went for historical books and copying fees, rather than for personal comforts or pleasures.

This notebook covers from September 13, 1844 to the latter part of August 1845. It is contained in a black leather pocket notebook, 5x3 inches, and in two improvised supplements; for at Mackinaw Parkman had exhausted his writing space, and wrote the rest of the journal, largely in pencil, on two large sheets of paper, folded and stitched into such form that they could be slipped into a pocket of the original notebook. Further notes on the law school, and on the Northwest and Pontiac, will be found in the 1846 Account Book, page 484.

The front end papers of the notebook contain some scribbled notes of names of books and authorities, and sources of reference material. Among those which can be deciphered are those of Gallatin,[1] the Philadelphia Society, the City Library, the Historical Society, Conyngham,[2] Ingraham, G. W. Baker,[3] Miller of 114 Cherry St., *Wars of North West*, Stone's *Red Jacket*,[4] Baumgarten's (?) *American Archaeologia*, Atwater's *Antiquities*,[5] Mr. Van Cleve (?) of Ohio ("is an investigator of antiquities"), and Stephens [Stevens][6] of 19 West Strand. There is also a note: "Read Dryden's Prose."

1844-1845

Sept. 13 [1844]. Muster at Concord—on a hill, with the tents with provisions for the companies on one side, and the booths, peddlers, oyster stalls, bookstalls, etc., on the other. Several companies of rangers in frocks and with rifles. The tall artillery sentinel—the gambling at the tavern, the congregation in the barroom. George P.'s [Parkman's][7] follies.

That remarkable constraint [to] which the presence of a person of inferior sense, acuteness, and energy will sometimes subject one far his superior.

A letter from Orne [Orme] describing the battle of the Monongahela. Winslow, p. 136.[8]

Another letter: The inhabitants of Nova Scotia, on whose quiet remaining on the soil, one of the French claims was founded—they remained, probably, on sufference, though they refused the oath of allegiance, except on condition that they should not be compelled to bear arms.

Winslow's Nova Scotia Journal—His Journal at Lake George.[9] Trumbull's Papers,[10] Mass. Hist. Soc.

Sunday, Sept 21. Some men are fools—utter and inexpressible fools. I went over to Dr. B[igelow]'s[11] last night to call on Miss—— [Prentiss?][12] Heaven knows I am quite indifferent to her charms, and called merely out of politeness, not caring to have her think I slighted her. But the Dr., in the contemptible suspicion that he is full of, chose to interpret other-wise. William Train was there, whom

285

I allowed to converse with Miss. P. while I talked with the Dr.'s lady. The Dr. watched me, though I was not aware of it at the time, till happening to rise to take a bottle of Cologne, out of a mere whim, and applying some of it to my handkerchief; the idiot made a remark, in a meaning tone about *"long walks* in the evening" injuring me. He soon after asked me to take a glass of wine, saying that it would make me *feel better.* He whispered in my ear that Train *would go soon,* and I better stay. What could I do or say? I longed to tell him the true state of my feelings, and above all what I thought of his suspicious impertinence. I left the house vexed beyond measure at being pitied as a jealous lover, when one object of my indifference to Miss ——— that evening was to prove, to her and the rest, how free I was from the influence of her attractions. Is it not hard for a man of sense to penetrate all the depths of a blockhead's folly? and to know what interpretation such a fellow will put on his conduct? I sent him a letter which I think will trouble not a little his jealous and suspicious temper.

Sept. 23. Watertown Miller[ite] Meeting,[13] which I went to with White.[14] At a private house. A dozen or so of men and oldish women were seated silently about the room. We sat down, and for a long time the silence was interrupted only by sighs and groans. At length a big stout fellow struck up a hymn, which was fervently sung by all. Then they dropped on their knees, while another prayed aloud in a hasty and earnest manner, responded to by sighs, exclamations, and cries of "Amen." Several other prayers were made. One large, broadfaced, stupid fellow was a long time getting under weigh, but grew at last very loud and fervent. A woman joined immediately in a voice still more rapid. Then there was silence. All rose from their knees. A moment after, the large man by the table rose slowly, and fixing his eyes on vacuity, exclaimed: "How bright the vision! Oh, how long shall this bright hour delay?" I at first thought this a burst of enthusiasm—it was no such thing, but a quotation from Dr. Watts.[15] The fellow went on with more quotations, gathered from far and near, describing the glories of heaven, etc. There was a good deal of spiritual pride about this man. He evidently thought himself a full match for any clergyman at expounding scripture, and gifted with a large share of grace. I set him down as a vain, proud fanatic, of a cold nature. Of course he was speaking from the immediate impulse of the holy spirit within him, and his discourse was rambling and bungling enough. He said he once went out West; and described, *à la* Yankee, the difficulties he encountered, and drew a parellel between his journey and the Christian heavenly journey. He then spoke of Christ, giving a sketch of his life, and remarking that though he might have "associated with the popularest men of his time," he preferred persecutions. He said that all true Christians must be persecuted; as he told a minister at Boston, if they were not persecuted they were not Christians.

"Well, now, I tell you what it is, brothers, and sisters, and *friends*, these here ministers, the (the) popularest men of their day, ain't Christians," etc. He thought that a "blazing stake would be set up here in Watertown, to persecute the true believers—yes, I do, and that are within three months, too."

The enthusiasm of the poor devils is exalted amazingly by the tricks played on them. He exposed their doctrine—Christ was to take the form of flesh—heaven was to be "located" on earth—and then he drew a bungling picture of the heaven.

Several speakers followed him. One woman modestly remarked that it was easy to endure the cross and the stake, and such like great evils, but it tried the Christian's soul when it came to parting with little ornaments and dresses. The Bible champion corrected some of her quotations as she went on. When she sat down, he said that for "them that hadn't got grace inside of 'em it *was* hard, as sister Stone said, to part with little worldly trifles—but if one has truly got the spirit of God, and is persecuted and shunned and despised of men, he don't want no more to do with them things. If a man or a woman sticks to his jewels, it's a sign he han't got grace, but goes by rule, like them that preach in meeting off of notes," etc., etc., etc.

With screams, ejaculations, and prayers, the meeting was going on when we left.

Nothing is more cheerful and bright than the clear sunny days of autumn, when the woods have changed—but it is a dull and chilling

sky—all is cold and cheerless. Blue jays are screaming and occasionally a squirrel chirrups. The shrubs have grown dark and dull with
last night's frost, and the cold puffs of air shake them in a melancholy
manner. The pines along the edge of the clearing, the piles of wood—
the rocky hill with its various colored shrubbery, and rough and
broken growth of wood along its top—all wear the same gloomy
aspect. A white spot on the dull sheet of cloud marks where the sun
should be.

The Methodists have bishops and a sort of hierarchy. There are
conferences to settle the affairs of the church, appoint ministers, pay
them, etc. The great annual conference at Baltimore confirms and
rejects the acts of the rest. Though the salary of the ministers is not
paid by the parishes, they meet great hospitality and attention, and
want for nothing during their stay.

More Blackstones were sold in the Colonies than in England, says
Burke.

Money more than their just proportion paid by the Colonies for
the last two F[rench] wars.

The Assemblies had always *paid* the Governors, and civil officers.
Assemblies expected to provide a civil list on the arrival of each
governor. This practise discontinued—Governors paid annually.

Folsom family,[16] Exeter, N.H., descendants of the officer in the
War. The editor of the *News Letter*[17] will probably know about it.

"*Cornwallis*"[18] at Brighton, Oct. *18*, '*44*. I was there before the
militia had gone off. Some had the large skirted coats of revolutionary officers; some wore battered helmets; some three-cornered
hats; some nothing. They had every variety of weapon, from
blunderbuss to rusty saw; and were of all ages and sizes. A more
ragamuffin assemblage I never saw.

"Officers to the front," exclaimed the general on his horse. The
long line of ragamuffins, who stood leaning on their rifles or muskets
in every variety of outlandish costume, looked as if they had never

an officer among them. But at the word a number of fellows straddled out from the line—with yellow breeches and red coats; or with false beards and dirty shirts; armed with axes, swords, or guns. These marched up to the front and faced gravely towards the general. "*Gentleman* officers," he began, etc.

The address over, the officers withdrew, and the music struck up, at which the whole line of ragamuffins got under way, and marched straggling off the ground, just as the sun went down.

In the space in front of the tavern was the usual congregation of idlers and loafers—with a gang of Indians firing their guns and yelling close by.

*Nov. 3*ʳᵈ. The family of ———. He himself is a generous, open, hospitable, kind-tempered man of vulgar birth and education who has got an enormous fortune. His delight is in liberality, and he scatters money like water. His lady—a very dull and vulgar personage—is chiefly solicitous to make a display of the "tasty" and "genteel." They have a score of half-gentleman hangers-on around them. The house is furnished with an elegance that would better befit a palace. ——— has brought from Europe a splendid collection of pictures, which he has not the cultivation to appreciate, but delights to listen to their praises. He has statues, splendid articles of *bijouterie* from Paris, some of which are most antirepublican in character, and piled together with a profusion akin to that of a warehouse. The damask curtains, the artificial flowers, the wax-candles, and the numberless and regal ornaments give his rooms a most remarkable aspect.

His children, who play at whist with the aforesaid hangers-on all evening, are much petted, and provided with lapdogs. ———, his son, educated in Paris, is particularly weak and senseless, placing the height of human glory in dissipation, in which he has of course indulged, though scarce sixteen. The mother and children are, indeed, all very weak and ill-informed, but the cordial hospitality and kindness of ——— may make up for all, though [he] is quite in want of tact and discrimination, as might be expected.

———

Where in America is to be found that spirit of sport and bluff hearty enjoyment, that is seen in English country gentlemen and others? Business here absorbs everything, and renders people incapable of every other *pleasure*.

Officers of the army and navy are sometimes an exception. There is an old retired navy surgeon at Medford,[19] who lives with his dogs and his guns like an English squire, enjoying himself in the same hearty manner. Business, too, swallows much that is noble. The somewhat chivalrous sentiments, the reference of all things to the standard of a gentleman's honor, a certain nobleness (though it may be joined with debauchery and blackguardism) is found among the officers of armies.

Our business men, on the other hand, have narrowed away all this. Thoughts bent on practical gains are not pleasant to contemplate, no matter how much virtue may accompany them.

Old Mr. Blanchard, who, though past eighty, toothless and grey, stumped about with more than the vivacity of a boy. He was all liveliness and excitement. Some one offended him. "Damn you," shouted the old man, thumping down his cane, and shaking his fist. A general laugh followed, at which he stumped off elbowing among the crowd, shaking his head in wrath. A moment more found him all light and cheerfulness again, amusing a group of bystanders with jokes and stories.

The theological discussion at the Medford barroom, between Wait the blacksmith, James the Irishman, and the Whig who had been invited to drink a glass of champaign with Dudley Hall.[20]

Jan. 8th, '45. One of the most amusing characters of "our table"[a] is Bigelow,[21] a man so nervous and excitable that he has no self restraint, and is constantly advancing strange propositions with a most absolute air. This morning, he was inveighing bitterly against the "aristocracy" of the cadets,[22] but his more usual expression is that of the most unmitigated contempt for "clod-hoppers." Tonight he pitched upon "counter-jumpers" as the subjects of his animadversion, roundly declaring, rolling back his head and bringing his fist

[a] At a law school eating club.—Ed.

down upon the table, that there was not a respectable "counter-jumper" in Boston. Cobb[23] remarked that Mr. Lawrence[24] had extolled to him the character of that respectable class, on which Russell[25] remarked that Mr. Bigelow's acquaintances were probably from the inferior ranks of counter-jumpers. "That's a damned imputation! I defy any man here to say that I ever associated with counter-jumpers—least of all, Mr. Russell, those whom it is your pleasure to denominate, in so highflown and grandiloquent a style, the *lower ranks* of counter-jumpers," etc.

Fitchburg, Jan. 18. A bad inn. Sitting in public-room with an old woman, an(d) old man, and Joe [Peabody].[26] Landlord came in with a quantity of wood, which he put on the fire. He wished to make excuse for the tardiness of his preparations for supper, which he did thus: "Well, I never see nothing to beat this!" "What's to pay?" said I. "What's to pay! Why there's them damned boys won't stir nor do nothing! Here I've been a slaving this fortnight, and them lazy cusses, sitting on their arses. I won't stand it—nohow. They pretend to do work, do they—they *shall* do work, I guess they'll find that out, pretty quick. I guess their wages 'll feel it; if they don't, I'm mistaken. I'll tell 'em what it is to be hiring out and then not doing work, arter all," etc.

S[now] and his family[27] on the hill.

Sunday. This morning all the trees were crusted with the sleet of night before last. Every little twig was cased in crystal, and the green spires of the pines which showed through the coating of ice, were like diverging bundles of pea-green icecles. The sun rising behind a wooded hill made a most gorgeous appearance. All seemed studded with diamonds.

Mahon's, *Eng[land]*, IV.[28]

Coll[ection] of Extracts,[29] Series of Letters on the Scheme of Invasion in '59.

Harrison, *Ind. Life*.[30]

Lee, *Britain, Cocking's War*, a poem.

W's [Williams'] *Vermont*[31]
Romans' *Florida*[32]
Catalogue, Worcester Lib'y[33]
There is a printed journal mentioned in Worcester Cat. of service on the Lakes in '63 or '64.[34]
Filson's *Kentucky*.[35]
Hudson's Bay Compy: Ellis[36] and Dobson [Dobbs],[37] etc.
The Importance of Gaining and Preserving the Friendship of the B[ritish] Interest Considered, 1751.
Waldegrave's *Memoirs*.[38] Sermon on Death of Titcomb
Pickering's *Wyoming*.[39]
Guizot, *Cours d'Histoire Moderne*.[40]
Dryden—Pope—Bolinbroke—Swift's *John Bull* and *Martinus Scriblerus*[41]

The two deaf and dumb men in the public-room of the Elm Hotel. The old stage-agent playing chess, with the man looking over his shoulder.

The Senate Chamber[b]—the thin, large-nosed man, who tried to know everybody—took the Prex's cloak, with an "how-de-do, Mr. Quincy,"[42] and whom the Pres., with his usual felicity of manner, cut. The mean-looking man who sat listening with his mouth open.

The Penobscot Squaw at Roxbury: "You come up here to see; not for buy. You must give something." A large woman with quite expressive features.

March 10. The trees this morning were covered in every twig with feathery chrystals of snow, which gave them a beautiful appearance.
"Pride goeth before destruction and a haughty spirit before a fall" —think of that!

Lyman[43]—his silence, his oaths, his indecencies, and filthy habits.
P——, his white coat at class supper—his squirt, and his . . . .

Sunday. March 15[16]. The caterpillars of the willow just diverging

ᴸ   [b] At the State House in Boston.—Ed.

from the bud. The long, stiff, awkward young shoots of Sumach. The beaded ends of the young maple-twigs. Q. Are the bright-red forked shrubs maples?

The crust of ice with the water run away from beneath.

J——y. His vanity and love of display, joined with energy, combine to make a fool of him. He affects the man of the world—goes always in full dress, and though he has no sportsmanlike propensities, keeps a breed of dogs about him, and affects the connoiseur: also a fine equipage. He is foolishly proud of money and his supposed rank in society, and lets drop no opportunity of showing his superiority. From constantly pushing himself into the foremost place, and affecting to command everywhere, he has raised a host of enemies. His vanity impels him to lie enormously. I suspect him of not being remarkably brave, though I should never have made the remark but for some boastful lies he has lately been telling about a street battle with some fellows who insulted him. He is hospitable and bountiful through ostentation.

March 16 [*17*]. The Navy Club[44] paraded today in a variety of costumes. The "Lord High" had an old Continental uniform; the drum-major flamed in red, the drum was carried by Dunlap,[45] who was plainly conscious of the dignity of the place. The band wore a variety of uniforms. The standard was borne by Grey [Gray],[46] who came little short of nine feet high, measured to the top of his plume. The "Rear-Admiral"—"the laziest fellow in the class"—walked behind in a Turkish dress, with two Negroes to carry a chair for him to sit in, and another with his pipe and handkerchief. The "digs" all wore square caps. The doctor was admirable, and had a whole hospital of bones and skulls hanging about him. The chaplain, too, was done to the life: he had a Bible in his hand, which on examination proved a cigar-box. One of the "Horse marines" was mounted.

Is a man a coward, because he feels less than himself in a crowd?

Lyman's freaks; his disgusting habits at table; windows broken and he will not mend them; goes to Brooks'[47] room, looks into his drawers —"Hulloa, you've got some gingerbread!"; invites himself to spend the evening there; stays till morning, and sleeps standing against the wall, like a horse!!

The theological controversy at Mrs. Sanders'.[48] Brooks is a good-natured, thoughtless, careless fellow, without either application, ambition, or any settled principle. He thought church-going was "horrid"—"such a damned bore to sit under a sermon 40 minutes—ministers ought to know better, damned if they hadn't," etc.

Ritchie[49] seriously and fervently upheld the Church of England, which seems in his eyes the receptacle of all holy and eccellent things, while J. Peabody laughed at B.'s random heedless remarks, at the same time taking an occasional part in the discussion like one who had deep feelings on religious subjects—perhaps he thinks he has. J. G. also came in with his silly boyish observations, but was immediately snubbed. "Oh, *there!* that's enough," said Brooks, "stop now, that's good fellows—nothing I hate like talking religion, because it never comes to good—you can't convince one another—here, Watch, come here, old boy, and get your supper!"

Halkett,[50] *Historical Notes respecting the Inds. of N[orth] A[merica] with Remarks on the attempts made to Convert and Civilize Them* (by John Halkett, Esq., 8vo., pp. 480, London, 1825) contains notes and references to authorities.

Letters in Pa. arranged by John Jordan, Jr. 91 South 3rd St. Member Hist. Soc., Philadelphia.

Letters of Bouquet, etc.

John Sonntag Havil[l]and

Bro(a)dhead[51]

Birbeck [Birkbeck][52]

Travels through that part of America previously called Louisiana. By Mr. Bossu, Captain in French Marines, *translated from the French by John Reinhold Forster,*[53] *F.A.S. Illustrated with notes relative chiefly to Natural History, to which is added by the Translator a systematic Catalogue of all the known plants in N. America,* etc., etc. (London, 1771).

Read Rich's *Catalogue*[54]—Cat. Phil. L'by.

Hartford Hist. Soc. Newspapers. New London Papers, in Mr.

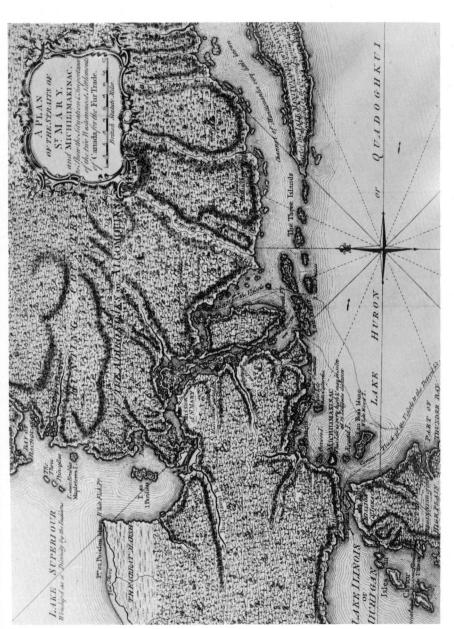

A Plan of the Straits of St. Mary and Michilimackinac

Engraved map

(Coverdale Collection No. 210)

Green's (Samuel?) hand. Putnam's letter originally published in a New London Paper?

Quebec Hist. Soc.[55]

Rich's *Catalogue*

Pouchot *sur la dernière guerre de l'Amérique.*[56] Very good.

Force[57] has authorities for Pontiac's notes of hand.

Lanman[58]

Little P.—about 13 years old—talks as if he were 50. "I do not think that seventeen is an appropriate age for entering college. The boy is too unexperienced. I agree entirely with my father that eighteen is preferable," etc., etc.

Brooks: "Law! Damn it, I never knew anything like it. Why, I can't take up a book without it puts me to sleep. I don't know what in the devil made me take Law—it's horrid! Greenleaf[59] met my father the other day and told him I was making fine progress; what does he know about it. Father swallowed it all; I wish Greenleaf would hold his tongue; I swear, it's horrid."

Law School Debating Soc. Batchelder[60] brought in numerous books from whence he read for three quarters of an hour, and made beside a most loose and ridiculous speech. He seems an instance of a man who is suspicious and timid, from *running* or *snubbing*, in private conversation, but will talk on forever, feeling a perfect independence in the debating club, where no one interferes with him.

Lee [Lea][61] of Louisiana spoke in the negative of the question which was that of nullification.

Hoadly [Hoadley][62] of Ohio, whom I have often remarked for a wretchedly sickly and feeble-looking person, spoke in the affirmative. His voice was like a lion's; and a supernatural energy seemed to animate his yellow, faded features, and give them an expression of fierce resolution.

Hooper[63] of South Ca. also spoke in the aff. He is a very gentlemanly southerner; pale, long-haired, well formed, and well-dressed; apparently haughty, proud, and aristocratic. He spoke with great fluency and not without taste; and was eminently courteous and stately in his manner.

Thayer[64] of Mass. took a *common-sense view* of the matter—every one of that assembly were *presumed to know* various things which he mentioned; the members of the convention were "*at least* men of ordinary abilities," etc.—a weak Yankee.

Ap. 23. D.D.S. [Daniel Denison Slade][65] on Fresh Pond—cross, childish, self-willed. He likes people whom he can direct, and who always yield to his selfish will. He is anxious to be treated with courtesy and consideration, yet is himself often very offency by his childish obstinacy and self-will.

Promised land of Canaan, to which the Israelites were entitled by right, but which was occupied by barbarous nations ordered to possess it. Application of this as a figure representing the kingdom of heaven—obstacles interposing to prevent attaining it—nevertheless sure. 1st-2nd Distrust of merits—2nd Distrust of power—3rd Worldiness—4th Fear of men, etc.

"They exchange opinions casually, and these are final. Councils generally deliberate upon what has been beforehand pretty well settled." [pp.] 27, 100.

Acct. of Chipawas by Cass.[66] Religious advantages, etc., [p.] 101. Pride in the *totem*: he is jealous of its honor and will avenge for insult offer(r)ed to it, [p.] 102; different totems different in political influence.

May 30, 1845. A great meeting of the Fourierites in Tremont Chapel. Most of them were rather a mean set of fellows—several foreigners— plenty of women, none pretty—there was most cordial shaking of hands and mutual congratulations before the meeting began. A dirty old man, four feet high, filthy with tobacco, came and sat down by me and was very enthusiastic. He thought Mr. Ripley, who made the opening speech, "one of the greatest men our country can produce." Ripley was followed by a stout old man, in a sack, who had previously been busy among the audience, welcoming, shaking hands, etc. He spoke with his hands in his pocket, and gave nothing but statistics, in a very dry, uninteresting manner. It surprised me to see these old fellows, who looked like anything but enthusiasts, attached to the cause. Horace Grant [Greeley]—the editor from N. Y.—spoke in a very weak, indecisive manner, seeming afraid of himself and his audience. He, however, gave some remarkable details of the working of the "present system of society" as illustrated by the working classes of N. Y.

Brisbane and Dana followed in a pair of windy speeches, and Channing was beginning a *ditto* when I came away. They say that there is a system of laws by which the world is to be governed "harmoniously," and that they have discovered those laws. F. Cabot was there, looking much more like a lunatic or a beast than a man.[67]

The Foot Race, June 17. There was not much excitement or enthusiasm. Thimblerig, etc., was going on. Among the characters most worthy of notice was the spectral puppy on horseback, with a patch over his eye, and the "special constable"—a perfect specimen of Yankeeism, with all its oddities and humors, internal and external.

Withers' *Cronicles of Border Warfare* (Clarksburg, Va., 1831).[68]
Doddridge's *Notes on the Ind. Wars* (Wellsburg[h], Va., 1824).[69]

Shallus's *Tables*, Hv'd [Harvard] L'by.

Napier's *History of the Conquest of Scinde*[70]
"Wiandots: by the Delawares called Delanatinos"—*Ettwein*.[71]
"The Six Nations[72] called the Mohicans, Delawares, and all the N. England savages, *Agozhaganta*"—Ettwein.

Toganawita—Mohawk. Otatscheehte—Oneida. Tatotarko—Onondaga. Tagahajon—Cayuga. Caniadario—Sataga-ranjes—Seneker. Six Nats.—Aquanophionihaga.—Ettewein (comp. the *printed* work— there may be mistakes in transcription!).

Delawares—Wapanachti. Oucheporiais—Chippeways. Chawainon —Shawnese [Shawnees]. Redmond Conyngham—Lancaster.

Prov[incial] Rec[ord] Bk., S[tate] P[aper?] 426, Colonial Recs.[73]
Plan of F[ort] Duquesne at Lancaster
1. Lancaster *Intelligencer*, 1843[74]

2. Chief Justice [J. B.] Gibson, Carlisle or Harrisburg, for Armstrong.[75]

3. Loudin's Work [Fort Loudon]—Carlisle

4. J. Francis Fisher,[76] Philadel., for admission to Phil[osophical] Soc., etc.

5. Plans of Ft. Pitt in Phil. Soc.?

6. James Ross at Pittsburg.[77]

7. Delaware *Register*. Wilmington.

8. Historical Coll. by Sherman Day.[78]

9. Bradstreet[79]—see notes to Letters of Junius.

Bouquet's[80] character—he employed Capt. Jack Smith and others.

The girl at table, who, probably afraid of being vulgar, made no answer when I offered to hand her what she was looking at with evident longing.

N. Y. [*New York*], *July 10.* The woman at Union Park who had dreamed of chairs, and after, on another night, of glass tumblers; and as she looked on the workmen at the fountain, felt a presentiment that she was destined to make her bread by means of it—so she bought chairs and a pitcher and glasses for water and lets them out for the people, as in the Champs Elysées. She also remarked upon the girls who made the park a place of assignation—spoke of the inconstancy natural to mankind—and was plainly up to snuff.

7535—*An Historical Review of Penna. from Its Origin, founded on authentic documents.*[81]

Chronicon Ephratense[82] (Lancaster, 1786), in German, but probably contains something.

Logan MSS., Vol. 3: a paper on Paxton Boys[83]—a paper on Ind. grievances, etc.

Ed. Shippen M.S. Col. [James] Bird's [Burd's], with Miss [Mrs.] Thom[p]son—Stevens[84]

Lancaster, Pa. A town of 9,000 inhabs.—laid out in a singular form, the main streets crossing each other thus:

The people chiefly Dutch—among them a number of Mennonists,[85] with long hair and beard. All the people here are as strong and hardy as any men I ever saw—seem to take life easily—have open and hearty manners, but are represented by Stephens [Stevens] as particularly close and miserly—as ignorant and stupid also, knowing nothing beyond their farms, and in the management of these following the manner of their forefathers. The land here is very rich, producing excellent wheat—there are a number of very rich people living in a plain manner here. Lancaster City is said to be the richest in the States. According to Stephens, this little place contains four distinct and separated circles of society.

Rode out to Paradise, to visit Mr. Redmond Conyngham.[86] Passed not many miles from the establishment of the "protestant monks" at Ephrata. Country rich and not very hilly—houses small, but many of them well built of stone, with very large and queerly shaped barns of the same, or on the poorer establishments of squared logs.

At Paradise stopped at the fine, old, whitewashed stone house of Mr. Whitmer, who came out, dressed like an ordinary laborer, and gave us a hearty Dutch welcome, inviting us to pass the night, which we promised to do. I was presented to his wife and daughter, who sat in the "stoup," after which the old gentleman hoped we would spare him the trouble of "bucking up"—he being evidently too lazy. We found his house stored with marine and mineral curiosities, etc.; he being a virtuoso after his fashion, and—a miracle for a Dutchman —a dabbler in science!

Going to Mr. Conyngham's who gave me much information on the Inds., we returned and found two young ladies, who quite deserved the title, invited to meet us. Having taken supper, during which the old gent. thrust in his head, and with a hearty grin, exclaimed ironically to his daughter who poured out the tea, "Hulloa, Laura, don't these fellers mean to be done eating pretty soon—they'll starve us out of house and home." Having taken supper we took a walk with the girls by the side of Peckway Creek—a small and not very clear stream, close by the house. Our apartment was quite sumptuously furnished—Stephens says the old man is worth $40,000—but S. exaggerates.

Found my classmate Baker[87] a schoolmaster here.

Returned to Lancaster in the morning—visited the famous jail[88] —explored the yard and the rooms—the *reputed* scene of the massacre. The prisoners are sometimes afraid to enter No. 13 or 14—which tradition points out (falsely?) as the place—no blood visible!

July 18. Came to Harrisburg. Walked at evening by the Susquehanna—a most broad and majestic stream—full of islands—with a fine prospect of mountains beyond—waters that ripple over a stony bottom, making a deep low murmuring. It is low at this season—though very wide, it seems not from the shore to have the majesty of *depth*, as the lines and streaks on its surface extend apparently from one shore to the other.

I saw a group of Dutchmen playing a game, something like quoits, with iron rings. Their faces bore no stamp of Yankee care and thought—they and the women were as stout specimens of flesh and blood as could be desired—a remarkable contrast to the puny Philadelphians.

July [?]. Canal Boat from Harrisburg to Williamsport. This is a new mode of travelling to me.

The old Baltimorean and his daughter, with the foreigner—the thin, meagre fop who said he looked like Tyler[89]—and a host of countrymen on board. The country beautiful, but not wild—the river very low.

At Harrisburg, locofocoism[90] has, of course, the ascendancy; consequently dinners are eat with a dispatch truly astonishing. Several men in the offices were true representatives of their party—blackguards of the first water, though one or two were quite gentlemanly men.

July [?]. From Williamsport, I came to Trout Run by a most wretched Rail Road. Trout Run is a little tavern among very wild mountains, not far from Lycoming Creek. Great Island, the scene of Armstrong's exped[ition], is about 26 miles above Williamsport— at least I am told so. The river there is said to be flanked by high hills, as it is below with wide intervales. The mountains on the south side of the river, near Wmsport, are called Laurel Rock.

Between Trout Run and a place called Blockhouse—*i.e.*, "Log-house"—the mountains are exceedingly wild and high, and without clearings—the chief one is called Laurel Hill.

A low and disagreeable set of fellows in the stage.

Dined at Blossberg, a mining place—very small—very rough— very dirty—and very disagreeable. It rained—went on thence by a wretched Railroad to Corning. Beyond Blossberg, the settlements are principally Yankee, along Tioga Creek.

A drunken, swearing puppy in the cars first amused and then disgusted me. Such a railroad I never saw before. Stopped at night at Corning, a new and flourishing place, and in the morning came to Seneca Lake, and took steamboat at Jefferson, a(t) town at its head.

Buffalo. Saw several Senecas[91] in the street.

The Detroit steamer was crowded—among the rest, a host of Norwegian emigrants—very diminutive—very ugly—very stupid and brutal in appearance—and very dirty. They appear to me less intelligent and as ignorant as the Indians. Besides these, a motley swarm of passengers of all nations.[92]

The shores of the lake consist of banks covered with trees, with now and then some land a little higher visible behind—but all is in general low and monotonous. A slight wind—yet the waves beat loudly on the shore

The group of Inds. at Detroit: the little squaw—the old one with her continual grin—the old man with his nose poxed away—and the rest. They had got a kettle of rum and were drinking it. They were miserably weak and slender. Evidently, their only enjoyments were eating and drinking. They laughed and were very happy over their liquor.

Hog Island has a border of marsh on the east side—so have the eastern and much of the western shores as you approach Lake Sinclair [St. Clair]. Flat, usually marshy ground in front—a line of forest behind—is the general appearance of the country. Isle à la Pêche is small, low, and in part marshy. Presqu'ile is a rising ground at the edge of the water, with marsh behind. The land in general is flat as a map.

The lands around the outlet of St. Clair River are very low— here the river splits into a multitude of ramifications, amongst flat marshy islands, interspersed with tracts of wood. The waters rise to the very brim, and seem ready to pour themselves upon the shore. On Lake St. Clair, a faint narrow line of distant woods, resting on the waters, divide the lake from the sky on the horizon. It is said that the waters never rise. No hills are visible—nothing but smooth green marsh, forests and the abundant waters.

Going towards Lake Huron, the banks become higher. Along the east shore is a thick group of trees, where a tribe of Inds. live, scattered along the bank in little log houses. Fort Gratiot,[93] a stockade work, stands close by the outlet of the lake. At the outlet the land is low and flat.

The western shore of Huron, near the outlet, at sunset—it presents nothing but a uniform dark line of forests, with a splendid display of purple and golden clouds behind, and the leaden colored waves below tinged with the evening colors. The woods stretched away into nothingness on each side.°

Thunder Bay. The land becomes a little higher before reaching Thunder Bay—though the Capt. says that it bears the same uniform flat appearance from this place to the Sinclair. The lands deep in Thunder Bay seem low and flat in the distance. Several islands are about its mouth, shaggy with firs. They tell me that thunder is very common here.

° Pp. 108-50 of the notebook consist of accounts and bibliographical references. This material is given in the Appendix to this journal.—Ed.

Mackinaw.[94] Approach from the low extensive island of Bois Blanc on the right—the main shore just visible on the north—another little island between Bois Blanc and Mackinaw.

The place is a picture of an ancient Canadian settlement—the little houses in Canadian style—some of them log, with roofs thatched with bark—the picket fences, of rough sharpened stakes, that surround them all—the canoes and Ind. huts on the shore give them a wild and picturesque air. Wild-looking half-breeds in abundance—a group of squaws and children, wrapped in their blankets, sat on the steps of a store—one little Canadian, three-quarters savage, had a red shawl tied round his head, red leggins, gay moccasins, and a blanket coat—another, who looked out from between his straight black locks with a wild and particularly vile expression, was staring at the steamer.

Sunday. This morning, before breakfast, walked round the shore. The lake beautifully clear—banks of limestone frequently jutting in rough spires, feathered with shrubs, from the midst of a thick growth of arbor-vitae, birch, and maple, etc., that cover the steep and high banks; while white and waterworn masses are strewn along the water's edge. The shore is most beautiful. Saw the "arched rock"— then walked over the island, which is covered with a thick growth, chiefly maple.

Capt. Martin Scott[95] inspecting his men on the parade.

Lieut. Whiting[96] showed me the "Sugar loaf," which is truly remarkable—an abrupt spire starting up ninety feet from the midst of the woods. Near at hand, is Fort Holmes,[97] on the highest point of land, commanding the present fort—and close to this, on the descent below, is the "Scull-rock" where Henry[98] hid.

The houses are chiefly thatched with elm bark—the sides of many are also covered with it, though they are for the most part of squared and whitewashed logs.

Lieut. W. gives the Canadians the following character: good natured—jovial—lazy, as far as regular work is concerned, but extravagantly fond of wandering about, fishing, etc.

The Ind. trade here is chiefly managed by pedlars who go into the Ind. country on their own account—the fir [fur] companies are used up[99]—Mackinaw is no longer an outfitting place—the voyageurs' occupation's gone.

Various deposits of sculls and bones have been found in different parts of the island, among the rocks.[d]

Scull Rock. The cave was once two or three feet deeper than at present—it was filled up by the Ind. boys at the Mission, each of whom as he visited the place, threw a stone in. Capt. Scott remembers to have seen bones there.

Passage to the Sault. Coast as far as the Detour low, wild, and covered with firs. The same around the Detour. Passage wide in many places and dotted with fir-covered islands—all wild, forlorn, and desolate—trees hung with mosses—many of them dead and leaf-less.

Farther on, the distant coasts and islands presented a strange appearance—by an optical illusion, they assumed the appearance of basaltic formations—then low and dimly seen islands would swell up into high peaks—then the top would be apparently detached and lifted like a cover from the base. Blue and distant coasts would alternately rise above and sink below the horizon; and on a long point that thrust itself out against the horizon, a few detached trees, and ragged firs, swelled up like the spires of a city, and soon after seemed pillars supporting a canopy over the land. Day a little obscured by piles of fleecy clouds.

We took the "Montreal Channel," that being the most picturesque. For a long time the shores were wide stretched apart. They gradually approached.

On a green beach connecting a rocky island with the shore, were the skeletons of what the pilot, Mr. Peck, called a Chippewa[100] encampment. Some of the poles were arranged in the peaked, some in the round form. On this place are the graves of the band. Peck say[s] he has known food placed on them at intervals for twenty years.

The channel grew narrower, and was filled with wild rocky

[d] At this point Parkman had filled up his notebook, and so continued his narrative on a sheet of paper headed "Journal of Part of Journey in August '45—No. 1. Commenced at Mackinaw, Aug. — 1845."—Ed.

islands—the bare rock sloped upward from the water, or rose sheer in precipices. The islands were shaggy with a growth of firs, large and small, dead and living—the channels between deep and black— opposing shores often abrupt and high, and covered with the rough and savage growth of firs. Some rocky and mossy promontories were almost bare—here and there rose a wild and battered tree from a crevice—shrubs were scattered around among dead trees standing and prostrate. Such was the passage for a long way, seeming narrow from the multitude of islands.

They tell me that there is good land inland, especially on St. Joseph's Island.

Met Mr. and Mrs. Arnold of New Bedford, with Miss Chandler and James Lawrence.[101]

The channel soon widens, and loses some of its picturesque character, though some highlands and precipices appear(s). Two Ind. lodges of bark on the shore. Suddenly we turned into a narrow winding passage where, toward evening, the scene was as wild and beautiful as any I ever saw. This was not many miles from the Sault.

At the Sault, everything full of copper speculators.[102] Found, with the party aforesaid, lodging at the Baptist Mission house—Mr. Bingham's.[103] Conversed with him on the Inds.—hope he is not a fair specimen of Ind. missionaries; he is stupid and ignorant, and said to have no influence. Protestant missionaries generally are said to be without power or respect.

Ft. Brady[104]—a square stockade with block-houses at two corners.

The inhabs. of the Sault are chiefly Canadian and half-breeds— always dancing and merrymaking—who live in houses resembling those at Mackinaw.

Ind. lodges, some round, some peaked, on the bank of the rapids. All Ojibway. Lodges covered with *pukivi*e mats and birch bark, the former very thick and warm. Saw Ind. fishing in the rapids.

Mr. Arnold failed in his attempt to get the ladies a paddle down the rapid. Lawrence and I went down together. A half-breed, educated at the Mission at Mackinaw, and named Joseph [Gurnae] directed the canoe. (The Chippewa birches are all large—they have small wooden canoes.)

e Bark.—Ed.

Joseph was remarkably intelligent. I afterwards conversed with him. All the Inds., he said, knew of Manabosho, and he mentioned several of his exploits, as recorded by Schoolcraft[105]—also those of Paupukeewis, whose name he mentioned with a laugh. He spoke of fasts, love philters (which he said were universally in the hands of the young women), charms, etc., etc. He evidently believed much of them himself, and cautioned me against ever letting an Ind. girl, to whom I might become attached, get possession of one of my hairs, as she would then have it in her power to do me mischief. He boasted to have once defeated a spell cast on a man by a conjuror.

Mr. and Mrs. Jones, copper-speculators grown elevated by prospects of wealth. The latter coolly introduced herself at Bingham's —on scarce any pretext—to Mrs. Arnold, and then presented her husband. She has been up to Copper Harbor, an exploit which increases her self confidence and complacency. She gives her opinion as to where *forts* should be built, etc.

We returned to Mackinaw by the Channel we came by—scenery appearing no less fine than before.

Whiting introduced me to Mr. Robert Stewart [Stuart][106] of Astoria memory. Mr. S. thinks Tanner's book[107] of much value, and that T., who at the time of dictating it had recently become a member of the church, told nothing but what he *believed* to be true—that however his superstition and savage imagination sometimes deceived —that he had been in the custom of telling stories till he believed them himself. Mr. S. said he had seen an Ind. who was convinced that he had changed himself into a rattlesnake, etc. He thinks highly of Tanner's native powers of mind and courage.

Mr. S. thinks that Schoolcraft's *Algic Researches* are a superstructure of falsehood on a true foundation—that having once caught the tone and spirit of the tales, he multiplied them *ad libitum*—though he thinks that many of them are genuine.[108]

Capt. Martin Scott, being bent on getting up a picnic, seemed little inclined to fulfil his promise of sending me to Old Mackinaw with a crew of his soldiers; so Whiting found an old Canadian, François Lacroix, who with his two sons carried us over in a fishing boat. The distance is about eight miles. We explored the ruins of the fort[109] (see *Miscellanies*), made a dinner there, and returned. The old

Canadian and his sons rowed with a quick easy stroke that carried
us rapidly; yet before we left the land, the thunder was growling
from a huge pile of black clouds to the southwards; and before we
were half over, a long flash leaped from the edge of a black curtain
of thunder cloud down to the dark waters at the horizon, and then

Old Fort Mackinaw
plan taken by Lieut. Whiting

(These points of the compass not very accurate)

64 y

8

5

54 y

58

100 y

5

8½

7

34 y 55 y

Mag.

Straits

the thunder bellowed over the waste. The shore of Michigan was
obscured by white mists and rain—then Bois Blanc grew dim also—
the old fort too was veiled, and it evidently rained there, though
away to the north the long undulating shore of Pt. St. Ignace was
easily seen, and the nearer white cliffs and green shrubbery of
Mackinaw. At last the drops fell fast upon us—another thunder clap
bellowed over the water—old François laughed and put on his

chapeau, and we pulled hard for the town. As we skirted the shore, the Canadians stood at the doors of their huts in the rain looking at us. Passing between an old wreck and the shore, the swells, which run high in the straits, nearly capsized Whiting, who stood in the boat. At length, we gained the beach—the boat was hauled up—and we found the picnic party had abandoned their purpose, though the storm was passing and a fine *arc-en-ciel*, as François said, rested on the water to the southwards.

Mackinaw seems to have been a great resort of Inds. I saw this morning at the fort, a box of bones found in various caves and crevices about the island. Some were discovered yesterday by a soldier who took refuge from the rain under a rock. A large number have been got from the cave Whiting and I visited day before yesterday.

Last night the Inds. in the lodges on the beach got drunk. I heard them singing for a long time in a mournful, maudlin fashion, repeating the same words, and varying the song with what seemed to be boasts or narratives of exploits. The same monotonous music rose from half a dozen lodges that stood in a line together.

This morning I found a group sitting among the ruins of a hut, which they seemed to have pulled down about their ears. They were still drunk, singing and laughing. One of them was a remarkably handsome squaw, with a good-looking young man, with his leggins and bare thighs, at her side. There was another drunken fellow coiled up singing on the ground. Then a tall, thin, savage-looking old fellow came along and seated himself in the midst. They turned rum out of a bottle into the cover of a tin pail, and tried to drink it raw, keeping up a constant laughing and maudlin merriment.

At another lodge, a squaw was making very neat mats out of rushes—much finer and neater than the *pukivi* mats.

Mr. Turner, the sportsman and boon companion at Mackinaw.

Palmer, Michigan, Sunday. Attended church—orthodox—clergyman a vile-looking fellow, tall and sallow, with a loud voice and a bad obtrusive face. A very pretty face in the choir. People really good-looking and strong. A severe thunder-storm came up, which detained the little congregation singing psalms for some time after service.

Reflected this morning on the disadvantage of republican governments, being led thereto by Backus's aspirations after a despotism!

The intelligent fellow with whom I conversed at Brown's Tavern, Palmer, and who told me so much of mines and steamboats.

The women at work making carpets in the large room of Whitman's house, where I spent a disagreeable day in overhauling *six trunks* of old McDougall's [M'Dougal's] papers.[110] They worked on in a dismal silence—not a word spoken. I found a fine engraving of General Washington in the trunk, which I gave to the elder woman, who declared she would not take a dollar for it: another woman came in, who, smitten with jealousy, tried to get a gift or a swap of it, but it would not do.

The dyspeptic man who insisted on helping himself to such morsels as suited him (with his own knife and fork). He had nursed himself till he had reached a state of egotistic selfishness.

The Canadian gentleman on board the steamer *Red-Jacket*, between Detroit and Palmer. Mr. Rice, the trader, lumberer, etc., who told his story of being left on an island in Thunder Bay—and of his hospitable reception by an Indian when he reached the shore. He said that this island, which he had set on fire in order to get a good crop of grass, burnt for several months, as the soil is, as he says, "sulphur rock."

As you approach the opening of Detroit River on leaving Lake St. Clair, Presqu'ile, projecting before Hog Island, seems like another island. Hog Island is covered with a thick growth of trees, but is bordered by much low, level, and grassy land.

M. François Baby[111] and his establishment at Windsor. A fine old brick house; the porch, the shrubbery, and the hall have a waste and picturesque air—books, guns, neglected tables, old clocks, chests of drawers, and garments and Indian equipments flung around. The little Negro girl, and the strange-looking half-breed, who were sunning themselves among the hens and hogs in the back yard.

Went to Sandwich. The old Canadian houses often have little square porches in front. Here men ride always at a canter, as far as my observation goes.

Canoes are often made of a peculiar shape of a bent log,[f] the hinder

---

[f] A very rough sketch of a canoe occurs here in the journal.—Ed.

end being elevated and squared—sometimes both ends are high and sharp, like the elegant log canoes of the St. Lawrence, but not so well made. The large Chippeway canoe is the perfection of the thing. The Chippeways use a small log canoe for hunting, etc. They have no small bark canoes. A Mackinaw boat is unique—it is a hugely magnified and elaborated skiff, moved by oars that are secured by leather thongs fastened to a single pin by way of rowlock, as also are the oars of the fishing skiffs at Mackinaw.

The old Huron church, just above Sandwich, is a most venerable and delapidated structure, with the green in front and the old buildings round. Here were congregated a host of little Canadian waggons, with corresponding horses. The people seem to have caught English manners, and their French complaisance has disappeared.

There are some English cottages. I stopped at one, mistaking it for Mr. Askin's.[112] The owner was an officer—his sword hung with his garments in the hall, and hard by was his gun and fishing rod. A fine pair of antlers lay on the window-sill of a little projecting room that seemed his study. So much for English tastes.

Mr. Askin(s), a little, dried-up, *distingué* man, received me with great courtesy, and expressed much interest in my objects. His mother was a Campeau. He talked incessantly, though almost unintelligibly from his front teeth being knocked out, and finally ushered me from the door with a profusion of compliments, etc.

The opposite shores are low, but beautiful—no high land in sight, but a line of woods rises behind the buildings and scattered Canadian cottages with a beautiful effect.

Below Detroit, the shores grow lower still. Fighting Island is almost without trees at present, its upper parts are elevated some feet above the water with here and there a clump of bushes or a tall tree; but as you go down, it changes to a complete marsh, beyond which the other arm of the river may be seen, and puddles of glistening water vary the surface of the rank grass. Turkey Island is all marsh. The shores in this part present the same uniform marshy appearance, and are almost level with the water, with which they seem imperceptibly to mingle, as the strong grass grows thinner along their edges.

Bois Blanc near Malden is raised some feet above the water.

Aug. 16. North shore of Erie, near Point Stanley. The bank is high and steep, and composed of earth work by the water and quite raw, with the forest along the top.

Sometimes the section of a ravine appears, filled with trees, seeming like a notch cut in the shore. In a wider and very pretty opening stands Port Stanley. East of this, the bank is high for many miles, but gradually becomes lower, and fifty or sixty miles further on, it is almost level with the water, at Long Point. Long Pt. is extremely low and flat. On the other side, about Erie, the land seems quite high, but where the opposite shores converge towards Buffalo, they are neither of them very high.

Conversed with an old emigrant from the north of England, who spoke highly of the advantages of Canada, and the yet greater advantages of the States.

The scene on landing at the Quay at Buffalo—it surpassed anything I ever yet saw for hubbub and noise.

Niagara, Aug. 17. The Cataract is a bloated noisy house—a set of well-dressed blackguards predominated at table. One fellow—very good-looking—I particularly noticed. He sent the waiter with a bottle of champagne to a friend of his at another table, who coolly helped himself, and then proceeded to fill the glasses of some ladies near him out of his friend's bottle. At this the latter's face became heavily overshadowed; he reddened with vexation, played uneasily with knife and fork, and turning to a neighbor remarked that he "always knew ——— for a damn mean fellow, but that was a little *too* sneaking." So he bowed across the table and sipped his glass with great gravity. When the bottle which had got into such dangerous hands was returned to him, his face wonderfully brightened. Poor fellow! He had come with a half year's clerk's salary to be gay and live fast for a week at Niagara; it was hard that his earning should be drank up in that unceremonious fashion.

Niagara. I have looked at the great cataract, but do not feel in the temper to appreciate it or embrace its grandeur. An old woman, who, for the pure love of talking and an itching to speak to everyone, several times addressed me with questions about she knew not what, filled me with sensations of particular contempt, instead of amusing me as they would have done, had not my stomach been disordered. I sat down near the rapids. "What's all this, but a little water and foam?" thought I. "What a pack of damned fools," was my internal commentary on every group that passed—and some of them deserved it. But, thank Heaven, I have partially recovered my good-humor, can sympathize with the species, and to some degree feel the sublimity of the Great Cataract.

How many of the visitors here deserve to look on it? I saw in the tower a motherly dame and her daughters, amid the foam and thunder and the tremendous pouring of the waters. "Oh, ma!" (half whispered), "He's looking at us! There, I've torn my sash; I must go home and pin it up, etc." Old Niagara pours bellowing on forever, as it has poured since the beginning of time, and generation after generation of poor little devils of human beings play their little pranks and think their little thoughts around him. He roars on undisturbed, while age after age of the manikins look at him, patronize him with their praises, and go to the devil before his eyes. What does he care for their pranks, their praises, or their fault-finding? His tremendous face never changes; his tremendous voice never wavers; one century finds him as the last did, in his unchanging power and majesty.[113]

Aug. 18th. Visited the Devil's Hole. A violent rain. It is the very place for an Ind. massacre.[114] The great cliffs that flank the river are here notched away, leaving an immense, deep gully withdrawn back from the river, with sheer, savage lime-stone fencing it on three sides, and the furious river on the other. Stand on the "Platform Rock" and look down into the gulf upon a mass of vegetation—bass-wood—white cedar (*arbor vitae*)—ash—sumach—iron-wood, rising together in the abyss, with now a savage, bristling spruce or hemlock shooting up above the rest. The man measured the height from the Platform—his line lodged at seventy feet, but it must be nearly twice as deep, measured from the centre of the gulf upwards. The old road, he says, followed the edge of the precipices somewhat thus[g]—the men that were precipitated must have fallen eighty feet or more into this

g A very rough pencil sketch has been omitted here.—Ed.

rocky and wooded den. Bloody Run dribbles downward near the platform, and is large enough to carry a mill in spring. According to the man, the attack was made just above or at the upper corner of the Hole. Here, on one side, is a hollow, probably filled with dense bushes in 1763, while on the other a hill rises, whence a rush could be made with great effect. Behind this hill is a ravine, the mouth of which is plainly visible a few rods down the road, and below the Hole. The man says that the foundation of a blockhouse is visible on the hill above the Hole.

The view from the Platform up and down the river, raging between its precipitous banks and compressed to a width of from 50 to 30 rods, is most extraordinary.

We descended among the rocks and dripping woods through the Hole to the bank. The surges run six or eight feet high—the channel seems filled with great rocks, though it must be extremely deep. The waters boil up from the bottom like a chauldron.

The man says that all that changes the height of the water are the winds of Lake Erie. He has known them to rise and fall from this cause, 9 feet. Indeed, the bushes have been swept away some height above the present level all along the banks. He has known the ice piled and frozen together the whole way across. The Falls themselves struck me less than these scenes.

The view from above the Whirlpool is no less magnificent—and that from Bellevue, including the distant cataract, is more sublime and beautiful than anything I ever saw. When the sun broke suddenly out upon the face of the Fall, and brightened the white and gushing foam, the Torrent fairly seemed to laugh.

The loafer near me at table. The poor devil was out of his element. He could not conceive why it was that the waiters were so attentive to his neighbors, while he was quite neglected. He sat embarassed and disconsolate, siezing upon, as a forlorn hope, every dish that happened to come within reach. At length, a waiter siezed upon a knife that lay by his plate and transferred it to some more favored individual, whose demands were imperative. When next the waiter passed, the neglected one said, "Now bring that knife back again, if you've mind to." Pitying his helplessness, I offered him dishes, for which I got no other acknowledgement than an instant siezure of the proffered viands, or a decisive "No!"

Went behind the "sheet," under the guidance of a nigger—an opposition. "They are generally reckoned the Seven Wonders of the World, sir!" he remarked, speaking of the Falls. "What a *preliminacament* a man would be, sir, on that 'ere rock, sir, wouldn't he?"

The world cannot match the view from the Table Rock.

I saw an old, withered, hollow-eyed, straight-backed Yankee peering at the Falls with a critical scrutiny, as if he was judging of the goodness of a bank note.

The view from the Lewisto(w)n railroad—the original of Bartlett's picture, "Forest on Lake Ontario."[115] River at Lewiston—the abrupt rocks here cease, though the banks are still high. The river wide deep and tranquil; headland after headland give it a very picturesque appearance. The rapids begin immediately above Lewiston.

Fort Niagara[116] stands on the point that projects from the shore at the outlet of Ontario. Behind it stretches away even now a great level forest, apparently unbroken, the same seen from the railroad. About this point, and all along the lake for a great distance, the land is quite flat and wooded, with abrupt raw banks of earth along the water. Looking back after passing the Fort, you see it standing on its point of land, with the more distant shore on the other side, the outlet stretched out like a promontory behind.

About Oswego, land rolling and in part wooded—forming a beautiful and graceful shore. The morning mist hung around it when I saw it. Entering the river, a hill on the right, another on the left, where the present fort stands.

Though now dammed up, the river was once stoney and rapid. In some places the banks are still high and wooded with chestnut, maple, beech, hemlock, pine, etc.

Passed Lake Salina—country undulating—farther south, hilly. Saw the large salt works about the salt springs near the Lake, mentioned by Bartram.[117] Lake itself fresh.

At Syracuse, took a horse and rode to Onondaga Castle, about nine miles distant. Descended into the valley at near sunset. Scenes formed by the wooded hills far and near, the rich flats bordered and dotted by trees, and the little stream Onondaga, very beautiful and romantic. Bartram's description will answer for the present day, except that there are many frame houses, possibly more cultivated land, and a frame council house in place of that seen by B. The smokes and houses may be seen far up on the borders of the woods— many good cornfields along the hills and intersecting the patches of woods—rich hay in the interval[e] meadow, through which among rich groves of trees winds the Onondaga, small and choked up, as described by Bartram.

I treated a man to cigars—he showed me the council-house, where by the way they are to celebrate the Green Corn Dance on Monday. (They have many dances in the course of the year.) It was a long, plain, one-story building, containing only one large room, with a fire-place at each end, benches placed around, a brass horn to convoke the people, and a large turtle-shell rattle to keep time to the dance.

I got the Inds. into excellent humor by presents of cigars and pipes. They are to hold a general council of the Six Nations at Tonawanda in the Fall.

They are the worst people in the world to extract information from: the eternal grunted "yas" of acquiescence follows every question you may ask, without distinction.

Pro[nounced] "Onondawga."

One old fellow whom I conversed with seemed to remember the council-house described by Bartram, with the partitions in it. It is impossible to say, however, whether he really did so. The present council-house, he told me, was erected eight years ago.

(Examine Barber's *N. Y. Hist. Coll.*[118] for an acct. of Onondaga.)

Fort Stanwix[119] stood in the midst of a very level country—the Mohawk is here quite small.

At Oneida, I saw several Indians (examine Barber's *H. Coll.*).

German Flats are a level and beautiful interval.

The Valley of the Mohawk has no pretension to sublimity. Its hills are not high, but the river winds like a snake in the interval between, with trees fringing its banks, forming a rich and picturesque landscape. (I am getting a stronger relish for quiet beauties.)

The lawyer with the sharp nose, thin face, and small mouth. His vehement narratives about himself, and the singular contortions of countenance with which he enforced them.

The noisy and vulgar party of girls, who sat on the backs of the seats and filled the cars with their cackling. The old fool of a woman, their mother, who rivalled the accomplishments of her daughter. Is not a *half*-educated, vulgar, weak woman a disgusting animal? Where there is no education at all, and no pretension, the matter is all very well—where high education and good sense are united, it is very well indeed—but the half-and-half genteel—damn them!

The fury of the man who saw the cars run over and kill a man and woman at Schenectady—his exclamations and threats against a man whom he took for one of the company. "I accuse you for a murderer!" Clenching his fists: "By G— I'll have the law on you. I want to know who you are. I want to know if you are a gentleman," etc.

The drunken fellow, who said he was wounded at Texas,[120] on board the steamer.

Appendix

Accounts
Previous Expenditures

Omnibus	.15
Brandy, etc.	.08
Cars from Medford	.15

(Received from C. in payment of debt: .75; carried over to account of funds on opposite page[below]).

Joseph Gurnae, Sault St. Marie

Funds at starting, Tuesday, July 8, 1845: $103.17[h]

July 8:	Cravat	.75
"	Shave	.06
"	Cider	.04
"	Ticket to N. Y.	2.00
"	Supper on board	.50
July 9:	Ale	.06
"	Boots	.12½
"	Porter	.11
		3.64

"	Carriage to Astor H[ouse]	.50
"	Baths	.25
"	Carriage	.50
"	Soda & Omnibus	.18
"	Waiter	.18
July 10:	Soda, etc.	.18
"	Porter	.06
"	Astor House	3.50

[h] "A bill of credit for $100. more."—F. P.

July 10:	Carriage & Porter	.37½
”	Passage to Philadel.	4.00
”	Supper	.50
”	Cab	.50
”	Waiter	.25
July 11:	Ale	.06
”	Tanner's *Am[erican Trav[els]*	1.50
”	Soda & Omnibus	.09
”	Bath	.35
		12.97

July 12:	Sundries	.18
”	Colombia H'se	3.63
”	Waiters	.70
”	Congress Water	.12
”	Dinner & Tea	.55
”	Bath	.25
July 13:	Breakfast	.15
”	Servant	.05
”	Soda	.06
”	Dinner	.35
”	Bath	.12½
July 14:	Breakfast	.28
”	Dinner	.58
”	Supper	.35
July 15:	Breakfast	.15
”	Sundries	.12
”	Dinner	.45
		8.54

”	City Lib'y	.25
”	Bath	.25
”	Tea	.20
July 16:	Breakfast	.15
”	Bath	.25
”	Franklin House	4.25
”	Waiter and Porter	.75
”	Soda	.18
”	To Lancaster	2.52
”	Porter	.12½

July 16:	Sundries	.25
July 17:	Books	4.00
"	Hotel and chaise	4.75
"	Lancaster *Intelligencer*	2.50
July 18:	To Harrisburg	1.50
"	Breakfast, etc.	.63

$100.00	$54.	$22.67
44.	20.	13.
56	34.	8.50
		$43.67

Papers copied	5.00
Hotel	6.95
Porter, etc.	.25
Boots	.12
Fare to Williamsport	3.62
Supper and fare to Trout Run	$1.00
Fare to Blossberg	1.50
Lodging at Trout Run	.50
Fare to Corning	1.50
Dinner	.25
Salts	.06
Lodging and Fare to Seneca Lake	1.50
Passage across	1.50
" to Rochester	2.00
Lodging and Porter	1.12
To Buffalo	2.50
Dinner & Tea	1.00
Bath, etc.	.37
Fare to Detroit	7.00
Cider	.12
Shoes cleaned	.12
Map of Michigan	2.00
Sundries	.25
Hotel at Detroit	6.22
Passage to Mackinaw	7.00
Lodging at "	2.70
Passage to the Sault	5.00
Lodging	.50

Canoe down the Sault	1.00
Ale and porter	.50
Passage from Sault	5.00
Key to Valise	.37
Boat to Old Mackinaw	2.00
Lodging at Mackinaw	3.00
Passage to Palmer	6.00
Shoes blacked & Cider	.18
Lodging at Newport	.87½
Supper at Palmer	.25
Porter	.12
Ale	.06
Passage to Detroit	1.25
Porter	.25
Daguerreotype	3.37½
Postage	.26
Tracing paper	.37½
Map of Wayne City	.50
Rhubarb	.06
Trip to Windsor	.15
Hotel	4.87
Steamboat *London*	6.00
Porter and Brandy	.30
Guide to Niagara	.25
Fare to Niag. (steamer)	.75
Porters	.37
Ferry to Am[erican] Side	.12
Goat Is[land] Bridge	.25
Bath	.25
Waiter	.12½
Man at Devil's Hole	.50
Driver	.25
Man at Whirlpool	.25
Buggy to Devil's Hole	1.00
Ind. chisel	.25
Brandy	.06
Ferry	.30
Museum	.25
Going under Falls	.50
Cane	.50

Ind. Curiosities	2.00
Hotel bill	4.87½
Porter and waiter	.37½
Fare to Syracuse	5.00
Breakfast	.50
Boots cleaned	.12
Cigars, etc., for Inds.	.30
Horse to Onondaga	1.00
Hotel at Syracuse	1.50
Porter	.25
Fare to Albany	5.50
Dinner	.25
Hotel at Albany	1.50
Sundries	.37½
Fare to N. Y.	1.50
Dinner	1.37
Omnibus	.12½
Lodging	.50
Breakfast	.30
Carriage	.37
Porter	.12
To Boston	2.00
Nigger	.12½
Supper	.25
Carriage	.25
Sundries	.37
Carriage	.25
Lodging at Pavilion	.50
Carriage (on Father's acct.)	2.00
Omnibus	.15
Stage	.25
Postage, etc.	.12½
Cars	.15
Boots cleaned	.10
H[asty] P[udding] Supper	3.00

(Owe to Rice for furniture removed 1.50—.75 for lamp, oil, etc., sold him)

Owe Wyman .75 for horse

    " Clapp[1] " " "

[1] "Began with Clapp. Sept. 1."—F. P.

Owe Clapp .75 for horse

Rcd. from Mother	.25
Omnibus	.15
Class Supper	3.55
Big Bear	.50
Joseph	1.00
Cars (on mother's acct.)	.15
Dinner	.31½
Stage to Medford	.18¾
,, ,, ,,	.18¾
Omnibus	.15
Stage	.18
Dinner	.44
Hornden's Ex[press]	1.25

4	1.00	.25
37½	2.12	.50
8	2.50	1.37½
	6.12	.65

1.00 ⎫
2.62 ⎬ ½
2.50 ⎭

.12½	Miss Adams
3.50	Seignourry C. Carol
.46	Miss Wood
.12½	Phillomine Seeds
.62½	
.62½	Miss Hall: Bryant
2.02	
3.00	
.25	
.37½	
.12½	
.50	

Historical Notes

Trumbull [Papers], II:
P. 30, Whitehall, Jan. 27, 1763
P. 44, St. James's, Oct. 19, 1763
P. 45. Norwalk, Conn. Nov. 10, '63

McKenney's *Memoirs*[121]—soon to be published
Dryden
Look up Military—Colonial
Franklin's *Hist. Rev[iew] of Pennsylvania.*[122]
Marshall's *Kentucky*[123]
Jefferson's *Notes on V[irgini]a*[124]
Chapman[125]
Jenessies—Senecas

Letters, '56-74, in State House (?). Page 415.

Letter from Ft. Pownal, Capt. Goldthwaite, to the hunters on Quontabagook Pond, warning them to leave it, as the I's [Indians] were dissatisfied. March 24, '64.

Journals, Page 328.

Acct. of C[row]n Pt.

Elinor Noble—page 330 and Military, May 16, '62.

Page 343. Letter from Capt. Goldthwaite, at Ft. Pownal, Me. Insolence of Inds. Sept., '67

Indian '57.—'75, let.[p] 295

A letter from Johnson, dated April 25, '64. An expedition against the enemy. 200 houses burnt.

Page 289. From Capt. Goldthwait, Penobscot Inds. discontented. Page 292.

Goldthwait. Penobscots. They had been infected. P. 294

Col. Lithgow to Dr. Gardiner, *Penobs.*

Oct. 7, '63. A Royal Proclamation about the I[ndian] trade.[126]

Van Schaack's *Reminiscences*[127]

Putnam's letter, *Conn. Courant,* '64.

A View of the Causes and Consequences of the Am. Rev.

A Second Letter to a friend on Dieskau's fight.[128] Boston, '55

General Review, '52

Martial Review by Boyce *excellent.*

N. Y. Hist. [Soc.] *Coll.,* vol. III, for character of Rogers.

Mrs. Coghlan, *Memoirs*[129]—a daughter of Major Moncrieffe.

Border Life, Lancaster, Pa.

London Mag[azine] for '63, etc., a Rev[iew] of the War.

Authorities on the Indians (from Bancroft):

Le Jeune. Chateaubriand—read it—6th vol. Joutel. Lafit[e]au. Brainerd. Marest. Le Clercq. St. [Mother] Mary of the Incarnation. Le Caron [Lecaron]. Benjamin Constant (ninth). Creuxius. Alloüez. Jarvis [Jogues] (in N. Y. Hist. Coll.). Purchas. Bernard Romans. Brebeuf. Du Pratz, *Hist. Louisiana.* Mackenzie.[130]

Acadia and Ft. W[illiam] H[enry] Hist. Worcester. Alloüez, Le Jeune, and Brebeuf—see *Relation de la N. France.* Le Clercq, *Rel. de la Gaspésie.*

Book of Collections in [Mass.] Hist. [Society] Lib'y, '20-'61. P. 172: Proceedings of Albany Congress, July, '54. Mass. Gen[eral] Court. Act for levying soldiers, April 5. Letters of Bollan to Hse. of Reps. and to W. Pitt, '57-'58. List of provincials who deserted from Ft. Cumb[erland], Chignecto, with a vessel. (This collection is principally of letters on domestic and church matters).

Col. Israel Williams Papers,[131] '56-80. This contains a great many letters, official and otherwise, chiefly details of the war. Burk to Williams; important details of Put[nam] and others July 2, '57, p. 29. Summons to aid of William Henry, p. 30. Alarm of the country at its capture, p. 41. Lt. Pierce's scout afterward, p. 42—Whiting to Williams.

Univ. Magazine[132]
Smith's *Journal*[133]
Sullivan's *Maine*[134]
Williams' life[135]
Belknap[136]
Peter Williamson[137]
Withers[138] (for Braddock, etc.)
Uni[versal?] Museum
Haz[ard] *Pa. Reg.*[139]
Gordon[140]. Entick[141]
Burk[e].[142] Churchman[143]
Heckewelder's *Narrative*[144]
Wright's *Hist.*[145]
Price[146]
Withers.[147] Humphreys[148]
Gibson's *Journal of Siege of Louisburg*[149]
Smith's N[ew] J[ersey][150]

Apx. [Appendix] of Dogsby's *An. Reg.*
Marston
Niles' Reg.[151]
Hewat[t].[152] Reissel.
Trumbull[153]
Wynne
Indian Miscellany
For Devil's Hole Massacre see *Ind. Miscel.—Bk. of Inds.*[154]*—An. Reg.—*
Maude's *Visit to Niagara.*[155] Mante.[156]

Lettre d'un François à un Hollandois au sujet des Differends entre la France, etc., 1755.
Lettre d'un Anglois contenant un rélation authentique of F. and E. negotiations at opening of the War, 1756.
Raisons que prouvent qu'il est impossible que les deux nations Angloise et Françoise puissent vivre en paix, 1670
De Lisle's "Carte de Nouvelles Découvertes."
Rélation de la Louisiane[157]
Bradbury's (*Travels?*)[158]
An Essay on the Government of the Colonies (said to be partial).
Coxe's *Carolina*[159]
Keith's *Virginia*[160] (1738).
Virginia and Carolio (1471 Liby.), containing a satirical poem on southern manners, etc. A very curious old collection, 1610.
Journal in N. Y., 1701
Louisiana. Père Vivier's letter, *Lettres Edifiantes,* v. 28.

Mémoir[e]s sur le Acadie

Loudon, etc. See Franklin's life by Sparks. Braddock, etc.—d[itt]o———.
Oct. 14[th], 1755. Rogers' scout, State House "Letters," 1755-'56, No. 25.
Letters of the '56 Campaigns in abundance.
Oct. 3[rd], 56. E[nglish] Fugitives from Canada arrive at No. 4, with news of Oswego. See 1755-'56, No. 483.
July 11[th], '56. Descent on Ft. Hoosuck. No. 375.

Ohio Defeat, Boston, '55.
A Reminiscence of Oswego.
New American Mag., 1759-60, by Sylvanus Americanus. Pa. Liby.
Mémoire[s] sur le Canada.[161] 3 vols. on the War

Martel's *Mémoire dans l'Affaire du Canada*, 1763.

Shirley's Statement, Mante (?)

Cape Breton—1760[162]—a large volume.

Porcupine's Works.[163] A MS. Journal of a soldier in '55 Battle.

Mr. Officer—Winwatts
Judge Reed   } Carlisle
Hepburn

M. W. F. [Monday, Wednesday, Friday]—Greenleaf

Tues. T. S. [Thursday, Saturday]—Story. 10–11 o'clock.

Story on Bailments, Tuesday from 10–11.

Blackstone on Wednesday, 11–12, 2nd and 3rd Sections especially.

Historic Authorities to be Consulted

Winslow's *Journal*,[164] Mass. Hist. Library

Philadelphia *Gazette*.

Cole's charges against Lyman.

Letters of Officers in the state house, by means of Dr. Palfrey[165]

A Letter to the People of England on the present Situation and Conduct of National Affairs. It contains charges against the ministry.

Bradford's *Am. Avt.* [*Advertizer*]

"The Indians of the different States, and a collection of anecdotes, etc., illustrating Indian manners." The whole a mere compilation. Barber, p. 69.[166]

Loskeil's *Hist. of Missions*[167]—an acc[ount] of I's [Indians].

Dieskau—Hoyt's *I[ndian] wars*

Smith's *Discourses on Public Occasions in America*. Frontiers of Pa., etc. '54–'63

The Iroquois—attempts to convert them. Humphrey's *Accnt. of Soc[iety] for Propagtn. of Gospel in Fgn. Parts*.[168]

Barton's *New Views*, a comparison of Indian Tribes.

Contest in America,[169] an acct. of the relative situation of the two colonies—causes of the war—and the most expedient measures to be taken, 1757.

True and Impartial State of the Province of Pensylvania—Its Govr., pro-prietaries, Assemblies, etc., etc., 1759.

Smith's *Hist. of N. Y.*[170] contains a sketch of Oswego, and descriptions of fur-trade—social character, &c., 1757.

Cooper's Sermon before the General Court on the Reduction of Quebec.[171]

Loskeil contains an acct. of Christian Inds. on the frontier in '50-64.

"English Discoveries in the Ohio Valley, '44-'74."[172] *N[orth] A[merican] Review*, vol. 49, p. 69.
General Sketch of Canada Gov. etc.[173] *N. A. Rev.*, [vol.] 46, p. 409.
American Magasine, '57-'58[174]
Contest in America by Mitchel[l].

Drake's *Chronological collection* mentions facts with the authorities, 1757. Price.[175] *Martin's Magazine*, '55, '56, etc.
Wright[176] contains Abercrombie's official letters.
There is a journal of Bradstreet's expedition against Frontenac by one of the volunteers.[177]
Col. Grant's expedition. Trumbull's *Connect[icut]*.[178] Burk's *Va.*—Cuming's *Tour*—Palmer's *Travs.*—Gordon's *Pa.*—Wynne—Knox—Holmes—*Life Arthur Lee*—Withers—Hazard's *Pa. Reg.*, VIII, 141—Mant[e].[179]

Montcalm's Jesuit paper is in the last edition of the *Lettres Edifiantes*.[180]

Cherokee War. Simms' *Life of Marion*[181]

Heriot's *Canada*[182] (description).
Athenaeum[183]

Elder
Miner[184]
Lee—Baker
Stephens [Stevens] and brother
Newton   *trio—famous*
Lee the Doctor   *laid* down

Baker's name ⎤
P. O.   ⎬ Cambridge
Room   ⎦

W. S. Pearce—Corner of Court St. and Tremont Row.

Indian regard for flags of truce.
1688, 1st F[rench] War: 74 years of war; 34 of active hostilities.
'88 K[ing] William's
Queen Ann[e]'s War
Spanish [Succession]
Old French

G. W. Baker   Postage [?]
                                Toll   [?]
                                Books   3½

Militia systems except *in Pa.* ¼ of colonists trained to arms. Their intelligence.

1690—Phipps' Expedition against Penobscot, etc., Quebec. Both Colonies left alone. Ryswick.

Phipps and Fletcher try to obtain command of the militia. Assemblies decided to have full power over the militia. *Volunteers* out of states. Requisitions to Govrs., for assemblies raised by offs. and given to E. officer in chief. 1 year

---

1710. Q. Ann[e]'s War—felt at the South. *Utrecht, 1713*—Nova Scotia gained.

Sp[anish Succession] War—Aix-la-Chapelle.

O[ld] F[rench] War. 1st American Dispute. There were causes in Europe.

English Monopolies—Companies—Colony Companies
Va. tobacco—King James—to be landed in England.

Restrictions long limited to Va.—prohibitions of foreign trade. Foundation of N[avigation] Act. Carrying trade by Englishmen; imports and exports to be sent but to E[ngland]. European commodities to be landed in E.

Timber, N. E. fish, etc., bounty.

Selfish policy of England.

Internal trade and trade to the W. I[ndies] islands—restrictions. Customs houses established by British law.

Resistance of Mass. Assembly and others to N[avigation] Act. They had not been consulted, nor were they represented.

Attempts to crush Colonial Manufactures

Smith's *Wealth of Nations*—Colonies

Whitman,   Sanderson
    Palmer   between 4th

Prov. Recs.

Stephens ⎫
              ⎬ Tremont Row.
Stevens ⎭

Notes

I. 1841 JOURNAL

¹ James Monroe Tower (1823-?) of New York was attached to Parkman's class of 1844 at Harvard during their sophomore year.

² Dr. Daniel Denison Slade (1823-96) of Boston was a classmate and lifelong friend of Parkman, and a favorite companion on tramping and hunting excursions during their college years. Slade was known to his fellows as "The Chieftain," while Parkman's college nickname was "The Loquacious." Slade studied medicine and became professor of applied zoology at Harvard in 1871. He was a pallbearer at Parkman's funeral.

³ Parkman and Slade traveled sixty-eight miles on the Boston & Maine to Dover.

⁴ Alton, New Hampshire, is twenty-eight miles from Dover.

⁵ Washington Irving (1783-1859), author of *The Alhambra* and at this period the dean of American letters, was a favorite with Parkman, both in youth and later life, because of Parkman's historical interests. Irving's *Tour of the Prairies* (1835), *Astoria* (1836), and *Captain Bonneville* (1837) may well have inspired Parkman's Oregon Trail trip of 1846.

⁶ Red Hill towers some two thousand feet above the head of Lake Winnipesaukee. S. A. Drake, in his *History of the White Mountains* (New York, 1881), comments: "This eminence would be called a mountain anywhere else. Its altitude is inconsiderable, but its situation at the head of the lake, on its very borders, is highly favorable to a commanding prospect. . . ." (pp. 14-15)

⁷ Parkman seemingly visited Lake Winnipesaukee and the White Mountains in 1838 with his father, but there is no known account of this journey.

⁸ There are innumerable variants of this romantic tale. See B. G. Willey, *Incidents in White Mountain History* (Boston, 1856) 54, 271-76.

⁹ Abel Crawford (1765-1851), who married the daughter of Captain Rosebrook and was the father of Tom and Ethan Allen Crawford, long kept a tavern, the Mt. Crawford House, at the southern end of the Notch

of the White Mountains. Later the Notch was named after his family, who did so much to make the region accessible to visitors.

Abel Crawford was the first guide to the White Mountains. At seventy-five, he rode the first horse to reach the summit of Mt. Washington, over the trail cut by his sons. He represented the district in the state legislature during the last five or six years of his life.

[10] From 1829 to 1852, Thomas J. Crawford kept the Notch House, which had been built in 1828 by his father Abel and his brother Ethan at the northern entrance of the Notch. It was long the center for excursions on the western side of the White Mountains and is not far from the present Crawford House. In 1840, Tom Crawford improved the footpath to Mt. Washington, which had been cut by Abel and Ethan in 1819, into a bridle path. This is now the foot trail known as the Crawford Path.

[11] The Willey House, for some time the only stopping place for travelers between Abel Crawford's and Captain Rosebrook's at Fabyan's, a distance of thirteen miles, was built by Leavitt Hill in 1792 and occupied by his brother Henry for some years after the opening of the turnpike through the Notch in 1803, being kept for part of the time as a tavern.

Later abandoned, it was occupied by Samuel Willey, Jr. (1788-1826) in October 1825. On the night of August 28, 1826, Willey, his wife, five children, and two hired men met death from tremendous landslides, which left untouched the house from which they had fled at the moment of danger. Hawthorne's story "The Ambitious Guest" is based upon this Willey Disaster, one of the most famous New England tragedies. A brother of the victim, the Reverend Benjamin G. Willey, gives a very detailed version of the story in his *Incidents in White Mountain History*, pp. 110-40.

[12] Professor Benjamin Silliman (1779-1864), Yale geologist and chemist, made the geological survey of Connecticut, the first of its kind in the United States. After taking law and medical degrees at home and traveling abroad, he published *A Tour to Quebec in the Autumn of 1819* (New Haven, 1820). Two years earlier he had founded the *American Journal of Sciences and Arts*, better known as *Silliman's Journal*, in whose number for April 1829 (No. 15, 217-22), he gives an account of his visit to Crawford Notch in May of the preceding year. But Parkman may have been thinking of Dr. Oliver Hubbard's ascent of the Willey Gorge in 1837, described in the same journal (Vol. 34, I, 105-24), where this Dartmouth professor says his "ascent was impeded by a perpendicular front six feet high."

[13] The first bridle path on the mountains was made by Ethan Crawford in 1821. A path from the Notch House to the summit of Mt. Washington

was opened by Tom Crawford in 1840. Another bridle path, following nearly the same course as the cog railroad, was opened by Horace Fabyan after 1840. The bridle paths were abandoned after the opening of the Carriage Road, on the eastern side of the mountains, in 1861.

14 Miss Pamela Prentiss (1821-?) of Keene, to whom Parkman paid his attentions two years later during a winter vacation spent in Keene, visiting his classmates George Silsbee Hale and Horatio J. Perry, is probably the original of the intrepid heroine of his novel *Vassall Morton*.

15 Probably Mt. Willard, which stands nearly 2,800 feet high in the jaws of Crawford Notch, which it commands.

16 George Blankern Cary (1824-46), Parkman's brilliant and frivolous classmate and clubmate at Harvard, died of pneumonia caught after a Boston ball while still in law school.

Henry Tuke Parker (1824-90), a classmate of Parkman both in college and law school, lived in London for many years, where he was a corresponding member of the Massachusetts Historical Society and London agent of the Boston Public Library. He distributed the American Relief Fund to the French after the Franco-Prussian War.

Edward Wheelwright (1824-1900), Parkman's college and law school friend, pallbearer, and first biographer, was an artist, man of letters, and antiquarian. He was art critic for the *Atlantic Monthly* from 1876 to 1879, and as class secretary he prepared biographical accounts of members of the Harvard class of 1844. His "Memoir of Francis Parkman," *Publications of Colonial Society of Massachusetts*, I, 304-5 (1894), is the best of the early biographic accounts.

17 The Basin, a mile from the Franconia Flume, is now regarded as quite as much of a spectacle as the Flume itself.

18 Fifield's tavern was called the Notch House.

19 John Prentiss (1778-1873) of Keene, the founder of the *New Hampshire Sentinel*, state senator, and a successful publisher of school texts, was the father of the girl who attracted Parkman's attention at Crawford Notch by her fortitude.

20 James Annance of St. Francis, Quebec, attended Dartmouth 1831-34, but did not graduate. He is quoted as having said of Dartmouth that it "spoiled a great many good Indians and made very poor white men." He became the best-known hunter and guide in northern New Hampshire and Vermont. An Indian called "Old Louis" Annance, a Congregationalist, was well known about Moosehead Lake, where he came in the early 1850's. He supposedly met Thoreau in 1857 at Northeast Carry. Whether or not James and "Old Louis" were the same man is a question. The St.

Francis Indians may have adopted the French-Canadian custom of bestowing double- or triple-barreled Christian names, on which there were many variations in English.

[21] Dr. Charles T. Jackson (1805-80), geologist and chemist, studied medicine in Paris and Vienna after graduating from the Harvard Medical School in 1829. He patented in 1835 a telegraphic apparatus similar to Morse's, and in the following year decided to devote himself to chemistry and mineralogy. In 1837 he surveyed the public lands of Maine and Massachusetts, and became the Maine state geologist, publishing reports 1837-39. In 1838 he made a similar survey of Rhode Island, and from 1840 to 1847 he conducted the New Hampshire state survey. In 1846 he patented his discovery of guncotton; and in the same year he discovered anesthesia and suggested its properties and applications to his pupil Dr. W. T. H. Morton. His claim to the latter discovery was recognized by the French Academy and Jackson was awarded a prize for observations and experiments, while Morton was given a similar award for introducing ether into medical practice in 1848.

[22] Moses B. Williams, a former pupil of Dr. Jackson, was his field assistant during the second year of the New Hampshire survey. Williams had spent the summer of 1840 measuring sectional profiles across the state and the following winter in laboratory research. Jackson pays tribute to Williams' volunteer service in his introductions to the 1841 and 1844 *Reports*.

[23] Baltimore was a publishing center in the 1830's and 40's, with Edgar Allan Poe as one of its notable editors.

[24] Captain James F. Bragg was the leading man of the tiny first settlement of Errol, New Hampshire, which was brought into existence by lumbering operations. The first town meeting was held in his house in 1831, and he long served as selectman. The town numbered only thirty-eight inhabitants in 1871, half a century after its settlement.

[25] No Bennet is mentioned in such fragmentary accounts of the early days of Errol as exist, but a Bennett Brook is shown on the topographical map, below Wilson Mills.

[26] Joshua Lombard is not referred to in the early accounts of Errol. Parkman corrected the spelling of the name in the 1842 Journal.

[27] Captain Wilson, like Captain Bragg, gave his name to the place where he settled, now known as Wilson Mills, Maine.

[28] Jerome, the nephew of James Annance, evidently lacked both the intelligence and the education of his uncle, although he appears to have been a pupil of Peter Masta, who walked three hundred miles from his

home on the St. Lawrence in order to attend Dartmouth, and upon his return taught at the St. Francis reservation.

[29] Mettallic, or Mettallak, was the son of a chief whose tribe dwelt on the upper Androscoggin. Some sickness gradually killed off the tribe, until only Metallak and his wife and children remained. His daughter married a St. Francis Indian, and his beloved wife died some time later. Mettallak put her body in his canoe and buried her on a small island in Lake Umbagog, where he mourned for three days and nights. After that, he lived alone, the last survivor of his people, fishing and hunting and acting as guide to the region. He had lost one eye in early life, and the other was put out one day when he fell against the stub of a tree. In 1846 he was found wandering blind through the forest by two hunters, who led him to Stewartstown, New Hampshire, where he spent his few remaining years as a public charge.

[30] By way of the fifteen miles of the Nashua & Lowell and the twenty-six miles of the Boston & Lowell. In the early days of rail transportation, New England was covered with a network of small roads, usually originating locally and constructed on strongly individualistic lines, with a fine disregard for their eventual place in a larger scheme.

II. 1842 JOURNAL

[1] The Boston & Albany was only completed in 1839, so the journey between the two cities by train was still regarded as a novel experience.

[2] Henry Orne White (1824-87) was a member of the class of 1843 at Harvard. His lack of interest in historical matters made him an unsatisfactory companion for Parkman, as the latter indicated in a letter of September 30, 1892 to Abbé Raymond Casgrain about this trip: "White did not sympathize with my ideas, and was sometimes rather disgusted at my persistency in searching after localities for which he did not care a pin." White's lack of endurance and his proneness to discouragement when things were going badly were still more serious liabilities on the wilderness part of this expedition.

[3] Fort Edward is near Glens Falls, New York, on the upper Hudson. A stockade fort was first built on this site—long known as the Great Carrying Place because it was the chief portage on the Hudson–Lake George–Lake Champlain–Richelieu water route—by Colonel Francis Nicholson

in 1790 and was named after him. Another fort, first known as Lydius after a Dutch settler and later as Fort Edward after the Duke of York, was built here by General Phineas Lyman of Connecticut in 1755, and was sometimes called Lyman's Fort. Its occupation by General Webb halted Montcalm after the French capture of William Henry in 1757. Fort Edward was also the goal of Marin's French and Indian raid earlier in the same summer. See *Half-Century*, I, 140; and *Montcalm and Wolfe*, II, 173, 205-7.

[4] Parkman first visited London two years later, but he was familiar with Dickens' accounts of it.

[5] Union College, which grew out of the Schenectady Academy (1784), was chartered in 1795.

[6] Saratoga Springs was a favorite summer camping ground of the Iroquois, particularly the Mohawks, who were attracted to the place by the medicinal springs long before white men visited the region. The district was the scene of several conflicts between the French and English and their Indian allies. In 1693 a French expedition was defeated by Governor Benjamin Fletcher and Peter Schuyler. In 1745 the settlers were massacred by French and Indian raiders. The battle of Saratoga during the Revolution was fought about five miles southeast of the present village. The first lodging house for visitors to the springs, a log cabin, was built in 1771, and by 1830 the place had become one of the most popular American resorts.

[7] In Fenimore Cooper's *The Last of the Mohicans* (Ch. 6-9) Hawkeye, Uncas, and Chingachgook hide Cora, Alice, Duncan Heywood, and David in these caverns while fleeing from the Mingoes. Cooper was Parkman's favorite novelist.

[8] The skirmish of Rocky Brook, which is referred to in the text, took place on the morning of September 6, 1755, when the French and Indians under Baron Dieskau and Le Gardeur de St. Pierre ambushed a portion of Sir William Johnson's forces, under the command of Colonel Ephraim Williams and Lieutenant Colonel Whiting. After the initial French success in this skirmish, they were defeated at Lake George by Johnson, and Dieskau was wounded and taken prisoner.

[9] Colonel Ephraim Williams (1714/5-55), who came to Stockbridge, Massachusetts, with his family in 1737 from the Connecticut Valley, commanded the line of frontier outposts known as the Massachusetts Forts, which ran from Fort Dummer in Vermont to Fort Massachusetts near Williamstown, where he usually resided. In 1755 he commanded the 3rd Massachusetts in Johnson's army, and headed the detachment

sent out from the main camp at Lake George to intercept Dieskau's lines of communication with South Bay. Early in the engagement at Rocky Brook he was shot through the head, when he mounted a rock to reconnoiter. He was buried near the spot where he fell, at the foot of a huge pine beside the military road linking the lake and Fort Edward. His grave was later marked with a boulder inscribed E.W. 1755. He made provision in his will for a free school at Williamstown, which in 1793 became the college called after him. There is a tablet to his memory in the Williams Chapel. See *Montcalm and Wolfe*, I, 301-4, 309-15.

[10] Sir William Johnson (1715-74), who was born in Ireland, came to America in 1738 to take charge of the New York estates of his uncle, Admiral Sir Peter Warren. He was appointed Indian agent in 1744 and obtained remarkable influence over the Iroquois. In 1755 he became Superintendent of Indian Affairs, and was also made major general in command of the expedition against Fort Frédéric (Crown Point). Braddock's ill-fated march against Fort Duquesne and Shirley's expedition against Fort Niagara were part of the three fold plan of this campaign. Johnson intended to build a fort at the head of Lake George, proceed up the lake and capture Carillon (Ticonderoga), and there await the rest of his army before attacking Fort Frédéric. But news of Dieskau's flanking attack by South Bay on Fort Edward forced him to give battle at Lake George on September 5. For his victory he received the thanks of Parliament, a baronetcy, and £5,000. He has been criticized for not following up his success and moving against Carillon and Fort Frédéric as originally planned, but it was late in the season and his army had been rudely handled before it won its triumph. See *Montcalm and Wolfe*, I, 296-329.

[11] Captain William McGinnis (?-1755) of Schenectady commanded the detachment from Fort Edward which encountered French stragglers at Bloody Pond, after the battle at the lake. During this final action of September 5, 1755, McGinnis was hit in the head by a ricocheting ball, but continued in command until the end of the fray. He died two days later. See *Montcalm and Wolfe*, I, 319-20.

[12] Bloody Pond, two and a half or three miles south of Johnson's camp at Lake George, was the place where two hundred men from Fort Edward under Captains Folsom and McGinnis fell upon the French and Indian stragglers and drove them to their boats at South Bay, after capturing their baggage and ammunition. The name of the pond commemorates the unceremonious burial in its waters of the victims of the fray.

[13] The first fortification at the head of Lake George, consisting of embankments of gravel surmounted by logs, was built by Sir William

Johnson in 1755 and named by him after the commander in chief, the Duke of Cumberland, younger son of George II, the victor of Culloden and the loser of Fontenoy. The site was an unfortunate choice, being swampy and easily commanded from the surrounding hills. The fort was captured by Montcalm on August 9, 1757, and most of its garrison were massacred by his Indians, who refused to abide by the terms of capitulation. The French burned the fort, which had been greatly strengthened since 1755, and stripped it of munitions and supplies.

[14] The Marquis de Montcalm (1712-59), who came to America as commander in chief in 1756, sent Rigaud de Vaudreuil to reconnoiter William Henry in March 1757, and then himself besieged it in form in the following August with 8,000 men. Landing at Artillery Cove on August 3, he opened trenches and parallels, and bombarded the fort, which surrendered six days later. His lines ran from Artillery Cove to within a few hundred yards of the fort, around the southwest corner of the lake. See the plan, "Siege of Fort William Henry, 1757," in *Montcalm and Wolfe*, II, 183.

[15] Fort George, a short distance southeast of William Henry, was surveyed by General James Abercromby and his engineer Montresor in 1758, but was not built until the following year under Amherst. It was solidly constructed of masonry on the hill which had formed part of Johnson's camp in 1755 and of a division of Munro's forces in 1757. The capture in 1759 of Carillon and Fort Frédéric on Lake Champlain eliminated its usefulness, and only one bastion was completed.

[16] William Caldwell was the son of General James Caldwell, an Albany merchant, who acquired 1,595 acres of upstate New York land in 1787.

[17] The legend of treasure buried at William Henry, probably at the time of its surrender to Montcalm in 1757, is referred to in Hoyt's *Antiquarian Researches*, which is quoted in Van Rensselaer, *Battle of Lake George*, 69.

[18] This was probably one of the trenches of Montcalm's siege works. See *Montcalm and Wolfe*, II, 192 & n.

[19] General James Abercromby (1706-81), called "Nambycromby" by the provincials for his excessive caution which bordered on poltroonry, came to America in 1756 and superseded Shirley and Webb in command of the army, being supplanted in turn by the Earl of Loudoun. In 1757 he commanded the second brigade in the Louisbourg Expedition, and in 1758 he became commander in chief on Loudoun's recall. He led the unsuccessful expedition of that year against Carillon (Ticonderoga), with Lord George Howe as his second-in-command. After the latter's death at

Trout Brook the campaign became a dismal failure, with Montcalm hopelessly outwitting Abercromby. After his disastrous attack on Carillon, Abercromby retreated to the head of Lake George, and burned his boats in the general panic.

[20] These batteries may have been part of Montcalm's siege works.

[21] In Cooper's *The Last of the Mohicans*, Chapter XX, Hawkeye, Uncas, and Chingachcook are pursued by the French Indians while conveying Colonel Munro and Duncan Heyward up the lake.

[22] Ethan Allen (1737/8-89), Revolutionary soldier and author, was born in Litchfield, Connecticut. He served at William Henry in 1757, and in 1769 became a resident in the New Hampshire Grants, as Vermont was then called. In 1770 he organized the Green Mountain Boys, whose "colonel commandant" he became. Acting on Connecticut orders, he captured Ticonderoga on May 10, 1775. In September, while serving with the American army of invasion in Canada, he was captured in a brash attempt to take Montreal by surprise. He was a prisoner in Quebec, England, and New York for the next two years, before being exchanged. Washington gave him the brevet rank of colonel on his release. After the fall of 1778 he was immersed in Vermont politics and commanded the militia in border warfare with the New York settlers. With his brother Ira, he negotiated with Governor Haldimand of Canada to make Vermont a British province rather than an American state. Aside from controversial works on political subjects, his claim to authorship rests on *Reason, the Only Oracle of Man* (Bennington, 1784), a curious deist production. He became one of the great folk heroes of the Revolution.

[23] Parkman's enthusiasm for historic spots here led him into rhetorical excess. Sabbath Day Point was merely the scene of the ambush of Colonel Parker's scouts by the partisan Corbière and his Indians on July 26, 1757, and a stopping place of Abercromby's army on July 5, 1758 as it moved against Ticonderoga.

[24] Captain Samuel Patchin was among the first settlers on Lake George, making his home on Sabbath Day Point. The veteran was fond of his liquor, and one winter day tried to sail a sled load of grist over the ice to the mill at Bolton. Relying too much on the local name of the sleigh—a "jumper"—he came to grief on Vicar's Island over which he had tried to jump his load.

[25] French Canadians, some of whom had served with the American invaders of Canada in 1775-76, began to settle about Lake Champlain after the American Revolution under land grants from Congress. More

drifted south after the Papineau Rebellion of 1837, which centered in the Richelieu district along the outlet of the lake.

[26] "Judge" Nathaniel Garfield's tavern was on or near the site of the Phoenix Hotel at Hague. He is said to have had "an intimate acquaintance with every deer on the hill-sides and every trout in the waters." His courtesy title was due to the fact that he was town supervisor for many years.

[27] Naumkeag was the Indian name of Salem, Massachusetts, and these bills were doubtless issued by a Salem bank. In 1842, that city was just beginning to lose its commercial importance as a great shipping center.

[28] Rogers Rock, or Bald Mountain, near the foot of Lake George, was so called because of "an unsupported tradition that he escaped [from Captain Hebecourt's ambush of March 1758] by sliding on his snowshoes down a precipice of Rogers Rock." (*Montcalm and Wolfe*, II, 220 n.)

[29] Colonel John Butler (1728-96), the hated Tory from Connecticut and the Mohawk Valley, served under Sir William Johnson in the 1755 expedition against Carillon, in the Niagara campaign of 1759, and in the Montreal expedition of the following year. He was also with Abercromby at Carillon and with Bradstreet at Fort Frontenac. During the Revolution he was the commander of Butler's Rangers, who displayed great cruelty in their raids on their former neighbors of the Mohawk settlements, notably at Wyoming. His son Walter, who was even more cordially hated than his father, was responsible for the Cherry Valley massacre. After the war the elder Butler was appointed Superintendent of Indian Affairs for British North America, with headquarters on the Niagara peninsula.

[30] Joseph Brant (1742-1807), or Thayendanegea, a Mohawk chief whose sister was Sir William Johnson's mistress, commanded the British Indians under St. Leger and raided the Mohawk Valley and northern Pennsylvania with the Tories of John Butler and John Johnson during the Revolution. He was at Oriskany in 1777 and at Cherry Valley in the following year, but is believed to have had no part in the Wyoming massacre. He was rewarded for his services with a colonel's commission in the British Army.

[31] Fort Stanwix on the Mohawk guarded the portage from Wood Creek and Lake Oneida. An old blockhouse known at Fort Williams stood near this place until 1756, when it was destroyed by General Webb in his panic after Montcalm's capture of Oswego. The new fort was built by General Stanwix in 1758. It was unsuccessfully besieged by St. Leger in 1777. Its site is now occupied by the city of Rome, New York.

[32] Fort Anne, named after Queen Anne, was built by Colonel Nicholson in 1709 to protect the route from Fort Edward on the Hudson to South Bay on Lake Champlain. It was later destroyed by the French, but subsequently rebuilt. Robert Rogers fought the French and Indians under Marin near by in 1758. The fort was captured by Burgoyne in 1777 and by Major Carleton in 1780.

[33] Sir John Johnson (1742-1830), a son of Sir William Johnson, was made a major general of the New York militia in 1774, but served with the British in the Revolution. He was St. Leger's second-in-command against Arnold in 1777, the year after he fled to Canada, and twice raided his old domain of the Mohawk Valley in 1780. He became Superintendent of Indian Affairs in 1783, thus succeeding his cousin Guy Johnson and his father in that office. He lived in Montreal during the latter part of his life.

[34] A. Loring Cushing was a prominent Boston lawyer of the day.

[35] William Caldwell owned almost all the town of Lake George, then named after him. He lived near the site of the Mansion House and built as an office the stone edifice now used as the post office.

[36] "Old Dick," who was also known as the "Old Man of the Fort," came originally from Massachusetts, but spent forty-five of his seventy-six years about Lake George. He worked at odd jobs on shore and on the lake boats, but his chief interest was in rattlesnakes, then plentiful about Black Mountain and Cobble Hill. He is supposed to have been able to extract the fangs of the snakes, which he sold and exhibited on the boats. His snake box was thus inscribed: "In this box a Rattell Snaick Hoo was Kecht on Black mountaing. He is seven years old last July. Admittance sixpence site. Children half price, or notten."

[37] Parkman refers to the abatis constructed across the peninsula of Ticonderoga, along the ridge about half a mile from the fort, in 1758, at the suggestion of a French officer named Guges. This position broke Abercromby's attack.

[38] Amherst began to besiege Ticonderoga in form on June 22, 1759, but on June 23 the French commander Bourlamaque retired to Ile-aux-Noix on the Richelieu, leaving Captain Hebecourt to blow up the fort on June 26. See *Montcalm and Wolfe*, III, 79-82.

[39] Ticonderoga, known to the French as Carillon, was built by Chartier de Lotbinière in 1755-56 on a promontory overlooking the junction of the outlet between Lake George and Lake Champlain. It was the key to the Hudson–Champlain–Richelieu invasion route, and the chief French outpost against British attacks on Canada. Abercromby was badly beaten by Montcalm in his attempt against it in 1758, while in the following year

it fell with ease to Amherst, Bourlamaque having been ordered by Vaudreuil to retreat rather than risk his whole army. Ethan Allen captured the fortress by surprise in 1775, thus opening the way for the American invasion of Canada by way of Champlain and the Richelieu. It was recaptured by Burgoyne in 1777 and remained British until the close of the Revolution. Under the peace treaty it became the property of the United States. Parkman thus describes the fort, basing his account on De Lotbinière's report to the minister, October 31, 1756: "It stood on the crown of the promontory, and was a square with four bastions, a ditch, blown in some parts out of the solid rock, bomb-proofs, barracks of stone, and a system of exterior defences as yet only begun. The rampart consisted of two parallel walls ten feet apart, built of the trunks of trees, and held together by transverse logs dovetailed at both ends, the space between being filled with earth and gravel well packed." (*Montcalm and Wolfe*, II, 64-5.) Only one bastion was destroyed by the slow match left burning in the magazine when Hebecourt retired from the fort. After years of the vandalism described in Parkman's notes, the site and its ruins were acquired by a conscientious and historically minded proprietor, who was largely responsible for the restoration of the fortress to its former impressiveness. Ticonderoga is now a public park and museum.

[40] Steam navigation on Lake Champlain was opened in 1809 by the *Vermont*, built at Burlington in the preceding year and the world's second successful steamboat. The *Burlington* (built in 1837) and the *Whitehall* (1838), of the Champlain Transportation Company, maintained a service between Whitehall, at the head of Lake Champlain, and St. John's on the Richelieu. The *Burlington* evoked one of Charles Dickens' few favorable *American Notes*, in the same year that Parkman sailed up the lake: "There is one American boat—the vessel which carried us on Lake Champlain from St. John's to Whitehall—which I praise very highly, but no more than it deserves, when I say that it is superior even to that on which we went from Queenston to Toronto or to that on which we travelled from the latter place to Kingston, or, I have no doubt, I may add, to any other in the world. This steamboat, which is called the *Burlington*, is a perfectly exquisite achievement of neatness, elegance, and order. The decks are drawing rooms; the cabins are boudoirs, choicely furnished and adorned with prints, pictures, and musical instruments; every nook and corner of the vessel is a perfect curiosity of graceful comfort and beautiful contrivance." (*American Notes*, Ch. XV.)

In 1909 the *Burlington* and *Whitehall* were still in existence at the graveyard for outworn ships at Shelburne Harbor. With the development of the railroads in the 1850's, the passenger traffic on the lake soon degenerated largely into excursions.

41 The University of Vermont at Burlington was founded in 1791. At the time Parkman visited it, the university's faculty boasted six members, of whom the most notable was the classicist and philosopher Joseph Torrey. There was a prevailing climate of theological controversy about the institution at this period, though it was nonsectarian.

42 Camel's Hump, known as Camel's Rump in the pre-Victorian era and as Lion Couchant to the French, is the third highest peak in the Green Mountains, its 4,088 feet being surpassed by Mt. Mansfield's 4,364 and Killington's 4,241. It would seem that Parkman confused Camel's Hump and Mansfield, for Mansfield lies to the left of one approaching the mountains from Burlington, with Camel's Hump to the right, south of the gap in the range formed by the Winooski Valley.

43 Tension between the United States and Great Britain had been prevalent along the Canadian border since 1837 because of boundary disputes, such as the War of Pork and Beans between Maine and New Brunswick in 1839, and the Indian Stream Republic incident in New Hampshire. The Webster-Ashburton treaty of August 9, 1842 settled these boundary questions.

44 Paul Chase of Stanstead was probably one of the Yankees who had migrated over the border from New England after the Townships were opened for settlement in 1792. The name is common in New Hampshire and Vermont.

45 William Miller (1782-1849), the Prophet of the Second Coming of Christ in 1843 or 1844, was born in Pittsfield, Massachusetts; brought up in Poultney, Vermont; served as an officer in the War of 1812; and became a Baptist preacher in Low Hampton, New York. About 1831, after fourteen years of intensive self-study of the Bible and elaborate mathematical calculations based upon the prophecies of Daniel, he began to preach that the year 1843 would usher in the millennium. His doctrine found ready acceptance in a New England fermenting with new sects and theological debate as the old Calvinistic system broke up. First farmers, then tradespeople and members of every class, were numbered among his followers, who probably never exceeded fifty thousand convinced believers. Three other Second Adventists flourished at this period: Joseph Wolff of Palestine and England, who set the date at 1847; Harriet Livermore of Massachusetts, whose views coincided with Wolff and who on four different occasions preached the approach of the Second Coming in the House of Representatives at Washington; and Lady Hester Stanhope, who installed

herself upon Mount Lebanon in Syria in order to be ready for the Advent, in anticipation of which she kept two white Arab horses ready, one for our Lord and the other for herself. The years 1842 and 1843 were marked by a feverish agitation among the Millerites, who were particularly numerous in New England, but the failure of the Advent to materialize on Miller's schedule rapidly broke up the sect.

[46] Peter Barnes came to Pittsburg, New Hampshire, from **Corinth, Vermont,** in 1822.

[47] James Abbot of Pittsburg, New Hampshire, was probably a son of the Elisha Abbot who was one of the group of Corinth settlers who came in 1822. His political views were exceptional for this region, for in the 1841 election for governor, Pittsburg tallied 51 Democrat and only 8 Free Soil Whig votes.

[48] William Henry Harrison (1773-1841) was elected to the presidency on the Whig ticket in 1840, after what is known as the "log cabin and hard cider campaign" because Harrison made the most of his frontier background. Harrison died one month after his inauguration.

[49] John Tyler (1790-1862), in his early career a Democrat of the Calhoun school, was nominated for the vice-presidency on the Whig ticket in 1839 and was elected with Harrison. Upon Harrison's death, soon after the inauguration, Tyler succeeded to the presidency. Harrison's cabinet resigned, with the exception of Daniel Webster who was then engaged in negotiations with Lord Ashburton for the settlement of the Canadian boundary dispute, when Tyler vetoed the "fiscal corporation" bill. He had the support of neither party and faced the opposition of a Congress controlled by Henry Clay. In 1844, Tyler was an irregular Democratic candidate for a second term, thus confirming Abbot's suspicion that he was not a true Whig.

[50] Parkman evidently did not regard this verbal tradition as trustworthy, for it does not figure in his account of the William Henry massacre in either *Pontiac* or *Montcalm and Wolfe.*

[51] The first settlements in the Connecticut Lakes region were made in the 1820's.

[52] The lunge is a fish usually found farther north than the Connecticut Lakes in North America.

[53] Ebenezer Oakes, the tavern keeper at Franconia, was a member of the family which operated the Franconia ironworks.

[54] Gurnsey, or Guernsey, was a pioneer settler in the Franconia region. His wife is credited with the discovery of the Flume, while out fishing.

[55] Captain Artemas Knight was one of the founders of Franconia in

1774, and the new keeper of the tavern at Lincoln may have been one of his three sons. This house was three-quarters of a mile from the Pool and one of the earliest inns, if not the first, in the Notch.

⁵⁶ The Reverend George Punchard (1806-80), who graduated from Dartmouth in 1826 and from the Andover Theological Seminary in 1829, was ordained at Plymouth in 1830 as a Congregational minister. After suffering throat trouble, he entered journalism, founding the *Daily Evening Traveller* and editing it from 1845 to 1857, and again after 1867. During the interim he was secretary of the New England branch of the American Tract Society. He was the author of the five-volume *View of Congregationalism* (1841-80).

III. 1843 NOTEBOOK

¹ Giles F. Yates of Schenectady, New York, was the son of Robert Yates (1738-1801), the Revolutionary patriot and jurist whose notes on the Federal Convention, *Secret Proceedings and Debates*, were published by his widow in 1821. A brother, John Van Ness Yates (1779-1839), edited and continued William Smith's *History of New York*. Albany, 1814. *Bib. Can.* 267.

² The Reverend John Williams (1817-99), who later became president of Trinity College, Hartford, and Episcopalian bishop of Connecticut, was rector of St. George's Church, Schenectady, from 1842 to 1848. He was the son of Ephraim Williams (1760-1835) of Old Deerfield, Massachusetts, who edited Volume I of the *Massachusetts Reports*; the grandson of Dr. Thomas Williams, Sir William Johnson's physician; and the great nephew of Colonel Ephraim Williams (1714/15-1755), the defender of the frontier in the French and Indian War. He was educated at Harvard and Trinity, and became professor of history and literature at the latter institution, so his interests were akin to those of Parkman.

³ Clermont is ten miles south of Hudson, New York.

⁴ The Palatine settlers of the Mohawk Valley were tenants of Sir William Johnson. Fonda was named after Lieutenant Jelles Fonda, a scout with Johnson at Lake George in 1755 and at Oswego in 1757.

⁵ Père Isaac Jogues, S.J., (1607-46) escaped from the Iroquois in 1642 through the aid of the Dutch of Rensselaerswyck (Albany). See his letters to Lalement dated August 30, 1643 and January 6, 1644, in Vimont's

Relation of 1642-43, Ch. XIV (Thwaites, XXV, 92-9); also Lalement's *Relation of 1647*, Ch. VII (Thwaites, XXXI, 92-9). The old Dutchman of the story Parkman heard may be Dominie Johannes Megapolensis (1603-1670), who was born a Catholic but became the Reformed Dutch minister of the place until 1649 and afterwards pastor of what was later known as the Collegiate Reformed Church of New York (Thwaites, XXV, 288 note 4). Père Jogues was sent home to France after reaching New Amsterdam (New York) in 1643; but returned to Canada in the following year, and in June 1646 came to Fort Orange (Albany) as ambassador to the Iroquois.

Schenectady was burned by the French and Indians under Le Moyne de Ste. Hélène and D'Ailleboust de Mantet on the night of February 8, 1690. No Jesuit accompanied the expedition. The house of John Sander Glen (known as "Captain Sander," a name rendered by the French as "Cendre," "Condre," and "Coudre") was alone spared because of his kindness to French prisoners (E. B. O'Callaghan, *Doc. Hist. of N. Y.*, I, 285-312; Parkman, *Frontenac*, 225-27).

It is probable that Parkman's informant confused the two local legends and linked them together to make a better story.

[6] Joseph Brant, or Thayendanegea (1742-1807) was a Mohawk chief and one of the most notable figures of his race. His sister Molly's relationship with Sir William Johnson helped him to rise to the leadership of his people. At the age of thirteen he fought under Sir William at Lake George in 1755; and later was sent through Johnson's interest to Moor's School, Lebanon, Connecticut, where Eleazar Wheelock began his educational work with the Indians. Brant fought with the whites against Pontiac in 1763; and served as secretary to Guy Johnson, who succeeded his uncle as Superintendent of Indian Affairs in 1774. During the Revolution Brant won the Iroquois to the British interest, and for his efforts was rewarded with a colonel's commission in the British Army. He went to London in 1775 and was presented at Court, entertained by Boswell, and painted by Romney. He commanded the Indians under St. Leger, and with the Tories of Butler and Johnson harried the Mohawk Valley, southern New York, and northern Pennsylvania. He was at Oriskany in 1777 and Cherry Valley in 1778, but is believed to have had no part in the Wyoming massacre of the following year. He frustrated Red Jacket's attempt to win a separate peace for the Mohawks from the Colonies, and got Canadian land grants for them from Sir Frederick Haldimand. On a second visit to England in 1785-86, he secured indemnities from the British govern-

ment for the losses suffered by the Mohawks during the Revolution. He died in Ontario, where he made his home after the Revolution.

7 The place where the Mohawks burned their prisoners at the stake. Prisoners were always brought home for this purpose by the Iroquois after a war party.

8 Fort George was constructed as a permanent fortification in masonry by Amherst in 1759; but its site had been occupied by part of Johnson's armed camp in 1755, by part of Munro's forces in 1757, and by Abercromby in the following year. The lines were traced by Abercromby and his engineer Montresor in June 1759, and the works were completed within a month; but the fall of Ticonderoga eliminated the fort's usefulness. During the Revolution it was held by the Americans, except for brief occupations by Burgoyne in 1777 and Carleton in 1780.

9 The Soeurs Grises, or Gray Nuns (Soeurs de la Charité de l'Hôpital-Général), are an order founded at Montreal in 1737 by Madame d'Youville. They devote themselves to the care of the old and infirm and of abandoned children, to hospital work and the visiting of the sick and poor, and to conducting orphanages, insane asylums, and institutions for the blind. The order has run the General Hospital at Montreal since 1747.

10 Parkman visited the third Cathedral of Montreal, built in 1825 by Bishop Lartigue at the corner of St. Catherine and St. Denis streets. This church was completely destroyed by fire in 1852, when a conflagration laid waste most of the city.

11 The 71st Highland Light Infantry was one of the famous regiments of the British Army, having served with distinction in the Peninsula campaigns and at Waterloo. In 1843 the service battalion had its depot in Montreal, while the reserve battalion was in garrison at Chambly. Lieutenant Augustus Terrick Hamilton, an officer of this regiment, did a fine series of drawings of Montreal and Chambly.

12 The 89th Regiment of Foot had served at Niagara in the War of 1812. Lieutenant George F. Ruxton, author of *Life in the Far West*, served in this regiment.

13 The 43rd Monmouthshire Light Infantry had a distinguished record in the Peninsula campaigns during the Napoleonic Wars.

14 The fort at St. John's, on the Richelieu River, after having been burned by the French in 1759, was rebuilt by the English ten years later. Under the gallant Major Preston, it finally surrendered to Montgomery's American army of invasion in 1775, after a siege of forty-five days. Between 1778 and 1784, £24,000 were spent on restoring the fortifications, but by 1804 they were again ruinous.

[15] This fort at Ile-aux-Noix on the Richelieu was constructed at the time of the War of 1812, but it saw little service and never underwent a baptism of fire.

[16] The Hope Gate, named after Sir Henry Hope (?-1789), lieutenant governor of Quebec from 1785 until his death, was built in 1786, ten years after Montgomery's assault. It was altered during the reconstruction of the fortifications in 1823-32, strengthened in 1840, and demolished in 1874.

[17] Richard Montgomery (1736-75), an Irishman who long served in the British Army—he was with Wolfe at Louisburg in 1758 and at Ticonderoga and Crown Point under Amherst in the following year—settled in New York, married the daughter of Robert Livingston, and was named one of the colony's eight brigadier generals under Major General Philip Schuyler. In 1775, while Arnold led 1,000 men against Quebec by way of the Kennebec and the Chaudière, Montgomery, under Schuyler, headed another army of 1,300 which advanced by the Hudson–Champlain–Richelieu route against Montreal. Schuyler fell sick and Montgomery was given the chief command. After taking the forts at Ile-aux-Noix, Chambly, and St. John's, whose capture resulted in the capitulation of Montreal, Montgomery joined forces with Arnold at Pointe-aux-Trembles on the St. Lawrence, above Quebec. After a siege of twenty-five days, a double assault was planned for the night of December 30, with Arnold leading one party by the Saut-au-Matelot and Montgomery another by Près-de-Ville, at the foot of Cape Diamond. The plan called for a juncture of the two parties after they had won the Lower Town, and a subsequent joint attack on the Upper Town by the Côte-de-la-Montagne. But Montgomery was killed at the head of his force while attempting to surprise the battery which commanded the passage under the Cape. By his friend Guy Carleton's orders, Montgomery was buried with military honors under one of the bastions of Fort St. Louis, not far from the present St. Louis Gate. His remains were removed to St. Paul's churchyard, New York City, in 1818, but memorial plaques mark both his death place and his temporary grave in Quebec.

[18] The Wolfe and Montcalm Monument stands in the Governor's Garden, adjoining the Chateau Frontenac and facing Dufferin Terrace. Lord Dalhousie laid the cornerstone on November 15, 1827, and the monument was completed on September 8, 1828, the day of his departure from Canada. A competition was held for the best inscription, and the prize medal was won by J. Charlton Fisher, LL.D., with the admirably concise text noted by Parkman.

[19] Wolfe's Monument stands near the Provincial Museum, in the center of a *rond-point*, in Battlefields Park. It is a plain round column, surmounted by a sword and helmet. A plate attached to the base reads:

Here Died
WOLFE
Victorious
Sept. 13
1759

Until Lord Aylmer raised a monument here at his own expense in 1832, neither the scene of Wolfe's victory nor that of his death was commemorated fittingly, though a simple memorial was built by the army in 1759 on this site. Aylmer's monument was replaced in 1849 by the officers of the garrison. The crown piece and inscription of the 1849 monument are preserved in the present one, which was set up in 1913 by the National Battlefields Commission.

[20] Frances (Moore) Brooke (1724-89), *The History of Emily Montague* (London, 1769. *Bib. Can.* 425.) This romantic novel, in the style of Richardson, is dedicated to Guy Carleton. The first Canadian novel, it depicts the scenery and social life of Quebec. The author, whose husband was garrison chaplain from 1760 to 1768, spent five years in Quebec, and had a good eye for scenery and character. She was also no stranger to psychology.

[21] The reference is probably to Charles Butler's *The Book of the Roman Catholic Church* (London, 1825), a reply to Robert Southey's anti-Catholic *Book of the Church.*

[22] See note 9, 1841 Journal, p. 330.

[23] Ethan Allen Crawford (1792-1846), known as "The Giant of the Hills" for his great height and strength, cut the first paths up the mountains in 1819 and 1821. He was nearly seven feet tall, and the tales of his feats are reminiscent of Paul Bunyan. He frequently carried weary excursionists home on his back from the mountains, and is supposed to have mastered a bear with no weapon but his bare hands. Guildhall was his birthplace and the former home of his maternal grandfather, Captain Eleazar Rosebrook.

[24] Dennison conducted a tavern at the Rosebrook house, near Fabyan's.

[25] See note 10, 1841 Journal, p. 331.

[26] The Aroostuck expedition arose out of a boundary dispute, sometimes known as the War of Pork and Beans. In 1838-39 the boundary between

Maine and New Brunswick was in question. Maine erected forts along the line she claimed; Congress authorized the President to resist any attempt of Great Britain to enforce exclusive jurisdiction over the disputed territory; and open conflict seemed imminent. Fortunately the level-headed General Winfield Scott was given command on the frontier, and on March 21, 1839, he arranged a truce and joint occupancy of the region until a satisfactory settlement should be reached. A compromise, allowing each party less than it had claimed, was attained in the Webster-Ashburton Treaty of 1842.

[27] The theologically-minded Russell came from Bethlehem (founded in 1790 as Lord's Hill).

[28] Daniel Pierce Thompson (1795-1868), *The Green Mountain Boys: a Historical Tale of the Early Settlement of Vermont* (Montpelier, 1839).

[29] Knapp had taken over the Notch House at Franconia, which Parkman had found deserted in 1842 and which had been kept by Fifield in 1841.

[30] Center Harbor, on Lake Winnipesaukee, was one of the chief gateways to the White Mountains, since roads led thence to both Crawford and Franconia notches. It was a favorite resort of the Abenakis, who feared the mountains and usually camped to the south of them. Ossipee and Fryeburg are rich in Indian burial mounds, in which some relics have been found.

[31] Charles Fenno Hoffman (1806-84), editor, poet, and novelist, began his journalistic career by writing for the New York *American*, which he later edited with Charles King. He was editor of the *Knickerbocker Magazine* (to which Parkman later contributed) for a few months in 1833; then left on a tour of the Northwest by horseback. His travel letters, first published in the *American*, were collected in the two volumes of *A Winter in the West* (1835). His "Scenes and Sources of the Hudson" were collected in *Wild Scenes in Forest and Prairie* (London, 1839; New York, 1843). He also wrote an undistinguished novel, *Greyslaer, a Romance of the Mohawk* (1839). At this period, his interests were close to those of Parkman.

[32] George Barstow (1812-83), *The History of New Hampshire from Its Discovery* (Concord, 1842).

[33] William Dunlap (1766-1839), *History of the New Netherlands, Province of New York, & State of New York to the Adoption of the Federal Constitution* (New York, 1839-40). Dunlap's best-known works are his history of the New York stage and his diary.

[34] John Milton Whiton, *Sketches of the History of New Hampshire* (Concord, 1834).

[35] Paugus, war chief of the Pequawkets, a tribe of the Abenakis, organized the famous ambush of Captain John Lovewell's party. Paugus was killed in the fight at Lovewell's Pond on May 8, 1725, by either Ensign Seth Wyman of Woburn or John Chamberlain, the honor being disputed. Cf. *Half-Century*, I, 256-71.

[36] There were several guidebooks entitled the *Northern Traveller* in circulation at this period. Theodore Dwight (1796-1866) published one in 1825 which was reprinted four times by 1841. *The Northern Traveller and Northern Tour; with the Routes to the Springs, Niagara & Quebec, and the Coal Mines of Pennsylvania; also the Tour of New England* was published at New York in 1831.

[37] Probably Thomas Starr King (1824-64), Unitarian clergyman, lecturer, and writer, who was a great lover of the White Mountains, which he celebrated in 1860 in his classic *The White Hills*. In 1843 he had just finished three years as a schoolteacher in Charlestown and Medford (the home of Parkman's maternal relatives), and had taken a job as bookkeeper in the Charlestown Navy Yard, which gave him more time for his studies. Three years later he became a minister in Boston, and soon rivaled Henry Ward Beecher as a lyceum lecturer.

[38] Lucy Howe Crawford (1799-1869), *The History of the White Mountains from the First Settlement of Upper Coos and Pequaket* (White Hills [Portland], 1846).

[39] Timothy Nash and Benjamin Sawyer were hunters who in 1771 "discovered" the passage through the White Mountains, doubtless long known to the Indians. In 1773 they received from Governor John Wentworth as reward a grant of 2,184 acres to the west of the range, but they did not long retain control of this enormous property. A route through the mountains to Portland was very important for the development of northern New Hampshire and Vermont at this period; hence the magnificence of their reward.

[40] Captain Eleazar Rosebrook (1747-1817), a native of Massachusetts, early settled in the north country, first at Lancaster and later at Colebrook, then thirty miles beyond the last settlements. He once traveled eighty miles on foot in order to get a bag of salt at Haverhill, which he carried home on his back through the trackless wilds. Later he lived at Guildhall, Vermont, where his family stayed while he served in the Revolution. In 1792 he sold this farm and became the first settler in Nash and Sawyer's Location. He built his house on the Giant's Grave (at Fabyan's) where he also had saw and grist mills. He opened the first hotel for summer

visitors in 1803. In 1817, Captain Rosebrook left his property to his grandson Ethan Allen Crawford, who had served as his hired man.

⁴¹ An account of the disaster appears in note 11, 1841 Journal, p. 331.

⁴² Susannah Willard Johnson Hastings (1730-1810). *The Captivity of Mrs. Johnson* (Windsor, Vermont, 1807.) (Cf. *Bib. Can.* 320.) Mrs. Johnson, a native of Charlestown, New Hampshire—then known as "No. 4" from its place in the chain of frontier forts—was captured in an Indian raid on the village in 1754, carried overland to Lake Champlain, and thence to Montreal and Quebec, finally returning home by way of London. Her book is a colorful epic of the French and Indian War, though the story doubtless gained in vividness during the long period that elapsed between the events and their chronicling.

⁴³ A Meserve was one of the first settlers of Jackson, New Hampshire, in 1790. Stephen Meserve of Bartlett represented that town and Jackson in the state legislature.

⁴⁴ Captain Samuel Willey (1754?-1844), the father of the victim of the landslide, was one of the first settlers of Upper Bartlett, and later lived in North Conway. He came from Lee, Massachusetts in 1777. Another son, the Reverend Benjamin G. Willey (?-1867), was the author of the best early book on the White Mountains (*Incidents in White Mountain History*, Boston, 1857).

⁴⁵ Colonel Joseph Whipple of Jefferson, New Hampshire, whose farm was near the mill on the Cherry Mountain road, owned most of the good land north of the mountains in the early days of settlement. He came from Portsmouth in 1772. He was a paternalistic landlord, and on his annual visits to Portsmouth acted as agent for most of the inhabitants of the region. Willey gives a different version of the corn story (*Incidents*, 71), saying that it was a famine year and that the colonel refused to sell grain to any save his neighbors, for fear that they should suffer. The "Indians" were from Bartlett, thirty miles away. Willey also has a happy ending for the Tory raid story. After his escape, the colonel "went directly to a meadow, where he had men to work, and, ordering each man to seize a stake from the fence and shoulder it as he would a gun, soon presented himself again to the Indians, who were already in search of him. Seeing him in the distance, as they supposed at the head of a large company of armed men, they hastily seized what plunder they could lay hands on, and fled." (*Incidents*, 72.)

⁴⁶ John Josselyn (1638-75). *New Englands Rarities Discovered* (London, 1672); *An Account of Two Voyages to New England* (London, 1674). Josselyn's observations on nature are to be found in *New Englands Rarities* (Transac-

tions of American Antiquarian Society, IV). The *Voyages* was reprinted in *Massachusetts Historical Society Collections*, Series 3, Vol. III (1833). A famous passage describes the view from Mt. Washington: "The country beyond these hills, northward, is daunting terrible; being full of rocky hills, as thick as mole-hills in a meadow, and clothed with infinite thick woods."

[47] See note 35, of this journal, p. 350.

[48] "About 1827, such of the Wolfe papers as had descended from General Warde, the executor of Wolfe's mother, to his nephew, Admiral George Warde, were placed in Robert Southey's hands, but a life of Wolfe which he had designed was not prepared, and the papers were lost sign of until they appeared as lots 531-32 of the Catalogue of the Dawson Turner Sale in 1858 . . ." (J. Winsor, *Narr. & Crit. Hist. of America*, V, 602, n. 4.)

[49] This was Parkman's favorite sister Caroline, who acted as his amanuensis and copyist during his early labors on *The Oregon Trail* and *The Conspiracy of Pontiac*, and who married the Rev. Dr. John Cordner of Montreal in 1852. Like her brother, she was troubled with weakness of sight, and underwent the attentions of the noted oculist, Dr. S. R. Elliott of Staten Island, a year before he did.

[50] The Penobscot mission village of Panawariské was above Bangor, at or near the mouth of the Passadumkeag River. After Colonel Westbrook burned it in 1723, the village was re-established nearer Bangor, a little below Old Town. This settlement became the nucleus of the reservation which Parkman visited, and which still exists. Cf. *Half-Century*, I, 244-45, 254.

[51] The Lord's Supper was probably a cyclorama, a popular form of traveling show at this period.

[52] The Caughnawaga Mission for the Iroquois was established by the Jesuits in 1667 on the south shore of the St. Lawrence at the mouth of the St. Jacques River, in the seigneury of Laprairie, near Montreal. It is still in existence as a reservation, not far from the original site opposite Lachine and once more under the direction of the Jesuits. Cf. E. J. Devine, S.J., *Historic Caughnawaga* (Montreal, 1922).

[53] Castine, Maine, at the mouth of the Penobscot, is named after the Baron de St. Castin (1650-1712), who established himself in a fort called Pentagoet at that place and took an Abenaki wife. He and his sons had great influence over the Indians.

[54] This account of the Mohawk raid on the Penobscots is mentioned in *Pontiac*, I, 10 n.

IV. EUROPEAN JOURNAL

¹ George Borrow's *The Bible in Spain* was first published in 1843. Since Parkman had a vague plan of wandering through Spain, to which he later refers in the journal, it was not surprising that he should be reading Borrow and *Don Quixote* on the voyage to Europe.

² Nathaniel Jarvis Wyeth (1802-56) of Cambridge, Mass., led a fur-trading party into the Oregon country in 1832 and again in 1834. In the latter year he was accompanied from the Missouri to Fort Hall by the first Oregon missionaries, Jason and Daniel Lee. An account of Wyeth's first journey by his cousin John B. Wyeth, *Oregon: or a Short History of a Long Journey* (Cambridge, 1833) is one of the early classics of Western history, although Nathaniel called it a book "of *little lies* told for gain." John Kirk Townsend's account of the second journey, *Narrative of a Journey Across the Rocky Mountains . . . in 1834* (Philadelphia, 1839) was also doubtless familiar to Parkman, as references in this journal and that kept on his Oregon Trail trip indicate. Wyeth's own account of his experiences was not printed until 1899 (G. E. Young, Ed., "Correspondence and Journals of Captain Nathaniel J. Wyeth," *Sources of History of Oregon*, I, 3-6, [Eugene, O., 1899]).

³ Cf. *Vassall Morton*, p. 394.

⁴ This description of the gale is taken over word for word in *Vassall Morton*, pp. 395-96.

⁵ Probably William F. Worthington of William Worthington and Co., merchants, of 20 Central Wharf, Boston, who either owned or chartered the *Nautilus*. The small merchant vessels of the eastern seaboard were very active in the Mediterranean trade at this period.

⁶ Don Alonzo Perez de Guzman (1256-1309), known as "*El Bueno*," defended Tarifa in 1296 and allowed the besiegers to kill his son, whom they held captive, rather than surrender the town. The Duke of Medina-Sidonia, the commander of the Spanish Armada, prided himself on his descent from Don Alonzo.

⁷ Sir George Augustus Eliott (1717-90), later Lord Heathfield, commanded Gibraltar during the four years' siege which was begun in 1789 by the Spanish and French.

⁸ See Appendix to this journal, p. 237.

⁹ See Appendix to this journal, p. 237.

¹⁰ Sir John Moore (1761-1809) was mortally wounded at Corunna

during the Napoleonic Wars. The familiar poem by Charles Wolfe about his burial in the ramparts has immortalized his name.

[11] Admiral Sir Peter Parker (1761-1811) was Nelson's first patron.

[12] Prince Gerhard von Blücher (1742-1819) was Wellington's trump card at Waterloo.

[13] Lorenzo Papanti of 21 Tremont Row, Boston, was the best known dancing master of the day in that city.

[14] See the Appendix to this journal, p. 237.

[15] Jehan Parisot de la Valette, Grand Master of the Knights of St. John, defended Malta in the great siege of 1565, which checked the advance of Mohammedan power in southern and western Europe. Under him the order reached its highest fame. He refused a cardinal's hat, preferring independence, and made Valletta the best fortified place in the world.

[16] The Albion on Tremont Street and Murdoch's Tavern were famous Boston eating and drinking places of the day.

[17] Matthew Gregory Lewis (1775-1818) was known as "Monk" Lewis for his celebrated romance, *Ambrosio or the Monk*.

[18] See the Appendix to this journal, p. 237-38.

[19] See the Appendix to this journal, p. 238.

[20] See the Appendix to this journal, p. 238-39.

[21] Don Mateo Lopez' card was found in Parkman's pocket notebook.

[22] See the Appendix to this journal, p. 240.

[23] See the Appendix to this journal, p. 239.

[24] See the Appendix to this journal, p. 239.

[25] See the Appendix to this journal, p. 239-40.

[26] See the Appendix to this journal, p. 239.

[27] See the Appendix to this journal, p. 240.

[28] The Sicilian Vespers were the massacres of the French at Palermo and elsewhere in 1282, as a result of the conspiracy of the Sicilians with the Greek emperor Michael Palaeologus and King Pedro of Aragon against the Angevin dynasty.

[29] King Ferdinand II of Naples and the Two Sicilies used the jealousy between the two parts of his kingdom to advantage in the revolutionary agitation of 1847.

[30] See the Appendix to this journal, p. 241.

[31] See the Appendix to this journal, p. 241.

[32] See the Appendix to this journal, p. 241-42.

[33] See the Appendix to this journal, p. 242-43.

[34] See the Appendix to this journal, p. 244.

[35] See the Appendix to this journal, p. 245.

[36] James Holman (1786-1857) became blind at the age of twenty-five, after serving in the British Navy. He then traveled widely, describing his journeys in three books: *Narrative of a Journey . . . 1819-21* (London, 1822), *Travels in Russia, Siberia, Poland, Austria, etc.* (London, 1825), and *Voyage Round the World* (London, 1834-35).

[37] Count Perolla was the grandson of Count Roger, the Norman who drove the Saracens out of Sicily.

[38] *Aeneid*, Book V.

[39] Agathocles, the greatest of the early rulers of Sicily, was tyrant of Syracuse and eastern Sicily (317-301 B.C.). He waged a long war with Hamilcar of Carthage; and in quelling a revolt led by Syracuse's rival Acragas, he laid Segasta waste.

[40] This incident serves as an episode in *Vassall Morton*, pp. 115-16.

[41] Theodore Parker (1810-60) was the great Unitarian preacher of his day. He was a man of great erudition and later advised Parkman in his first historical work.

[42] Carnival was a period of from three to ten days of merrymaking, just before the beginning of Lent. The custom is probably a survival of the Roman Saturnalia, and Rome was the headquarters of it, although all the principal Italian cities had carnivals. The throwing of sweetmeats and flowers was the result of the reform by Pope Sixtus V of the old custom of throwing dirt, dust, and flour.

[43] Masaniello led a revolt at Naples in 1647 against Spanish rule.

[44] Shrove Tuesday.

[45] John Adams Dix (1798-1879) served in the War of 1812 and was adjutant general of New York in 1830. He soon became a prominent leader of the Democratic Party, and was a member of the "Albany Regency," which controled the party from 1820 to 1850. From 1841-43 he was editor of *The Northern Light*, an Albany literary and scientific journal.

[46] George Washington Greene (1811-83), a grandson of General Nathaniel Greene of Revolutionary War fame, was the American Consul at Rome from 1837 to 1845, when he returned to America. In later life he was a teacher and historian.

[47] Samuel Gridley Howe (1801-76), who had taken part in the Greek Revolution and founded the Perkins Institute for the Blind in Boston, was traveling in Europe in 1844 on a prolonged tour of philanthropic institutions. He was accompanied by his wife, Julia Ward Howe, later the author of "The Battle Hymn of the Republic," whom he had married in the previous year.

[48] A fuller account of the Virginian St. Ives is given in Parkman's article, "A Convent at Rome," (*Harper's Magazine*, August 1890 [LXXXI, 448-54]), which was based on this journal.

[49] Johann Friedrich Overbeck (1789-1869), the German painter, was a leader in the nineteenth-century revival of Christian art. He went to Rome in 1810, and for the rest of his life it was the center of his labors.

[50] William Morris Hunt (1824-79), the painter, was Parkman's classmate at Harvard, but had been suspended for inattention to his studies. His brother John was a freshman at Harvard. The Hunt family decided to remain in Europe, where William studied painting for ten years, before he returned home to become the apostle of the Barbizon School and the dean of the Boston art world. When Parkman encountered him, Hunt had already begun to study in Rome with Henry Kirk Brown, the American sculptor.

[51] Claude of Lorraine or Claude Gelée (1600-82), the great French landscape painter. His works in the Altieri and Colonna palaces at Rome were probably fresh in Parkman's memory.

[52] Cyclopean masonry, the chief survival of the prehistoric period in Italy, is characterized by polygonal stones set in irregular courses.

[53] By "General Confession" Parkman probably meant the obligation of all Catholics to confess and to receive Holy Communion at Eastertime.

[54] Cf. *Jesuits*, I, 197 n. 2.

[55] Probably Mr. William English of Castlerock, Dublin, whose card was found in Parkman's pocket notebook.

[56] Hiram Powers (1805-73), the American sculptor, settled in Florence in 1837. His "Greek Slave," completed in 1843, made his reputation as one of the leading artists of the day.

[57] The disorder that brought Parkman to Europe is described by Edward Wheelwright, one of his Harvard classmates, as "heart-strain" brought on by overexertion in the college gymnasium. A mule-back tour through rugged Sicily and rambles in the Alps were hardly calculated to help a bad heart. It is possible that the doctors told Parkman to go easy because of his heart, when they really wanted him to relax because of the nervous hypertension from which he undoubtedly suffered at this period.

[58] Ethan and Tom Crawford, the giant sons of old Abel Crawford, kept taverns in the White Mountains which Parkman had frequented in 1841-43.

[59] Cf. *Vassall Morton*, p. 244.

[60] Cf. *Vassall Morton*, p. 194.

[61] *American Notes*, Ch. III.

[62] The Jardin Mabille was one of the most notorious pleasure-places in the Paris of the period. Parkman seems to have had a very knowing uncle.

[63] Charles Matthews (1803-78) was one of the most famous English actors of his day. He played at the Haymarket during much of 1843 and 1844.

[64] The repudiation of foreign debts in the great financial panic of 1837 made as many enemies for the United States as did insistence on the payment of the war debts of 1914-18.

[65] Catlin's "Indian Gallery," first shown in New York in 1837 and in London in 1839, did much to arouse the interest of both Americans and Europeans in the Far West. George Catlin spent six years painting the Indians and collecting this valuable mass of relics in the West and South. Many of his paintings were reproduced in lithograph in his *North American Indian Portfolio* (London, 1844), and have found a permanent home in the National Museum at Washington, D. C.

[66] Tom Thumb, later known as "General," was one of a celebrated line of dwarfs who have gone by this name.

[67] The dwarf Jeffrey Hudson (1619-82) was a favorite of Henrietta Maria, wife of Charles I of England. He saw service against Cromwell in the Rebellion.

[68] George Atkinson was a brother of William P. Atkinson, Parkman's brother-in-law.

[69] In Scott's *The Heart of Midlothian.*

[70] James Ballantyne printed Scott's first book, the *Minstrelsy*, in 1802; and later was his partner, first as a printer and then as a publisher. The collapse of the Ballantyne firm involved Scott in bankrupcy, out of which he struggled through his writing.

[71] In *Waverly.*

[72] Daniel Denison Slade, Parkman's companion on his first excursion in the White Mountains in 1841.

V. BOSTON & BERKSHIRE JOURNAL

[1] The front end papers of this notebook contain a note to "Pay Pratt"; and some scribbled names, mostly of Harvard classmates; and the note "Third Wednesday of August be at Cambridge." This was Parkman's

graduation day, as commencement was then held in the autumn. The rear end papers contain some illegible law and sermon notes, and the following list of equipment for his Berkshire expedition:

shoes
waistcoats
card for gun   Knapsack to contain
knapsack

three shirts
two stockings
flannel drawers
fishing apparatus
Powder & shot
Hist. of B[erkshire]

There is also a list of names: "Hall, Hamilton, Trollope, Cooper's *Works*, Bird's *Works*, *Green Mt. Boy*, Leatsfield, Miss Leslie—Pencil sketch."

[2] In 1840 Albert Brisbane, the father of the late Arthur Brisbane of the Hearst press, published *The Social Destiny of Man*, a book which introduced the social ideas of Charles Fourier to an America already interested in Robert Owen's ideas of association. In April 1841 George Ripley, who had recently resigned from the Unitarian ministry, launched the Brook Farm experiment at West Roxbury, which Emerson referred to as "a French Revolution in small and an Age of Reason in a patty pan." By 1844 Brook Farm had become a Fourier phalanx, with a membership of about a hundred.

[3] Parkman's classmate, Charles B. Snow of Fitchburg, Mass.

[4] George Blankern Cary (1824-46), a brilliant figure of Parkman's class at college.

[5] John (Dawson) Gilmary Shea (1824-92), after studying law and being admitted to the New York bar in 1846, entered the Jesuit novitiate in 1848 and spent six years in the order, being closely associated with Père Félix Martin, the historian and first rector of St. Mary's College, Montreal. Soon after leaving the Society of Jesus, Shea began a systematic study of the Indian missions in America. He won notice with his *Discovery and Exploration of the Mississippi Valley*. In 1854 he published his *History of Catholic Missions, 1529-1824* which brought him into correspondence with Parkman and in 1857 he initiated his series of Crémoisy reprints of early voyages. He was considered the best-informed American on Indian questions of his day.

[6] Rolland Green of Mansfield, Massachusetts?

[7] John Norton (1716-78), *The Redeemed Captive, Being a narrative of the taking and carrying into captivity of The Reverend Mr. John Norton When Fort Massachusetts Surrendered . . . August 20, 1746* (Boston, 1748). *Bib. Can.* 203.

[8] Montague City is on the east bank of the Connecticut River, opposite

Greenfield and near Turner's Falls, Massachusetts, where Captain Turner killed 300 Nipmucks in 1676.

⁹ Probably Horace T. Clark (1823-?), who is listed in the West Stockbridge records as a "machinist."

¹⁰ John Sergeant (1710-49) of Newark, New Jersey, abandoned his tutorship at Yale to become the first missionary to the Stockbridge Indians in 1734. He was ordained at Deerfield in the following year. His first church stood on the green, "a few rods north-east of the present South Church," and was opened on Thanksgiving Day, 1739. Sergeant gave himself so zealously to the task of educating and converting the Indians that he came to an early death. He was much loved by his flock.

¹¹ During King Philip's War (1675-76), Major Talcot of Connecticut and some Stockbridge Indians defeated two hundred hostile savages on the Housatonic, midway between Westfield and Albany.

¹² Dr. Oliver Partridge (1757-1848), who was born in Hatfield, came to Stockbridge as a young man. He was a son of Colonel Oliver Partridge, the sheriff of Hatfield.

¹³ Agrippa Hull (1759-1848), a resident of Stockbridge from childhood. He served over six years in the Revolution, four of them as Kosciusko's body servant. He was long in the service of Judge Sedgwick. In later life he was one of the noted characters of the village.

¹⁴ Mrs. Stephen Jones was the widow of the son of Captain Josiah Jones (1725-?), who was referred to by the Stockbridge Indians as "Good man, always kind to Indian." When the tribe left Stockbridge for the West, they gave the Captain the old conch shell which had always been used to call them to the mission church.

¹⁵ A grandson of Captain Jones.

¹⁶ Actually Dr. Partridge was eighty-seven in 1844.

¹⁷ Colonel Ephraim Williams (1715-55) early went to sea and visited England, Spain, and Holland, but abandoned the sailor's life at the request of his father, who had removed from Hatfield to Stockbridge in 1737. The son acquired considerable land holdings and represented the town in the General Court, before returning to Hatfield in 1748 to serve as deputy sheriff under Colonel Oliver Partridge. In 1746 he was given charge of the line of frontier forts running from Fort Dummer on the Connecticut River to Fort Massachusetts near Williamstown. Since he was engaged in preparing an invasion of Canada to check the French and Indian raids, he was not at the latter place when it was attacked by Rigaud de Vaudreuil in 1746; but successfully defended it against a second attack in 1748. He was promoted from captain to major, and at

the end of the War of the Austrian Succession settled again in Hatfield. In 1755 Williams commanded a regiment in Sir William Johnson's army and was killed at Rocky Brook. Cf. *Half-Century*, II, 232, 241-42; *Montcalm and Wolfe*, I, 301-14.

[18] Colonel Oliver Partridge of Hatfield was sheriff in peacetime and soldier in wartime.

[19] General James Abercromby (1706-81) became British commander in chief in North America in 1758; and led the unsuccessful expedition against Ticonderoga in that year, which ended in Montcalm's great victory of Carillon. Most of the colonial officers regarded his Scottish caution as cowardice.

[20] Brigadier General George Augustus, Viscount Howe (1724-58) came to Halifax in 1757 as commander of the 60th Regiment, and was transferred in the same year to command the 55th. He was Abercromby's second-in-command on the expedition against Ticonderoga in 1758; and was killed in a preliminary skirmish on July 8, near the junction of Trout Brook with the outlet of Lake George, by the French advance party under Langy and Trepezec. (See *Montcalm and Wolfe*, II, 295-304.) He was a brother of General William Howe and Admiral Lord Howe of Revolutionary War fame.

[21] Cf. *Montcalm and Wolfe*, II, 300-4.

[22] Major General Jeffery, Baron Amherst (1717-97), a former aide-de-camp of the Duke of Cumberland in the German campaigns, came to America in 1758; and with Admiral Boscawen captured Louisbourg in that year. He was colonel of the Royal American Regiment and succeeded Abercromby after the latter's recall. Amherst captured Ticonderoga and Crown Point in 1759; in the following year he moved against Montreal down the St. Lawrence from Lake Ontario, while Brigadier Haviland proceeded by Lake Champlain, and Brigadier James Murray came up from Quebec. Amherst was thus responsible for the final capitulation of Canada on September 8, 1760. He was appointed commander in chief and governor general in North America in 1761.

[23] No Morrison from Stockbridge is listed among Rogers' Rangers.

[24] Captain John Konkapot, the leader of the Stockbridge Indians, sold a good part of the Berkshire Hills country to Connecticut Valley proprietors in 1724, "in consideration of £450, 3 barrels of cider, and 30 quarts of rum." Konkapot lived on the east side of the Great Barrington road, a few rods north of the brook still called after him. Under missionary pressure he evinced some desire to become a Christian; but objected that if he did so, his people might discard him, and also that "the conversation

of the Christians about him was even worse than that of the heathen."
Konkapot, who was given a captain's commission by Governor Jonathan
Belcher, was nonetheless instrumental in the establishment of the mission
at Stockbridge, which he befriended. He and his family were the first
Stockbridge Indians baptized by Sergeant in 1735.

[25] Parkman probably refers to the massacre of Lieutenant Colonel
Monro's garrison at William Henry in 1757 by Montcalm's Indians. Cf.
Montcalm and Wolfe, II, 184-203.

[26] An auxiliary of the American Temperance Society, formed in 1826,
was established shortly after the original society was formed at Stockbridge.
It was particularly flourishing from 1840 to 1843, with a total abstinence
program.

[27] Rogers' Rangers were organized by Major Robert Rogers from among
the frontiersmen and hunters of New England for service during the
Seven Years' War. Their most famous engagements were on Lake George
and Lake Champlain; and their most notable achievement was the
destruction of the Indian village of St. Francis on the river of the same
name near the St. Lawrence, which had served as headquarters for many
of the French and Indian raids on the New England settlements.

[28] The anti-rent agitation in New York began during the first term of
William H. Seward as governor (1838-40). Its center was the Hudson
River counties, where most of the land was included in the vast estates
of Rensselaerswyck, Livingston, Scarsdale, Phillipse, Pelham, and Van
Cortland manors, under the leasehold system with perpetual leases, leases
for 99 years, or leases for one to three lives. Feudal dues and alienation
fines were part of the system. The agitation reached its climax in 1845,
when the anti-rent associations elected Governor John Young, who was
favorable to their cause, and were responsible for the calling of the
constitutional convention of 1846, which abolished feudal tenure and
destroyed the leasehold system, thus breaking up the great estates.
Fenimore Cooper wrote three anti-rent novels: *Satanstoe* (1845), *The Chain-
bearer* (1845), and *The Redskins* (1846).

[29] Plattsburg, New York, on the west shore of Lake Champlain, was the
headquarters of the American Army on the northern frontier in the War of
1812. On September 11, 1814 the British fleet was defeated by Commodore
Macdonough in Plattsburg Bay.

[30] "Captain" Edmund Badger of North Adams, Massachusetts was
honorably discharged from the U. S. Army in 1815 as a first lieutenant.
Like other retired officers, he seems to have risen in rank after the days
of his active service.

[31] Colonel Ephraim Williams (1714/5-55) of Stockbridge and Hatfield made a will at Albany on July 22, 1755, in which he provided for a free school in Williamstown, near where he had been stationed at Fort Massachusetts. This school was incorporated in 1785, and in 1793 became Williams College.

[32] Since no Jones of Stockbridge was an officer in the Revolution or War of 1812, the reference is probably to Captain Josiah Jones (1725-?).

[33] Fort Massachusetts was the most exposed of the line of frontier posts built to defend the New England settlements against the French and Indian raids. Colonel Ephraim Williams usually made his headquarters there, after he was placed in charge of the forts; but he was absent when the place was attacked in 1746 and its garrison of fifty was overcome by Rigaud de Vaudreuil's force. In 1748 he successfully defended the fort against another assault.

[34] This "country Professor" was Albert Hopkins (1807-72), the astronomer, who was a resident of Stockbridge and an early graduate of Williams. He returned to Williams to teach mathematics and natural history in 1829. In 1834 he went to Europe to purchase apparatus for the college, and upon his return built with his own means the first astronomical observatory in an American university. A great botanist and a pioneer in the organization of field trips for students of the natural sciences, he was a correspondent of the Royal Astronomical Society of London, and a brother of Mark Hopkins, the famous president of Williams.

[35] Colonel Ephraim Williams divided his time between Stockbridge and Hatfield.

[36] Stephen W. Williams (1790-1855), *American Medical Biographies* (Greenfield, Massachusetts, 1845). Dr. Thomas Williams, brother of Colonel Williams, was appointed a surgeon in the army raised for the Canada expedition in 1744, and also for the line of frontier forts commanded by his brother. He was a member of his brother's staff at Bloody Brook, and dressed Dieskau's wounds.

[37] A life of Israel Putnam by Oliver W. B. Peabody was published in Sparks' *Library of American Biography*, Series I, Vol. 7. The "Stephens" of Parkman's note may be either Henry Stevens (1819-86), then at the Harvard law school, who went to London in the following year and became a famous bookseller and authority on Americana and Canadiana, or his brother Simon, with whom Parkman visited the Pennsylvania frontier in 1845. Henry Stevens had spent his college holidays ransacking New England and the Middle Atlantic states for material for Peter Force's *American Archives*, so he is probably referred to here.

[38] Dr. Stephen W. Williams (1790-1855) carried on researches into local history, botany, and chemistry, as well as his medical practice. He wrote many papers for the New York Historical Society and the Massachusetts Medical Society. His memoirs of medical men were collected in *American Medical Biographies* and two years later he published a family history.

[39] The "Molang" of Humphreys' account of Israel Putnam was Marin, the famous leader of French and Indian raids, who was defeated by Putnam and Rogers near Fort Anne in 1758. Cf. *Montcalm and Wolfe*, II, 329-34.

[40] Robert Rogers (1731/2-95), the famous partisan, was born at Methuen, Massachusetts, but grew up on his father's farm near Concord, New Hampshire.

[41] Major General Epaphras Hoyt (1765-1850) of Deerfield, Massachusetts, was at various times postmaster, justice of the peace, register of deeds for Franklin County, high sheriff, member of the constitutional convention of 1820, and a ranking officer of the state militia. He wrote extensively for *Silliman's Journal*, and his *Treatise on the Military Art* (1798) went through several editions. His *Antiquarian Researches* (1824) was his best-known work. He never published the copious notes on the Indian wars and Burgoyne's campaign, which were his chief concern for some years before his death.

[42] This story of the ranger at Bloody Pond was not used by Parkman in the histories.

[43] Either Henry or Simon Stevens may have had Samuel Blodget's "A Prospective Plan of the Battle Near Lake George," which was published at Boston soon after the battle in 1755.

[44] This account of Montcalm's advance against William Henry in 1757, by Père Roubaud, S.J., missionary to the St. Francis Indians, is found in *Lettres Edifiantes et Curieuses*, VI, 189 (1810). Parkman uses it largely in *Montcalm and Wolfe*, II, 168-203.

[45] The two officers were Captain Pringle and Lieutenant Roche. See *Montcalm and Wolfe*, II, 215-20.

[46] Cf. note 39.

[47] Possibly Engineer Lieutenant Thérbu's map, "Attaques du Fort William-Henri."

[48] Samuel Williams (1743-1817), *The natural and civil history of Vermont* (Walpole, New Hampshire, 1794).

[49] Zadock Thompson (1796-1856), *History of Vermont, natural, civil, and statistical* (Burlington, Vermont, 1842).

[50] Hendrick, chief of the Mohawks with Johnson at Lake George in

1755, was killed in Dieskau's ambush of Colonel Williams at Bloody Pond. He was one of Parkman's Indian heroes, and one of the horses on the Oregon Trail trip was named after him.

[51] Epaphras Hoyt (1765-1850), *Antiquarian Researches, comprising a History of the Indian wars in the country bordering the Connecticut River* (Greenfield, Massachusetts, 1824).

[52] These maps were doubtless in the Harvard Library. It has not been possible to identify them without full titles.

[53] John Huddlestone Wynne (1743-88), *The History of the British Empire in America* (London, 1769).

[54] Robert Rogers (1731-95), *A Concise Account of North America* (London, 1765). Rogers' *Journals* were also published at London in the same year, and this may be the book Parkman had in mind.

[55] John Mitchell (?-1768), *The Contest in America between Great Britain and France* (London, 1757).

[56] John Warner Barber (1798-1885), *The History and Antiquities of New England, New York, and New Jersey* (Worcester, 1841).

[57] Timothy Dwight (1752-1817), president of Yale, traveled widely through New England and New York from 1796 to 1815. His *Travels* were published in 1821-22 at New Haven.

[58] Sir Charles Augustus Murray (1806-95), *Travels in North America* (New York, 1839).

[59] Colonel John Winslow's *Journal* and *Letterbook* are invaluable sources on the expulsion of the Acadians in 1755. Parkman used them in *Montcalm and Wolfe*, I, 243-95.

[60] The Massachusetts Archives, in the State House at Boston, are rich in manuscript material on the French and Indian Wars.

[61] The reference may be to the renegade Roubaud's forgeries, which he placed in the hands of the King when he went to England, and which were partially printed at London in 1777. See *Montcalm and Wolfe*, III, 170-1 n.

[62] General John Taylor Cooper presented a large collection of Johnson MSS. to the New York state library; and W. L. Stone (1793-1844) procured many more from the Johnson family in England and other sources. These have been printed by the State of New York in nine volumes (Albany, 1921-39).

[63] Jared Sparks was Parkman's historical mentor and adviser at Harvard.

[64] Roubaud's account, in *Lettres Edifiantes et Curieuses*, VI, 189.

[65] Soon after the battle at Lake George in 1755, Samuel Blodget published at Boston *A Prospective Plan of the Battle Near Lake George, with an*

Explanation thereof, containing a full, though short, History of that important Affair, by Samuel Blodget, occasionally at the Camp when the Battle was fought. This is reproduced in E. B. O'Callaghan, *A Documentary History of New York*, IV. The "Explanation" is only found complete in the original. Cf. *Montcalm and Wolfe*, I, 328-29 n.

66 Dieskau's account of the battle of Lake George has been printed in O'Callaghan, *Documents relating to the Colonial History of New York*, X, 316-8. Cf. *Montcalm and Wolfe*, I, 307-29.

67 Jean Victor Varin de La Marre was Commissaire de la Marine at Quebec 1734-47 and at Montreal 1747-54. He served as substitute for the Intendant Bigot, in whose fraudulent operations he was involved after 1749.

68 Pierre de Rigaud, Marquis de Vaudreuil, was the last French governor of Canada.

69 The Agniers were the Mohawks, a tribe of the Iroquois Confederacy. They generally fought for the English in the French and Indian War.

70 The Chevalier de Montreuil served as adjutant general in Canada from 1754 to 1758. He later played a part in the defense of Quebec in 1759 as a major general.

71 Doreil was Commissaire de la Guerre with Vaudreuil in 1755 and 1757.

72 Fort Edward on the Hudson was first known as Fort Lydius, after a Dutch resident of the place.

VI. OLD NORTHWEST JOURNAL & PONTIAC NOTES

1 Albert Gallatin (1761-1849), Swiss-born American statesman and scholar, abandoned public life in 1827 and settled in New York City, where he devoted himself to science and literature. In 1836 he published, in the second volume of the *Transactions* of the American Antiquarian Society, his notable *Synopsis of the Indian Tribes within the United States East of the Rocky Mountains and in the British and Russian Possessions in North America*. In 1842 he founded the American Ethnological Society with H. R. Schoolcraft, John R. Bartlett, Branz Mayer, and E. G. Squier, all of whom became correspondents of Parkman. In 1843 Gallatin was president of the New York Historical Society, to which Parkman was elected as an honorary

member four years later, on the strength of *The Oregon Trail*. In *Pontiac* (9 n.) Parkman refers to a conversation with Gallatin.

² Evidently Parkman planned to visit the chief Philadelphia libraries, and to consult Redmond Conyngham of Paradise, Pennsylvania, a member of the state legislature and a historical amateur who published documents on the Pennsylvania part of Pontiac's conspiracy in the Lancaster *Intelligencer*.

³ George Washington Baker (?-1895) was a member of the class of 1844 at Harvard.

⁴ William Leete Stone (1793-1844), *Life and Times of Sa-go-ye-wat-ha, or Red Jacket* (New York, 1841).

⁵ Caleb Atwater, "Description of the Antiquities Discovered in Ohio and other Western States," in *Archaeologia Americana*, I (Worcester, 1820).

⁶ Probably Parkman's correspondent Simon Stevens, a brother of Henry Stevens; the latter was the famous bookseller and bibliographer, who at this time was combing attics for old books as the agent of James Lenox of New York, whose collection formed the nucleus of the New York Public Library.

⁷ George Parkman (1823-1908), Harvard 1844 and Dane Law School 1846, was Parkman's cousin. He was the son of the Dr. Parkman who was murdered by Dr. John Webster in the Medical School Laboratory at Harvard.

⁸ This letter of Captain Orme, Braddock's aide-de-camp, dated July 18, 1755, is cited in *Pontiac*, I, 118.

⁹ Colonel John Winslow (1702-74), a descendent of the early governors of Plymouth, Massachusetts, served in the expeditions against Crown Point and the Kennebec, but is best known for his connection with the deportation of the Acadians in 1755. His journals are in the possession of the Massachusetts Historical Society. They were extensively used by Parkman in *Montcalm and Wolfe*, I, 243-95.

¹⁰ The Jonathan Trumbull Papers, formerly in the Massachusetts Historical Society (portions published in M. H. S. *Collections*, Series 5, IX & X) consist of twenty-eight folios and two quartos of miscellaneous papers, dating from 1750 to 1783. They are now in the Connecticut Archives at Hartford.

¹¹ Dr. Jacob Bigelow (1786-1879), Rumford Professor and Professor of Materia Medica at Harvard, was a prominent Boston physician and an amateur botanist of some note. He shared Parkman's love for the White Mountains, and made several botanical expeditions there as a young man,

while preparing his *Florula Bostoniensis*. Parkman married his daughter Catherine Scollay Bigelow in May 1850.

12 Parkman's early attachment to Miss Pamela Prentiss of Keene, New Hampshire, was evidently waning. Cf. 1841 Journal, p. 12-17.

13 The Millerites were disciples of William Miller (1782-1849), leader of the Second Adventists in America. From 1831 onward Miller preached the Second Coming of Christ in 1843, and when the Advent failed to materialize on schedule, set the date for the following year. The Millerite meetings were a notable feature of New England life during 1843-44. Parkman had already encountered some members of the sect on the Vermont frontier. Cf. 1842 Journal, p. 66.

14 Henry Orne White (1824-87), Harvard 1843, was Parkman's companion on his 1842 excursion to Lake George and northern New England.

15 Dr. Isaac Watts (1674-1748), the noted English divine and writer of hymns.

16 The Folsoms of Exeter, New Hampshire, were descendents of that Captain Folsom who shared with Captain McGinnis the command of the scouting party to Fort Lyman, at Bloody Pond in 1755. Cf. *Montcalm and Wolfe*, I, 320.

17 The Boston *News Letter* (1704-75), modeled on the London *Gazette* and one of the longest-lived newspapers of the eighteenth century, had several later namesakes.

18 Such historical pageants as this were popular in the United States up to World War I.

19 Medford, Massachusetts, was the home of Parkman's mother. In his youth he frequently visited his grandfather Hall's farm there.

20 Dudley Hall was probably one of Parkman's Medford cousins.

21 Samuel Cutler Bigelow (?-1904), a Williams graduate of 1845.

22 The First Corps of Cadets was Boston's crack milita outfit. At this period each American city had at least one such socially notable military unit.

23 Moses Gill Cobb (?-1903), Harvard 1845.

24 Abbott Lawrence, the magnate of the Lowell cotton mills, was the prophet of commercial Boston at this period.

25 Thomas Hastings Russell (?-1911), Harvard 1843.

26 Joseph Peabody (?-1905) of Salem was a great college friend of Parkman.

27 Charles H. B. Snow (?-1875), Parkman's college classmate, belonged to one of the old Fitchburg families who lived on the hill overlooking the mills.

[28] Philip Stanhope, Viscount Mahon (1805-75), *History of England from the Peace of Utrecht to the Peace of Versailles, 1713-83* (London, 1836-54). Mahon became involved in a controversy with Parkman's historical master, Jared Sparks, over the latter's editing of *Washington's Writings* (Boston, 1837).

[29] This *Collection of Extracts*, frequently referred to by Parkman, may have been Jared Sparks' compendium of European documents, made during his studies in the French and English archives.

[30] William Henry Harrison's "Discourse on the Aborigines of the Ohio Valley, in which the Opinions of its Conquest in the Seventeenth Century, by the Iroquois or Six Nations, supported by . . . Colden . . . Pownall . . . Franklin . . . Clinton . . . and Haywood . . ., are Examined and Contested" was printed in the first volume of the Ohio Historical and Philosophical Society's *Transactions* (1839).

[31] Samuel Williams (1743-1817), *The Natural and Civil History of Vermont* (Walpole, New Hampshire, 1794).

[32] Bernard Romans (c. 1720-84), *A Concise Natural History of East and West Florida* (New York, 1775).

[33] The Catalogue of the Worcester Library was published in 1836-37.

[34] Captain Morris kept a journal of his embassy to the Illinois in 1764, which was printed in *Miscellanies in Prose and Verse* (1791). Cf. *Pontiac*, II, 208 n.

[35] John Filson (1747?-88), *The Discovery, Settlement, and Present State of Kentucky.* (New York, 1793).

[36] Henry Ellis (1721-1806), *A Voyage to Hudson's-Bay . . . in the Years 1746 and 1747* (London, 1748). *Bib. Can.* 207.

[37] Arthur Dobbs (1689-1765), *An Account of the Countries adjoining to Hudson's Bay* (London, 1744). *Bib. Can.* 193.

[38] James, second Earl Waldegrave (1715-63), *Memoirs* (London, 1821). Waldegrave was an intimate friend of George II, and for a time "governor" or tutor of George III. In 1755-57 he negotiated on the part of the king with Newcastle, Devonshire, Pitt, and Fox about the formation of a ministry.

[39] Timothy Pickering, *A Letter from Colonel Pickering, containing a Narrative of the Outrage committed on him at Wyoming, with an Account of the Controversies respecting the Lands claimed by the states of Pennsylvania and Connecticut, which led to that Event* (Salem, 1819).

[40] François Pierre Guillaume Guizot (1787-1874), *Cours d'histoire moderne* (Paris, 1829-32).

[41] Jonathan Swift (1667-1745) was a kinsman of Dryden, the bosom

friend of Bolinbroke, and with Pope and Arbuthnot established the Scriblerus Club, writing parts of both *Martin Scriblerus* and *John Bull*.

[42] Josiah Quincy (1772-1864) was president of Harvard from 1829 to 1845. He was also active in Federalist politics.

[43] George Theodore Lyman (?-1908) did not graduate from the law school.

[44] The Navy Club seems to have been a Harvard social organization.

[45] Robert Hartly Dunlap (?-1847) was a graduate of Bowdoin in 1842.

[46] George Gray (?-1850) graduated from Harvard in 1845.

[47] Francis Brooks (?-1891).

[48] Mrs. Sanders' was one of the numerous Cambridge boardinghouses of the period.

[49] Harrison Ritchie graduated from Harvard in 1845.

[50] John Halkett (1768-1852) was Lord Selkirk's brother-in-law and supported him in his dispute with the North-West Company. Halkett also wrote the *Statement respecting the Earl of Selkirk's Settlement of Kildonan, upon the Red River* (London, 1816).

[51] Jordan and Havilland were pillars of the Pennsylvania Historical Society, whom Parkman consulted about the Alleghany frontier. John Romeyn Brodhead (1814-73), while attached to the American Legation at The Hague, became interested in the early Dutch history of New York. Governor Seward appointed him agent of the state to procure materials bearing on its early history. Brodhead spent four years in the Dutch, French, and English archives; and returned home with eighty volumes of copied documents. These were edited by E. B. O'Callaghan and B. Fenn, and published as *Documents Relating to the Colonial History of New York* (Albany, 1856-86).

[52] Morris Birkbeck, the English associationist, founded the colony of New Albion, Illinois, in 1817. His *Notes on a Journey in America* (London, 1818) would have interested Parkman.

[53] Forster was also the translator of Peter Kalm's *Travels*.

[54] Rich's *Bibliotheca Americana* (London, 1832-44) was the best bibliography of Americana before Sabin's monumental work.

[55] The Quebec Literary and Historical Society was founded in 1824 through the influence and generosity of Lord Dalhousie, then governor general. The library was started in 1828 and now includes a valuable collection of Canadiana, both French and English. The society's series of *Transactions* (1829-1924) and *Historical Documents* (1838-1906) are full of important historical materials. For a fuller account of the society's history and activities, see *Centenary Volume, 1824-1924* (Quebec, 1924);

for a calendar of its publications, see Colonel William Wood's *Index* (Quebec, 1924).

[56] Pierre Pouchot (1712-69), *Mémoires sur la dernière guerre de l'Amérique, 1755-60* (Yverdon, 1781). Cf. *Bib. Can.* 330.

[57] Peter Force (1790-1868), *American Archives* (Washington, 1837-53). But in *Pontiac*, I, 265, Parkman gives Robert Rogers as his authority on this point.

[58] James H. Lanman, *History of Michigan* (New York, 1839).

[59] Judge Simon Greenleaf (1783-1853), Royall Professor of Law from 1833 to 1846 and Dane Professor from 1846 to 1848, was Judge Story's great colleague at the Dane Law School, the precursor of the Harvard Law School. Greenleaf was noted for the thoroughness of his legal knowledge.

[60] Eugene Batchelder (?-1878) left law school before graduation.

[61] John B. Lea (?-1846) was a graduate of Princeton in 1843.

[62] George Hoadley graduated from Western Reserve in 1844.

[63] Charles Edward Hooper (?-1914).

[64] Andrew Eliot Thayer (?-1873) graduated from Harvard in 1842.

[65] Daniel Denison Slade (1823-1896) was Parkman's companion on his 1841 journey.

[66] Lewis Cass (1782-1866), *et al.*, *Historical and Scientific Sketches of Michigan* (Detroit, 1834). Cass was the first governor of the territory of Michigan, and did some admirable pioneer work on the history of the region. His collection of documents bearing on the siege of Detroit proved of great value to Parkman for *Pontiac*. Schoolcraft, Henry Whiting, and John Biddle also collaborated on this volume. General Cass wrote many articles on the Indians in the *North American Review*.

[67] The Fourierites, as the Brook Farmers were called because of their adoption of the ideas of Charles Fourier, were viewed with alarm by right-thinking Bostonians of the day. In 1841 Emerson noted: "The view taken of Transcendentalism in State Street is that it threatens to invalidate contracts." George Ripley, who had earlier resigned from the Unitarian ministry, launched the Brook Farm experiment in community living in April 1841. Horace Greeley, editor of the New York *Tribune*, was drawn into the movement through the enthusiasm of his collaborator, Albert Brisbane, who had introduced Fourier's ideas to America with *The Social Destiny of Man* (Philadelphia, 1840). Charles Dana, later editor of the New York *Sun*, was one of the early members of the community. The Reverend William Henry Channing longed to join the group, but yielded

to his wife's opposition. 1845 saw the highwater mark of the movement, which shortly after dissolved.

68 Alexander Scott Withers' *Chronicles of Border Warfare* (Clarksburg, Virginia, 1831), a valuable collection of legends of the frontier, was edited and annotated by R. G. Thwaites in 1895.

69 Joseph Doddridge, *Notes on the Settlement and Indian Wars of the Western Parts of Virginia and Pennsylvania, 1763-83* (Wellsburgh, Virginia, 1824).

70 Sir William Francis Napier (1785-1860), *History of the Conquest of Scinde* (London, 1845). Napier's *War in the Peninsula* (1824-40) has established his fame as the greatest British military historian.

71 Bishop John Ettwein (1721-1802) compiled a dictionary and phrasebook of the Delaware tongue. In 1788 he wrote an account of the traditions and language of this tribe, which was published by the Pennsylvania Historical Society in its 1845-47 series of *Bulletins*, after Jared Sparks had found the MS. among Washington's papers. Parkman evidently used Sparks' transcript.

72 The Iroquois Confederacy, originally known as the Five Nations, became the Six Nations after the Tuscaroras joined the Mohawks, Oneidas, Onondagas, Cayugas, and Senecas.

73 The *Colonial Records of Pennsylvania, 1683-1736*, were printed at Philadelphia in three volumes in 1837-40. In 1852 these three volumes were reprinted and thirteen more added, covering up to 1790.

74 Matthew Smith's account of his massacre of the Conestogas was published in the Lancaster *Intelligencer* for 1843. See *Pontiac*, II, 131.

75 Colonel Armstrong destroyed an Indian village at Great Island on the west branch of the Susquehanna in October 1763. See *Pontiac*, II, 108-9.

76 J. Francis Fisher (1807-73) of Philadelphia was a well-to-do lawyer who never practiced his profession. He was very active in the Pennsylvania Historical Society from 1828 to 1865, and his own special interest was in the early history of the state. Parkman saw him to get admission to the Philosophical Society.

77 James Ross (1762-1847) of Pittsburgh, lawyer, land speculator, and U. S. Senator, was a staunch Federalist, and hence known to Parkman.

78 Sherman Day, *Historical Collections of the State of Pennsylvania* (Philadelphia, 1843).

79 Colonel John Bradstreet (c. 1711-74), an Englishman or Nova Scotian, distinguished himself at the attack on Louisbourg in 1745 which owed its origin partly to him. He defended Oswego and captured Fort Frontenac in 1758. In 1764 he was sent to punish the Western Indians for their part in Pontiac's uprising. See *Pontiac*, II, 174 *ff.*

[80] Colonel Henry Bouquet (1719-66), a Swiss professional soldier, came to America with Haldimand in 1754, when the latter took command of the second battalion of the Royal Americans at Philadelphia. In 1758 Bouquet marched with General Forbes against Fort Pitt, which he commanded until 1762. In the following year he returned and raised the siege. After Bushy Run he organized an expedition into the Indian country, which penetrated to the Delaware towns and resulted in a treaty of peace. Bouquet did not have the usual British officer's contempt for Indian methods in warfare, which he adopted. Captain James Smith, having been a captive among the Indians for some years, trained his men to fight Indian fashion.

[81] *An Historical Review of the Constitution and Government of Pennsylvania, from its origin . . . founded on authentic documents* (London, 1759). This work is generally attributed to Benjamin Franklin, though disowned by him in a letter of September 27, 1760 to David Hume. It was published at Franklin's expense. See P. L. Ford, *Franklin Bibliography* 109-11.

[82] Brother Lenneck (?-1767) *Chronicon ephratense* (Lancaster, 1786). An English version of this history of the "Protestant monks" was published at Lancaster in 1889.

[83] The Logan MSS. were deposited in the Pennsylvania Historical Society in 1840. The Paxton Boys were the Pennsylvania settlers who banded together to repress Indian outrages on the frontier in 1763. Cf. *Pontiac*, II, 130-67; 392-404.

[84] The Edward Shippen MSS. are quoted in *Pontiac*, II, 136 n., and Appendix E. The Burd MSS. were given to the Pennsylvania Historical Society by Mrs. Thompson of Thompsonville, Pennsylvania, and form part of the Shippen Papers. They include Colonel James Burd's letter-book, 1756-58, and two volumes of military papers, 1755-95.

[85] The Mennonites, so called after their leader Menno Simons (1492-1559), originated in Zurich in 1523 among the Anabaptists. Their strongholds were long in Holland, Germany, and France, but intolerance toward their beliefs in all European countries but Holland drove many of them to America. Their first colony was established at Germantown, Pennsylvania, in 1683; and by the middle of the eighteenth century Lancaster County was a Mennonite stronghold, as it remains today.

[86] Redmond Conyngham of Paradise, an antiquarian, employed himself in collecting documents on the Paxton Men, which he published in the Lancaster *Intelligencer*, and which are used largely by Parkman in *Pontiac*, II, Ch. 24-5.

[87] George Washington Baker, Harvard 1844.

88 For an account of the massacre of the Indians in the Lancaster jail, see *Pontiac*, II, 133-38.

89 John Tyler (1790-1862), tenth president of the United States (1841-45).

90 Locofocoism was a left-wing movement within Jacksonian democracy of the 1830's, so called because its adherents relit with locofoco matches the gas which the Tammany Democrats had turned out in the hall where both groups assembled in 1835. As a Whig, Parkman had no use for the extremists of a party which he regarded with horror for its levelling tendencies.

91 The Senecas were one of the Six Nations of the Iroquois Confederacy, and eventually the most important tribe. Their home was in western New York, between Seneca Lake and the Genesee River. The majority of the tribe still lives on reservations in this region.

92 Norwegian emigrants came to the United States as a result of the struggle during the 1820's and 1830's between the peasantry and the old ruling class. Immigration from Europe to the Great Lakes region began in the 1830's, and in 1845 immigrant vessels sailed three times a day westward from Buffalo.

93 Fort Gratiot was built in 1814 on the site of old Fort Joseph.

94 Mackinaw (Michilimackinac) was the great Western center of the fur trade, a role for which its geographical position at the crossroads of the Lakes admirably suited it in the days of canoe and bateau transport. The Mackinac Company was organized about 1784. It operated from Cahokia to the sources of the Mississippi, and from northern Illinois into Spanish Louisiana, west of the Missouri. In 1811 John Jacob Astor bought out the Canadian company and merged it with the Southwest Company, which became the American Fur Company in 1816. The first trading post was established at Michilimackinac in 1668, while the Jesuit mission of St. Ignace dates from 1670. Mackinaw was the chief rendezvous of the winterers in the heyday of the Hudson's Bay Company, and the field headquarters of northern division of the American Fur Company.

95 Captain Martin Scott (?-1847), a Vermonter who had served as a lieutenant in the War of 1812 and subsequently in the Fifth Infantry, was breveted major in May 1846, for gallantry at Palo Alto and Resaca de la Palma, and lieutenant colonel that fall for his conduct at Monterrey. He was killed the following year at Molino del Rey.

96 Lieutenant Henry Whiting (?-1851) of New York served in the Fifth Infantry from 1840 to March 26, 1846, when he resigned. He had collaborated with General Cass in studying the early history of the region.

[97] Fort Holmes, or George, was built by the British after their capture of Mackinaw Island in the War of 1812. After the recovery of the place by the United States, the fort was named after Major Andrew Holmes, who was killed in the American assault of August 4, 1814.

[98] Alexander Henry (1739-1824), a pioneer fur trader of the Northwest, came to Montreal with Amherst's army in 1760, and in the following year reached Michilimackinac with a fur-trading permit. His experiences in the West for the next sixteen years are described in his *Travels and Adventures in Canada and the Indian Territories* (New York, 1809). Henry's account of the massacre in 1763 is the chief source of Parkman's account in *Pontiac*, I, 351-75, which describes his taking refuge in the Skull Rock cave. Henry returned to Montreal in 1776, and became a dormant partner in the North-West Company.

[99] The fur trade of the old Northwest, after a century of French exploitation and a century of cutthroat competition among the Hudson's Bay Company, the North-West Company, and the X Y Company, was finished as far as large-scale operations were concerned by the middle of the nineteenth century. Beaver, the most profitable fur, was becoming scarce; and the development of modern felting methods by hatters had eliminated the great demand for it. The American Fur Company, whose main business was now in buffalo robes rather than in beaver, wound up its operations at Mackinaw in 1842. With the growth of steam navigation and the railroads, the voyageurs who had carried trade goods from Montreal to the Western posts and returned with cargoes of fur, became victims of technological unemployment.

[100] The Chippewas or Ojibwas were a large tribe of Algonkin stock who occupied the country around lakes Huron and Superior. They were allied with the Ottawas and Potawatomies, and their language was long used for trade and diplomacy by the other tribes of the Great Lakes. Their myths were the basis of H. R. Schoolcraft's *Algic Researches* (1839), upon which Longfellow founded *Hiawatha*.

[101] James Lawrence (?-1875) graduated from Harvard in 1840 and was an overseer of the university from 1866 to 1870.

[102] The Lake Superior copper boom began in 1844 when mines were put into production, after the geologist Douglas Houghton had revealed the presence of the precious metal in his report of 1841.

[103] Abel Bingham was one of the missionaries who made their headquarters at the Soo, where the Indian agent for the Lake Superior tribes resided.

[104] Fort Brady was built by the Americans on the south side of the strait between Lake Superior and Lake Huron.

[105] Henry Rowe Schoolcraft (1795-1864), Indian agent for Lake Superior, recorded the Algonkin legends in his *Algic Researches* (1839) and *Oneota* (1844-5). His work is no longer taken seriously by anthropologists, but was widely hailed at the time. Robert Stuart's comments recorded by Parkman and the latter's reviews in the *North American* for July 1865 and July 1866 (CI, 28-64 & CIII, 1-18) were dissenting opinions.

[106] Robert Stuart (1784-1848), a Scot educated in Paris, came to Montreal in 1806 to join his uncle David, who was in the fur trade. Both joined Astor's Pacific Fur Company and sailed in the *Tonquin* for the Columbia River in 1810. Robert Stuart returned in 1812 with the Astorian overland party to St. Louis and New York. After 1819 he represented Astor at Mackinaw as manager of the Northern Department of the American Fur Company. He retired in 1833 and made his home in Detroit. Parkman was fortunate to catch him on a visit to his old headquarters. This encounter doubtless played a part in determining Parkman to make the Oregon Trail trip in the following year.

[107] John Tanner (1780?-1847), *A Narrative of the Captivity and Adventures of John Tanner, U. S. interpreter at the Saut de Ste. Marie, during thirty years' residence among the Indians in the interior of North America* (New York, 1830). *Bib. Can.* 1612. Tanner was captured by the Indians in Ohio in 1790, and fought, hunted, and traded with them in the Middle West until 1820. His narrative ends about 1830.

[108] Parkman adopted this opinion in an article in the *North American* for July 1865 (CI, 28-64).

[109] P. J. B. F. X. Le Gardeur de Repentigny built a fort on the southern shore of the strait in 1751, which was destroyed by fire in 1762. In 1780 Major Sinclair, the British commander, moved the fort and village from the south shore to the island. The North-West Company's post on the north shore was burned by the Americans in 1814. Parkman probably visited the south shore ruins.

[110] Lieutenant M'Dougal was captured while on an embassy to Pontiac in the spring of 1763. His son's papers, "which were very voluminous and contained various notes concerning the Indian war," came into the possession of a Mr. Whitman of Palmer, Michigan, "who permitted such of them as related to the subjects in question to be copied by the writer" (*Pontiac*, I, 263 n.).

[111] François Baby, Jr. of Windsor, Ontario, was the grandson of Jacques Duperron Baby (1731-89), the Detroit trader who was a friend of Pontiac

and aided Major Gladwin's garrison with supplies during the siege of Detroit in 1763. See *Pontiac*, I, 269 n.

[112] John Askin (1738-1815) of Albany was a trader at Detroit and Mackinaw after 1762. In 1772 he married Marie Barthe, whose mother was a member of the Campeau family, and in 1796 he moved to Windsor when the Americans took over Detroit. His son Charles lived in Windsor from 1812 to 1862, and was probably Parkman's informant.

[113] Beginning of "Journal of Part of Journey in Aug. '45—No. 2."

[114] On September 13, 1763 a British wagon train from Fort Schlosser was ambushed by the Indians at the Devil's Hole. See *Pontiac*, II, 82-5.

[115] William Henry Bartlett (1809-54), an English artist, traveled widely through the United States and Canada in the late 1830's, making drawings for the well-known engravings of *Canadian Scenery* (1840) and *American Scenery*.

[116] Fort Niagara stood at the mouth of the Niagara River, on the American side. The first fortification on the spot, built by La Salle in 1678, was burned two years later. Chaussegros de Léry built a fort in stone in 1726, which replaced the blockhouse of 1721. The fort was rebuilt again in 1749, but was captured by Sir William Johnson ten years later. Like the other frontier outposts which were important in the Indian trade, it was not surrendered to the United States until 1796. During the War of 1812 it was the American base of operations for the Niagara campaign, until its capture by Colonel Murray in 1813. It was restored to the United States by the Treaty of Ghent.

[117] John Bartram (1699-1777), *Observations on the Inhabitants, Climate, Soil, Rivers, Productions, Animals, and other matters worthy of Notice* (London, 1751). *Bib. Can.* 186. Bartram's description of the long house of the Iroquois— the council chamber of the Five Nations—at Onondaga, which he visited in 1743, is quoted in *Pontiac*, I, 20-1 n. Onondaga was the capitol of the Iroquois Confederacy, and is still a reservation.

[118] John Warner Barber (1798-1885), *The History and Antiquities of New England, New York, and New Jersey. Collected and compiled from authentic sources* (Worcester, 1841).

[119] Fort Stanwix on the Mohawk River guarded the portage from Wood Creek and Lake Oneida. It was built by General Stanwix in 1758, and was unsuccessfully besieged by St. Leger in 1777. Its site is now covered by the city of Rome, New York.

[120] Texas revolted from Mexico in 1835-36, and was admitted to the United States in March 1845. Since fighting in the Mexican War did not

begin until the spring of the following year, Parkman's "drunken fellow" must have seen service against Santa Anna in the revolt ten years before.

[121] Thomas Loraine McKenney (1785-1859), *Memoirs, official and personal* (New York, 1846). Cf. *Bib. Can.* 998.

[122] [Benjamin Franklin (1706-90)?], *An Historical Account of the Constitution and Government of Pennsylvania* (London, 1759).

[123] Humphrey Marshall, *History of Kentucky* (Frankfort, Ky., 1824).

[124] Thomas Jefferson, *Notes on the State of Virginia* (Paris, 1782).

[125] Probably Thomas Jefferson Chapman, *The French in the Alleghany Valley* (Cleveland, 1887). Studies collected from historical magazines.

[126] The Proclamation of 1763 prohibited the intrusion of settlers upon the Indian reserve of the Ohio Valley and adjacent regions.

[127] Henry Crugar Van Schaack, *Life of Peter Van Schaack* (New York, 1842). Van Schaack's Onondaga campaign was a phase of General Sullivan's expedition against the Six Nations in 1779.

[128] Charles Chauncy (1705-87), *A Second Letter to a Friend* (Boston, 1755). *Bib. Can.* 234. Chauncy was pastor of the First Church. This letter is also attributed to Timothy Walker. See *Montcalm and Wolfe*, I, 328 n.

[129] Margaret Moncrieffe Coghlan, *Memoirs* (London, 1794).

[130] Paul Lejeune, S.J. (1591-1664), *Jesuit Relations, 1632-40.*

François, Vicomte de Chateaubriand (1768-1848), *Travels in America & Italy* (London, 1828).

Henri Joutel (1640-1735), *Journal du dernier voyage de M. de la Salle* (Paris, 1713).

Joseph-Henri Lafiteau, S.J. (1681-1740), *Moeurs des Sauvages Amériquains* (Paris, 1724).

Jonathan Edwards (1703-58), *Memoirs of David Brainerd* (Boston, 1749).

Gabriel Marest, S.J. (1662-1714), "Lettre au Père de Lamberville," *Lettres Edifiantes et Curieuses*, X, 268-327 (Paris, 1732).

Chréstien Leclercq (1641-95?), *Premier établissement de la foi dans la Nouvelle France* (Paris, 1691); *Nouvelle relation de la Gaspésie* (Paris, 1691).

Marie de l'Incarnation (1599-1672). *Lettres* (Paris, 1681).

Joseph Lecaron, S.J. (1586-1632), *Relation de 1624.*

Benjamin Constant, *Oeuvres*, IX.

Creuxius [François Ducreux (1596-1666)], *Historia canadensis* (Paris, 1664).

Claude Alloüez, S.J. (1622-89), "La continuation de ses voyages [Marquette]," in Thevenot, *Récueil des voyages* (Paris, 1681).

Isaac Jogues, S.J. (1607-46), "Papers," New York Historical Society *Collections*, II Series, 3.

Samuel Purchas (1575?-1626), *Purchas, His Pilgrimes*, III & IV (London, 1625-6).

Bernard Romans (1720-84), *A Concise Natural History of East & West Florida* (New York, 1775).

Jean de Brébeuf, S.J. (1593-1649). See Rageneau, *Relation des Hurons, 1649*.

LePage du Pratz, *History of Louisiana* (London, 1763).

Sir Alexander MacKenzie (1755-1820), *Voyages, 1789-93* (London, 1801).

[131] The Colonel Israel Williams Papers in the Massachusetts Historical Society consist of two volumes of letters and papers (1730-80), dealing with the French and Indian Wars, together with letters from Governor Hutchinson and material concerning the founding of Williams College.

[132] The *Universal Magazine* was published in London in the 1730's.

[133] Colonel James Smith, *Account of the Remarkable Occurences in the Life and Travels of Colonel James Smith during his Captivity with the Indians, 1755-59* (Lexington, Kentucky, 1799).

[134] James Sullivan, *History of the District of Maine* (Boston, 1795).

[135] John Williams, *Biographical Memoir of the Rev. John Williams; with Papers relating to the Early Indian Wars in Deerfield* (Greenfield, Massachusetts, 1837).

[136] Jeremy Belknap, *History of New Hampshire* (Philadelphia and Boston, 1784-92).

[137] Peter Williamson (1730-99), *French and Indian Cruelty* (Glasgow, 1758); *Occasional Reflections on the Importance of the War in America* (London, 1758).

[138] Alexander Scott Withers, *Chronicles of Border Warfare* (Clarksburgh, Virginia, 1831).

[139] Samuel Hazard (1784-1870), *Hazard's Register of Pennsylvania* (Philadelphia, 1828-36).

[140] Thomas F. Gordon, *History of Pennsylvania to 1776* (Philadelphia, 1829).

[141] John Entick, *et al.*, *General History of the Late War in Europe, Asia, Africa, and America* (London, 1763-64).

[142] Edmund Burke, *Account of the European Settlements in America* (London, 1757).

[143] Joseph White, *An Account of the Gospel Labours and Christian Experiences*

. . . of *John Churchman, late of Nottingham, in Pennsylvania* (Philadelphia, 1781).

[144] John Heckewelder, *Narrative of the Mission of the United Brethren among the Delaware and Mohegan Indians, 1740-1808* (Philadelphia, 1820).

[145] John Wright, *A Compleat History of the Late War* (Dublin, 1763).

[146] Richard Price, *Observations on the Nature of Civil Liberty, the Principles of Government, and the Justice and Policy of the War with America* (London, 1776).

[147] See note 138.

[148] Colonel David Humphreys, *Essay on the Life of the Honorable Major-General Israel Putnam* (Hartford, 1788).

[149] James Gibson, *A Journal of the Late Siege* (London, 1745).

[150] Samuel Smith, *History of the colony of Nova Caesaria, or New Jersey, to 1721* (Burlington, New Jersey, 1765).

[151] *Niles' Register* (Baltimore, 1811-49).

[152] Alexander Hewatt, *Historical Account of the Rise and Progress of the Colonies of South Carolina and Georgia* (London, 1779).

[153] Henry Trumbull, *History of the Indian Wars* (Boston, 1841).

[154] Samuel G. Drake (1798-1875), *The Book of Indians* (Boston, 1841).

[155] John Maude, *Visit to the Falls of Niagara* (London, 1826).

[156] Thomas Mante, *History of the Late War in America* (London, 1772).

[157] Henri de Tonti (1650-1704), *Relation de la Louisiane* (Amsterdam, 1720).

[158] *Bradbury's Transcript Copy of the Early Court Records and other Important Documents pertaining to the Settlement (of Maine), 1636-1686* (Portland, 1843-45).

[159] Daniel Coxe, *Description de la Carolana*. In Margry, *Découvertes & établissements*.

[160] Sir William Keith, *History of Virginia* (London, 1738).

[161] *Mémoires sur le Canada, depuis 1749 jusqu'à 1760* (Quebec, 1838). *Bib. Can.* 326.

[162] Thomas Pichon (1700-81), *Lettres et mémoires pour servir à l'histoire . . . du Cap-Breton* (La Haye, 1760).

[163] William Cobbett, *Porcupine's Works: a Faithful Picture of the United States of America . . . 1783-1801* (London, 1801).

[164] Colonel Winslow's *Journal of the Expulsion of the Acadians*, long preserved in the Massachusetts Historical Society, was printed by the Nova Scotian Historical Society in Vol. 3 of their *Transactions*.

[165] John Gorham Palfrey (1796-1881) was a Unitarian clergyman who devoted much of his life to education and history. He was a classmate of Jared Sparks at Harvard and shared his love of early colonial history.

Palfrey wrote much for the *North American Review*, substituting for Sparks as editor in 1825 and acquiring control of it in 1835. He edited the magazine from that year to 1843, when it passed into the hands of Francis Bowen. Palfrey's *History of New England* (1858-75) incorporates much of his historical labors and is a monument to his scholarship.

[166] John Warner Barber, *Connecticut Historical Collections* (New Haven, 1836).

[167] Georg Heinrich Loskeil, *History of the Mission of the United Brethren among the Indians in North America* (London, 1794).

[168] David Humphreys, *An Historical Account of the Incorporated Society for the Propagation of the Gospel in Foreign Parts* (London, 1730).

[169] John Mitchell, *The Contest in America between Great Britain and France* (London, 1757). *Bib. Can.* 264.

[170] William Smith (1728-93), *The History of the Province of New York* (London, 1757).

[171] In *Montcalm and Wolfe*, II, 337-38, Parkman cites Jonathan Mayhew's sermon rather than Cooper's.

[172] J. H. Perkins, "English Discoveries in the Ohio Valley, 1744-74," *North American Review*, XLIX, 69, is a review of Captain Jonathan Carver's *Travels* (1780) and his *Travels in Wisconsin* (1838).

[173] J. H. Lanman, "General Sketch of Canadian Government," *North American Review*, XLVI, 409, is a review of John McGregor's *British America* (1833) and Schoolcraft's *Narrative of an Expedition to Itasca Lake* (1834).

[174] The *American Magazine, or Monthly Chronicle for the British Colonies*, was published in Philadelphia by William Bradford in 1757-58. The Rev. William Smith was the chief editor.

[175] See note 146.

[176] John Wright's *A Compleat History of the Late War* (Dublin, 1763) contains Abercromby's official letters.

[177] *Impartial Account of Lieutenant-Colonel Bradstreet's Expedition, by a Volunteer* (London, 1759). Cited in *Montcalm and Wolfe*, II, 135 n.

[178] Benjamin Trumbull, *Complete History of Connecticut* (New Haven, 1818).

[179] John Daly Burk, *History of Virginia* (Petersburg, Virginia, 1804-5).

F. Cuming, *Sketches of a Tour to the Western Country* (Pittsburgh, 1810).

J. Palmer, *Journal of Travels in 1817* (London, 1818).

Thomas F. Gordon, *History of Pennsylvania to 1776* (Philadelphia, 1829).

John Huddlestone Wynne, *A General History of the British Empire in America* (London, 1770).

John Knox, *An historical journal of the campaigns in North America* (London, 1769).

Abiel Holmes, *Annals of America, 1492-1826* (Cambridge, 1829).

Richard Henry Lee, *Life of Arthur Lee* (Boston, 1829).

Alexander Scott Withers, *Chronicles of Border Warfare* (Clarksburgh, 1831).

Samuel Hazard, *Register of Pennsylvania* (Philadelphia, 1828-36).

Thomas Mante, *History of the Late War in North America* (London, 1772).

[180] *Lettres Edifiantes et Curieuses* (Lyon, 1819).

[181] William Gilmore Simms, *Life of Francis Marion* (New York, 1844).

[182] George Heriot (1766-1844), *Travels through the Canadas* (London, 1807).

[183] The Boston Athenaeum, a private library rich in historical materials.

[184] Charles Miner, *History of Wyoming* (Philadelphia, 1845).

Parkman's
EUROPEAN TOUR
1843-4

HIGHLANDS
Glasgow   Edinburgh
O   Galashiels   Tweed R.
Abbotsford   Melrose
CHEVIOT
HILLS
Carlisle   Penrith
Coke Tees   Darlington

IRELAND

GREAT
BRITAIN   Amsterdam

Liverpool
Mersey

London
Folkestone   BELG

To Halifax and Boston

Boulogne

Paris

F
R
A
N

ATLANTIC   OCEAN

Bordeaux

PORTUGAL

SPAIN

Madrid

Lisbon

MED

From the Azores

Granada
SIERRA
NEVADA MTS.
Algeciras   C De Gata
Tarifa   Gibraltar
C Spartel   Ape's Hill

0   100   200   300
Scale in Miles